The Dramatic Censor;

or,

Critical Companion

[Francis Gentleman]

Volume Two

Benjamin Blom, Inc.

1972

S. Taylor inv. sculp.

THE

DRAMATIC CENSOR;

OR,

CRITICAL COMPANION.

————Si quid novifti rectius iftis,
Candidus imperti : fi, non, his utere mecum.

VOLUME THE SECOND.

LONDON:

Printed for J. BELL, near *Exeter Exchange*, in the *Strand*;
and C. ETHERINGTON, at *York*.

M DCC LXX.

First published London, 1770
Reissued 1972 by
Benjamin Blom, Inc.
New York, N.Y. 10025

Library of Congress
Catalog Card Number 77-91902

Printed in the
United States of America

2

THE
DRAMATIC CENSOR
dedicates with esteem and respect, this
SECOND VOLUME
of humble Criticisms
to the
LIBERALITY of SENTIMENT,
ORIGINALITY of GENIUS,
AFFLUENCE of CONCEPTION,
PLEASANTRY of EXPRESSION,
WIT, HUMOUR, and INSTRUCTIVE SATIRE,
which so peculiarly unite to ornament the
private and public character of

Samuel Foote, Esq;

ADVERTISEMENT.

A Sincere *esteem for the* Drama, *ardent wishes for the prosperity of the* Stage, *admiration of the beauties, and concern for the defects, both in composition and action, first dictated this work ; which from many flattering instances of approbation, has, we apprehend, been conducted with some share of ability, upon commendable principles : wherefore, the same plan will be pursued that we have hitherto adopted. Not one objection has been offered to our criticisms on the plays which have fallen under our notice ; as to our strictures on the performers, we have been accused by some of too much lenity, by others, of too much severity ; a few of the most inconsiderable objects mentioned, have taken great umbrage at the supposed injury done their imaginary merits ; of their ignorant, illiberal resentment we have heard, with an equal mixture of pity and contempt ; resolved neither through fear nor favour to abate the smallest particle of that critical prerogative we have assumed ; however, the most abject, discontented murderers of common sense in either house, may rail at the* Dramatic Censor, *secure from any trace of resentment for so doing, in this work, if as it is eagerly hoped some of the deficiencies pointed out are reformed, the ultimate view of this and the former Volume will be fulfilled.*

In the wide field of observation before us, several passages and circumstances must no doubt escape, though equally deserving regard with several of those we note : however, we flatter ourselves, nothing material has

as

ADVERTISEMENT.

as yet flipped us, or will hereafter be omitted ; and that a review of the work when compleated will prove, that interest and malevolence, the two worst influences authors can write under, have been equally distant both from our heads and hearts.

JULIUS

THE

DRAMATIC CENSOR.

JULIUS CÆSAR.

A TRAGEDY by SHAKESPEARE.

IF powerfully inculcating one of the nobleſt principles that actuates the human mind, the love of national liberty, can ſtamp additional value upon works of genius, we may venture to pronounce the tragedy now before us, as to the ſubject of it, highly deſerving of attention from an Engliſh audience; in reſpect of the executive part, a review of the ſeveral ſcenes will, we hope, furniſh a competent idea.

At the commencement of this piece, the author introduces two Romans of character and public ſpirit reproving the mob with great energy for making holiday on Cæſar's account, in whoſe ambition the freedom of their country had found a grave. The remonſtrances of Marullus and Flavius are pathetically perfuafive, and the mob reply with humorous, characteriftic bluntnefs ; however, we are not fond of fuch ludicrous matter in a tragedy, and wifh the piece could have been faved from the intrufion of inadequate characters, without enervating feveral paffages, which as they ftand at prefent difcover peculiar force.

As Cæfar goes to the Courfe he is accofted by a Soothfayer, who warns him to beware of the Ides of March, this prediction, however, he treats with contempt, and paffes on to the games, leaving Brutus and Caffius on the ftage ; from the former's declining to join the public feftivity, his friend takes occafion to hint a gloominefs which feems to have hung for fome time on his difpofition ; Brutus being fo touched, confeffes that paffions of fome difference cloud his mind ; upon this foundation Caffius works with great fubtlety to feel the pulfe of his political principles ; a diftant fhout occafions Brutus to exprefs apprehenfion that the people are conferring royalty upon Cæfar, whom Caffius, in a long, fpirited, and picturefque fpeech endeavours to depreciate, by an unfavourable comparifon with himfelf ; however, there is more of oftentatious vanity than found argument in it, for the ftrength of a very brave and good man might fail in fwimming, and his tongue, parched with feverifh thirft, call for drink without any juft imputation againft his courage ; the next fpeech of Caffius, where he accufes the Romans of enflaving themfelves, and compares Brutus with Cæfar, applies clofely to the point in view.

Brutus perceiving the drift of Caffius, replies with fenfible referve, but delivers one pofitive and

noble

noble declaration, that he would prefer a state of
rural obscurity rather than confess himself a citizen
of Rome, under a disgraceful state of public affairs. Here their conversation is judiciously interrupted by the return of Cæsar and his train : what
the conqueror of the world says in this scene is very
unimportant, and we heartily concur with BEN
JOHNSON, that his quaint remark upon the leanness
of Cassius deserves to be sneered at ; indeed, some
good reasons for suspecting that senator of gloomy
designs are subjoined, but how the author could
carry Cæsar off the stage with an unessential, ridiculous remark on the deafness of one of his own
ears, we cannot conceive.

⁕ In the next scene Casca, with a blunt peculiarity,
informs Brutus and Cassius what happened while
the people were offering Cæsar a crown ; his picture
of popular vehemence, irregularity and weakness,
is just and striking, but sweaty nightcaps need not
have been mentioned : upon Brutus's observing
that Cæsar is liable to the falling sickness, Cassius
makes a most emphatic and comprehensive reply
in two lines : at the conclusion of this interview,
our author has, with singular judgment, given Cassius a soliloquy, which fully explains his own principles and character, while it throws some distant
light on the contrast disposition of Brutus, which
being generous, open and unsuspecting, Cassius
justly thinks well calculated for him to work upon,
thereby to gratify his personal resentment against
Cæsar.

Casca and Cicero are next brought in view, a-
larmed at violent, elementary concussions and
strange prodigies ; the descriptive part is powerful

and

and poetical. When Cicero retires, Caffius appears, who feems to rejoice in the aftonifhing circumftances which furround Rome, and infers from them, matters of important dependancy relative to the ftate : upon mention of Cæfar, as king, Caffius proclaims a refolution of never fubmitting to what he terms flavery ; to this Cafca agrees, and hence a dawn of the confpiracy, againft Cæfar breaks upon the audience ; when Cinna enters, Caffius declares him one of his faction : Brutus being mentioned as a moft defirable addition to the party, Caffius gives fome papers calculated for that purpofe, and directs how they may be thrown in the way of Brutus's obfervation ; with which preparative circumftances, and a fhort, but energetic elogium on the popularity of Brutus, the firft act properly and agreeably concludes.

Brutus is introduced at the beginning of the fecond act, as meditating by ftar-light ; and his foliloquy refpecting Cæfar's greatnefs, is finely imagined, efpecially that part of it which touches on ambition. Upon Lucius's bringing fome papers found in his mafter's ftudy, Brutus queftions him, whether to-morrow is not the Ides of March ; this, though apparently a trifling point of interrogation, muft be confidered as a good preparative for the death of Cæfar, which has been predicted at that time.

Upon perufal of what Lucius has brought him, he finds a dark, yet forcible infinuation, relative to the enflaved ftate of Rome, and his own inactivity. He explains the matter, takes the point home to himfelf, and with juft, patriotic feeling, determines to attempt the redrefs of his country's wrongs :

upon

upon being told that Caffius and fome other perfons are come to wait upon him, he concludes, we think rather too haftily, that they are the confpiracy; he has reafon to apprehend much public difcontent, but there does not appear any foundation for his fuppofing an actual confpiracy is formed.

When the confpirators enter, Caffius introduces them feverally, and the reception they meet is cordial. Our author manifefts great judgment in communicating the matter they come upon a-fide, and happily threw in to fill up, the digref-fion of where the fun rifes. At the propofition ot an oath to bind mutual fidelity, Brutus characterifti-cally refufes fo fufpicious an obligation upon noble, generous minds, and eloquently fhews why the caufe alone is fufficient to bind them, or if not that, nothing can; the manner of debating who are fit for their purpofe is very natural, and Brutus's ob-jection to cutting off Antony, merely as a friend to Cæfar, heroically humane; the knowledge De-cius difplays of Cæfar's difpofition, and the ufe he propofes to make of it, fhew deep policy; the warning Brutus gives his friends to wear difengaged looks, is prudent: upon calling to Lucius, and per-ceiving that he is afleep, Brutus fhews moft plea-fing benevolence of difpofition, by leaving his boy's flumber undifturbed.

Introducing Portia, though what fhe fays cannot affect an audience much, is judicious, as it is a re-lief to the other fcenes, and approaches the pathetic, though it cannot touch the tender feelings. Her method of founding the care which lies heavy on him, and his method of declining an explanation, are fenfibly natural; however, to foften the prefent
referve,

referve, he promifes future information, and fends her off to make way for a vifitant, Caius Ligarius, with whom a very unimportant conference enfues, which we think is left out and properly in the reprefentation.

Cæfar appears next in his palace, evidently a-larmed at the turbulence of the preceding night, and orders the priefts to do prefent facrifice ; Calphurnia approaches, filled with dreadful apprehenfions, and by drawing a ftrong picture of thofe prodigies which have been recounted to her, endeavours to diffuade Cæfar from going to the capitol ; however, he feems to treat omens with fenfible contempt, and even rejects the unfavourable opinion of the Augurs ; at laft, Calphurnia's tender remonftrances prevail, and he confents that Antony fhall acquaint the fenate with his refolution not to go.

Matters thus circumftanced, Decius Brutus appears, as being deputed to folicit Cæfar's appearance at the capitol, which, after fome refufal, by touching Cæfar's vanity, and alarming him with the imputation of fear, he works him up to go ; the reft of the confpirators coming to attend him, he refolves to accompany them, and propofes previous refrefhment, which occafions Brutus to make a moft beautiful reflection on Cæfar's unfufpecting mind, and their own fatal diffimulation.

> That every like is not the fame, oh Cæfar !
> The heart of Brutus yearns to think upon.

In the next fcene we meet Artemidorus, a foothfayer, perufing a paper defigned for Cæfar, wherein he warns that monarch of all the confpirators by name. Portia, anxious for the great event depending,

Julius Cæsar.

ing, comes on in a state of very natural confusion, dispatching Lucius for intelligence ; her disjointed manner of speaking is well imagined ; upon questioning Artemidorus, she collects fresh fear of a discovery, and retires confessing the full force of womanish apprehensions.

The third act opens with Cæsar entering the senate, when he is addressed by Artemidorus, who urges attention to the paper he offers, as being of near concern to himself, which Cæsar therefore very nobly declines, as being least worthy of present regard ; those doubts which SHAKESPEARE has furnished the conspirators with, are naturally the consequence of feelings concerned in such an important and precarious undertaking.

When Metellus kneeling adulates Cæsar with multiplied titles, the monarch replies like a truly great man, but uses some terms too much in the bashaw stile ; upon the repeated solicitations of different senators to favour Cimber's suit, he well describes and manifests his own firmness : upon his confirmed refusal, Casca, according to appointment, gives the first stab, upon which all the rest follow his blow, and the world's great conqueror falls beneath a multitude of wounds, seeming to disdain every messenger of fate, but that sent by Brutus ; here our author's judgment deserves great praise, in giving Cæsar no more to say than history authorizes ; but after speaking English through every scene and speech before, why he should introduce *et tu Bruté* is not so obvious as might be wished.

The exultation of the conspirators, and the methods they propose for reconciling this great, unthought of event to the people, are well conceived ;
however

however we may applaud the glorious impulfe of patriotifm which caufed Brutus to facrifice fo fincere and powerful a friend to the liberties of his country, yet we heartily concur with Mr. POPE, that the fpeech concerning dipping their hands in Cæfar's blood, is much more fuitable to any other confpirator than him.

SHAKESPEARE was judicioufly fond of realizing mimic reprefentation as much as poffible, for which purpofe the following lines in this piece were certainly and happily intended.

> How many ages hence,
> Shall this our lofty fcene be acted o'er
> In ftates unborn, and accents yet unknown ;
> How many times fhall Cæfar bleed in fport,
> Who now on Pompey's bafis lies along,
> No worthier than the duft.

Antony's fervant, in a very plaufible ftile, offers from his mafter conciliating motives to the confpirators, who promife him fafety for his appearance ; he is introduced much too foon, as there are but three lines from the fervant's going till he comes on, which muft oblige us to imagine him waiting at the door, where he would by no means have trufted himfelf, after he had fled to his houfe amazed, without fome credible affurance of protection.

When Mark Antony enters he follows an amiable, natural impulfe, which directs him to pay his firft regard to the dead body of his royal friend, without even cafting a glance at his furrounding murderers ; his addrefs to thofe real or pretending patriots is pathetic and fpirited, Brutus's reply cordial and fenfible ; there is fomething hypocritical, yet politic,

politic, in fhaking hands with the blood-ftained
confpirators, the action leffens him in our efteem,
yet the defign, which may be eafily perceived, commands our approbation. Caffius pinching him
clofe, he makes a fecond ferious declaration of attachment to the popular party, which rather lays
him low in the view of truth, but to be upon a level
with rogues, efpecially thofe in power, integrity
muft become flexible, and fometimes fubmit to wear
a mafk.

Antony's defire of leave to pronounce Cæfar's
funeral elogium, ftrikes even flow perception with
a more extenfive meaning than is expreffed, which
Caffius very prudently adverts to ; however, Brutus gives a reafon, favouring of felf-fufficiency, why
it is not dangerous to give Antony the privilege of
the roftrum ; therefore configns Cæfar's corpfe to his
care, only referves to himfelf the firft opportunity
of fpeaking to the people : this point being fettled,
the confpirators retire, and leave Antony to vent his
feelings more at large, which he does in a very mafterly foliloquy, admirably fuited to his fituation.
Upon the appearance of a meffenger from Octavius
Cæfar, he warns the young Prince to avoid the danger of entering Rome in fo critical a ftate of affairs, mentions the trial he intends to make of popular affection, and then goes off with his imperial
mafter's body.

Brutus, attended by the Plebeians, next ftrikes our
view, he mounts the roftrum, and difpatches Caffius to divide the multitude ; in his addrefs to thofe
who ftay to hear him, his oratory difcovers itfelf in
that warm glow of fentiment, that nervous, yet un-
adorned flow of expreffion, which diftinguifhes elo-

quence, founded upon confcious honefty : he appeals to feelings of a focial, virtuous and patriotic
nature ; he appeals to the dulleft conception, by a
beautiful antithefis of his great love for Cæfar, and
his fuperior regard for the liberties of Rome ; fubmitting, at laft, with tempered dignity, and juft
confidence, his part in the affaffination of great Julius, to public opinion, even among the loweft clafs
of the people ; fuch as fome of our prefent, fmart
Englifh fenators have called the *fcum of the earth.*
Upon Antony's approach with Cæfar's body, he,
according to promife, gives place, and retires with
a glorious obfervation, that the fame weapon which
ftabbed his beft friend, is ready to affail his own
heart, if ever the public fafety fhould require it.

Upon Antony's mounting the roftrum, it immediately occurs, that a great contraft of manner,
ftile and argument, fhould be adopted ; this arduous variation we hope SHAKESPEARE will appear
amply qualified for upon due infpection. The
Plebeians feem to have received fo ftrong a prejudice in favour of the confpiracy from Brutus's oration, that to imprefs an oppofite opinion, appears almoft impracticable ; infomuch, that upon Antony's
even mentioning the name of Brutus, a jealoufy of his
meaning ftarts up amongft the mob ; this circumftance is a very artful and natural preparation for
what follows.

In the firft fpeech of Antony, we difcover a beautiful, yet modeft elogium, upon the merits of Cæfar, mingled with ironical compliments to the confpirators, particularly Brutus ; he clofes it with a
proper, pathetic appeal, to his own mournful feelings on the occafion, which evidently touches the

Plebeians,

Julius Cæsar.

Plebeians, and lays their hearts open to the impreffion he apparently wifhes to work upon them. In the next fpeech, our orator, with deep policy, obliquely hints, that he could communicate fome inflammatory intelligence, but through his refpect to Brutus, declines the office; he then plays a principal engine againft their prejudice, by mentioning the will of Cæfar, as a moft interefting concern to them; with the true violence of mobbifh fpirits, they defire the will may be read, this the orator moft fhrewdly evades to increafe their eagernefs, and that it may work the more powerful effect, fhews them the feveral wounds in Cæfar's coarfe, pointing out each man who ftabbed him, by name.

The piteous fpectacle inflames the mob to fudden exclamations of defperate tendency; this agitation of mind Antony avails himfelf of, by feeming to foften their refentment, which, like an inadequate quantity of water thrown upon powerful flames, tends to make it rage the fiercer. Thus roufed, he confirms their fury, by reminding them of, and reading to them Cæfar's will, wherein they find a refpectful and confiderable remembrance of the Roman citizens; this corroborates all preceding circumftances, and they go off, denouncing moft terrible threats againft the confpirators. This fcene finely exhibits the mutability and inconfiftency of popular affection, which an artful, plaufible orator, can warp from attachment to antipathy, from the moft worthy to the moft worthlefs object of human confideration: an excellent leffon this for all ftates, more efpecially free ones.

By a fervant Antony is informed of Octavius's arrival at Rome, and goes to meet him at Cæfar's

houfe:

houfe : after this, comes a moft uneffential fcene, omitted in reprefentation ; a fcene without any meaning, unlefs from the treatment Cinna meets with : we deduce a truth, moft generally known, that an enraged mob, in the midft of precipitation, will as foon facrifice an innocent as a guilty object, fo wild, fo unprincipled are in general their refolutions.

At the beginning of the fourth act, we find the bloody triumvirate, Octavius, Antonius and Lepidus, confulting who fhall fall the victim of their difpleafure, or ambitious views, in which cruel fcheme we perceive they proceed upon principles of great condefcenfion to each other ; however, when Lepidus difappears, we find he is made a mere tool to the other two, particularly Antony ; they go off, determining to make head againft the warlike preparations of Brutus and Caffius.

In the next fcene Brutus appears, encamped near Sardis ; after fome previous converfe with Pindarus and Lucilius, by which we are informed, that he fufpects a decline of friendfhip in Caffius ; the accufed perfon appears, and recriminates a charge of wrong upon Brutus ; an explanation is warmly urged, when the latter prudently advifes an abftracted difcuffion of their affairs, that their armies may not be acquainted with fo important and prejudicial a diffention : for this powerful reafon they retire to Brutus's tent, where the matter is refumed with great eagernefs by Caffius, and maintained with much philofophical dignity by Brutus.

A money matter feems the point in difpute : Brutus, with a noble elevation of mind, expreffes his contempt of fordid felfifhnefs, and with confiderable

asperity,

asperity, reproaches Caffius, not only for refusing him some supplies he had solicited, but even with venality in selling public offices ; such stinging allegations would rouse a more patient spirit than Caffius seems to have : in short, the whole scene is a powerful, beautiful, instructive contrast ; shewing the great advantage cool deliberation of mind has over intemperate rashness. Their reconciliation is brought about in a very becoming manner. SHAKESPEARE, immediately after this noble interview, for what reason we cannot divine, has introduced a poet, to speak some as trifling and superfluous lines as ever were penned ; so disgraceful a rhimer is justly banished the stage.

The circumstance of Portia's death is well mentioned, and Brutus's behaviour quite characteristic ; we also much approve the short debate which arises upon marching to Philippi, as it brings to view the main story. If we could relish ghosts, Julius Cæsar's, in the tent of Brutus, would be very admissible ; in action, it certainly gives solemnity, and makes a striking conclusion to the fourth act. This ghost is introduced upon the stage, and we think very absurdly, a second time.

Antony and Octavius begin the fifth act, in the fields of Philippi ; after a few short speeches, Brutus, Caffius, and their party appear, when a parly and conference ensue ; it may perhaps be an instance of overstrained delicacy, to make an objection to what passes between the hostile leaders upon this occasion, but we apprehend the terms of reprobation they exchange, are not quite consistent with such exalted characters.

What

Julius Cæsar.

What Caſſius ſays to Meſſala, after Octavius and Antony go off, concerning unfavourable omens, is very preparative for the cataſtrophe of the piece; the parting of Brutus and Caſſius, from the poſſibility of never meeting again, is truly pathetic, and well performed, muſt deeply ſtrike every generous mind.

The battle now begins, Caſſius's party gives way; unable to bear the idea of defeat, that chief, with the ſame precipitation of temper which has all along marked his character, determines upon death; and commands Pindarus to perform, what amongſt the Romans was deemed an act of friendſhip, adminiſtring of fate: from what follows, it appears, that a miſtake has led him into this irreparable ſtep, which affects Titinius ſo much, that he puts an end to his own burthenſome being with Caſſius's ſword. The ſcenes between this, and that of Brutus and his friends, after a total defeat, are very trifling; nor can we think that SHAKESPEARE has taken ſo much care to render his amiable hero's fall important, as he might have done: in the laſt ſcene Antony pronounces a very juſt and conciſe, yet copious elogium upon Brutus.

The ſubject of this tragedy is of a very intereſting nature, and its tendency ſingularly uſeful in a ſtate like that of Great Britain. The unities are no doubt ſadly mutilated, yet does it not appear in repreſentation ſo irregular as it really is; the characters are very numerous, and thoſe of any conſideration, ſupported with great conſiſtency.

Julius Cæfar appears poſſeſſed of ſuch intrepidity and openneſs of mind, as recommend him, though the enſlaver of his country, to the reſpect of an

audience:

audience ; as a part, there is no opportunity for an actor to difplay capital abilities; the beft perfonators. of him we remember were Meffrs. BRIDGWATER and SPARKS.

Brutus is a character of fingular dignity, amiable in every point of view, except that violent breach of gratitude, confpiring againft, and perfonally affailing the life of a man, who, upon moft difinterefted principles, had proved himfelf his faft friend ; this is a point of doubt, which has been often debated, and as often left undetermined : however, as the Roman idea of patriotifm, not only juftified, but applauded a man, even in the act of fuicide, where the good of his country was effentially concerned. It may eafily be admitted an eftablifhed rule, to facrifice the deareft friend, nay, the neareft relation, for the fame glorious caufe ; and, in this view, Brutus ftands exculpated, for Cæfar's ufurpation of power, moft certainly broke off all focial connection between him and every citizen, influenced by the principles of liberty.

After this defence, we are forry that he appears only as a tool of Caffius's policy, in the piece before us ; his own virtue and fenfibility do not poffefs fufficient activity to lead in the caufe of patriotifm; though, when roufed, they join the general concern with cordiality and firmnefs. A mind of fpotlefs integrity, feems to poffefs him through the whole ; and though there is a flight charge of weaknefs againft him, yet there is an engaging uniformity which preferves him in our efteem while alive, and renders his fall an incident of tender concern.

Brutus requires good, but not extenfive powers of reprefentation ; a graceful figure, with full, placid

cid articulation of voice, muft, in this part, fufficiently gratify a fenfible fpectator. Mr. QUIN having much lefs monotony in Brutus than any other
tragedy part, that is the verfe not affording him fo
many opportunities for periodical cadences, he appeared more refpectable, and lefs offenfive than the
bufkin generally rendered him. His oration to the
Plebeians had great, and his fcene with Caffius very
fingular merit ; in feveral other places he was heavy
and infipid.

Mr. SHERIDAN, curtailed by nature of almoft
every favourable, adequate, external requifite, yet
manifefted great judgment in this character, main-
taining ftricter equality through the whole than Mr.
QUIN ; if he could not rife fo high in the view of
criticifm, neither did he fall fo low. His perfon,
though unimportant, by the aid of drefs, was not
totally void of refpect : but a ftiff famenefs of
action, frequently rifing to extravagance, fuper-
added artificial to natural deficiency. SHAKE-
SPEARE's meaning he clearly conceived, and fully
conveyed, but frequent, ungracious fnip-fnap breaks
of voice, and a painful attempt to keep up the laft
fyllable of every fentence, his peculiar fault, gave
ftrong fpecimens of oratorical diffonance. Mr.
WALKER, within thefe few years, made a decent
fhift with the part at Covent Garden ; at prefent,
there is not the flighteft trace of it to be found at
either houfe.

Caffius is in every refpect a ftriking contraft to
Brutus ; an enemy to Cæfar rather from envy and
private pique, than public fpirited principles :
proud, impatient, fubtle, irafcible, without any kind
of virtue, but the military one of courage, to recommend

Julius Cæsar.

commend him ; yet from some spirited and plausible declarations in the cause of freedom, an audience are induced to view him as a more valuable object than he really is, andthough his fall appears to be an unjustifiable effect of impetuosity, yet we are apt to lament it.

As a part, the reprefentation of Caffius is more difficult, and requires much greater powers of expreffion than Brutus ; however, this is to be remarked, that an indifferent actor can much more easily catch applause from an injudicious audience in the former, than the latter ; indeed, if two capital performers, of equal merit, prefent themselves to the public in these characters, the odds are great but Caffius outstrips his competitor in noisy approbation. In the course of our theatrical observation, we recollect but one good Caffius, Mr. RYAN ; the techy degree of paffion described in this part, and the general mode of mind which actuates it, he hit off in a very characteristic manner. Mr. Mossop, in attempting this fiery Roman, shewed much power, but very little nature ; and every other candidate we have feen funk below contempt ; he is, like Brutus, fo unhappily fituated, as not to have the shadow of a reprefentative at either theatre,

Cafca's cynical roughness was admirably defcribed by Mr. SPARKS, nor did he fustain much injury from Mr. RIDOUT's abilities ; yet even this confpirator would find but indifferent fupport from any exifting fon of the bufkin.

From the outlines of Mark Antony's character, as drawn not only by his friend Cæfar, but the confpirators alfo, we should be apt to deem him a mere trifling, unimportant reveller ; yet, when circum-

ftances

ftances call for ferious attention, we perceive him to
be a very fhrewd, plaufible and deep politician ; a
perfuafive orator, an active and refolute foldier :
his manner of working up the Plebeians is mafterly,
and fhews a thorough knowledge of life.

Mr. BARRY, beyond a doubt, ftands foremoft in
our approbation for this part, as poffeffing a very
adequate figure, an harmonious voice, and all the
plaufibility of infinuation that SHAKESPEARE meant;
however, we think that critic an enthufiaftic admirer, who, fpeaking of him in the roftrum, ex-
claimed, that Paul never preached fo well at Athens.
It is certain, nature in this, as well as all his dramatic undertakings, furnifhed him with almoft irrefiftable recommendations ; but judgment did not feem
fo much his friend as might have been wifhed.
Mr. DIGGES figured, and imagined the part extremely well, but wanted that flow of voice effential to fmooth oratory. Mr. DEXTER was pretty
and inoffenfive, but very faint and lukewarm. Mr.
ROSS ftands next to what Mr. BARRY was, and has
it in his power to make a very eftimable Antony ;
but with refpect to the ftage, this gentleman's inclination and abilities feldom accompany each other.

As to the long, &c. of male characters in this
tragedy, they are not worth regard ; and as to the
ladies, all we can fay of them is, that Mrs. WOF-
FINGTON, in Portia, deferved more notice than any
other lady we have feen.

To differ with great men, or eftablifhed opinions, is rather hazardous ; however, we muft venture
to blame Dr. JOHNSON's feelings, which confider
this piece as cold and unaffecting ; we readily admit
there is a total want of thofe tender paffions which

are

Julius Cæsar.

are effential to move and pleafe female fpectators, which prevents it from commanding that fuccefs on the ftage it deferves: however, we are hardy enough to contend, that the fubject is truly interefting, that the thoughts are noble and inftructive, the verfification fuitable, the orations happily contrafted, the characters well preferved ; and that the whole together refembles a beautiful fabric, which in general ftrikes with fingular fatisfaction, in fpite of fome fmall irregularities and blemifhes which appear : had the fifth act been adequate to the other four, we fhould not hefitate to pronounce SHAKESPEARE'S JULIUS CÆSAR, a very capital ornament to the ftage, and a moft defirable companion in the clofet; containing many paffages and circumftances which may improve, not one which can taint the mind.

SCHOOL

SCHOOL for RAKES.

A COMEDY. ANONYMOUS.

BY a converfation between Frampton and Willes, at the beginning of this comedy, we find, that Sir William Evans, a Welch baronet, and his family, are arrived at the town-houfe of Lord Euftace ; and from what occurs, efpecially from what Willis lets fall, we may infer that they are not very agreeable guefts ; the baronet's daughter Harriet is mentioned, and fome defign, relative to her, dawns upon us : the pertnefs of a valet, buoyed up by a mafter's confidence, is well defcribed in this fcene ; and the infults a dependant upon quality is liable to, equally well fet forth.

Frampton, who appears a man of principle and fenfibility, though by a decay of circumftances reduced to humour and affift the licentious purfuits of a diffipated young nobleman, in a very rational foliloquy, after Willis retires, reflects upon his painful fituation, but expreffes fome fatisfaction, that he has efcaped an iniquitous affair then on the tapis, and goes off with a commendable refolution, not to abandon his patron, while furrounded with perplexities, nor to affift him further than honour and peace of mind allow.

Sir William Evans, his fifter Winifred, and daughter Harriet, as frefh from a journey, next appear : the baronet feems difpleafed at his lordly hoft, but is rallied by his fifter for not having notions of politenefs

litenefs and family confequence equal to her own ;
he feems loth to incur obligations ; fhe confiders an
interchange of civilities as none. Their altercation
fubfiding, Sir William addreffes himfelf to Harriet,
who appears unexpectedly thoughtful and grave,
which, being queftioned, fhe attributes to fatigue ;
however, a fmall intimation is dropped afide, fignifying, that the houfe without its owner, cannot be
very agreeable to her.

Mrs. Winifred's defire that all their acquaintance
fhould know of the intimacy with Lord Euftace, is
a well applied ftroke of fatire againft the ridiculous
admirers of elevated ftations.

Upon the baronet's mentioning a defign of vifiting Captain Lloyd, the maiden lady expreffes great
apprehenfions at the gentleman's coming to Lord
Euftace's ; this Sir William is furprized at, the captain being uncle to the perfon intended for Mifs
Harriet's hufband ; here a frefh altercation arifes
between the brother and fifter, which is terminated
by the former going on his propofed vifit to Captain Lloyd. When the baronet difappears, Winifred drops a piece of information, by which we
learn, that her niece's hand is already difpofed of,
and therefore beyond the father's power. Here
Mifs Harriet appears, and from what paffes between
the young lady and her aunt, we perceive that the
former entertains uneafy fenfations for two reafons
firft, that her marriage is concealed from the baronet, and next that her hufband has not been in town
to receive them ; from which laft caufe fhe draws
fome difagreeable doubts of his conftancy. This
delicate agitation of mind, Mrs. Winifred endeavours to compofe, by defcanting on her noble connection,

nection, her supporters, coronets, &c.   Robin acquaints Harriet that Mr. Frampton defires to speak to her, the ladies go off to meet him immediately in the parlour.

Frampton, in two short foliloquies, previous to the appearance of the ladies, intimates a strong uneasiness of mind at a business he has in hand, and makes this just, instructive remark, that it is the lowest, we may add the most cruel baseness, to be capable of admiring, and betraying an innocent young creature in the same moment.

From the succeeding scene we learn, that the illness of Lord Euftace's father has been the cause of that absence which Harriet takes unkindly ; Frampton delivers a very plausible exculpation of his friend, and expressing a hope of his speedy arrival, the ladies go off to mend their external appearance against my lord's approach.

Frampton is now again in foliloquy, which Lord Euftace interrupts by his approach ; a conversation ensues between the friends, which plainly shews, that Lord Euftace has sensibility to know that he acts upon very culpable principles, respecting Harriet ; especially by drawing her into a feigned marriage, and wanting to cast her off.   Frampton's remonstrances are candid, persuasive and well applied ; among other points of perplexity, Lord Euftace expresses strong apprehension that his villainy will be discovered to Sir William Evans and family, by the compunction of a steward who is dying, and has declared an intention of confessing his own guilt, in acting the part of a clergyman.   To defeat the chance of a letter from this man reaching improper hands, Lord Euftace defires that Frampton

3   ton

ton may stay in the house, and take care that all
letters are first brought to him ; Frampton remarks, that it is an irksome and hateful undertaking,
but having promised, he seems willing to give all
possible assistance towards preventing a discovery ;
Lord Eustace expresses a desire of seeing Harriet, but
Frampton, for prudential reasons, dissuades him, and
the first act concludes here with some just remarks on
the essential, preparatory grounds of amendment in
tainted minds ; indeed, this entire scene may be
called a good, agreeable lesson of moral and social
instruction.

Lord Eustace begins the second act, ruminating
on his own disagreeable situation, and the pride of
family, which reduces him to such a dilemma ; Robert, as messenger, acquaints him that the ladies are
approaching ; after a few lines Harriet appears, and
with a very natural eagerness of mind, approaches
to embrace the man she considers as her husband ;
but from a sudden check of delicacy stops short, and
discovers marks of confusion for having appeared so
forward : Lord Eustace questions the cause of her
timidity, and upon Mrs. Winifred's entrance immediately after, apologizes for his absence at the
time of their arrival in town ; the old lady grants
her excuse with great readiness ; Harriet, however,
cannot shake off her concern entirely, which occasions her aunt to make some tart observations on
such unbecoming behaviour.

A proposal is made to Lord Eustace, of opening
the marriage affair to Sir William, and Mrs. Winifred's kind interposition is solicited, but having promised his lordship to maintain secrecy, she goes off,
determined to fulfil the treaty, as she phrases it, and
leaves

leaves the young couple to a tete-a-tete, wherein Harriet continues to urge unfolding the matter to her father; this encreases his lordſhip's embarraſſment much, from which he at length makes a temporary eſcape, by ſuggeſting a deſign of going into the country, on pretence of joining his regiment, and promiſing that he will there comply with her requeſt. On being queſtioned why in his letters to Harriet he has never ſtiled her wife, the danger of diſcovery by his father, Lord Delville, is urged as a reaſon, and thus the tender, believing, deceived lady, is quieted for the preſent.

Mrs. Winifred re-enters haſtily, and announces the approach of her brother Sir William, who ſpeaks at his entrance ſome rough but ſenſible truths againſt the prevalence of luxury ; after making ſome juſt remarks on the general relaxation of military duty, and the partial indulgence that is ſhewn to officers of quality in particular, the baronet comments upon his daughter's evident alteration, and unuſual depreſſion of ſpirits ; being interrupted upon that point by Mrs. Winifred, he paſſes on to the report of Lord Euſtace's approaching marriage, as ſet forth in one of the public papers. At this unexpected piece of intelligence, Harriet very naturally takes an alarm, while Mrs. Winifred treats the matter with contempt ; Lord Euſtace puts a good face on the affair, laughs at news-paper information, and obſerves, that it is one conſequence of the liberty of the preſs, for paragraph-writers to marry couples who have ſcarce ſeen each other ; however, he admits ſome grounds for the report relative to himſelf, as Lord Delville had expreſſed great liking to Lady Ann Mountfort's

large

large fortune. Sir William, in his rough ſtile, com‑
ments upon the unneceſſary pains of explanation
Lord Euſtace has taken, as not thinking the mat‑
ter of any concern to him or his family. An en‑
gagement of buſineſs calling the young lord away,
he goes off, ſoliciting leave to viſit the ladies, which
is granted. We think the requeſt a little odd, and
imagine the author forgot that the Evans's were
lodged in his lordſhip's houſe.

Mrs. Winifred, after chiding her neice for en‑
couraging groundleſs apprehenſions, dips into her
favourite theme politics, and by diſplaying groſs
abſurdity, ſtands before us a ſevere ſatire upon thoſe
who buſy themſelves with concerns out of their
ſphere, and quite beyond their conception.

Sir William re-entering with Robert, queſtions
him firſt about my lord's valet, who is ſaid to be a
very uſeful creature in his way ; and next concern‑
ing Frampton, of whom Robert can ſay no more
than he believes him honeſt, becauſe Willis does
not like him. Towards the end of this converſa‑
tion, with his truſty domeſtic, the baronet declares
he will leave town in a few days, and that his only
remaining care is the marriage of his daughter Har‑
riet with Colonel Lloyd, which he determines ſhall
ſoon take place.

Frampton and Willis next claim our attention,
the latter giving an arch account to the former of
the precautionary orders left by Lord Euſtace, to
watch cloſe and exclude all Sir William's friends.
In the courſe of this interview, Willis gives his
tongue ſeveral pert liberties reſpecting Harriet,
which occaſions Frampton to check him with be‑
coming ſpirit ; an account of Captain Lloyd's con‑

nection with Lord Euftace, and the foundation of
it' occurs, when a knocking at the door calls off
Willis ; Frampton is left to meditate alone ; what
he utters is to the purpofe, and has force, but we
could wifh this gentleman had not been loaded with
fuch a number of foliloquies ; however, his views
being worthy a man of honour, every good, tender
mind muft fympathize with and applaud him.

We are now introduced to Sir William and Harriet, he appears to be engaging his daughter's approbation of Colonel Lloyd as a hufband ; Robert
mentions the approach of Captain Lloyd, and the
blunt tar enters clofe at his heels ; after a fhort compliment, he complains of fome difficulty he had in
getting to his friends, and in the fea phrafe fays, he
was near tacking about, had not Robert, by clearing
the deck of my lord's impertinent valet, got convenient entrance. Upon pointing out the ladies as
his fifter and daughter, Lloyd ludicroufly replies to
Sir William, that they are much altered fince laft
he faw them, one being grown a young, and the
other an old woman ; the latter part of this obfervation affecting Mrs. Winifred, fhe retorts upon the
captain rather churlifhly, by remarking, that he is
not *grown* a brute, for he has always been one; this
feems the prelude to an altercation of fome bitternefs, but the captain gives it a turn, by afking for
Sir William's fon, the young colonel, who, by his
account, has made a flip to London from his quarters in Ireland, and therefore, to fcreen the affair,
has changed his name to Wefton ; this intelligence,
with the additional hint that fome female has occafioned his journey, ruffles Sir William.

A frefh

A frefh point of debate arifing between the captain and Mrs. Winifred, Lord Euftace is mentioned, with whom they both claim a particular intimacy; his lordfhip's approaching marriage being again fpoken of, Harriet feels a frefh alarm, which her aunt endeavours to fupprefs; but Captain Lloyd's declaration that he has feen the equipage, jewels, liveries, &c. preparatory to the wedding, the young lady's fears appear confirmed, and her confufion proportionably rifes, till at laft mention being made of fome eafy, country girl, who has been made a fool of by Lord Euftace, fhe lofes every trace of refolution, and faints; this puts her father into a flurry of fpirits, fhe is conducted off by Mrs. Winifred, Captain Lloyd goes in fearch of the colonel; and Sir William, in a foliloquy, which concludes the fecond act, endeavours to account for this fudden and extraordinary emotion; however, he fhoots wide of the real mark, and might as well have faid nothing, but for the following remark, which is very pregnant with truth and good fenfe. " The foibles of youth fhould rather be counteracted than oppofed, left in endeavouring to weed them out, we may deftroy a kindred virtue."

Frampton begins the third act with a few uneffential lines before Willis comes on with fome letters he has intercepted; the voluble valet paints his own political dexterity in pleafant, fpirited terms, and feems to urge a claim of reward for his affiduity very home to Frampton, who confidering him as a kind of villainous, though neceffary utenfil, difmiffes him the room in pretty rough terms, after fecuring the letters, which latter circumftance Willis feems to regret, and goes off grumbling deeply.

Frampton

Frampton now again foliloquizes, and entertains us with exculpatory meditation refpecting himfelf, as intermeddling with the difhonourable purpofes of Lord Euftace, and to relieve his mind refolves upon delivering the letters to Sir William ; at which crifis Lord Euftace enters to him, enquiring eagerly if he has fecured thofe letters ; this draws on a full and emphatic explanation of Frampton's fentiments, wherein the breach of hofpitality, as well as common civility, is charged home againft his lordfhip, who offers no palliation but the neceffity of his fituation, and warmly defires to fee the letters ; this Frampton commendably evades, and baits him with feveral inftructive reproaches ; the young peer replies in a ftile of warm farcafm, and the matter rifes to fuch a pitch, that Frampton refigns his charge, and renounces his lordfhip's friendfhip, finding it muft be held on unworthy terms, and retires.

Willis now comes forward, full of expectation to work on his noble mafter's weaknefs for the reward of his diligence, but Frampton's fpeedy and unexpected return interrupts his defign ; he is ordered out of the room, and a frefh converfation between Lord Euftace and Frampton enfues, wherein the latter fhews a very delicate fenfibility for his patron's perplexed fituation, and impreffes him with a ftrong idea of his own mifconduct ; this produces a great conceffion from his lordfhip, and a cordial reconciliation is the confequence ; it is alfo refolved, that all Sir William's letters, fave that from Langwood, the dying fteward, fhall be delivered him, for this purpofe they are delivered to Willis.

When his lordfhip and Frampton retire, the active valet, with a true fpirit of intrigue, determines

mines to fee what the important, excepted letter
contains; and fiddling about the feal, breaks it
before he is aware. This rather alarms him, but a
gratification of his curiofity foftens the accident, and
he explores the contents with fome laughable obfervations, drawing favourable hopes of advantage
from the difcovery he has made.

Harriet is next difcovered alone, expreffing much
love for, with painful doubts of Lord Euftace; entering upon fo folemn an obligation, in direct breach
of offilial duty, adds to her irkfome fenfations. Sir
William enters upon her meditation, and fhews a
letter he has received from her brother, confirming
Captain Lloyd's infinuation, that a lady is the caufe
of his vifiting London. Speaking of his fon's matrimonial views, the baronet utters a fentiment every
parent fhould invariably adopt, that worth and virtue are fuperior to every confideration of fortune.
Strong marks of melancholly ftill hanging upon
Harriet's countenance, her tender father wants to
come at the caufe, which again brings Lord Euftace
under confideration; the fubject works fo ftrongly
upon the young lady, that fhe aftonifhes Sir William
with falling at his feet, and works him into ftrong
perplexity by foliciting, in broken fentences, his
pardon, for having become Lord Euftace's wife
without his knowledge. This circumftance deeply
impreffes the old man, whofe good fenfe perceives a
ftrong objection, his lordfhip's diffipated, licentious
difpofition, which cannot afford the profpect of
much conjugal felicity. Harriet, however, purfues her tender folicitation, and urges fome exculpatory arguments in her lord's favour, which work
the wifhed for effect, and obtain Sir William's forgivenefs;

givenefs ; this fends off the young lady in perfect harmony of fpirits.

By the fcene which immediately follows between Sir William and Robert, we learn, that the latter has made fome difagreeable obfervations, and even heard of the impofition which has been paffed upon Harriet. This diftracting explanation roufes the baronet, who hearing that Willis is confidante, orders Robert to call him : upon the valet's appearance he is at firft queftioned mildly, then with a degree of intimidating warmth, concerning Lord Euftace's marriage ; he hefitates for fome time, but having a fword pointed to his breaft, and fancying Sir William has had information from Langwood, pulls the letter Frampton had charged him to fecrete from his pocket, which the baronet fnatches ; after puzzling each other for a few fpeeches longer, the valet, terrified for what he has done, makes a confufed and laughable retreat.

Here Sir William, refolving to have a further explanation, after reading the fatal letter, calls for his fifter and daughter, who both appear on the inftant ; he immediately pronounces the deceit, which overpowers Harriet, and gives Langwood's letter to Mrs. Winifred, who, with her ufual felf-fufficiency, confiders it as a falfe, forged affair ; and feems to wonder that her brother can be fo eafily impofed upon. This but enflames the baronet's paffion more, and caufes him, after fome ftinging reproaches vented againft his daughter, to hurry off the ftage.

Harriet, in the midft of her confufion, propofes to fly from Lord Euftace's dwelling, but Mrs. Winifred perfifting in her opinion, that there is fome impofition in the affair, advifes her neice to fend

Lord

Lord Euſtace a letter; this, though warmly urged, is obſtinately refuſed, ſo that when Harriet retires to avoid further importunity, the aunt determines to write herſelf; and though ſome doubts reſpecting Lord Euſtace intrude upon her, yet ſhe cheriſhes the comfortable idea, that he dare not deceive her, or, if he does, that the ap Evans's are not to be injured with impunity.

At the beginning of the fourth act, a new character is preſented to us, Colonel Evans. In the converſation between him and Captain Lloyd, the latter, after blaming young Evans for leaving his regiment ſo abruptly on a woman's account, apologizes in ſome meaſure for the indiſcretion, by telling what influence a Donna Iſabella at Gibraltar, had once like to have gained over himſelf; after this, the talkative tar enquires minutely into the circumſtances of the colonel's fair one, to which he only obtains the general reply, that ſhe is young, handſome, and of rank above her admirer's expectation; expoſition of her name is declined. After theſe gentlemen diſappear, who, in our opinion, have ſaid nothing any way eſſential to the piece, nor much to place them in eſteem with an audience, Mrs. Winifred and Robert appear, when ſhe receives further proof of Lord Euſtace's treachery. After a few lines, ſhe diſpatches the honeſt domeſtic to watch a private door in the garden; here Sir William joins his ſiſter, who wants to argue matters with him, but his temper of mind not ſuiting her purpoſe, he at firſt anſwers rather churliſhly; however, ſhe forces her diſcourſe on him, and propoſes to try her influence and Harriet's tears upon Lord Euſtace. This deſign the baronet treats with contempt, and thereby

thereby irritates his vain fifter; befides, with becoming pride, he difdains the thought of his daughter's fuing fo bafe a man. Another thought arifes
in Mrs. Winifred's prolific brain, that as Lord
Euftace has a place at court, Sir William fhould
complain of him to the king; this romantic idea
produces fome juft compliments to virtuous royalty,
but Sir William cafts fo ineffectual a proceeding afide,
and determines upon taking perfonal fatisfaction,
with which fpirited refolution he withdraws.

Another very immaterial foliloquy occurs here,
at the end of which Robert appears, and informs
Winifred, that he has heard the private door in the
garden unlocked, this hurries her off to prevent
Lord Euftace's meeting her enraged brother.

Colonel Evans, who as we find has been affault-
ed by footpads, enters with Lord Euftace, by whom
he has been refcued; thanks are returned for the
fervice. By a converfation which enfues, we find,
that upon being told the title of his deliverer, Colonel Evans looks on him as a rival in the affections
of Lady Ann Mountfort; a meeting is propofed,
but declined, as each of the gentlemen is otherwife
particularly engaged: Lord Euftace partly unfolds
his critical fituation with Harriet, but as her name is
not mentioned, the colonel remains ignorant that
fhe is his fifter.

The next fcene Mrs. Winifred brings on Harriet,
when Lord Euftace immediately enters, and endeavours to footh that heavy concern which hangs on
the young lady; for fome time the aunt harangues
him on the charge of infidelity, which he evades
with tolerable effrontery, but is reduced to a painful dilemma upon her producing Langwood's letter;

2 · however,

however, he profeffes an honeft defign, dictated by ardent love, in the clandeftine marriage effected him; this ftrikes Mrs. Winifred with the pleafing hopes of repairing every thing, and fhe goes off to prevent Sir William from coming abruptly upon the young couple, as they feem to be in a fair train of reconciliation; but this female politician appears much out in her calculation, for Harriet's offended virtue and delicacy remain inexorable to entreaty, and fhe retires, difclaiming every idea of connection with fo unworthy a betrayer: here Sir William enters, full of the injury done him through his daughter, and a very warm altercation enfues, which is fupported on Lord Euftace's fide with as much decent fpirit as the circumftances will admit; to Sir William's violent decifion, he very properly oppofes his own confcioufnefs of error, which is a fufficient reafon why courage fhould not exert itfelf againft an injured perfon; however, the baronet's perfifting in aggravation, compels him at laft to accept the challenge, in confequence of which, a meeting is appointed at eight o'clock the next morning, with feconds.

After Sir William has expreffed fatisfaction that his fon the colonel is abfent, as this affair of the duel muft have fallen upon him, Mrs. Winifred bolts in, and accufes her brother of turning matters topfyturvy; fhe alfo mentions Harriet's haughty refufal, which feems to give the old gentleman fingular fatisfaction. His fifter's wifh for being attached to nobility at any rate, gives rife to fome pertinent reflections upon the mingled pride and meannefs which mark her character; Sir William treats her notions with afperity and contempt, and then haftes to

Vol. II.   F   comfort

comfort Harriet, whofe rejection of Lord Euftace, has replaced her in his favour. Mrs. Winifred, in a high miff at the flight fhe has received, wants to affert her own infallibility, by cafting the blame of what has happened upon others, and concludes, with applying to herfelf Lord Chatham's declaration, of not being accountable for meafures that fhe is not fuffered to guide.

Lord Euftace and Frampton begin the fifth act, conferring on the unlucky circumftance of the former having met Sir William, and the challenge confequential to it, which Frampton fenfibly obferves, ought not to be fulfilled; however, Lord Euftace folicits him to act as a fecond, which for fubftantial reafons he denies. Marriage of Harriet is urged as a palliative, but the young peer dreads an imputation of cowardice. Upon Frampton's abfolute denial to be concerned, Lord Euftace requefts his delivery of a letter, in cafe he fhould fall, to his father, and goes off to fearch a lefs fcrupulous friend to act as a fecond. Frampton defcants fome time on the contrariety of Lord Euftace's difpofition, and goes off, refolved to avert, if poffible, thofe perils which hang over his head.

Harriet, accompanied by her aunt, gives vent to an unequalled, and apparently incurable perplexity of mind, occafioned not only by the bafenefs of her fuppofed hufband, but by the impending duel, which fhe urges Mrs. Winifred to prevent at any rate, for which purpofe the old lady retires juft as Sir William appears : he perceives Harriet's concern, and tenderly tries to foften her, but endangering his life on her account, prevents the defired effect; as the baronet will not relax thofe ftrict notions of honour,

which

which urge him on to fo defperate a mode of fatisfaction.

Captain Lloyd's approach occafions the afflicted
Harriet to retire ; we find that the captain has been
fummoned to act as Sir William's fecond; to this
end the baronet acquaints him with the duel he is
engaged in ; a circumftance which draws from the
fon of Neptune fome whimfical remarks on fighting, for which he feems to have a very good ftomach,
but thinks breakfaft an effential preparative. This
caufes Sir William to take him into another room,
and leaves the ftage open for Lord Euftace, who
comes on with Colonel Evans, as his fecond.

By what drops from the colonel, we find, his lordfhip, through romantic notions of juftice, has determined to ftand Sir William's fire, without returning it. At the fame inftant, Harriet and her
father enter at oppofite doors, the colonel is immediately faluted with the titles of fon and brother,
but is reproved as appearing the abettor of that
man who has difgraced his fifter; this young Evans
difclaims, and treats Harriet with rough contempt ;
then takes the quarrel upon himfelf, and gives Lord
Euftace a regular challenge, which, upon finding
Harriet's innocence, he feems more warmly bent to
enforce. As he and Lord Euftace are going off,
Frampton enters, who, hearing Harriet exclaim,
" when will my miferies end," replies, " I hope
this moment, madam." This dawning of an e-
clairciffement occafions furprize in all the parties,
and enquiries of what he means ; when he declares,
that he has been with, and is juft come from Lord
Delville, who approves Harriet for a daughter-in-
law, and has charged him with a letter to Sir Wil-

liam

liam Evans upon that subject. This letter being
perused, the baronet pronounces it a mark of honour in the old peer, yet says it cannot atone for
the misconduct of his son Lord Euftace; this ftarts
a fresh difficulty, which however is removed by a
declaration, that Lady Anne Mountfort never was
an object of serious attention to Lord Euftace, and
is in reality the lady whose hand is deftined for Colonel Evans: hence a reconciliation and mutual
congratulations enfue on all sides.

Captain Lloyd, upon feeing such an affemblage
of unexpected characters, feems difappointed that
the proposed engagement is not likely to take place;
however, like an honeft, good natured man, fympa-
thizes in the general joy, with which the comedy
concludes. But what could induce the author to
tag half a dozen very indifferent lines together, by
way of deducing a moral, we fhall not pretend to
fuggeft; let it fuffice to fay, that we could wish nature and the eftablifhed mode, which rejects rhimes,
had been more ftrictly regarded.

Upon a general view of this comedy, it appears
to be written with a good intention; the dialogue
has confiderable eafe, but not much fpirit or elegance; the plot is tolerably interefting, and the
fcenes regularly enough difpofed, but the cataftrophe
is rather huddled up; and the delicacy which Sir
William Evans and his daughter feem fo ftrongly
poffeffed of, at laft vanifhes almoft imperceptibly.

The characters, without a grain of originality,
are well imagined, and fupported with tolerable
confiftence; Lord Euftace is an odd medley of virtues and weaknefs, for his errors are certainly more
the effect of warm paffions and inadequate judgment

ment than abfolute vice ; there is a face of meannefs
in his propofed connection with Lady Anne, which
cafts a fhade that refts on him, even when matters
are made up. In reprefentation, he is what performers call a tolerable walking gentleman, and is
not much beyond the abilities of Mr. CAUTHERLY,
who, by never attempting any thing higher, would
deferve fome degree of praife.

Sir William is a perfon of nice feelings, and a
fond, without being a foolifh father. Mr. HOL-
LAND, who was certainly better calculated for a particular caft in comedy, than any thing he ever did,
or could do of a tragic nature, gave juft and fingular fatisfaction in the Welch baronet ; fince his
death, Mr. HURST has undertaken him, with fome
degree of fuccefs, which could not happen without
fome merit ; though certainly the audiences of London have lately been much weaker in their judgment, or more extenfive in good nature, than they
were feven years ago. May the difpofition continue till there is a frefh fupply of intrinfic merit to
ftand the teft of criticifm.

Colonel Evans is a very immaterial object, and
can never gain any credit for either author or actor ;
what can be done for him in action Mr. PALMER
fupplies agreeably enough.

Frampton is certainly a well drawn child of nature ; one who, notwithftanding the want of prudence to preferve his circumftances in a ftate of
comfort and refpect, neverthelefs has a heart which
fcorns, even in the midft of dependance, to flatter or
promote for intereft, the vices of an opulent patron;
nay, who hazards the favour of that patron by labouring to fave him from himfelf : he is a moft amiable

able agent in the piece, and fhould not after his effential, good offices, have been left in fuch an unprovided
ftate at the conclufion. We know not any character
more chaftely or more agreeably performed on either of the ftages than this by Mr. REDDISH, from
whofe expreffion the valuable fentiments flow with
peculiar grace and fenfibility.

Captain Lloyd is well defigned, but underwritten,
the leaft entertaining of any fea character on the
ftage, and moft evidently borrowed from all who
went before him; nothing but the happy conception
and exquifite talents of Mr. KING, could render
him fo agreeable as he now appears.

Willis feems drawn with judgment and vivacity by the author; nor is the effential whim and
fprightlinefs of reprefentation any way deficient in
Mr. DODD's very pleafing performance of this
laughable and fpirited valet. Mr. W. PALMER has
upon emergencies made a tolerable fhift.

Robert has an agreeable, blunt fimplicity, and
commendable honefty of character in his compofition; and ftood much indebted for the notice he
obtained to Mr. BADDELY's characteriftic naivetè of
action.

Mrs. Winifred is a painful, miferable copy of
Mrs. Margate Maxwell, in the DEVIL upon two
STICKS: fo flat, fo impoverifhed, that Mrs. CLIVE's
powerful talents alone could have rendered her bearable: poor Mrs. HOPKINS is as much afleep in the
performance, as the author was in writing this part.

Harriet is a tender, fenfible, delicate young lady,
and in every one of thofe ideas received ample juftice
from the interefting appearance, and pathetic expreffion of Mrs. BADDELY.

Being

School for Rakes.

Being much difgufted, both in the theatre and clofet with a fuperabundance of foliloquies in this piece, we have taken pains to count them, and find no lefs than twenty-two; the greateft part of which, or at leaft half, falls to Frampton alone ; the plot muft be very hard ftrained which requires fuch aid ; however, the SCHOOL for RAKES, from its moral tendency, and the excellent fentiments with which in feveral places it is fprinkled, may be recommended as a comedy more deferving of attention, both in public and private, than many other pieces of much greater critical merit ; virtue is patronized and inculcated through the whole, without being once put to the blufh, or in the leaft degree facrificed to applaufe catching humour.

The

The O R P H A N.

A TRAGEDY by OTWAY.

IF the author now before us could not lay claim
to the nobleſt, yet he has been generally, and juſtly
allowed ſome of the tendereſt flights of genius that
ever graced dramatic compoſition : his beauties are
many, and thoſe he principally derived from the liberality 'of nature, which had conferred feelings,
conception and expreſſion, well adapted to a ſubject
of the queen of tears. He had alſo ſeveral glaring
faults, but thoſe were totally derived from the licentiouſneſs of taſte, and depravity of manners, which
prevailed when he wrote ; indeed, by his life, as
well as his pen, we perceive him to have been deeply tainted, but our remarks muſt be applied to him
as a poet, not a man.

It is uſual to omit the firſt ſcene of this tragedy in
repreſentation, which is a ſtretch of theatrical prerogative we do not altogether approve ; for though
what paſſes between Erneſto and Paulino is not ab-
ſolutely eſſential, yet their converſation is beyond
doubt a very good introduction to the piece, better,
as we apprehend, than that with which it now commences ; however we ſhall not give the ſubſtance of
what is ſo little regarded, but begin with the two
brothers, who being juſt returned from the chace,
mention ſome danger that Caſtalio has been in, and
then paſs on to other matters, till they come at laſt

to

Orphan.

to mention Monimia, their father's ward. The attachment of each to this young lady, occasions an appearance of disagreement between them, but a softening concession from one, draws from the other a most solemn declaration of unalterable friendship; uttered partly according to the taste of the day, in rhime, and very little above the degree of doggrel.

When Monimia enters with the page, we soon perceive that her heart is considerably prejudiced in favour of Castalio; all her questions and observations strongly indicate it. Cordelio's replies to her questions are in an arch characteristic stile, but in one speech rather licentious; his account of what he has heard from the brothers, in regard to their love for Monimia, is distinct and natural; we think Monimia's resentment against the design of Castalio's introducing Polydore to a private conference, is very becoming; indeed, there does not seem any colour for such a paltry condescension in the former, as the latter might have gained an interview without such an introduction.

When the brothers appear, and Castalio, according to promise, stands master of the ceremonies, the lady expresses confusion; but why she should seem to entertain such dreadful, previous apprehensions of Polydore, we cannot say. Castalio's sudden, and we may add, strange departure, ruffles her extremely, and seems to be the only cause for her ungracious charge of ill gature against Polydore's countenance, even before he has spoke a word; such treatment is rather cavalier on her side, yet at first occasions no return but warm declarations of amorous passion, which are well expressed, and suitably replied to: however, when Monimia comes to a peremptory refusal of sacrificing her honour, why she should suppose his professions dishonourable, we know not. Polydore throws off every trace of the gentleman, and shews himself the brute Monimia seems to have imagined him. His general sarcasm against the whole sex is illiberal, but not without some truth and considerable fancy; her reply is couched in very proper and strong terms: what Polydore speaks after she goes off, his allusion to the bull, &c. is almost too gross for a satyr to utter, or a Billingsgate fish-wife to hear; it is highly shameful that somewhat more bearable has not been substituted, instead of such sensual, filthy trash.

At the beginning of the second act, Acasto, with his two sons, are presented to our view; the old gentleman descants on the pleasures and dangers of that day's chace; particularly remarking his own critical situation from the attack of a wild boar, and his fortunate conquest over that furious animal. Recital of this last circumstance draws from Castalio a complimentary line, which his father justly considers as bordering on flattery; a depravation of mind he treats with asperity, dismissing it with great propriety from social connections, to the interested dependance of court sycophancy; a dissembling dependance, which he illustrates in very strong colours, and corrects with a keen lash of satire: but poets may exhaust their imaginations, and moralists declaim on the subject till they are weary; yet modest merit will never gain an equal share of favour at any court, with servile effrontery and low artifice.

Serina bringing on the news of Chamont's arrival, gives Acasto singular pleasure; he having, as appears, a warm attachment to that young soldier, whom

whom he welcomes with the moft cordial tendernefs. Chamont replies with manly feeling, interchanges fome kind expreffions with his fifter Monimia, and then pays a delicate compliment to Acafto's daughter Serina, which fhe feems to receive with fome degree of tender fenfation.

Acafto, in the flow of domeftic happinefs, and in refpect of his royal mafter's birth-day, orders feftivity through all his houfe ; and upon his fon's letting fall fome expreffions of ardent loyalty, he manifefts a little of the vanity of age, in proclaiming an anecdote of once killing a rebel who uttered difrefpectful terms of his monarch. The laboured panegyrics upon royalty in this fcene, were fo many fugar-plumbs dropped by our bard to fweeten the leading character of his day.

As Acafto is going off to receive fome guefts who are arrived, Chamont defires a conference upon matter of ferious concern, which being granted, he draws a pathetic, preparative picture of his dying parents, to introduce more ftrongly the old gentleman's kind patronage to himfelf and his fifter ; he then fuggefts a doubt concerning Monimia's fituation and behaviour, which Acafto defires him to clear up, adding a moft friendly declaration, that he will defend her caufe, even though it fhould fubject his own children to prejudice.

Here a conference enfues between Chamont and his fifter, from whence we may infer, that he poffeffes honour to almoft a romantic degree ; but is unaccountably credulous, and unpardonably choleric. His account of their dead father is truly amiable ; the dream is fanciful, but a ftrange foundation for a man of even tolerable underftanding to ground jea-

lous

lous apprehenfions upon ; and the picture of the old hag, who gave his fears confirmation, is inimitable, fo worthy regard, as a beautiful defcription, that we beg leave to tranfcribe it ; though after all, we judge it a fufficient proof of Chamont's weaknefs, and wonder at our author for inculcating fo ridiculous an idea of witchcraft.

> Through a clofe lane as I purfu'd my journey,
> And meditating on my laft night's vifion,
> I fpied a wrinkled hag with age grown double,
> Picking dry fticks, and mumbling to herfelf ;
> Her eyes with fcalding rheum were galled and red,
> Cold palfy fhook her head, her hands feemed wither'd ;
> And on her crooked fhoulders had fhe wrapped
> The tatter'd remnant of an old ftrip'd hanging,
> Which ferv'd to keep her carcafe from the cold,
> So there was nothing of a piece about her ;
> Her lower weeds were all o'er coarfely patch'd
> With different colour'd rags ; black, red, white,
>   yellow,
> And feem'd to fpeak variety of wretchednefs.

Upon Monimia's folemn declaration of ftrict adherence to virtue, Chamont's ftrange paffion cools, and gives her fome friendly, fenfible hints, refpecting the diffimulation of men in fubjects of love. He retires, and the young lady, irritated by Polydore's ungenteel treatment, determines, even at the expence of her own peace, to treat Caftalio with feverity. His immediate appearance gives her an opportunity of putting this refolution in practice, which fhe does in part, by quitting the ftage as he comes on ; this occafions Caftalio to utter his diffatisfaction in foliloquy, as alfo to fuggeft, that he has

a natural

a natural pliantnefs of temper which his miftrefs
plays upon ; he alfo confeffes himfelf wrong in trifling with his brother, where fo ferious a matter is
concerned ; but flatters himfelf, that as it is his firft
tranfgreffion, no ill confequences will enfue.

Polydore here enters, and places that young agent
of intrigue, the page, as a fpy upon his brother and
Monimia ; when the lovers come forward, we find
the lady in a fit of warm refentment, much beyond,
as we think, any provocation fhe has received, and
the gentleman for fome time tenderly condefcending ; however, ftung with reproaches which arife
from mention of Polydore, his temper rifes on the
fret, yet his refolution fhortly fails, and he finks again
into the whine with fuch effect, that Monimia foftens
into forgivenefs, and a fudden reconciliation, in the
true love ftile, enfues ; this caufes Caftalio to vent
his extraordinary fatisfaction in the full flow of poetical frenzy, rhiming himfelf and the fair Monimia
moft harmonioufly off the ftage.

Polydore, with his little fpy, begin the third act,
when a full difcovery is made to the former by the
latter, of all that paffed in the foregoing fcene ; the
page having told his tale, is fent off, when a fervant
enters with intelligence that Acafto has been fuddenly and violently taken ill at the banquet ; the
old gentleman foon enters in a ftate of weaknefs,
but recovery ; having his children about him, he
declares the difpofition of his fortune, in cafe of deceafe, to be an equal divifion of his eftate between
the brothers, fave a referve of ten thoufand crowns
for Monimia. This fcene furnifhes a ftrange con-
tradictory lapfe in Acafto's conduct ; for after an
equal divifion of his fortune between Caftalio and

Polydore,

Polydore, he allots one third of it to Chamont, in case of his marriage with Serina, who, in the first difpofition of affairs, poor lady ! was totally forgot. Thefe points fettled, Acafto retires to reft, attended by all the characters, except Chamont and the Chaplain.

Our young foldier's phrafe of addrefs to the clergyman, ftiling him Sir Gravity, is rather an unpolite, ludicrous beginning of converfation ; the intention of Chamont evidently appears to be getting at the connection, if any, between his fifter and Caftalio ; however, not being anfwered fo fully, nor fo foon as he wifhes, he breaks out into the fquib and cracker ftile of paffion, uttering fuch a train of illgrounded, irrational, ungentleman-like abufe, upon the clerical profeffion in general, as cannot be juftified : however, the Chaplain, with a moft eafy, condefcending nature, teeming with Chriftian forgivenefs, for the groffeft abufe, trufts one he has great reafon to think half a madman, with what at prefent feems effentially a fecret, the marriage ; this foftens the frantic red-coat, and they part upon very obliging terms.

Caftalio and Monimia now appear, he fully fatisfied with being in poffeffion of the idol of his heart ; fhe confeffes fome female fears from ominous circumftances which fhe has taken notice of ; thefe apprehenfions the bridegroom imputes to her tender nature, and urges a fpeedy confummation of his blifs. Here Polydore fhews himfelf, in the mean office of liftening at the door : Monimia reprefents fome probable ill confequences from her new hufband's coming to her bed chamber ; however, being clofely urged, fhe gives him a fignal to fecure

his

his admittance, and leaves him full of satisfaction at
the near completion of his happiness.

Polydore presenting himself, as if casually, to the
view of Castalio, and enquiring rather particularly
after Monimia, he receives equivocal answers, which
warm him into an absolute assertion of his passion ;
he delivers himself with warmth and roughness of
expression, while his evasive brother treats the matter with affected indifference, and retires sneeringly:
this behaviour, and his own licentious disposition,
prevail on Polydore to attempt a fatal imposition
upon hapless Monimia; having heard the appointed
signal, he derives from thence strong hopes of success ; for the purpose of gaining time, he calls the
page, and instructs him to attend Castalio while he
is undressing, and to stay with him till he is gone to
bed.

Matters thus disposed, he approaches the chamber
door, and by giving the signal, brings Florella to the
window, who, supposing him Castalio, tells him Monimia wonders at his *unkind* delay ; tho' it is certain,
as the stage has not been vacant since she went into
her chamber, that she has scarce had time to get un-
dressed ; Polydore being admitted, with a very fulsome address to his limbs, Castalio enters, followed
by the page, whom he wants to get quit of ; however, true to his master's instructions, he perseveres
in attendance, and obliges Castalio to hear some
proofs of his archness, though not much to the credit of his modesty ; indeed our author seems indu-
strious to call a blush upon the cheeks of delicacy as
often as possible ; for he has made this page, which
is generally represented by a child, utter some very
gross sentiments.

Being

Being at length difmiffed, Caftalio prepares for admittance to the manfion of his joy ; but, we think, if lefs had been given him to fay, where abfolute filence feemed fo neceffary, it would have been more confonant to the nature of things. Upon Florella's coming to the window, fuppofing him an impoftor, fhe treats him contemptuoufly ; this unexpected and provoking difappointment of his hopes, enflames him fo much, that being abfolutely refufed, he throws himfelf upon the ground, exclaiming againft the fuppofed faithlefsnefs of Monimia. Here Ernefto, an old fervant, following, as he fays, the found of forrow, finds his young mafter in that melancholy ftate ; with dutiful tendernefs he ftrives to footh his anxiety : on being told a woman is the caufe, he declares a hatred of the fex; this pleafes and flatters Caftalio's perturbed ftate of mind, which caufes him to exclaim in fevere, general terms, againft women, from whom hiftorically he deduces fome of the moft fignal mifchiefs which ftand recorded ; and with this rhapfodical, frenzied exclamation, he concludes the third act, in fuch a vociferous manner, as we might reafonably expect to draw the whole family about his ears.

Acafto, in foliloquy, commences the fourth act, congratulating himfelf upon a reftoration of health, which he imputes to a happy reft, and yet in the lines immediately after, complains of painful, ominous dreams, which are the bane, the imbitterers of nature's fecond feaft, hag-riding his imagination all night ; this is fo grofs a contradiction, that it is wonderful how the author could fall into it. Polydore appearing, his father enquires for Caftalio, and defires to meet him in the chapel ; then

Orphan.

then in a fecond foliloquy, fpeaks of having heard Caftalio's voice, during the night, conveying melancholy founds.

Here Monimia approaches the old gentleman, who, after fome kind obfervations upon her engaging looks, afks if fhe has not heard fome particular noife at night, being anfwered in the negative, he goes off to make further enquiry.

Our Orphan now left with Florella, declares apprehenfion that her marriage is difcovered, which muft operate much to the difadvantage of her hufband ; a kind of complaint is dropped at the bridegroom's cool method of taking leave in the morning. Upon feeing Caftalio fhe retires for fake of meeting him in her chamber, we think it would have been more natural to have met his fteps half way : however, her leaving the ftage, affords him an opportunity of fpeaking a very poetical, defcriptive foliloquy ; but a moft unnatural effufion for one under fuch a violent ftate of mental perturbation as Caftalio is.

Monimia, who has but juft now retired, without any frefh reafon returns, and flies into the arms of her lord, as fhe fhould have done before the uneffential differtation upon mountains, fhepherds, flocks, huts, birds, trees, &c. which he has fo fancifully entertained us with. Confcious of her own innocence and virtuous affection, the reception fhe meets naturally gives her a great fhock ; and though we confefs Caftalio's provocation poignant, yet we think the author has confulted the progrefs of his plot more than nature, in making him vent his paffions fo outrageoufly, without the minuteft article of enquiry why he was refufed admittance, as common

fenfe

fenfe might fuggeft fome caufe for fuch refufal, though not the real one; be it as it may, the bridegroom behaves in a moft tyrannical, unintelligible manner, and leaves his unhappy bride in a ftate of diftracted grief, which circumftance, however it may offend our reafon, neverthelefs touches compaffion very feelingly.

Chamont, at this interefting, alarming crifis enters, and finds his fifter in a fituation of the moft affecting nature : he tenderly enquires the caufe, and hearing Caftalio named, very juftly takes fire, but fomewhat checks the tumult of his mind, till the whole affair is explained in very pathetic terms; upon which he flames irrefiftably, and vows vengeance on Caftalio. This dreadful refolution Monimia is endeavouring to avert juft as Acafto enters; Chamont's impetuofity caufes him to affail the old man in a blameable, though natural manner.

Giving the epithet of villain to one of his fons, impreffes the old man ftrongly, and the fcene is agitated with warmth on both fides; the firmnefs of age, and flightinefs of youth, are finely contrafted; foftening Chamont, and then precipitating him again into ungovernable rage, are well imagined, well executed tranfitions; finely drawn, but rather too highly coloured for ftrict adherence to nature. On being promifed juftice, the young foldier retires, leaving Monimia to receive a very ftinging, though brief obfervation from Acafto; importing, that her firft complaint fhould have been to him as a father, which might have prevented fuch domeftic combuftion.

Thus wretchedly circumftanced, ill treated by her hufband, and in fome meafure caft off by his

father,

father, Monimia is left comfortless, amidst a thousand apprehensions for both her brother and Castalio, when Polydore comes in, and endeavours to
sooth the distressed fair one with tender expressions ;
however, not being a very agreeable object, it is not
likely his kindness should take the desired effect.
Upon mentioning that he knows Castalio to be the
cause of her sighs and tears, and urging his own
passion, Monimia reproaches him with having attempted to enter her chamber, under semblance of
his brother ; upon which, with a degree of precipitate triumph, he not only avows the design, but
boasts his absolute success. This raises a tremendous alarm in the heart of Monimia, and she cautions him to avoid such a dreadful assertion ; however, upon a clear, explicit declaration, of having
passed the night in her bed-chamber, nature faints
under so violent a shock, and Monimia is rendered
for a moment insensible of her horrid situation.

On the revival of her senses, she breaks out into a
general execration, and acquaints Polydore with the
dreadful crime his precipitate inadvertence has
hurried him into. Their intercourse now takes the
affecting turn of deep, mutual contrition, and pun-
gent sorrow. One thought of Polydore's, which suggests murdering, if any, the fruit of their guilty
joys, is detestably shocking, and the more so, as
there is no reason for mentioning such a thing ; and
of all extravagant excursions of fancy which have
offended criticism and propriety, we know not one
more hateful and unnatural, than Polydore's conclusive speech to the fourth act ; the notion of
witches, at any rate, is contemptible, but to introduce a picture of their noisome rendezvous, and to

present

prefent them as feeding upon imps, fattened with the blood of babes, is as difguftful as it is unnatural. The ftage has, we think, commendably foftened this moft cenfurable paffage.

The fifth act begins with Caftalio lying on the ground, and, as we underftand from his words, taking a view of deer which are paffing; from whence he draws a fhort comparifon between the tranquil ftate of brutality, and the perturbed fitua-tion of rational beings. His foliloquy ends with a very grofs and fuperfluous remark : being called upon by his father, he enquires who is fo wretched but to name him ; Acafto's defign is that of a fen-fible, benevolent parent, to reconcile the breach be-tween his fon and daughter-in-law ; this defirable point he urges warmly, and infifts upon Caftalio's condefcending to a perfonal interview with Moni-mia, but cannot prevail. While they are in debate, Chamont appears, full fraught with injuries : Caf-talio having heard the rough treatment his father has received from the young foldier, is prepared to meet him on the moft defperate terms ; from mu-tual heat, and aggravating expreffions, a fatal deci-fion feems impending, the fearful effects of which are prevented by Acafto's manly, fpirited interpo-fition, and the timely appearance of Serina ; how-ever, the ftorm feems to be lulled only for the pre-fent, and the young men part on very angry terms. Acafto here again renews his fuit, in favour of Mo-nimia, but without effect, till Florella enters with a pathetic account of her diftrefs, and an urgent foli-citation to fee Caftalio ; this melts all his obdurate refolves, and he hurries off to footh her anguifh. To fay truth, he has fhewn himfelf more than fuffi-ciently

Orphan.

ciently inexorable for any provocation he has received, as the material circumstance, of which she is innocent, as yet remains unknown to him.

Monimia enters in soliloquy, seeking distractedly for Castalio, who comes on with all the ardor of revived passion, with every trace of resentment sunk in oblivion.

Throughout this whole scene there is an affecting pathos of expression, and considerable variety of action: Monimia hints unintelligibly some hidden cause of distress, some unseen bar to the happiness he aims at, and which he supposes rests totally in her power. Grief and tenderness agitate him alternately, in a pitiable manner ; at length Monimia leaves him without any explanation, an entire prey to doubts and fears.

. At this gloomy period, upon this perilous temper of mind, Polydore enters, meditating on his own deplorable condition, which justly makes him weary of life. The brothers encounter, Castalio enquires for Monimia, of whom Polydore gloomily affects a total ignorance ; the word friendship being mentioned, Polydore catches at it, and throws out terms of suspicion against Castalio ; this urges the latter to a very affectionate declaration, and a solicitation of comfort from the former, who intimates he has none to give. At length, Castalio enters upon a perplexed explanation of his marriage with Monimia, this causes Polydore to break into violent resentment, which he gives scope to in very gross terms : Castalio manifests an extraordinary spirit of forbearance ; till, at last, being repeatedly stigmatized as a coward, he draws his sword, upon which Polydore voluntarily rushes, to end a being which the effects of his own

intemperance

intemperance has rendered hateful to him. Upon Caftalio's perceiving the fituation his brother is in, all enmity vanifhes, and he laments the circumftance which occafions Polydore to own his defign, to explain the occafion. Monimia comes in upon this blood-ftained fcene, and feeing the fatal circumftance which has happened, very juftly ftarts at the object. Caftalio now viewing her as an object of fingular guilt, feems to threaten death ; the expiring brother exculpates our unfortunate orphan in fuch a manner, that her unhappy hufband perceives his diffimulation has been the original and ultimate caufe of fuch fad difafters. Thus the plot comes to a moft interefting crifis ; Caftalio becomes convinced of his own mifconduct, and its fatal effects; while the innocent object of his rage and ill-treatment dies of poifon, adminiftered by herfelf---A circumftance we could have wifhed our author to avoid, as fuicide fhould never be rendered pitiable.

Chamont immediately enters upon the deceafe of his fifter, fraught with the fame vindictive rage as poffeffed him when laft he left the ftage; but the irrefiftable tempeft in Caftalio's breaft overbears him, till that unhappy victim of violent love and a weak mind, falls by his own hand. Polydore, who has lingered much too long on the ftage, yields his breath on Caftalio's receiving the fatal ftab, and Caftalio himfelf expires in a few lines, lamenting the forrows which are brought upon his aged, kind father, and bequeathing his birthright to Chamont ; who, after being a madman through all preceding fcenes where he has been concerned, immediately commences moralift, and concludes the piece with a moft uncomfortable, vague and indefenfible pofi-

tion,

Orphan.

tion, that heaven maintains its empire by the miseries of mankind; whereas, we think, that the bounties and indulgences of providence, as they are much more extenfive and worthy of divine power, fo they are infinitely a greater proof of it than thofe difagreeable, painful circumftances, which the follies and vices of mankind bring upon themfelves and fociety.

In this tragedy we meet with many ftrokes of peculiar fenfibility; the ftory affords great opportunity for fuch, and yet the plot not only abounds with improbable irregularities, but is originally founded upon a moft grofs and offenfive principle; every idea of delicacy is caft afide, and licentioufnefs made the vehicle of melting impreffions; the ftage is fo incumbered with blood and death, that it becomes a fpectacle of real horror; the characters give us in general a very unfavourable idea of human nature; however, they are well fupported, according to the principles on which each appears to be founded.

Acafto is an elderly nobleman, who has paffed part of his life in a ftate of honourable activity; but being like many other worthy objects, neglected to make way for the preferment of more pliant, courtly tempers, now abftracts himfelf from all public concerns, and means to enjoy the comforts of domeftic felicity. He appears to be poffeffed of a good underftanding, and a liberal mind; to his children a tender parent, to Monimia, as the daughter of a deceafed friend and dependent on him, a kind protector. No great requifites are wanting to render him refpectable in reprefentation, yet have we never feen any performer equal to our idea of this character; Meffrs. SPARKS and BERRY, were neareft the mark. Meffrs. BRANS-

EY

BY and GIBSON, are at prefent very poor apologies for it. Whatever ideas theatrical gentlemen may form of Acafto, we are perfectly of opinion, that he merits a capital actor to give him due confequence.

Caftalio is diftinguifhed by a foft, amorous turn of mind, whofe want of generous, open confidence, caufes all the diftrefsful circumftances which happen ; he is much more an object of partial pity than eftimation. With refpect to his brother, he certainly acts a mean, evafive part ; and with Monimia, he alternately fhews himfelf a fool and a tyrant : his circumftances give great fcope for the exertion of various capital powers, which were amazingly well fupplied in the elegant figure, bewitching voice, and excellent acting of Mr. BARRY ; who, in this part, defied the fevereft criticifm, and juftly claimed what he always obtained, the warmeft applaufe that enchanted feelings could beftow.

Mr. Rofs, tho' much fainter, has yet confiderable merit ; he figured the part well, his voice had the merit of harmony, but wanted extent of power for the moft impaffioned fcenes. Mr. REDDISH is heavy and inadequate through the whole ; neither his love, grief nor rage, keeps pace with the author's meaning. Mr. SMITH's conftant failing, famenefs, lies remarkably heavy on him in this part ; it is true, he rifes above infipidity, but does not ftrike out a gleam of leading merit. Mr. POWELL hit off the tender paffages much better than any other competitor, except Mr. BARRY ; but in the fcenes of mere dialogue, he fell very fhort of Mr. Rofs ; who perhaps for characteriftic eafe and gentility in them fhould be placed firft.

Polydore

Orphan.

Polydore is bold, open, licentious, rather brutal, both in character and expreffion ; ungenerous and bafe in his conduct to Monimia to the laft degree ; an object of much diflike, and very little efteem ; defpifed, or rather detefted in life, unpitied in his fall, more againft the actor than for him.

Mr. Sparks was the moft characteriftic performer out of many that we have obferved ; the fpirit and fubtlety of this part, he marked with peculiar merit. We remember to have feen Mr. Sheridan make a moft lamentable attempt at this character, and are bold to fay upon recollection, that except the bare meaning of thofe words he uttered, the whole was fuch 'a piece of impotent, difguftful performance, as fcarce any actor of repute ever fhewed before or fince. Meffrs. Cautherly and Wroughton are pretty equal competitors for the palm of infipidity ; to fay which is worft would puzzle the acuteft criticifm, and imagination is almoft at a lofs to conceive the wretchednefs of either.

Chamont, in our account of the piece, has been marked as an oddity, and an extraordinary one he really is, but well calculated to fhew an able actor advantageoufly. The quicknefs and fire of look, as well as expreffion and gefture, which fo eminently diftinguifh Mr. Garrick from all his cotemporaries, no where operate more happily than in Chamont ; paffions which are really abfurd and laughable, as the author has drawn them, are by him rendered refpectable and ftriking ; the calmer paffages he delivers with unequalled fenfibility, and his tranfitions to the impetuous ones are fo mafterly, that all attempts to defcribe his excellence muft injure it.

It will perhaps fcarcely be credited, yet is moft folemnly true, that we have feen Mr. QUIN, when at leaft fixty years old, and of fuch corpulence as to weigh twenty ftone, roll on for the young Chamont, in a fuit of cloaths heavy enough for Othello ; a pair of ftiff-topped white gloves, then only worn by attendants on a funeral, an old fafhioned major wig, and black ftockings ; yet odd as this external appearance may feem, his performance was not one jot lefs fo ; and, without exaggeration, we may affert, that there never was any thing fo like burlefque, except the thing itfelf, as this veteran's dronifh apology for the juvenile foldier.

Mr. SHERIDAN-- why, why did we ever meet him in this play, except for Acafto ? was untunably formal and ftiff in the mild fcenes, irkfomely boifterous in the impetuous ones ; not a glimpfe of merit appeared through the whole, except his defcription of the witch, and the account of his father's integrity. Mr. HOLLAND would have been equally difagreeable, but that his expreffion was more lively, and his powers, as well as figure, more adequate ; though the buckram of affectation ftiffened him moft abominably.

The Chaplain is as well fupported by Mr. LOVE, as any audience can poffibly wifh.

The page we have feen done extremely well by feveral different children, but apprehend, Mifs ROSE, who played laft fummer at Mr. FOOTE's, with fo much and well deferved applaufe, would from her diminitive fize, archnefs of look, and peculiar fhrewdnefs of expreffion, furpafs any who have come under our notice.

3

Monimia

Orphan.

Monimia is drawn a character of great estimation, and touches the feelings of pity in a very peculiar manner ; her attachment to Castalio is open, generous and constant ; in some passages, it is true, she discovers a temper bordering on the violent ; however, she undergoes circumstances of peculiar provocation, and is at last thrown into a most desperate state. It is hard to say how any human mind, especially one possessed of sensibility, could sustain so distracting a situation ; but we could heartily wish that the author had found a more justifiable method of releasing her from care, than by the act of suicide, which takes off much from the regard she has obtained, and manifestly casts a heavy shade on her fall ; her taking poison in such violent perturbation of mind, may be authorized by too many examples in real life, and therefore is not unnatural, but it should have been avoided, as not only highly immoral, but irrational also.

The opinion we gave of Mrs. CIBBER and Mrs. BELLAMY, in Belvidera, may nearly point out the merits of those ladies in this character ; equal in the error of sing-song, we think the latter looked and spoke all passages of amorous feeling, much better than the former ; but in rage and distress Mrs. CIBBER was no doubt equal to every degree of conception. In the first, second and third acts, we have very little doubt of Mrs. BELLAMY's superiority : In the fourth and fifth, her great competitor, or rather example, took the lead considerably.

Mrs. YATES, though possessed of powerful and pleasing talents for tragedy, has a certain studied haughtiness of look, and stiff mechanism of gesture, very ill adapted to such a personage as Monimia ;

I 2   therefore

therefore we never tasted critical pleasure from her performance of it; the mode being much better suited to Roxana than our orphan.

Mrs. BARRY rather overfigures Monimia, but by uniting every excellence of the two first mentioned ladies, except Mrs. CIBBER's amazingly descriptive countenance, wherein every feature spoke; she appears to us the best in our recollection. We have seen Mrs. W. BARRY make such a shift with the part as might do well enough on a country stage, but must be very insipid upon a Theatre Royal. Miss MILLER, who appeared at Covent Garden last winter in Monimia, has agreeable capabilities; but, as we apprehend, will never become a capital, standing dish for criticism to feast upon.

Serina being merely introduced to give Chamont a sweet-heart, and Florella to joke upon the disappointment of Castalio, they cannot be supposed of sufficient note to fix any actress in remembrance; therefore we shall pass them without further remark.

After admitting much of the pathos in this tragedy, so much as even to render it a good acting piece, we are again to complain of gross licentiousness, without the shadow of a moral; wherefore we deem it highly censurable, and sincerely lamenting such a vile prostitution of OTWAY's masterly talents, most sincerely wish it banished by general consent, both from the closet and the stage.

The

The LAME LOVER.

A COMEDY by Mr. FOOTE.

BEFORE we investigate the comedy now in view, we hope our readers will concur in opinion, that as the author of it is at present living, and has had heavy charges of personality in characters laid against him, it may be an essential point of that impartiality we profess, to take a short view of the comic Muse's prerogative; and having established her power within due, that is salutary limits, a fair trial of the modern Aristophanes may ensue.

We first then lay it down for an irrefragable principle, that as satire could have no just existence without vices and follies, all knaves and fools, of whatever country or denomination, are the natural, lawful game of comedy; general ideas of both may be struck out to the proper ends of amusement and instruction; but how faint are the effects of such compared with those where individuals have sat for a well drawn picture? but then, say some persons, possessed of false delicacy, is it not cruel to render any particular character laughable or obnoxious? to this we readily answer, that it is really nature or habit, not the satirist, that furnishes the cause of such effects. For instance, a printer, with one leg, could never have been rendered the butt of ridicule, if a coxcomical vanity of appearing quite the fine gentleman, and a wit, with intellects very little a-
bove

bove common fenfe, had not marked him out as a
character of rifibility. If fuch a perfonage as Cad-
wallader ever lived, of which there is no doubt,
could there be richer or more defirable food for genius to feaft on ? his convulfed motion is not the
foundation of the mirth he occafions, his boafted
courage, learning, love for, and contempt of his wife,
are fuch an olio of whim, that it would have been
unpardonable in a writer of Mr. FOOTE's talents,
not to have facrificed him at the fhrine of fatire ;
however fome may argue of cruelty, we affert, that
a dramatic author, as well as a critic, or judge on the
bench, fhould be proof againft all influence of affi-
nity, intimacy, and partial connections. If you apply the rod to a favourite child, it muft wound your
feelings ; but will you therefore refrain due correction, and let him vegetate a wild, uncultivated,
and perhaps poifonous weed in the field of nature.

If then an acquaintance, or even a friend, who would
perhaps take umbrage from advice in private, renders
himfelf ridiculous or hateful, what more probable
method of working a reformation, than by fhewing
him a ftrong reflecting mirror of his own defects or
deformities ? thus then, fuppofing the perfon aimed
at takes it to himfelf, it bears a ftrong probability
of rendering him fervice, though by a painful method ; if, as is moftly the cafe, he joins the public
laugh at his own picture, without knowing it, then
there can be no cruelty, becaufe he fuffers no pain
from it ; indeed, if a man's circumftances were invaded, or any branch of trade injured, except that
moft pernicious one, methodift preaching, the cafe
would alter much, and even ftrict truth, too pub-
licly fpoken, be cenfurable.

That

Lame Lover.

That writer who comes neareſt the grand point of teaching us to *know ourſelves*, is certainly the moſt uſeful ; and in the dramatic ſphere, if he ſuperadds peculiar humour, deſerves the greateſt ſhare of praiſe. The ſtage has for ſeveral years dwindled into an almoſt total loſs of character and ſpirit, inſtead of which is ſubſtituted a ſoft, ſimpering, vague, declamatory chit-chat, to which is politely given the unmeaning title of ſentimental dialogue.

The LAME LOVER opens with Serjeant Circuit, we fear a very common character, and his daughter Charlotte, in warm conference about ſome gallant, which the former favours, but to whom Charlotte makes ſome ſtrong and ſenſible objections. The old ſplitter of cauſes, as he is afterwards emphatically called, argues humorouſly in quaint terms of litigation, and endeavouring to explain the matter, by a caſe in point, he puzzles himſelf in a very laughable manner, leaving the point more unintelligible than he found it.

Upon mention of Sir Luke Limp, the young lady ſuggeſts that he has other motives of attraction than his pretended paſſion for her, to bring him to the ſerjeant's houſe ; upon being interrogated concerning her meaning, ſhe hints a view upon her mother-in-law, Mrs. Circuit ; this, as ſhe cannot bring any poſitive proof, the lawyer treats with indifference, and imputes it to her jealouſy of the baronet. Here a deſcription of that gentleman drawn in lively terms occurs : ſpeaking of Sir Luke's being vain, even of defects, we meet this excellent remark ; " To be ſure, ſuſtaining unavoidable evils with conſtancy, is a certain ſign of greatneſs of mind ; but then, to derive vanity from a miſfortune, will not, I am afraid, be

be admitted as a vaft inftance of wifdom, and indeed
looks as if the man had nothing better to diftinguifh
himfelf by." The abfurd defire of hunting after,
and being attached to people of fortune, merely for
fake of their titles, is alfo alledged againft Sir Luke,
whom Charlotte ftiles, and ludicroufly proves a mere
nobody, upon very ample arguments. With thefe
preparatives he enters, full of vivacity, loquacity,
and felf-opinion ; his very outfet, defcribing his
companions, and the new chriftening of Charlotte,
as he calls it, has a ftrong zeft of humour. Upon
the lawyer's obferving that Sir Luke is nothing
worfe for the lofs of a leg, our whimfical baronet
turns his misfortune to advantage, by obferving,
that a falfe limb is free from all the apprehenfions
of injury and fenfations of pain, which commonly
attend a real one ; there is fomething extremely
whimfical in his remarks upon what he calls the
redundancies of human nature, and his challenging
the hot-headed Swifs to run corking pins into the
calves of their legs, is not only laughable from the
oddity of idea, but a juft and fevere farcafm a-
gainft boafters of courage and ftoicifm.

A fervant here enters with Sir Gregory Goofe's
complimentary invitation to Sir Luke, who mentions a previous engagement; but, upon hearing that
Sir Greg. is returned a member of parliament, he
throws afide his promife to Alderman Inkle, and
complies with the requeft of his brother baronet.
In a very fhort fpace the footman returns with a
letter, which proves to be a folicitation of Sir Luke's
company from Lord Brentford ; this occafions an
embarraffment, how to get off with Sir Greg. but
he fends an apology for that purpofe. Charlotte
takes

Lame Lover.

takes notice how the gradations of rank muſt give way to each other ; upon which, Sir Luke, by way of defence, pays ſome compliments to the attractive qualifications, eſpecially the wit of Lord Brentford, of which .ſome very laughable proofs are given ; ſuch as taking ready furniſhed lodgings, and hiring a coach by the month to evade a late act, which limits privilege, alſo paying his debts alphabetically ; nothing can be more whimſically pleaſant than the ſtory of his lordſhip and the coachmaker.

Upon Serjeant Circuit's appearing loth to part with Sir Luke, the loquacious baronet enumerates ſeveral curious engagements which call for his immediate attention. As he is going off, the ſervant returns in violent haſte, with compliments from a duke ; this puts Sir Luke into an irreſiſtable flutter ; his promiſes to Sir Greg and Lord Brentford throw him into great perplexity ; but being informed that the duke is waiting for him in his *own coach*, with the *coronets* on, every idea of his other friends is ſacrificed, and he frames a moſt extraordinary excuſe for Lord Brentford, no leſs than his being rendered incapable of attending, as two bailiffs had arreſted and carried him into the Borough.

Mrs. Circuit finding upon her entrance that Sir Luke is gone, throws out ſome oblique hints as if her abſence had haſtened his departure. The ſerjeant mentioning that he had been ſolicited to attend Kingſton aſſizes, for one of the judges, aſks if his going will be agreeable to his lady, who ſeems well pleaſed at the idea of getting rid of him for a little time. The name of his ſon Jack occurring, Mrs. Circuit objects to the lad's being brought up to the bar, and gives it as her opinion, that a commiſſion

in the army would enliven his natural ſtupidity with
a little fire ; to which the ſerjeant makes this very
pregnant reply, " True, love ; and a knowledge of
the law, may'nt be amiſs to reſtrain his fire a little."
Where this excellent ſtroke points it is needleſs to
explain.

The ſerjeant intimating that he ſhould be glad if
Mrs. Circuit would ſtay to hear his ſon's improvement, is anſwered by the lady, that ſhe has buſineſs
of much concern to engage her attention ; particularly as ſhe expects to be ballotted for as a member
of the ladies club. She then enquires when her
huſband intends to let her have money for the diſ-
charge of her gaming debts : to this, in the law
phraſe, he rather demurs, and with a true petifog-
ing ſpirit, propoſes to avail himſelf of the ſtatutes
againſt gaming, by which not only all demands a-
gainſt his wife may be prevented, but money made
into the bargain ; this the lady treats with very ſpirited contempt. In their altercation the following
valuable remark relative to the effect gaming among
the higher has upon the lower claſſes of life, occurs,
" Whilſt ſuperiors are throwing away their fortunes
and independence *above*, you can't think but their
domeſtics are following their example *below* ; the
conſequence of which is, the ſame diſtreſs that
throws the maſter or miſtreſs into the power of any
who are willing to purchaſe them, by a regular gradation ſeduces the ſervants to actions though more
criminal, perhaps not leſs *atrocious*." We know not
any paſſage of ſimilar length, in any author, which
conveys more uſeful ſatire, ſtricter truth, or more
comprehenſive good ſenſe.

The

Lame Lover.

The lady, not at all pleafed with her hufband's reafoning, infifts peremptorily on a pecuniary fupply to
fave her *honour*, as fhe phrafes it. This draws from
the ferjeant a differtation upon the word honour, fo
highly pleafing to us, that we cannot refift the temptation of tranfcribing, as worthy the perufal and
recollection of every reader.

" My honour is in pawn! Good Lord! how a
century will alter the meaning of words: formerly,
chaftity was the *honour* of women, and *good faith* and
integrity the *honour* of men; but *now*, a lady who
ruins her family by punctually paying her loffes at
play, and a gentleman who kills his beft friend in a
frivolous quarrel, are your only tip-top people of
honour. Well, let them go on, it brings grift to
our mill; for while both fexes ftick clofe to their
honour, we fhall never want bufinefs, either at
Doctor's Commons or the Old Bailey." Never was
a truer, bolder, or more inftructive picture of the
times drawn than in this fpeech; which alone is
worth whole fcenes of thofe dialogue novels called
comedies.

Act the fecond begins with the ferjeant and his
hopeful fon Jack; Mr. Fairplay, an attorney, is introduced, who recommends the cafe of one Mr.
Woodford to the ferjeant, who, after fome interrogations and doubts, defires Fairplay to call on him
fome other time. This gentleman being difpatched,
Jack acquaints his father of clients who have called
for his affiftance in two very fingular cafes; upon
which the ferjeant makes fome very laughable, characteriftic remarks, and then proceeds to queftion
his fon upon fome points of litigation, to which fuch
anfwers are given, as manifeft a fund of irrefiftable

humour;

humour; particularly the cafe of the cow, which, however ludicrous it may feem, certainly gave a hint of the moft ferious importance for prefervation of that worthy gentleman who was tried lately for fetting his houfe on fire; whofe acquittal depended upon fomething extremely fimilar to the fhrewd affertion, that though cattle may be cows, it by no means follows that cows muft be cattle.

After the ferjeant's departure for Kingfton, Charlotte enters, for whom Jack has a letter from young Woodford which he delivers, and recommends to his fifter's notice, with a confiderable fhare of boyifh humour; upon reading the tender epiftle, Charlotte difclaims all knowledge of its author.

After Jack has exerted his fimple eloquence in favour of Woodford, and prevailed upon his fifter to give fome gleam of hope, Mrs. Circuit enters, and difmiffes both the brother and fifter from her prefence; then enquires after a letter or meffage, and orders a collation for fome company fhe expects to be got ready. Being alone, fhe meditates on her fituation as candidate to be a member of the female coterie, and throws out fome curious remarks on the difpofition of time amongft fine ladies. In the midft of a moft pleafing reverie, Betty brings on a letter, which being opened with great eagernefs, unfolds the lamentable chance of having loft the very interefting election; this fo much overpowers her agitated fpirits that fhe faints, a circumftance which neceffarily occafions much buftle and confufion; in the midft of it Sir Luke enters, and exerts all his care to recover the diftreffed lady. This being effected, the fervants are difmiffed, and Mrs. Circuit defires the knight to read the letter, which he does,

2 and

Lame Lover.

and at the bottom finds what he thinks a circumftance of great comfort, viz. that fhe has had fixteen
almonds, and but two raifins againft her. This
fcene is juftly and pleafantly pointed at an eftablifh-
ment ridiculous to the higheft degree, which has
been fuggefted and countenanced by fome ladies of
leading fafhion.

Upon the appearance of Colonel Secret and Mrs.
Simper, who mention Mrs. Circuit's difappointment, fhe affects great indifference, and declares,
that the matter has happened entirely through her
own defign, then invites her guefts to the collation
in another room; this makes room for Jack and
Woodford, the former introduces the latter to his
fifter's room, and then returns to keep watch; his
foliloquy is fraught with real humour, arifing from
very pleafant and characteriftic tranfitions: while
he is making obfervations Betty, the maid, furprizes
him, and feeing young Woodford in Charlotte's
room, declares fhe will acquaint the ferjeant; this
alarms Jack, who endeavours to diffuade her, but
finds fome difficulty, as Mifs has offended Betty by
mentioning her drums. Some good ftrokes are
thrown out againft the ignorant vanity of fervants
apeing the extravagancies of their mafters and mif-
treffes; when this pert chamber-maid is called off,
by the ringing of her miftrefs's bell, Woodford re-
enters, and is queftioned by Jack, in low terms, whether he has gained his fuit, to which replying, that
he thought it too hard to prefs for fentence fo foon,
Jack reproves his diffidence, and is going to fuggeft
fome affiftance, when fight of his father frights them
into Charlotte's chamber again.

At

At the beginning of the third act, Sir Luke, &c.
are discovered at the collation, and a very entertaining burlesque upon the disjointed nothingness of polite chit-chat ensues ; at length the serjeant being mentioned, Sir Luke offers to introduce him, which surprizes Mrs. Circuit, as she supposes him at King-ston. The baronet, with a degree of whim very suitable to his character, brings forward a block with one of the lawyer's large whigs on it, this Mrs. Circuit salutes, as the image of her lord : being determined to have him at table as an object of mirth, she goes off for a serjeant's gown ; the mock figure being thus complete, Sir Luke's prolific brain suggests another stroke of humour, which is to plead a cause before the serjeant, as an indulgence to his darling passion. No sooner said than agreed to, when the two ladies and gentlemen go off to get proper habiliments. While they are preparing Serjeant Circuit comes on, ruminating on the hint Charlotte had given him, respecting Sir Luke and her mother-in-law ; seeing the collation, he is resolved to partake, and for that purpose going to a chair, he sees his own similitude at the head of the table, which at first startles and puzzles him to know the meaning ; however, he puts the favourable construction upon it, that his wife's singular regard makes her studious of having something in his absence to resemble him ; happy in this idea, he sits down and enjoys the wine, &c. very freely : approaching feet interrupt his jollity, when looking out, and seeing the appearance of four lawyers, he determines to secrete himself, and slips to that end under the gown, with this very poignant remark, that it is not the first fraud it has covered.

Prepa-

Lam's Lover.

Preparatory to the pleading, Sir Luke throws out some cutting farcafms againft perverfions of law, by firft obferving, that they are only to debate upon the cutting down of a tree, without taking any notice of a borough, which is the real point in difpute; and next by expreffing his hopes that none of his brethren have *touched* on *both* fides.

Mrs. Circuit, as counfel for Hobfon, the plaintiff, with moft loquacious volubility and abundance of circumlocution, not only ftates but illuftrates the cafe; fhe defcribes the utility and beauty of the plumb-tree in queftion, giving alfo an account of the clandeftine and injurious manner in which it has been cut down; from thence deducing in the ufual manner, ftrong hope that a verdict will be found for the plaintiff.

Sir Luke, for the defendant rifes, and after fome imagined interruptions, proceeds with much formal pompofity, to fet afide his antagonift's arguments, which he traces with ftrict method, purfuing, as he phrafes it, the probable and the pofitive proofs, both which he controverts in a very ludicrous manner; contending, that the plumb-tree which has been reprefented as fo beautiful and fo excellent, was not only leaflefs, limblefs, and almoft lifelefs, but alfo of an impoverifhed fpecies, far inferior to feveral other he mentions. Here, by a kind of inftinct, the real ferjeant bolts forward, and mentions green-gages as of fuperior quality; the fight of fo unexpected a perfon concludes the trial, and leaves only the ferjeant, with his friend Sir Luke, on the ftage; the former has been fo delighted with the pleadings, that in full glee he infifts upon the baronet's fitting down and taking a chearful glafs with him; both of thefe
gentlemen

gentlemen being previously fluftered, a few bum-
-pers force the flow of fpirits to intoxication.

Arrived at this critical point, Sir Luke begins to
unbofom himfelf, and by very natural degrees for
fuch a fituation, furnifhes the ferjeant with very intelligible hints of his intimacy with Mrs. Circuit:
the ferjeant for fome time, poffeffed of a particular
portion of confident ftupidity, forms no clear idea
of what he hears ; at laft, having fuch an explanation as he cannot poffibly refift or mifapprehend, he
breaks out in terms of high refentment againft his
wife, but thoroughly exculpates Sir Luke, and a
moft whimfical compact of friendfhip is entered into
by the offender and offended ; when Mrs. Circuit,
who, as it appears, has been liftening to this curious
tete-a-tete, bolts in, and rates her intimidated, credulous hufband moft foundly ; upon which, he
joins her in attacking Sir Luke, and bids him with
terms of infamy get out of his houfe : thus Sir
Luke is driven into Charlotte's chamber, whence his
appearance draws Jack, Woodford, and the young
lady ; frefh furprize here breaks in upon the ferjeant,
however, upon recognizing Woodford, and hoping
that the young man's view of fortune may be at-
tainable, hearing from Sir Luke alfo that the ftory
of his wife was to prevent the baronet's marriage
with his daughter, matters fubfide into a tolerable
calm, and the comedy ends with a promife of conjugal obedience from the ferjeant to his dear, injured
lady.

Having thus traced the fcenes and general purport of this piece, we are now to confider the unities and the characters, in a more diftinct manner ;
as to the former, Ariftotle himfelf could not have
                                            wifhed

Lame Lover.

wifhed them more ftrictly adhered to, as to the latter they have confiderable force, variety and novelty: the moral of this piece is rather complicate than fingle ; more deducible from the perfonages of the drama diftinctly, than the general action.

In the Serjeant we find abufe of law and equity fatirized with a very keen and pleafant degree of humour; in his wife the falfe fpirit of wifhing to join in even the vicious diffipations of high life, is laughably ridiculed ; and by Sir Luke Limp, buftling, talking infignificance, united to a ridiculous affection for titles, is admirably fet forth. The dialogue of this piece is lively, pregnant and terfe, to a confiderable degree of excellence.

Serjeant Circuit is one of thofe deteftable practitioners who ftudy the wrong fide of law more than the right, and prefer perverfion to juftice ; as knowing, according to an obfervation in this comedy, that a bad caufe is more profitable than a good one ; he is a knave in fociety, yet credulous and a dupe to his wife ; an admirer of Sir Luke's oddities, which he miftakes for wit, humour, fpirit and politenefs. This character is drawn with great ability, and poffeffes a kind of dry, intricate pleafantry, fomewhat difficult to hit off fuccefsfully ; notwithftanding which Mr. VANDERMERE gave us confiderable fatisfaction ; and we doubt whether his performance of the Serjeant would be mended by any gentleman of either houfe, unlefs Mr. YATES undertook him, whofe talents in fuch a vein of humour are inimitable.

Sir Luke Limp is as laughable a compound as ever was mingled, made up of vanity, affurance and verbofe nothingnefs, an obfequious appendage of quality, and the humble fervant of any body who will gratify his bufy difpofition, by tranfacting any commiffion, however trifling or ridiculous ; it is impoffible to read this part without tafting its high relifhed ingredients, but we are very certain that the fineft conception which has not been prefent at the animating action of Mr. FOOTE, muft have but a very faint idea of the baronet ; his vivacity, variety, and force of expreffion through the whole, rather furpaffes than falls fhort of his ufual excellence.

Jack Circuit is a well drawn piece of fhrewd fimplicity, and enlivened by Mr. WESTON's peculiar humour, fo forceable to an audience, afforded rich food for laughter.

Mrs. Circuit is a mixture of vanity and weaknefs, which indeed are commonly united : to fay that Mrs. GARDNER fhewed talents peculiarly happy, efpecially in pleading the caufe of the plumbtree, is rather too faint praife for her rifing and extenfive merit.

Charlotte, the Serjeant's daughter, feems to be a fenfible young lady, and rallies her father, in the firft fcene very agreeably ; her ftrictures upon Sir Luke Limp, and fome other characters, difcover difcernment, underftanding and humour. Mrs. JEWELL, whofe chief fault is a little want of effential fpirit in expreffion, fupported the delicacy of this part in an agreeable manner.

The Chambermaid, who varies little from the general run of that caft, was well enough perfonated by Mrs. READ. The reft of the characters are too inconfiderable to fay more, than that the performers did them as well as could be expected.

Upon

Lame Lover.

Upon the whole, this comedy, well acted, muſt ever pleaſe the general ear, but in the cloſet, if we judge right, it will only be acceptable to the intelligent few who can taſte the poignancy of its ſatire, and comprehend the bent of its humour ; a ſtrong proof of ſterling worth is its- having- every night riſen above a capricious prejudice which attended the firſt repreſentation.

CYMBELINE

CYMBELINE.

A TRAGEDY.

Altered from SHAKESPEARE by GARRICK.

NO author's works were ever inveftigated by fo many, and fuch able commentators, in the fame fpace of time as SHAKESPEARE's have been, within the laft half century: in many places he ftands indebted to their elucidations, in many others they have rather clouded than thrown light upon his ideas; feveral of his pieces have undergone advantageous alteration, and we repeat a wifh already mentioned, that an edition of his plays, cleared from the abundance of fuperfluous, trifling, offenfive, incoherent paffages which incumber them, was prepared for, and given to the public.

Reconciling any play written by fo unparalelled a genius to the ftage, deferves particular praife, as thereby public entertainment is much enriched, and noble flights of genius brought to a general knowledge; the tafk is arduous, and attended with much hazard; in this light we are to confider the piece before us, and fhould rather give Mr. GARRICK general approbation for his bold attempt, than point out induftrioufly the defects of his alteration; but however goodnaturedly inclined the DRAMATIC CENSOR may be, yet ftrict juftice, as heretofore, muft be aimed at, void of all prejudiced praife or cenfure.

CYM-

Cymbeline.

CYMBELINE opens with Pisanio and a gentleman conversing on the state of affairs at court; from their conference we learn that the old monarch is uneasily situated, as his daughter, by a former wife, whom he intended for the son of a widow lately espoused by him, has given herself in marriage to a person of much inferior rank, but great worth as a man : the account of Posthumus's birth and qualifications prepare an audience well for admitting him to favour ; mention is made of two of Cymbeline's sons lost in their infancy, which as one of the characters observes, is a circumstance calculated to strain credibility.

The Queen entering with Posthumus and Imogen makes fair-faced professions of friendship to the young pair ; but the princess rightly sees through the thin veil of her hypocrisy, and tenderly intimates it to her husband, whose departure she requires, yet pathetically laments ; his return is affectionate. The royal step-dame re-enters, and seems apprehensive of the king's seeing Posthumus, yet mentions aside her intention of bringing him to the view she feigns to dread so much ; a ring and bracelet, as mutual remembrancers of affection are interchanged, with expressions of delicate softness. Cymbeline's abrupt entrance and terms of reproach, hurry Posthumus off the stage ; Imogen sustains many harsh terms from her enraged father, and the Queen gets her share for suffering the interview with Posthumus.

From Pisanio, who was sent to see his lord on board, we learn that he has sailed ; it appears to us, that the alterer of this play might, without throwing any weight on representation, have furnished

nifhed matter to give Pifanio more probable time
for what he defcribes; what paffes between the
princefs and him refpecting her hufband's departure is pathetically picturefque.

The Queen next appears, with Cornelius a phyfician, from whom fhe receives a phial of fuppofed
poifon, which with moft murderous intention fhe
forces upon Pifanio, under a mafk of friendfhip,
foliciting him to influence his miftrefs Imogen in
favour of her fon ; this female monfter is truly offenfive, and rather difgraceful to human nature ;
however, the feeling mind has a comfort in prophe-
tically perceiving that her abominable defigns are
not likely to take effect ; for Pifanio, as well as the
phyfician, appears to have a right idea of her, and
faithfully profeffes attachment to his exiled mafter
Pofthumus.

By the power of poetical magic we are inftantaneoufly conveyed from the Englifh court to Italy,
without even the intervention of a chorus, which
though an imperfect, is yet a plaufible apology for
fuch palpable breaches of time and place.

Philario, Jachimo, and a Frenchman---why was
not the latter equipped with a name ? prefent themfelves ; their converfation, which is expreffed in
a cramp, obfolete, quibbling ftile, turns upon and
in favour of Pofthumus, who fhortly appears, and
is recommended to a cordial intimacy with the other
characters by Philario. A fubject of debate arifing
upon the qualifications of females, Jachimo expreffes himfelf lightly, and Pofthumus warms into
an elogium upon Imogen, without naming her ; the
oppofition of opinions at length increafes fo much,
that Pofthumus, we muft fay very foolifhly, enters

into

into a wager upon the impracticability of Jachimo's
obtaining any countenance from his wife. This
point being agreed between the abfurd gallant Jachimo, and the more abfurd hufband Pofthumus,
we are brought to the conclufion of the firft act, by
a forced, chimerical incident, fet forth in a fcene of
quaint, unimportant expreffion, which cannot help
the fpeakers, nor pleafe a judicious audience, unlefs
fupported by very agreeable capabilities.

At the beginning of the fecond act we find Imogen in foliloquy upon her unhappy fituation; after
a few lines Pifanio introduces Jachimo, as bringing
letters from Pofthumus. By the by, courtly eti-
quette is laid entirely afide, and fomething of a
queftion arifes how a ftranger fhould gain fuch ready,
cordial admittance to a princefs, watched in all her
motions, and labouring under the difpleafure of her
royal father. However, the adventurous Roman
was to be introduced, and SHAKESPEARE thought
the manner of little importance, elfe by charging
him with fome commiffion from Rome, which
might have been mentioned in the preceding fcene,
Jachimo's journey would not have been founded
upon fo romantic and improbable a crcumftance as
the wager alone, and his free accefs to court would
in fuch cafe be very natural.

From the part of Pofthumus's note which Imogen reads, it appears, that he gives Jachimo's villainous defign the faireft profpect of fuccefs, by re-
commending him to the lady's confidence in terms
of very kind refpect. The forward gallant, ftruck
with her beauty, and willing to make trial at once,
arms himfelf with uncommon confidence, and begins
his attack politically enough, by defcanting on the
superior

Cymbeline.

superior value of *her* charms, and the depravity of
human nature, particularly in Posthumus ; who being possessed of such matchless excellence, can prostitute his attention and regard to objects of far less
estimation.   There is art discovered in this part of
the scene, and fancy gilds the conduct, but we think
Imogen too tame, too dull of conception ; and Jachimo stands reprehensible for several very indelicate ideas, which we imagine the alterer of this play
should have softened : how could delicacy let slip ?

            should I—damned then——
Slaver with lips as common as the stairs
That mount the capital ?——

Base and unlustrous as the smoaky light,
That's fed with *stinking* tallow.

      —— with *diseased venturers*
To play with all infirmities for gold
That *rottenness* lends nature——

Live like Diana's priestess 'twixt cold sheets,
While he is *vaulting variable ramps.*

      —— to mart
As in a Romish *stew,* and to expound
His *beastly* mind to us——

Not one of the preceding passages has the least
gleam of poetical beauty, to apologize for fulsome-
ness ; and to make a chaste princess violate her own
modesty, by mention of Roman stews, though highly provoked, is a violent trespass upon decorum :
the turn which Jachimo gives to his intention upon
Imogen's resentment, is well imagined, and has in
action a very pleasing effect.   His request of place-
ing a trunk in care of the princess is odd enough,
                    and

Cymbeline.

and her immediately refolving to place it in her *bed-chamber*, ftill more ftrange; this circumftance we muft fuppofe Jachimo has thought of previoufly, in cafe other means fhould fail, and the unfufpecting princefs meeting his defign half way, they part for the night in friendly terms.

Cloten, the Queen's fon, next enters, with two namelefs lords---Sure titles were very fcarce when this tragedy was written, elfe SHAKESPEARE could never have incumbered it with fuch a parcel of a-nonymous peers. The fhallow-pated prince and his companions, are engaged in converfation upon a moft important quarrel, occafioned by Cloten's fwearing at a game of bowls. This fhort fcene ap-pears to be merely introduced as a fpecimen of this royal fprig. Upon Cymbeline's entering with the Queen, the obftinacy of Imogen is mentioned, but hopes given that when Pofthumus is a little worn from her recollection, fhe fhall be difpofed of ac-cording to their wifhes. Here intelligence is brought in of Caius Lucius's arrival, the Roman ambaffador; Cymbeline propofing to give him audience on the morrow, retires.

Upon being told of Jachimo, as one of Leona-tus's friends, Cloten difplays his mental abilities more at large; fhews himfelf perfectly the incohe-rent, vain fool, and goes off, leaving one of the lords to defcant on his weaknefs; and to tell in half a dozen fuperfluous lines, what even the dulleft au-ditor is already fufficiently acquainted with.

We are now conducted to the bed-chamber of Imogen, who expreffing wearinefs of reading, and ripenefs for fleep, fends her attending woman to reft, and with becoming piety commends herfelf to ce-

leftial

leftial protection. When she is locked in the soft
femblance of death, Jachimo rifes from the trunk,
in which he has lain concealed; and in a fpeech of
great variety, judgment, and poetical fancy, takes
into his poffeffion and remembrance, fuch ftrong
proofs of particular freedom and intimacy with the
innocent princefs, as cannot be controverted : this
done, he retires to his covert.

What the fhort fucceeding fcene between
Cloten and lords is introduced for we cannot
apprehend, unlefs to give an opportunity of clearing
the bed, &c. away. When the mafquerade is over---
fuch an entertainment feems rather improper for a
morning.---the fimple prince makes a very characteriftic fpeech, but we wifh the phrafe, *unpaved eunuch,*
had not been retained, underftood it is fhamefully
grofs; if unintelligible, it deferves the cenfure of
obfcurity. In his foliloquy, previous to knocking at the princefs's chamber-door, Cloten makes
fome remarks on the power and influence of gold,
too fhrewd for fuch a fuperficial coxcomb; what
paffes between him and the princefs is fhallow foppery on his fide, and peevifh quibble on hers; the
fpirit fhe fhews in favour of Pofthumus, is indeed
pleafing and commendable; her miffing the bracelet, and the contemptuous manner of leaving Cloten, conclude this act with tolerable propriety and
fpirit.

Now, by the irrefiftable power of dramatic con-
juration, we are---hey!---prefto! pafs!---carried a-
gain to Rome; where we find Philario and Pofthumus in conference. The latter drops a hint of his
confidence in Imogen's invincible modefty; they
then pafs on to the fubject of Caius Lucius's em-

2   baffy,

bafly; demanding tribute from Britain : this gives
Pofthumus an opportunity of paying a pretty compliment to the courage and independant principles
of his countrymen ; to which the poet has added a
forced panegyric upon living royalty; we call it
forced, becaufe applied to Cymbeline, who from
what is faid of him in the beginning, and his conduct through the piece, can fcarcely be deferving of
this paffage, which we think inelegant as well as
fuperfluous.

> *and more than that,*
> They have a KING whofe love and juftice to them,
> *May afk and have* their treafures and their blood.

The firft hemiftich in Italics, is not only impoverifhed but ungrammatical ; the laft faint and
vulgar. Befides, bringing this trite, thread-bare
compliment down to the prefent day, is taking a
large jump over feventeen centuries, to draw a fimi-
litude by no means defirable, in courtly terms of
very fteril praife.

. The obfervation of Pofthumus, on feeing Jachimo,
is a pretty fanciful apology for his miraculous
fpeed, and deferves to be particularly noted,

> The fwifteft harts have pofted you by land,
> And winds of all the corners kifs'd your fails,
> To make your veffel nimble.

After perufing fome letters delivered by Jachimo,
Pofthumus enters directly upon the grand point,
their wager. The fubject is fported with for a few
fpeeches, at length his rival enters upon proofs,
which his good opinion waves, while the room, its
furniture, and fuch dubious externals are mentioned.

At

At length the bracelet is produced, which strikes deep; however, the confidence of sincere love suggests that she might have delivered it to Jachimo for Posthumus's use : this gleam of comfort is clouded with one short question, and the unhappy husband is harrowed with passion; when Philario intimating she might have dropped the jewel, another pause of calmer reason ensues, and he desires some corporal sign; jealous relapses nevertheless break in even before the most substantial proof of disloyalty is uttered. At length, when Jachimo mentions the mole, cinque spotted, upon Imogen's breast, her distracted lord is so swelled with rage, as to be scarcely capable of utterance, wherefore he is judiciously carried off the stage in a state of outrageous dubitation.

In the soliloquy of Posthumus, succeeding the last mentioned scene, there are many fine opportunities afforded the able actor for striking transitions of tones, look and gestures; and his virulent charge against the character of woman in general, emphatically natural, for a man in his distracted state of provocation. But we must lament retaining the following passages, for the same reason, licentiousness, that we have censured some preceding ones;

> —— *some coiner with his tools*
> Made me a counterfeit—yet my mother seemed
> The Dian of that time——

> ——perchance he spoke not, but
> *Like a full acorn'd boar, a German one——*

Cymbeline giving audience to the Roman ambassador, next strikes our view; here we have instantaneously

Cymbeline.

ftantaneoufly travelled, even without an act tune, from Italy to Britain. The notion of tribute is treated with contempt by Cymbeline, as echo of his Queen, and the worthy Cloten ; who, to fay truth, fteps in this fcene a little from himfelf, and fpeaks with fome degree of fenfe and fpirit, though in a quaint ftile.

Whether in a royal audience any perfons are allowed to fpeak but the monarch and the ambaffador, we are not courtly enough to determine, but we apprehend not ; if fo the Queen and her fon are improperly introduced, without any neceffity ; for the matter in agitation might have been as well fettled in their abfence, unlefs it was deemed neceffary to fhew female influence over public councils.

Pifanio fucceeds the fcene of embaffy, perufing a letter from Pofthumus, who, in the heat of jealous rage, has directed him to murder the fuppofed adultrefs Imogen ; and for this defperate purpofe, has alfo fent a letter to his unfufpecting wife, advifing her that he is at Milford Haven, and wifhes to fee her there. Pofthumus here manifefts a cruel, premeditate, vindictive, rather than generous fpirit of refentment ; an injured hufband, with quick and warm feelings, might naturally facrifice an abufer of love and honour with his own hand ; but to play the hypocrite, and become a political murderer, favours much more of the Italian than Britifh difpofition. However, fuch our author has drawn his hero ; and Imogen, with all the eager impatience of a tender, loving wife, falls into the fnare, at once refolving to fet out with Pifanio on the journey : if the tender-hearted domeftic had not in his foliloquy expreffed proper deteftation of his mafter's bloody

command,

Cymbeline.

command, the audience muſt here have been in a
ſtate of very painful apprehenſion for Imogen; even
as it is, our ſuſpenſe muſt be touched with tender
concern.

Three freſh characters now offer themſelves to
view; Bellarius, an old man, and his two ſuppoſed
ſons, Guiderius and Arviragus. After a ſhort, ſignificant and poetical oriſon, applicable to their low-
ly and abſtracted ſtate, the old man takes occaſion
to mention mountain ſports, and deſcants with a
pleaſing, deſcriptive degree of philoſophical inſtruction, upon the elevated and humbler ſtations of
life, preferring the latter to the former; to this the
youths reply, with a ſenſible activity of ſpirit, that
their years require a more buſtling ſphere: we
could gladly tranſcribe this whole ſcene as teeming
with beauties, but ſhall confine ourſelves to the following lines of Bellarius, in anſwer to what Arviragus and Guiderius have urged:

> Did you but know the city's uſuries
> And felt them knowingly—the art *o'th'* court
> As hard to learn as keep, whoſe top to climb
> Is certain falling—the toil *o'th'* war,
> A pain that only ſeems to ſeek out danger
> *I'th'* name of fame and honour; which dies *i'th'*
>   ſearch,
> And hath as oft a ſlanderous epitaph
> As record of fair Act———
> When a ſoldier was the theme, my name
> Was not far off—then was I as a tree
> Whoſe boughs did bend with fruit—but in one night
> A ſtorm, or robbery——call it what you will,
> Shook down my mellow hangings—nay, my leaves,
> And left me bare to weather.

We

Cymbeline.

We have marked some diſſonant contractions by italics in the preceding lines, which might and ſhould have been ſoftened.

Bellarius's account of his own exile and the young princes, is alſo very 'nervous and pleaſing; however, his ſoliloquy is a palpable piece of explanatory information to the audience, and therefore cenſurable: by it we find, that Bellarius, in revenge of his unjuſt baniſhment, ſtole Cymbeline's two infant ſons, and that they know nothing of their real birth, but imagine themſelves his children, as being brought up from two and three years old with him and his wife Euriphile.

In the ſucceeding ſcene we perceive Lucius taking leave of Cymbeline: after the ambaſſador's departure, the old monarch enquires for Imogen, and complaining of her undutiful abſtraction, orders her into his preſence. The Queen faintly apologizes for her cold diſtance: on being informed that her chambers are all locked, Cymbeline confeſſes fear of what may be the meaning, and goes off; Cloten follows by the Queen's direction, while ſhe, in a ſoliloquy, expreſſes hope that Piſanio has taken the quieting draught which ſhe gave him; as to Imogen, the hopeful ſtep-mother encourages flattering ideas, that deſpair or voluntary exile has put her ſo effectually out of the way, as to leave the Britiſh crown entirely at her diſpoſal.

Piſanio, and his royal miſtreſs, appear next, on their journey; a ſtrong perplexity of countenance, apparent in him, cauſes her to queſtion the reaſon of it. Being urged cloſe, he gives Poſthumus's letter into her hands with diſtreſsful reluctance; the paper, or rather the matter it contains, proves dag-

gers

gers to her fight, and fhe is ftruck dumb, while Pifanio exprefles warmly his invincible confidence and good opinion refpecting her innocence.

The remaining part of this fcene is truly interefting; her folicitation for fulfilling her hufband's barbarous command, and the ftruggles of Pifanio, play powerfully on our feelings. His advice for her to join the Roman ambaffador's train in difguife, from thence deriving a probability of being near Pofthumus, is politic and humane. Imogen refolves to take his friendly counfel, and being told he has garments fit for the purpofe in their cloak bag, fhe agrees to put on a mafculine appearance.

The parting of Pifanio from his royal miftrefs, his leaving her to profecute the propofed pilgrimage alone, though there may be fome colour of reafon for it, is rather indefenfible; for we muft fuppofe that a faithful fervant, who had dared to elope with her, would have continued his attachment, by partaking her difguife and future fortunes; however, the poor princefs is left to encounter alone a precarious and perilous adventure: Pifanio prefenting her with the phial he received from the Queen, as a benign and fpirit-cheering cordial, they feparate and conclude the third act.

At the beginning of the fourth act, we find difappointed Cloten teeming with refentment againft Imogen. To him Pifanio enters, and is accufed of abetting her elopement; urged with heavy threats, he delivers a paper to Cloten, importing, as he fays, the ftory of her flight, but in reality calculated not only to deceive, but to lead him into danger. The royal gudgeon fwallows the bait laid for him, and bribing Pifanio to become his friend, refolves to

purfue

Cymbeline.

purfue his miftrefs in a fuit of Pofthumus's cloaths; declaring alfo, an intention of killing that unfortunate man, upon meeting him at Milford Haven.

Imogen, now in boyifh habiliments enters, and having loft her way, approaches the cave of Bellarius; into which, after ftrong marks of natural intimidation, fhe enters, to feek or obtain fome refrefhment to fupport languifhing nature. The huntfmen returned from their fports, Bellarius looks into his cave, and difcovers an unexpected gueft, upon whofe beauty and innocence he paffes a kind and comprehenfive compliment.

Upon being feen, Imogen enters from the cave, and prettily apologizes for her intrufion, offering alfo to pay for what fhe has had. Inquifition being made concerning her name and deftination, fhe affumes the title of Fidele, and fays fhe is following a relation bound to Italy from Milford. After this explanation, the good old man, cafting afide every confideration, but the pleafure refulting from hofpitality, invites her to better cheer; and, as night is coming on, to take up her repofe with them. Being prefented to her unknown brothers, a kind of inftantaneous, fympathetic regard rifes between them, and terms of mutual regard are exchanged; after which they retire into the cave.

Cloten next appears, upon the hunt for Pofthumus, and in his foliloquy, declares terrible intentions againft Imogen, when in his power; relying for exculpation from any crime he can commit, upon his mother's influence over Cymbeline. The fop and fool, in this adventure, feems to have a ftrong tincture of the defperado, which, according to our idea, is making him a kind of paradox in character.

Upon

Upon returning from the cave, Imogen declares herself sick, and is therefore left behind, while Bellarius, &c. go to the chace, one of the young princes having previously offered to stay with her as an assistant : by way of restorative, she applies the cordial furnished by Pisanio.

As the hunters are going off, Cloten enters, and from his using the word runnagates, Bellarius apprehends a discovery of their retreat ; the old gentleman's immediate knowledge of this prince, after an absence from court of twenty years, disguised too in Posthumus's cloaths, is rather an encroachment on probability. Guiderius, by his own desire, is left to encounter Cloten, while his brother and supposed father, look out to see if he has any attendants ; after a tart altercation, Guiderius and Cloten engage, fighting off the stage. After a few intervening lines, the former returns victorious, acquainting Bellarius and Arviragus that he has conquered, by the death of his antagonist.

The circumstance of Cloten's death, alarms Bellarius with just fears of fatal consequences ; Guiderius resolves upon committing Cloten's corpse to a neighbouring creek of the sea, and retires for that purpose ; while Arviragus receives instructions to go and assist Fidele in preparing some provisions. The old man's soliloquy, respecting his two adopted sons, is so beautiful, that it would be an unpardonable omission not to gratify the readers taste, by transcribing it.

Oh thou goddess !
Thou divine nature ! how thyself thou blazonest
In these two princely boys ; they are as gentle

As

Cymbeline.

> As zephyrs blowing beneath the violet,
> Not wagging his sweet head, and yet as rough
> (Their royal blood enchafed) as the rudeſt wind,
> That by the top doth take the mountain pine
> And make him ſtoop to th' vale—'tis wonderful
> That an inviſible inſtinct ſhould frame them
> To royalty unlearned, honour untaught,
> Civility not ſeen from other ; valour
> That wildly grows in them, but yields a crop
> As if it had been ſowed.

After Guiderius has acquainted us with his committing Cloten's body to the ſtream, Bellarius is
ſtruck with the found of folemn muſic from his
cave, occaſioned, as we foon learn, by Arviragus
having diſcovered Imogen in an apparent ſtate of
death. This circumſtance proves of much concern,
interment is ſpoken of, and Bellarius, with true dignity of ſpirit, reſolves that Cloten, though a foe,
ſhall in his remains be treated with reſpect, wherefore, he directs that his body may be found and laid
by Imogen's.

Cymbeline now preſents himſelf, deeply agitated
for the perilous, ſickly ſtate of his queen, the elopement of Imogen, the abſence of Cloten, and the
near approach of war. Perſuaded that Piſanio has
aided his daughter's flight, he breaths heavy threats,
but is foftened by one of his attendant lords, who
draws his attention to the public danger, from the
Roman legions being landed on his coaſt.

When Cymbeline goes off, Piſanio, in ſoliloquy,
gives us to underſtand, that though he has wrote to
Poſthumus, ſignifying Imogen's intention, yet no
anſwer has reached his hands. In the midſt of a

perplexed,

perplexed, dubitable ftate, he refolves to prove himfelf, by acting in defence of his country, a good citizen, and a loyal fubject.

Imogen and Cloten, by a change of fcene, are
difcovered ; the former awaking from the trance
fhe had been thrown into, by the liquid which Pifanio gave her, utters disjointed expreffions, pointing,
however, to the chief object of her attention and regard : upon difcovering the dead body befide her,
and fuppofing it, through knowledge of his cloaths,
the actual coarfe of her hufband, fhe breaths out
heart-felt lamentation for his fate, notwithftanding
the relentlefs fentence he pronounced againft her
life. While fhe is in this pitiable ftate, Lucius enters, with fome other Romans ; on feeing the dead,
headlefs body, and Imogen proftrate over it, tender
feelings impel them to feek a little further in the
matter. Upon queftion, the princefs fays it is her
mafter, who lies flain by mountaineers ; the faith expreffed by Imogen works a favourable impreffion
upon Lucius, who, with his affociates, determine to
give the fuppofed Pofthumus as refpectable interment as their fituation and means will admit : the
ambaffador's confolative addrefs to Imogen, with
which the fourth act concludes, is humane and philofophical :

———— be chearful, wipe thine eyes,
Some falls are means the happier to.arife.

Bellarius, and his adopted fons, begin the fifth
act ; alarmed at an unaccuftomed buftle they hear
round them, the young princes manifeft a becoming
fpirit, by wifhing to mingle with the war : by the
glow of their expreffion, and the warmth of their

I   eager

Cymbeline.

eager example, the old man kindles into fimilar feelings, and they unite in refolution to take an active part in the field.

Pofthumus now prefents himfelf, ruminating on the death of his wife, and feems deeply to repent the too harfh obedience of Pifanio, in executing his fanguine order; it appears, this unhappy man has been brought from Italy to fight againft his native foil; fo ungracious a tafk, however, he refolves a-gainft, and utters a defign of obfcuring himfelf in peafant's weeds, that under fuch cover, he may turn his fword againft the enemies of Britain, and meet that death his diftrefs of mind makes him wifh for. We are amazed why the alterer of this piece fhould have retained fo many infignificant, jingling tags, at the end of fcenes, fuch as want even the merit of harmony.

Immediately after a general encounter of the Roman and Britifh armies, Pofthumus meets and dif-arms Jachimo, but difdains to take his life. This is generous, yet, if we confider that Jachimo has been the foundation of all Pofthumus's woes, and that he is a capital enemy to his country, the incident does not appear fo natural as we could wifh; however, fuch we find it, and the effect it has on Jachimo, is fuitable to a mind filled with confcious guilt.

In the fhort fcene which follows, Pifanio gives us to underftand, that Cymbeline's victory was almoft folely derived from the intrepid behaviour of four perfons, who, from his defcription, appear to be Bellarius, Arviragus, Guiderius and Pofthumus.

Wearied with glorious action, dead to the charms of fame, and torn with perturbation of mind, Pofthumus

humus determines, in foliloquy, to reaffume his Italian garment, that he may fall by Britifh hands.

Cymbeline is now difcovered in his tent, delivering gracious thanks to Bellarius, and the two young warriors ; at the fame time, lamenting that the brave peafant who fhewed fuch heroifm is not to be found. We think the omiffion of what concerns Cymbeline's vile queen, and bringing on Lucius, &c. immediately the monarch has conferred knighthood on his unknown heroes, is perfectly right.

When Cymbeline acquaints the Roman leader that a facrifice is to be made of all the captives, to atone the flaughter of his fubjects, Lucius not only fhews great magnanimity of mind, but tendernefs of feeling, by confining his folicitation of mercy to Imogen, in the character of Fidele ; ftruck by his daughter's countenance, the old monarch readily grants the requeft, and admits the fuppofed page even to clofe conference with him.

While Bellarius, &c. are expreffing their furprize to fee the boy alive whom they fuppofed dead, Imogen moves her father to queftion Jachimo ; this being granted, fhe afks him concerning a ring he wears ; terms of compulfion are ufed to draw an anfwer from him ; this brings on gradually an explanation of Pofthumus's worth, Imogen's innocence, and Jachimo's villainy ; the circumftances related, though already known to the audience, bear repetition very well ; what Jachimo relates, works upon Pofthumus's grief and warmer paffions fo ftrongly, that he abruptly difcovers himfelf, and follicits punifhment for the deftruction of his wife ; on Imogen's interpofing he cafts her fo rudely off, that Pifanio inadvertently

ly

Cymbeline.

ly difcovers Fidele to be the real Imogen ; here a
moft agreeable eclairciffement ftrikes us, while
Cymbeline and Pofthumus become inftantaneoufly happier than fo harfh a father, and fo precipitate a hufband could deferve to be.

Cloten being mentioned, Guiderius avows having put him to death, and is for that action ordered into cuftody by Cymbeline ; hence arifes Bellarius's difclofure of the two young Princes, to
the great aftonifhment and joy of the old monarch,
after their being received into the arms of paternal affection, Cymbeline again mentions the poor
foldier, when Pofthumus confeffes himfelf the
perfon, and appeals to Jachimo, as having been
vanquifhed by him ; this the Italian corroborates,
at the fame time, begging death from that hand
which he has fo grievoufly provoked : but the Briton wraps his injuries in oblivion, and by an example of generous humanity, prevails on Cymbeline to
grant a general pardon, with which the piece concludes.

The plot of this play has too ftrong a taint of
romance, and the abfolute annihilation of unities is
rather offenfive ; notwithftanding Mr. GARRICK's
pains, there are abfurdities of a very grofs nature.
We remember to have feen an alteration of this
play by one Mr. HAWKINS, played at York, and
think it has confiderable merit ; however, we view
SHAKESPEARE between thefe gentlemen as a ftately
tree, abounding with difproportionate fuperfluities ;
the former has been fo very tender of pruning, that
a number of luxuriances remain ; and the latter admired the vegetation of his own brain fo much, that
he has not only cut the noble plant into the ftiffnefs

of

of an yew hedge, but decked it like a may-pole, with poetical garlands, which prove rather gaudy than useful ornaments. Mr. GARRICK's is, no doubt, best calculated for action, but Mr. HAWKINS's will stand a chance of pleasing every fanciful reader better, because he has in many places harmonized the expression, and rendered the obscure passages more intelligible; however, we wish he had retained more of the original, and Mr. GARRICK less.

. In point of character, this play is well supplied with a judicious variety, the lights and shades are so blended as to furnish a picture of human nature, both striking and instructive. As to Cymbeline, he is drawn, what we have strong reason to believe several monarchs have been, and what no doubt many in future will be, a fool; easily wrought upon, by designing persons, to actions totally below and inconsistent with his rank in life. Upon the stage, he is no more nor less than a very poor creature, having nothing to say as a counter-balance to the contemptible light in which he appears.

If an actor can have any merit in the part, we are willing to allow Mr. HURST some; indeed, this gentleman seems to have good capabilities for parental feelings. As to Mr. GIBSON, we have mentioned him so often disadvantageously, that we are absolutely weary of finding fault with his performance; and therefore shall only say for the present, that he is second best in this simple monarch.

Cloten is a strange and hateful composition, trifling, coxcomical, malevolent, pert and proud; yet possessed, which is somewhat strange in such a creature, of resolution. His circumstances mostly
present

Cymbeline.

prefent him as an object of contempt, mingled with
laughter, and his fall is a very fit facrifice to poetical juftice. This empty-headed prince can never
gain much favourable notice from an audience, Mr.
KING and Mr. YATES, both make more of him than
criticifm fhould expect, nor is Mr. DODD any way
deficient.

Pofthumus, as drawn by the author, has two moft
amiable qualities, conftancy in love, and courage in
the field; yet, if we examine them narrowly, we
fhall perceive the former ftrongly tainted with jealoufy, the latter impelled by defpair. That he is
weak in his underftanding, we need only appeal to
his ftrange wager with Jachimo, on which the plot
is founded; a circumftance, which would lead us
to think, that in SHAKESPEARE'S days, as well as
at prefent, it was the method to determine arguments, not by reafon, but betting. That this
hero is clouded with rafhnefs and a mixture of cruelty, witnefs his commiffion to Pifanio; however,
his fituation is fuch, that through the whole we find
him an object of very interefting concern, and are
led to pity, even where we muft blame.

A multitude of inftances concur to prove, that no
performer ever knew his own abilities better, or
ftrove more earneftly to keep them in the proper
channel, than Mr. GARRICK; his revival of this
play, were there no other motives but a frefh opportunity of difplaying his unparalelled powers, merits
a large portion of public praife; for, we are bold to
affirm, that confidering an actor muft make the
part, not the part an actor, his aftonifhing talents
were never more happily exerted; this affertion becomes more evident, by confidering that the falling

off from him to any other perfon who has fince done it, is greater than in any other character; the tenderneſs of his love, the pathos of his grief, the fire of his rage, and the diſtraction of his jealouſy, have never been ſurpaſſed, and poſſibly, in Poſthumus, will never be equalled.

Mr. POWELL, who paſſed through this part with a conſiderable ſhare of public eſtimation, was in his merit confined to tenderneſs alone; he much wanted eſſential rapidity of expreſſion, and the natural variety of ſudden tranſitions, incident to jealouſy, rage and deſpair. Notwithſtanding general opinion, we are inclined to think this gentleman's voice and features fell very ſhort of the bolder paſſions, for which reaſon his Poſthumus, though an agreeable piece of acting, could never be juſtly deemed great. Mr. REDDISH, whoſe general merit we are glad to allow, is ſtill more deficient. Laſt winter a remarkable piece of managerical ignorance or cruelty, was manifeſted at Covent Garden, by *popping* on a young perſon, who had never played before; in this arduous, ticklifh, and, as we think, unfavourable character; had he been tried in one of many more practicable parts, which the people are uſed to ſee murdered, ſucceſs might have been the conſequence. Mr. BENSLEY has fince done it, ha! ha! ha!

Bellarius is an old gentleman, well worthy of that reſpect he generally meets; virtuouſly philoſophical, cooly brave, ſenſible, humane and benevolent; his ſentiments and expreſſions are ſuch as muſt pleaſe and inſtruct; for this reaſon he is acceptable even in Mr. BURTON's repreſentation, which we deem for the moſt part very dry and unaffecting. Mr. CLARKE renders him much more agreeable; but

Cymbeline.

but we are obliged to travel as far as YORK for the
beſt that we have ſeen, one Mr. ORAM, whoſe merit
both in tragedy and comedy, ſhould have tranſplant-
ed him to the capital many years ſince.

Arviragus and Guiderius are in no ſhape remarkable, nor are any forcible requiſites wanting to re-
preſent them ; wherefore, the four following *charm-
ing* performers, whom we lump together from equality and ſimilarity of merit, may continue to *do* them
without much offence ; Meſſrs. CAUTHERLY and
BRERETON, at Drury Lane ; PERRY and WROUGH-
N, at Covent Garden.

In the alteration of this play by Mr. HAWKINS,
Palador, the eldeſt prince, is made rather more conſpicuous than Poſthumus, and we remember an ec-
centric genius at YORK, Mr. FRODSHAM, who performed him with ſingular merit. This perſon,
though he never reached a Theatre Royal, had extenſive powers, good feelings, and the advantage of
a liberal education to improve natural underſtanding, yet was often as great an oddity as ever preſented itſelf to the public eye ; wild and uncultivated, his beauties and faults reſembled a paterre of
flowers, choaked up with weeds ; the ſtage is ſeldom enriched with ſuch a genius, had he been early
placed under critical limitation.

Piſanio we muſt regard as a ſteady, prudent,
faithful ſervant ; he is a very amiable object in the
drama, and is ſupported at both houſes with pleaſing propriety by Mr. HULL and Mr. PACKER.

Jachimo is a villain of the deepeſt die, who from
a principle of oſtentatious gallantry, frames the moſt
iniquitous falſhood ; and lays the foundation, not only of miſery but murder, merely to win a paltry wa-

ger.

ger. Iago, Shylock, Richard, &c. have some colour for their abominable behaviour, but this Italian none. Confidered in a ftate of action, the part
deferves a capital actor ; Mr. SMITH poffeffes that
eafy elegance and fpirit which the character requires;
but, we muft be of opinion, that Mr. HOLLAND,
notwithftanding his affectation, claimed a fuperiority, efpecially in the laft act. Mr. PALMER, though
not equal to either of thefe gentlemen, ftands better
in this part than could be expected from his ftation,
and his experience of the ftage. We cordially recommend moderation in acting to this young performer, loudnefs of fpeaking, and violence of action, under the falfe notion of fpirit, are, with few ex-
ceptions, very offenfive.

Philario Lucius, &c. may be done with fo fmall
a fhare of executive abilities, that the mention of
any particular perfons in fuch parts would be totally fuperfluous.

The Queen is a finifhed female monfter, deceitful, ambitious, and cruel, without any one recommendation, either from word or fentiment ; a terrible weight upon any actrefs, and an offence to humanity. She generally falls to the fhare of a third
and fourth rate performer, and indeed deferves no
better ; we think a total omiffion of her would have
mended the piece : Mrs. REDDISH and Mrs. VIN-
CENT are paffable enough in this hateful, immaterial weed of royalty.

Imogen, for tender, fteady affection, is a compliment to her fex, and opens a fair field for happy
talents to difplay themfelves with fuccefs ; fhe poffeffes great force and variety, but falls off unpardonably towards the conclufion. Mrs. CIBBER's very

affecting

affecting capabilities, were much better fuited to this character than thofe of any other lady we have feen; Mrs. YATES has great merit in reprefenting the princefs, but wants an effential, elegant innocence; Mrs. BULKLEY has given us more pleafure than could be expected, from a lady fo little feen; and Mifs YOUNGE has fome title to praife, though a proper melifluous flow of expreffion and eafe of action, are wanting.

Upon the whole, CYMBELINE, as it is now performed, ftands a good chance of being a ftock, or living play, as long as theatrical entertainments are in efteem. To atone for grofs irregularities, the incidents are well imagined, the language nervous, the fentiments elevated, and the characters, except in the laft fcene, where there is a ftrange huddle of difcoveries, well fupported; as to moral, we cannot difcover any, but that providence, by unfeen means, reftores fuffering innocence to happinefs: judicious readers will ever find pleafure from this tragedy in the clofet, but decorations and action will moft recommend it to general tafte.

MAID

MAID of the MILL.

A COMIC OPERA. By Mr. BICKERSTAFF.

A Chorus and duett in praife of rural compe-
tence, pleafure and content, open this opera; after
which, Fairfield, the miller, expreffing fatisfaction
at fuch chearfulnefs, as gives fpirit to labour, orders
his fon Ralph to load flour for Lord Aimworth's;
to this the lad replies churlifhly, and remarks on a
partiality to his fifter Pat, both in refpect of education, and her manner of living. His obfervations
are pleafant and pertinent; the old man fuggefts
from fuch a glibnefs of tongue, that his fon is drunk,
but Ralph denies the charge, though he acknowledges having been treated with fome wine by a
gentleman from London; to whom he fpeaks of
returning, and therefore in defiance of all his father's
threats, determines not to do any work for the day,
concluding their difputes with a fong characterifti-
cally worded, and well calculated for comic expreffion.

Patty, called by her father, comes forward, and introduces herfelf to our acquaintance with a fong,
intimating that love, and of a hopelefs nature, has
invaded her breaft: from the converfation between
Patty and her father, we learn, that a match is depending between one Mifs Sycamore and Lord
Aimworth; fome obfervations occur refpecting a
melancholly which hangs round our Maid of the
Mill,

Maid of the Mill.

Mill, and Fairfield, like a prudent, affectionate father, proposes farmer Giles to her as a fuitable hufband ; her reply is complacent and dutiful ; on the
miller's mention that he may prove a much better
man than many who move in the character of gentlemen, Patty corroborates his fentiment in an agreeable air, which has both good fenfe and a fhare of
fancy to recommend it, for which reafon we fhall
prefent the reader with an opportunity to perufe it.

What are outward forms and *fhows*,
  To an honeft heart compar'd,
Oft the ruftic wanting *thofe*,
  Has the nobler portion fhar'd.

Oft we fee the homely flow'r,
  Bearing, at the hedge's fide ;
Virtues of more fov'reign pow'r,
  Than the garden's gayeft pride.

The word *fhows* in the firft line, and that which
rhimes to it in the third, we apprehend exceptionable ; not only as mere makefhifts, but alfo being
unchafte, and rather ungrammatical.

Upon Patty's going off, farmer Giles enters, and
enquires what hopes ; Fairfield encourages him, by
feeming to think there is no doubt of his fuccefs, but
intimates, that her peculiar obligations to Lord
Aimworth's family, requires their confent to every
material ftep fhe takes. Giles from hence hints a
prevailing report that Lord Aimworth, as he phrafes
it, has a fneaking kindnefs for Patty ; this fuppofition her father treats as an idle tale, and immediately advifes to follicit the peer's confent to his propofed match ; this the hearty ruftic gladly confents
to,

to, but wishing to pay his mistress a personal compliment, the miller points her out in the next room; upon which he addresses her in a song of some humour, and without waiting for any reply, or any immediate interview, he retires.

Patty now appears, and receives from her father the painful information, that her disgustful admirer is gone to solicit Lord Aimworth's approbation of the depending match; this throws her into a strong agitation of mind, and by hesitative intimations she signifies it; however, upon the miller's warm remonstrances, she seems to acquiesce, when he leaves her to a soliloquy, in which she discovers the real bent of her passion is to Lord Aimworth; who, according to her supposition, does not hold her indifferently; nevertheless, several irksome doubts arise, which in the true operatical stile, are composed for the present with a song, very languid, both in versification and sentiment.

Sir Harry Sycamore, and his daughter Theodosia, now mount the stage; by what passes, we are informed, that love is playing cross purposes in this family also. Theodosia upbraids the old gentleman with having encouraged her to receive the addresses of one Mr. Mervin, and having discarded him to make way for a treaty of alliance with Lord Aimworth; the baronet's defence is rather evasively ludicrous than rational, and he is at last obliged to own, that he has sacrificed his own opinion to that of Lady Sycamore. Such condescension the young lady rather objects to, as the effect of good nature improperly extended; and, with a becoming spirit of disinterestedness, upon being asked if she could give up the view of titles and ample fortune, declares

Maid of the Mill.

clares fhe would moft willingly ; rather chufing to embrace a cupid of her own liking, in the humbleft garb, than one with golden wings contrary to her free, generous inclination.

Lady Sycamore now enters, full of the dazzling appearance of jewels her daughter is to become miftrefs of, and calls them with other appendages of quality, the bleffings of life. Theodofia's more rational idea of things brings on an altercation, and fhe is taxed with lownefs of fpirit, in preferring a pitiful citizen to a noble peer ; there is a confiderable fhare of pleafing humour in what paffes here, and Sir Harry is brought into a kind of dilemma by Theodofia's obferving, that he is not averfe to her match with Mervin ; however, the old lady prevails, and the knight fings forth his refentment for the young lady's contradicting her mama.

Lord Aimworth comes forward, introducing Giles ; after paying a fhort compliment to Sir Harry, his lordfhip enters upon the farmer's bufinefs : being informed it is for his leave to marry, he gives it with condefcending cordiality, and adds his hopes, that Giles has made a prudent choice. After fome fimple, ludicrous circumlocution, the ruftic names his fweetheart ; upon which the peer pronounces her a deferving object, but feems a little particular, in afking whether the girl is willing, whether fhe fent to afk his confent, and whether her genteel education may not render her unfit for fuch a match. Giles's fong in praife of his miftrefs's notable qualifications, has fpirit and humour.

After Giles is gone off, Sir Harry flily infinuates, that a tenant to take off a caft miftrefs, is very convenient ; then talks of his own youthful gallantry pleafantly enough, but carries the joke too far when

his matrimonial chaſtity is mentioned ; for which
Lady Sycamore, with ſtrict propriety, drives him
out of the room.

Lord Aimworth left alone, meditates on, and
acknowledges his embarraſſed ſtate between Theodoſia, to whom he is engaged by promiſe, and Patty,
to whom he is attached by inclination ; ſome pretty
remarks upon the hard reſtrictions of birth and ſtation occur, but his lordſhip's ſong we are not very
fond of, as the idea is ſomewhat forced, and the ſimilitude rather obſcure, though trite.

Ralph and Mervin here enter, followed by Fanny, who, as a gypſey, preſſes the latter hard for
charity, but her ſuit is not attended to immediately,
as his attention is engaged by Theodoſia's ſuppoſed
falſhood ; however, he is at length ſung out of a
bounty, at which Ralph ſeems very angry, and
threatens to take it from her. By the following
part of this ſcene we find, that Ralph has a particular tendre for her, which he communicates as a
profound and important ſecret. Mervin, through
Ralph's intimacy with the gypſies, ſtrikes out a
ſcheme of diſguiſing himſelf as one of the gang,
that he may thereby get a ſight of his miſtreſs ;
Ralph promiſes him what he deſires, the cit then
makes a muſical exit, and aptly compares his hazardous metamorphoſe to the ventures of a merchant, who runs known hazards in purſuit of what
he admires.

Giles enters with Patty and Fanny, full of his
ſucceſs with Lord Aimworth, which he relates ; but
does not meet with the reception he ſeems to expect.
Churliſh Ralph throws in a remark, that his ſiſter
ſhould change her cloaths for ſuch as ſuit her ſtation

tion better ; she promises to obey her father, and a
quartetto, which concludes the first act, is sung ; as
to pieces of this sort, the words being mere passive
instruments for music and action, should not be cri-
ticised.

Lord Aimworth opens the second act with a soliloquy, expressing sentiments of virtuous tendency,
and a delicate attachment to Patty ; songs are necessary to make an opera, else what his lordship
sings here might as well have been omitted. Our
Maid of the Mill, with very natural awe and palpitation of heart, approaches her noble admirer ; the
encounter is well managed, and their conversation
opens in an easy, pleasing manner ; her thanking
him for favours conferred, and his manner of receiving those thanks, are prettily conceived ; his
lordship's remark upon the change of her dress,
shews that she has some interest in his thoughts, and
aptly introduces the indulgence his mother had
shewn the girl. There is a well connected chain of
gradation from one subject to another in this scene,
and Lord Aimworth's dubitable, round-about mention of farmer Giles, with Patty's replies, are, we
conceive, a good picture of nature in such circumstances ; his lordship's declaration of turning the
honest, well-meaning rustic off his farm, may be a-
pologized for as a probable start of jealousy, but it
infringes upon generosity of principle ; however,
there is some reason to think he does it merely to
try whether she has a positive regard for his rival
or not. The feelings of two youthful minds in love
with each other, yet ignorant of the mutual attachment, is very well described in this tete-a-tete ; his
lordship being good-naturedly peevish, and Patty

timorously

timerously obscure ; the transition to a marriage
with Theodosia is well introduced. At the conclusion of this scene Lord Aimworth's feelings rise
into a just degree of perplexity, and he goes off with
a very tolerable song.

Upon the peer's departure Giles enters, informing
Patty of some rural honours the tenants are going to
pay Lord Aimworth's arrival, and soliciting her as
a partner in the festival dance, being, as he says,
intended his partner for life ; upon mention of this
last circumstance, Patty enters into a serious remon-
strance against Giles's hopes of a matrimonial union
with her ; nay, she goes so far as to declare an absolute dislike, which even the authority of her father
cannot remove, or, as she expresses it in her song,
fears of the greatest hardships ; leaving him with
an earnest request not to harrass her with so irksome
a subject : she throws poor Giles into a consternation ; his supposition that learning has cracked her
brain, is extremely characteristic ; and his method
of accounting for the repulse she has given him, we
hold in the same view ; his song is nothing but a
repetition of what he has said before, however, possesses a degree of humour that must recommend it.

In the next scene we are entertained with some
agreeable remarks on rural felicity, of which Patty
and Theodosia seem to have a just and spirited idea :
Fanny, at Mervin's desire, approaches Theodosia,
and addresses her in the right gipsey, begging, for-
tune-telling cant, but without effect. Mervin, under favour of his disguise, pretends to pick up a paper, which is in reality a letter from himself to Theodosia ; upon reading it, she eagerly desires to be
conducted to the writer of it ; this induces the lover

to

to difcover himfelf, which he has but juft done when Sir Harry and Lady Sycamore come upon them. The knight happening to cough is humouroufly reproved by his lady for not obferving her directions concerning health : upon mention of gypfies, Sir Harry affumes the magifterial ftile, and rates them foundly; however, urged and led on by Mervin, they prefs after him ; this occafions Lady Sycamore to exprefs apprehenfions, while her valorous fpoufe fings forth his refentment in a rhapfody of abufe againft the mendicant crew ; a circumftance which throws the gypfies into a confternation, left he fhould be a juftice of peace.

Mervin, who had followed Theodofia, returns much chagrined at her departure, drives off the gypfies, and is in violent agitation about his miftrefs, who unexpectedly appears in the pavillion ; upon feeing her, with the true phrenzy of impatient love, he is for climbing up to her ; however, this fhe prudently forbids, and, as time preffes clofe, fhe comes at once not only to a declaration of love, but of her readinefs to elope with him. Here a frefh difficulty arifes, how to carry the lady off, having no carriage or horfes ; fhe defires him to expect her at the Mill, and to devife in the mean time fome method to accomplifh their mutual wifhes ; the amorous ditty fhe fings is made up of agreeable nothingnefs, founded on the pilfered idea of Juliet's calling Romeo back, and forgetting what fhe has to fay.

When Theodofia difappears, Fanny claims from Mervin the reward he promifed her fociety, which he gives her, fuggefting to himfelf a fcheme of getting Theodofia difguifed as a gypfy alfo. To further this purpofe, and to make Fanny a fafter friend,

he

he gives her a guinea, as earneft of twenty more, if
fhe will fulfil his defires ; Fanny, by miftaking
Mervin's meaning, gives the fcene an arch turn, favourable to acting merit.

Ralph's appearance makes Fanny refolve, that
unlefs he fulfils his promife of marriage, he muft
converfe no more with her ; feeing his miftrefs look
gloomy, and receiving very fhort anfwers from her,
the young miller enquires the caufe, and intimates
his having a bout with the gentleman, if he has been
uncivil to her. This brings her to an explanation,
and fhe claims his promife ; hence a well-conceived
fquabble arifes, and very ungentle terms enfue :
quite cock-a-hoop with her views from Mervin,
Fanny rates him foundly, and he in return treats her
with as good as fhe brings. This whole fcene is
perfectly founded in nature, and expreffed happily ; Ralph's foliloquy, wherein he vows revenge
againft his fuppofed rival, Mr. Mervin, is fpirited,
humourous, and very much in character.

We are now conducted to the Mill, where we
meet Fairfield and Giles over a pot of beer, the former lamenting that his daughter is deaf to all perfuafion, refpecting the marriage ; while the latter,
with a blunt, generous degree of compofure, imputes it to the right caufe, her liking another better.
His difinterefted fentiments in this fcene recommend
him much, and his fenfible refignation of the hopes
he had formed, fhew a good head, as well as an honeft heart.

Lord Aimworth coming unexpectedly, Fairfield
is rather puzzled to pay his refpects with propriety,
but is relieved by the peer's affable condefcenfion ;
who fhortly introduces the fubject of Patty's mar-

2   riage,

riage, and obferves, that nothing but the fudden
death of his mother could have prevented a genteel
provifion being made for the girl ; to repair which
lofs, with very delicate generofity, his lordfhip prefents to the Miller a bill of a thoufand pounds, and
takes on himfelf the expence of Patty's nuptials :
Fairfield, after expreffing fuitable gratitude, acquaints Lord Aimworth with his daughter's averfion to the match, and begs his influence to reconcile her. This intelligence and requeft caufe his
lordfhip frefh perplexity ; however, the miller fends
in Patty, between whom and the peer a fcene of critical delicacy enfues.

The manner in which Lord Aimworth founds
Patty's real inclination, his playing moth like round
the flame of his own paffion, her diffidence and tre-
mor of heart, his avowal of love, her declining the
firft wifh of her heart, to prevent any difgrace from
falling on his rank, by an inadequate connection,
all do the author of this piece great credit. Matters are left in an undetermined ftate when Sir Harry enters, fluftered with an idea that his daughter
was near being carried off by a gypfey man ; after
expreffing his refentment, he takes Lord Aimworth
afide, in favour of Giles, who has been relating his
difappointment ; while the peer and her father are
in converfe apart, Theodofia lets us hear her approbation of the gypfey fcheme.

Sir Harry acquaints Giles of my lord's good difpofition towards him, and declaring that he will
make all up, a quintetto, expreffive of their feveral
feelings, concludes the fecond act.

Lady Sycamore, and her mate, at the beginning of
the third act, are much agitated about their daughter's

ter's elopement with a gypſey ; Lord Aimworth endeavours to ſoften matters, and deſires that he may
have the management of the affair, eſpecially as he has
been the cauſe of Miſs Sycamore's uneaſineſs. The
knight's remarks upon ladies are rather harſh, and
not very charaƈteriſtic for a man ſo much under the
dominion of a crooked rib as he ſeems to be. Ralph,
under apprehenſion of having done ſomething
wrong, apologizes to Lord Aimworth, who acquits
him, and ſeeing the miller, enquires his buſineſs ;
Fairfield, from a very delicate principle, acquaints
him, that as talkative people have thrown out ſcan-
dalous inſinuations, reſpeƈting the thouſand pound
note given to him for Patty, he begs to return it ;
adding, that farmer 'Giles has been prejudiced a-
gainſt Patty by means of it. Lord Aimworth con-
deſcends to take back the note, and having been,
though inadvertently, the cauſe of Patty's loſing one
huſband, promiſes to get her another, for which
purpoſe he deſires the miller to bring her immediately, but detains him to take a letter he is going
to write ; then gives the audience a hint of his intention by a ſong.

In the next ſcene Fanny becomes petitioner to
Ralph, who humorouſly retorts upon her the rough
treatment ſhe gave him, and ſtands proof againſt all
her ſolicitation ; we apprehend his ſong, eſpecially
the firſt verſe, diſcovers a delicacy of ſentiment and
expreſſion rather out of charaƈter for maſter Ralph.
Fanny, finding his obduracy, laments her own for-
ſaken ſtate ; when ſhe mentions the gentleman,
though an enraged gypſey might ſay, *the devil run
away with him,* yet we apprehend it a very blameable mode of expreſſion for the ſtage.

Farmer.

Maid of the Mill.

Farmer Giles now appears, nettled at something Patty has said to him, and from the warmth of conversation declares, that he wont have her; this alarms her pride, lest he should think her temper moved on that account, she declares that nothing but painful neceffity could have obliged her even to a seeming confent; here Giles exhibits a touch of the brute, and very juftly irritates Patty till her paffion gets vent at her eyes, when she sings the following air, which we think worth tranfcribing.

Oh leave me, in pity, the falfhood I fcorn,
 For flander the bofom untainted defies;
But rudenefs and infult are not to be borne,
 Though offered by wretches we've fenfe to defpife.

Of woman defencelefs how cruel the fate,
 Pafs ever fo cautious fo blamelefs her way;
Nature and envy lurk always in wait,
 And innocence falls to their fury a prey.

Mervin, provided with a difguife for Theodofia, comes on here, and she, after rallying him for letting her be at the appointed place before him, goes into a clofet to put on the gypfey garment; which done, she fings an air in the ftile of thofe itinerant gentry, and is going off with her lover, when they are interrupted by the approach of Fairfield and Giles: the miller seeing two of gypfey appearance in his house, threatens them with punifhment, when seizing Theodofia, to fee if she has ftolen any thing, he knows her, and expreffes aftonifhment at her difguife. On the difcovery, Mervin offers to bribe the miller, who rejects the propofal with proper fpirit, and giving him a letter from Lord Aimworth, advifes their going to his lordfhip's. On perufal of the letter, their fcheme of running away is laid afide, and they refolve to obey the peer's fummons. Theodofia throwing out a good-natured doubt of Mervin's fincerity, he anfwers by a fong, founded upon one of the moft hackneyed fentiments in poetical compofition.

Giles, in a foliloquy of fome humour, acquaints us that he has heard of Lord Aimworth's promife to get Patty a hufband, and throws out his conjectures who it may be ; he alfo expreffes his fatisfaction at having efcaped the noofe, with one he fuppofes a caft miftrefs, and refolves to live a batchelor, that he may avoid the chance of being a cuckold.

From the Mill we are again conveyed to Lord Aimworth's houfe, where we meet with his lordfhip removing Fairfield's uneafinefs, at the attack which has been made upon his daughter's reputation. When the miller declares himfelf content, and is going home, the peer furprizes him with a propofition of taking Patty for his lady ; the old man's fwell of heart at fuch unexpected honour, the young woman's aftonifhment at fuch unforefeen happinefs, with his lordfhip's tender declarations, render this fcene affecting ; and, we venture to affirm, that what Ralph fays upon his fifter's wanting a proper acknowledgment, is as natural, comprehenfive, and fine an effufion of fimplicity, as ever fell from any author's pen, " Down on your knees, and fall a crying."

After a duett, in the bill-and-coo ftrain, between the happy pair, Sir Harry, Lady Sycamore, Mervin and Theodofia appear ; from what the knight fays, we learn, that by the interpofition of Lord Aimworth,

Maid of the Mill.

worth, the wifhes of Theodofia and her lover are to be fulfilled. Upon his lordfhip's prefenting Patty as his intended bride, fome objections are ftarted by Sir Harry and his lady, which the peer genteely and fenfibly fets afide ; then proceeds to provide for his honeft father-in-law, and declares an intention of getting Ralph a commiffion. The forward young ruftic's refolution of keeping Fan when he is an officer, and his elevated pertnefs, are circumftances highly in nature. Giles joining the company, is introduced to his former fweetheart, and promifed remiffion of a year's rent ; all parties thus accomodated, the piece concludes with an alternate fong.

With refpect to the plot of this opera, it is fimple, uniform and interefting ; the fcenes are ranged in an agreeable fucceffion, and the fongs flow naturally from the dialogue, which we think well varied for, and adapted to the characters ; neither the fentiments nor verfification of the fongs deferves much praife, and we fuppofe the author only meant them as mere inftruments for combining and conveying mufical founds.

In a review of the characters, we find Lord Aimworth what every nobleman fhould be, and what we fear very few are, humane, generous, virtuous and difinterefted ; poffeffing too much good fenfe to be fwayed by an irrational pride of birth, and too much delicacy of fentiment to approach the object of his love upon unworthy terms. As the part in reprefentation requires more of the feeling actor, than the harmonious finger, however we may like Mr. MATTOCKS in the airs, we muft rather object to him in the dialogue ; nervelefs expreffion and unvarying features, throw a great damp on this part.

We

We are forry to fay, that the fame remark is equally
applicable to Mr. DUBELLAMY, who has confeffedly much merit as a finger, not one grain as a fpeaker. Mr. REDDISH did it for his benefit, as we remember, and appeared the exact reverfe of thofe
gentlemen we have mentioned ; fuppofing his view
was more to get money than fame, and that he did
not mean to impofe himfelf on the public as a mufical performer, his Lord Aimworth was refpectable.

Sir Harry Sycamore is a talkative, vain, ignorant baronet, well calculated for Mr. SHUTER, who
certainly exhibits him with whimfical pleafantry ;
however, though we give him the foremoft praife,
juftice obliges us to fay, that Mr. PARSONS treads
clofe on his heels and fhews himfelf a very capable
fervitor in the temple of Momus.

Mervin is a loving gentleman, of very little merit,
and at each houfe has fallen into very feeble hands ;
Meffrs. BAKER and FAWCET do, if poffible, lefs for
him than the author has done ; fo that what Mr.
BICKERSTAFF has faintly conceived, they as infipid-
ly execute.

Fairfield, the miller, is a moft amiable ruftic, poffeffed of feelings and ideas equal to a more exalted
character, a kind parent, and an honeft man ; the
fituation he is placed in, and his mode of behaviour,
render him an object of refpect and concern. We
are extremely pleafed at meeting an opportunity of
giving Mr. GIBSON our approbation in this part, and
we have never mentioned him difadvantageoufly,
but his worth in private life made us peculiarly lament his deficiencies on the ftage. Mr. JEFFERSON
having the advantage of much freer expreffion than
Mr. GIBSON, we muft give him fo far the preference.

Giles

Giles is an extreme well-drawn, rural character, and Mr. BEARD did that honest, unaffected simplicity which distinguish him, particular justice ; his humour was natural, forcible and intelligible. The farmer has never been quite himself since that very excellent singing actor has left the stage ; however, impartiality demands that we should allow Mr. BANNISTER a very happy share of execution, both in the speaking and singing, considerably more than any competitor since the original. Mr. REINHOLD has performed the part with a considerable share of merit, but wants an essential mellowness of humour; and Mr. BARNSHAW has exhibited the farmer, but having more of the Clare Market knock-me-down knowing-one, than rustic simplicity, was by no means an agreeable representative.

Ralph is drawn with much pleasant propriety, and supported equally through the whole. Whatever merit Mr. DIBDIN may have in composition, he certainly has not the shadow of any in acting; wherefore, we are hardy enough to say, the young miller could scarce have fallen into worse hands.

Mr. DYER has some degree of spirit and nature, yet, if we may allude to painting, his performance is little more than dead colouring the character. If Mr. KING had not necessarily a cast of parts, which scarce allows him proper relaxation, the young miller should most certainly be rendered a public favourite, by the recommendation of his truly comic powers.

Lady Sycamore is a vain, positive old lady, who holds her lord and master in that light we fear many wives do ; and thinks her own understanding is shewn to more advantage, by taking him into the

leading-

leading-ftrnigs of her direction. Her overftrained modefty in catching at the flighteft appearance of licentious ideas, is very chara&teriftic ; her formality and falfe confequence, are excellently fupported by Mrs. PITT ; and Mrs. BRADSHAW, though inferior, cannot fail to gratify an audience.

Theodofia, who has nothing particular to mark her chara&ter, and is like moft other marriagable young ladies, fuffers no injury from Mrs. BAKER, or Mifs RADLEY , but we apprehend the fuperior fenfibility of Mrs. MATTOCKS, renders her more pleafing.

Patty appears to be an obje&t of the author's particular attention ; he has drawn her with fo many amiable qualities, that even pride muft allow Lord Aimworth juftifiable, in defcending fo much below his rank to fecure happinefs. Mrs. PINTO's execution of the fongs has been fo generally allowed, and had fuch amazing influence at the original performance of this piece, that we doubt whether in that refpe&t, the ftage will ever find her equal ; as to the fpeaking, fhe was much worfe than any one we have ever heard : however, be her deficiencies what they may, Covent Garden theatre, in common gratitude, owe; her a penfion of two hundred a year, for immenfe advantages received, even though fhe was never to fpeak or fing a line more. Mrs. MATTOCKS has given us more pleafure in Patty than Mrs. PINTO, but beyond all doubt the feelings and expreffion of Mrs. BADDELY, rank her firft in critical efteem.

Placed between thofe very engaging and fpirited gypfies, Mrs. THOMPSON and Mifs POPE, we may fay with Macheath, " Which way fhall we turn us,

how

how can we decide ;" however, if the scale must turn, Mrs. THOMPSON's merit, in our view, gives it the cast.

The author of this opera has candidly acknowledged taking his plan from Pamela, and we are happy to congratulate him on having made a very good and agreeable use of the materials furnished by that romance; his humour is not tainted with licentiousness, and the nicer feelings are wrought up with a probable and instructive delicacy ; upon the whole, we think the MAID of the MILL possesses such charms, such a chaste, pleasing simplicity, that both in representation and perusal, she must have many admirers.

DOUGLAS.

DOUGLAS.

A Tragedy.   By Mr. John Home.

L A D Y Randolph, formerly married to a chief
of the name of Douglas, but at the time of this tragedy espoused to Lord Randolph, opens the piece,
with a soliloquy, expressing that settled grief which
hangs upon her heart, for the loss of her deceased
lord, and infant son.   While in this state of mournful meditation, her living lord appears, and in mild
terms reproves the melancholy she wears; nay, is
so very moderate in his expectations, that he only
requires from her a decent affection; failing of
which, his wish is to mingle with the war, threatened
by a Danish invasion.

The lady here lets a ray of kindness break through
the clouds of sorrow, and speaking of war, she makes
a just and pleasing distinction between that waged
with a foreign power, and different ends of the same
island, which nature has united, conflicting with
each other.   There is a pretty compliment to the
union, and the courage of South and North Britain,
in this speech: Lord Randolph retiring, Anna appears; this kind confidant, by striving to balm her
lady's wounded heart, probes and pains it the more;
the pretence of grief being for a lost brother, Anna
asks, what her feelings must be, had a tender, be-
loved husband been snatched from her arms. Touching upon this master-string of her heart, she leads

I   Lady

Douglas.

Lady Randolph to a full difclofure of her mind : the narration of her fecret marriage, and the fate of her hufband is natural and pathetic ; her grief for expofing her child to the fate fhe fuppofes he met, is well defcribed. When Lady Randolph obferves, that a fore knowledge of the evils which had embittered her paft life, would certainly have broken her heart, Anna makes this very fenfible and moral reply :

> That God whofe minifters good angels are,
> Hath fhut the book in mercy to mankind.

This converfation, which we think rather too much extended for ftage action, is interrupted by the approach of Glenalvon, a perfon, who, from what fhe fays, is rather difagreeable to Lady Randolph, for which fhe affigns fufficient reafon, by fketching his character, and retires. A very immaterial foliloquy, trite in fentiment, but tolerably well expreffed, intervenes between Lady Randolph's exit and Glenalvon's entrance ; this enterprizing blade queftions Anna refpecting the thoughtfulnefs of her afpect, and pays fome compliment to her charms ; this fading advantage fhe holds light, from Lady Randolph's woes, and with dutiful feeling for her miftrefs's painful ftate, follows to relieve her.

When alone, Glenalvon lays himfelf open to the audience for a confummate villain, declares himfelf Randolph's fecret rival, and fignifies, that there is a fcheme on foot to deprive the unfufpecting baron of his lady, fortunes and life.

At the beginning of the fecond act, a peafant, fear ftruck, is brought on by fervants, and immediately after Lord Randolph enters with Douglas, as a young shepherd, who has rescued him from the desperate assault of four assassins: after thanks returned to the gallant stranger, both by the baron and his lady, enquiry is made concerning who the brave deliverer is; to this Douglas replies with a modesty peculiar to great minds, that his name is Norval, and that his father is a shepherd on the Grampian Hills, that an attack made upon their property, by a band of ruffians, some days before, had given his active spirit an opportunity of exerting itself, that his suceess in defeating the banditti, had inspired him with martial ideas, and that having heard of an impending war, he proposed entering the field in his country's cause, as a volunteer. On Lord Randolph's promising him protection and patronage, he replies with a manly sense of favour, and his noble friend takes him off to visit and view the camp.

The feelings of maternal sympathy dawn in this scene, and the following one with Anna, they are judiciously manifested in Lady Randolph's regard for her unknown son; well knowing the treachery of Glenalvon's heart, and his jealousy of any one who may rival him in Randolph's esteem, she determines to be young Norval's guardian. The following similitude of herself to a flower, is fanciful and pretty, but poetical allusions we deem unnatural to a mind diseased; perusal however may not be unpleasing:

I'll be the artist of young Norval's fortune;
'Tis pleasing to admire! most apt was I
To this affection in my better days:
Though now I seem to you shrunk up, retired
Within the narrow compass of my woe;

2

Douglas.

> Have you not fometimes feen an early flow'r
> Open its bud, and fpread its filken leaves
> To catch fweet airs, and odours to beftow;
> Then by the keen blaft nipp'd—pull in its leaves
> And though ftill living die to fcent and beauty?
> Emblem of me; affliction like a ftorm
> Has kill'd the forward bloffom of my heart.

Upon Glenalvon's appearance and enquiry after Randolph's welfare, Matilda gives him to under-ftand, we think too plainly, her knowledge of his character and real feelings; ftartled with her charge and confcious guilt, he endeavours to apologize, but by the mention of love, increafes her contempt and deteftation. At length, fhe acquaints him, rather indifcreetly, with Randolph's attachment to his de-liverer, and by threats alarms his jealoufy; this, upon going off, plainly appears, for in the fucceeding foliloquy, he determines to aggravate his former crimes, by removing young Norval at any rate; and, for that purpofe, refolves to try the cowardly attendant who forfook him in refcuing Lord Ran-dolph, fhrewdly obferving, that the greateft daftards are capable of harbouring dangerous revenge.

At the beginning of the third act, we meet Mrs. Anna foliloquizing to very little purpofe, as all fhe fays amounts to no more than telling us in a diffufe, flowery ftile, that Lady Randolph is afleep, and that fhe heartily wifhes her a good nap; indeed, fhe prays for it prettily enough, but placing immortal fpirits upon *golden beds,* favours too much of grofs mortality; befides, if we take the idea literally, a bed of ftraw is preferable to a bed of gold, if figu-ratively it means nothing: but poets are wedded to

R 2

fancy,

fancy, and too often confider propriety as a mere domeftic, to be employed or difcarded at pleafure.

A fervant acquaints Anna that one of the affaffins is fecured, and produces fome jewels taken from the prifoner, which are ftrong prefumptive proofs of his guilt. Upon viewing the jewels, Anna difcovers the family creft of Douglas, and goes off to acquaint her lady with fo alarming a circumftance.

Here an aged peafant is brought on, afferting his own innocence and ignorance of the crime laid to his charge : upon Lady Randolph's entrance, we find, that fhe expects to hear how her child perifh- ed; the old fhepherd folicits Lady Randolph's pro- tection from the torture with which he is threatened, which fhe grants, on condition that he truly relates the manner of his obtaining the jewels found upon him ; this he would gladly evade, but through fear of compulfion, enters upon the narration, which we think happily related, and the following defcriptive lines we particularly approve.

> —— whilft thus we poorly lived,
> One ftormy night, as I remember well,
> The wind and rain beat hard upon our roof;
> Red came the river down, and loud and oft
> The angry fpirit of the water roar'd.

From Norval's tale it appears, that he found a child floating in a bafket, that he brought up the child as his own, keeping from him every idea of noble birth ; that this adopted fon had left him fome days, purpofing for the camp, and that he was following to deliver him the jewels that were found in the bafket, as from them the real lineage of his charge might

might poffibly be traced. The whole of this relation is well conducted, and free from fuperfluity ;
the interruptions thrown in by Lady Randolph during the progrefs of it are natural ; and upon full
conviction that the young fhepherd is her identical
child; the burft of overflowing fatisfaction is very
defcriptive of maternal affection. From Anna's
advifing a prudent reftriction of her joy for fear of
difcovery, and her agitation, Norval fuggefts that
fhe is the daughter of his ancient mafter, which fhe
acknowledges, as alfo that the refcued child is hers.
Lady Randolph defires that the old man, till matters
are ripe for a difcovery, may go to an old fervant of
her father's, who lives retired from the world ; and
charges him, if he fhould meet Douglas, not 'to acquaint him with the difcovery that has been made.
Thefe precautions taken, fhe orders the fervants not
only to fet the old fhepherd at liberty, as being innocent, but to conduct him fome part of his way, as
reparation for the injury of having detained him as
a prifoner.

When all are retired but her confidant, the en-
raptured mother gives a fcope to joy, expreffing her
ideas in a pleafing flow of expreffion ; and fhe determines upon an interview with Douglas, not only to
indulge her tender feelings, but alfo to concert with
him proper meafures for afferting his rank and
birth-right. Here Glenalvon enters, with intelligence that the Danes are landed upon the Eaft coaft
of Lothian : Lady Randolph's remark upon the
mifery war brings to mothers and wives, is pleafingly compaffionate. By Glenalvon's obfervation, that
fcorn from thofe we love is more wounding than the
fword, the fubject of his paffion for Matilda arifes,
which

Douglas.

which fhe replies to with fenfible and friendly advice, couched in terms of politic complacence ; with hypocritical penitence he receives it, and not only promifes to lay afide his guilty paffion, but alfo to become the guardian of young Norval in the field. Pleafed with this promife, the lady retires, affuring Glenalvon, that upon fuch terms he may rely on her friendfhip, or, what is much more than any other degree of reward, the confcious approbation of his own heart.

Glenalvon alone, and fit for mifchief, cafts off the occafional veil of virtue affumed for a few moments, and triumphs in the effects he thinks his fmooth artifice may work upon the lady. He fuggefts, that his own dependance and fituation are ticklifh, wherefore, he determines to make young Norval an inftrument for raifing jealoufy in the breaft of Lord Randolph ; fo finifhed a rafcal as Glenalvon appears to be, would no doubt be capable of faying, as well as doing any thing vile. Yet his illiberal remark upon the female fex, with which the third act concludes, might as well have been omitted.

At the beginning of the fourth act, Lord and Lady Randolph are brought forward, converfing upon the Danifh invafion ; fhe expreffing female apprehenfions, he manifefting the fpirit of a brave man. Upon Douglas's entrance, Lord Randolph afks how he has learned fo much of military fciences in the midft of rural obfcurity ; this he accounts for by a very picturefque narration, but rather tedious to that part of an audience, who are not furnifhed with a conception as fanciful as the author's ; and burthenfome to a fpeaker who is not poffeffed of flowing, variable, declamatory expreffion.

on. The account of why his inftructor became a hermit, is, we apprehend, quite fuperfluous, and we have a ftrong objection to the following remark made by Lady Randolph :

There is a deftiny in this ftrange world,
Which oft decrees an undeferved doom ;
Let fchoolmen tell us why.

However ftrange the world may be, this affertion is equally fo, having no meaning at all, or a very dangerous one, accufing eternal juftice of a partial difpenfation---Deftiny ! we need go but a fhort time to the fchool of reafon for proof that there is no fuch principle in the providential fcheme of life ; wherefore, it cannot be thought harfh to confider fuch a pofition as inconfiftent with found philofophy, and rather an infult upon our fober fenfes. Let fatalifm be buried in the fame oblivion and contempt with witches, fairies, ghofts, goblins, and every other phantom of gloomy, troubled minds.

Here feveral fpeeches occur, no otherwife effential than to indulge the poet's fancy with unneceffary mention of a warrior who never appears. Indeed, through this whole fcene the plot ftands ftock-ftill, merely that the hobby-horfe of genius may prance about in the parterres of flowery defcription ; this will evidently appear by obferving, that if all which paffes from the beginning of the fourth act, to the fcene between Lady Randolph and her fon, was cut out, fuch an omiffion would not occafion the leaft chafm.

Left alone with her fon, impatient to make the difcovery, fhe enters upon the fubject, though diftantly

ftantly at firft, and invites him to a place of more
fecrecy, yet proceeds without removing. The explanation of his birth is brought about with fome
merit, but the effect of this fcene is anticipated, and
much weakened by what paffed between her and
the old fhepherd in the third act; befides, the converfation is ftretched out to a length which no force
of action can fupport : feeling fhould not be kept
long on the ftretch, for in fuch cafe it moft affured-
ly dulls.

After the tender tumults of joy fubfide, fhe tells
Douglas of his claim to the caftle and demefnes
which Lord Randolph holds in right of her ; then
mentions a defign of putting him in poffeffion of
his birth-right by means of the king ; fhe prudently checks fome impetuous ftarts which break forth
from him. After advifing him to conduct himfelf
ftill as Norval's fon, and to beware of Glenalvon,
he retires, leaving her to make a pious and very
emphatic fupplication to heaven in his behalf; a
fupplication which could have no effect if deftiny
prevailed. The following lines relative to the difficulty fhe finds to diffemble, are very fignificant
and pleafing ;

———— how do bad women find
Unchanging afpects to conceal their guilt,
When I by reafon and by juftice urged,
Full hardly can diffemble with thefe men,
In nature's pious caufe ?

Lord Randolph, who, from his firft appearance,
has talked of nothing but the Danes and battles,
here enters with the fame fubject ; wherefore, we
think his lady, upon going off, gives him a very
proper

Douglas.

proper hint, *to talk of war no more.* From what occurs between Randolph and Glenalvon we discover, that the latter has infected his patron and kinsman with jealousy; and that Randolph has in a letter from his lady to Norval, appointing a meeting, plausible proof of what Glenalvon has suggested. The villain, with great depth of policy, advises Lord Randolph to wait for more particular proof, and for that purpose to forward the intercepted billet to the young-swain, that by watching their motions he may have ocular demonstration of their behaviour: this counsel the baron approves, while his pretending friend desires leave to sound Norval on the subject, as from the weakness and vanity of youth some discovery may be made; this bait his lordship also catches at, and leaves Glenalvon to pursue his insiduous purpose.

By a short soliloquy it appears, that even he is deceived into an opinion that Lady Randolph entertains a criminal passion for the young stranger: by premeditate irony, Glenalvon works up the temper of Douglas to warmth, for which his mother's account of the villain has prepared him. The terms run high and reproachful on both sides, till at length their dispute is referred to the decision of the sword; when Lord Randolph re-entering interposes, and enjoins peace, demanding also the cause of quarrel, and offering his arbitration. This, with becoming spirit, Douglas declines; another alternative is then proposed, that their private quarrel shall rest undecided till the fate of war is known; the parties agreeing to this, the act concludes.

Douglas begins the fifth act with a soliloquy, wherein, though the characters must labour under

S strong

ftrong agitation of mind, yet we meet the author a-
gain fporting wantonly with his imagination, and alfo introducing the ridiculous, irrational idea of fu-
pernatural fpirits converfing with mortals, in the re-
tirements of night and folitude : we can forgive
poets any degree of fiction but this, which we hold
pernicious as well as contemptible,

Old Norval wandering in the wood, feeing the
fondling of many years, approaches, and notwithftanding Lady Randolph's caution to the contrary,
accofts him in his real character, and begs excufe
for having fo long kept him in a ftate of obfcurity ;
this tender condefcenfion of the old man, draws affectionate expreffions of regard from Douglas, who,
with great good fenfe and humility obferves, that in
his fylvan ftate, he learned fome inftructive leffons,
which he will ever retain ; particularly to treat his
inferiors with refpect, remembring that he once was
fhepherd Norval.

The old fhepherd having heard fome defigns a-
gainft his young lord's life, warns him of Lord
Randolph and Glenalvon, who have vowed revenge ;
unconfcious of having done any injury, the noble
youth is at a lofs to know their inftigation, but promifes to acquaint his mother with the danger, and
to take her advice. The old man here adminifters
a bleffing, and retires.

Again the hero of our piece foliloquizes in a luxuriant, poetical, and therefore, for his fituation, unnatural ftrain. There is an elevation of fpirit in
fome of thefe fentiments well worthy a great mind ;
but others are trifling excurfions of a luxuriant
mufe. Lady Randolph entering, a converfation follows, in which her fon repeats what old Norval informed

Douglas.

formed him of; from this she draws fearful apprehensions that the secret of his birth is discovered,
and that he consequently stands in much danger;
for which reason she advises him to seek the camp,
which he with a courageous glow of mind disdains,
and proposes to drive the treacherous spoilers from
possession of his father's house.

The fond mother admires his intrepidity, yet
fearing for his life, and assuring him of her own safe-
ty, she persuades him to seek his kinsman Lord
Douglas, in the camp; this, after some hesitation,
he complies with, and in compassion to maternal
fears, promises he will restrain his ardor in the approaching fight, as far as the honour of his endangered country and great name will admit. Here, as
the mother and son are affectionately separating, Lord
Randolph comes forward, with his murderous asso-
ciate Glenalvon; however, disdaining assassination,
the baron determines to attack him singly, and for that
purpose follows Douglas, while Glenalvon remains,
and discloses his intention of finishing them both.

A scuffle and clashing of swords is heard behind
the scenes, which calls Glenalvon off to execute his
fell purpose. Lady Randolph enters in wild confusion, and soon after Douglas, having disarmed
Lord Randolph, and slain Glenalvon, returns, but
not before the bloody villain had effected the design
of treacherously stabbing him. This incident produces a short scene of melting tendency, and every
generous mind must give a tear of pity to suffering
virtue. Upon her son's decease, Lady Randolph
very naturally loses sensation some moments,
through excess of grief; during which interval, her
husband receives the painful intelligence from Anna,

that

Douglas.

that he who was deemed a rival, was his wife's son. This throws Randolph into deep concern ; when the unhappy mother revives, she gives some vent to woe in frantic, disjointed expressions, and precipitately hurries off the stage to make way for old Norval, who comes to view and weep over the melancholy scene ; being checked by Lord Randolph for intrusion, his grief vents itself at large, in terms of bitter lamentation, over the corse of Douglas. Anna, who followed her mistress, returns with the lamentable intelligence of her having closed a wretched life, by precipitating herself headlong from a rock ; this heaps additional woe upon her husband's head, who considering himself as the principal cause of her distraction, resolves, after giving Anna directions for all funeral respect, to rush into the field of war, wishing never to return.

Thus ends a piece which has regularity of plot and unity of action to recommend it ; the incidents are few, and some trifling ; the scenes long, and in several places they run too much into a flattening similarity ; the sentiments are moral and poetical, but want originality ; the language is easy and chaste, and the versification well broke for those who speak the parts to avoid monotony ; the number of characters is small, hence some weight on action, however they are well chosen and uniformly supported ; time and place are also adhered to strictly enough.

Lord Randolph is so situated, that we can hardly collect the component parts of his character ; from what are distinguishable, he seems to be a lover of his country, a friend to merit, and as far as his lady's coldness will allow, a tender husband ; brave,

but

Douglas.

but weak ; with a heart to oppofe and conquer open foes, but wanting a head to difcern and counteract fecret ones. Till the touch of jealoufy he feels in the fourth act, and the laft fcene, what he fays is entirely compofed of unimportant declamation ; it is not eafy for an actor to render him pleafing to any audience, reprefenting him may be called rowing againft tide ; wherefore, Mr. YOUNGER, who was the original at EDINBURGH, and Mr. RIDOUT in LONDON, both merited praife for fteering clear of offence ; yet fo far as recollection will authorize comparifon, we think it a duty to place Mr. JEF-FERSON foremoft.

Glenalvon is, as we have already obferved, a horrid picture of deformed humanity, capable of vile actions upon the flighteft views. The author has in working up this part, mingled fubtlety with fpirit, and given a capable performer favourable opportunities to gain from humane feelings the applaufe of deteftation.

Mr. LOVE, the firft murderer of this murderous villain, was hateful indeed ; not from marking the character with propriety, not as Glenalvon, but as himfelf ; there never was fure a more rumbling, infipid, uncharacteriftic exhibition fince the days of Thefpis. Mr. SMITH was a very great contraft to this gentleman, yet as much out of character ; one growled like a thunder ftorm, the other fimpered like an April fit of funfhine. Mr. PALMER has capacity, well inftructed and reftrained, to do Glenalvon with propriety ; but if the play could be otherwife adequately caft, Mr. REDDISH would certainly do him that juftice he has hitherto been wronged of, and give the

I   author's

author's full meaning with fuitable force to an audience.

Douglas is drawn an object of great refpect, as to his filial, focial fentiments, and peculiarly fo for his ideas of glory ; but the author too often fpeaks in this part, forgetting character. The young hero's fituation is interefting, and his fall claims pity, but we wifh it had been effected by fome other means, or rather that he had been faved, as his death is a violent breach of poetical juftice, and might have been avoided, even to an amendment of the plot. There is fome fire and confiderable pathos in him, yet we think if he had faid lefs, he would have meant more.

Mr. BARRY never fhewed lefs of capital merit than in this part, almoft the whole of it feemed to drag upon his tongue, for which we can affign only two reafons ; that he did not think the writing and delineation equal to his execution, therefore was negligent ; or, which we think moft probable, the paffions not being wrought up to that degree of expreffion in which he excells, the part flipped from him without any perception of his own deficiency.

Mr. DIGGES was extremely pleafing and happy in the narrative and defcriptive parts, nor was he any way deficient in the ftrokes of tendernefs ; the author ftood very much indebted to this gentleman for the profperous exiftence of his piece. Mr. BRERETON may walk through it to fill up time before a pantomime or the jubilee, but fure neither the managers, nor he himfelf, would wifh to fee the whole of our opinion refpecting this attempt.

Old Norval's fimplicity, fenfibility, and tender fidelity of heart, engage us deeply in his favour ; he

is

Douglas.

is extremely well imagined, and finished in a masterly manner. As it is hard for a performer to render Lord Randolph respectable, so we think it would be difficult to find one of even decent capacity, who could be flat and unaffecting in the old shepherd: Mr. SPARKS discovered judgment and masterly strokes of acting, but was too mechanical and laborious; his simplicity wore strong marks of affectation, and his grief, in general, was discoverably pumped up by artificial feelings. Mr. PACKER, avoiding such faults, and successfully pursuing the path of nature, deserves preference.

Mrs. WOFFINGTON, whose tragic utterance was, in general, the bane of tender ears, never appeared to less advantage than in Lady Randolph; flat in the calm, and dissonant in the impassioned passages; who Mr. HOME might mean the part for originally, we cannot say, but Mrs. WARD, into whose hands it fortunately fell, did it as much justice as the poet or audience could wish, and deserves the praise of having exhibited in this tragedy, a very correct and affecting piece of performance. Mrs. BARRY, at present, who conceives the part equally well, having more power of expression, surpasses the last mentioned lady in execution.

Anna we have seen by Mrs. HOPKINS, Mrs. VINCENT, and Mrs. REDDISH, if there is any difference, we prefer the latter.

The persecution this tragedy underwent in its infant state, from some rigid, malevolent enthusiasts, was singular and severe; yet, from a very sensible and laudable exertion of public spirit, the author, to our great satisfaction, and the honour of the Edinburgh audience, received unexpected and extensive

advantage

advantage from the malevolence of his narrow-minded, illiberal foes; who abſurdly confine religion to auſterity of features, formality of ſpeech, and abſtraction from public amuſements. May ecclefiaftic tyranny ever find ſuch a fate, through the ſenſe, ſpirit and independancy of mankind.

Though we have objections to Douglas for want of buſineſs; to ſome of the ſcenes for trifling too long with the paſſions; to a ſuperfluity of deſcriptions; and to the cataſtrophe, which ſweeps off the innocent with the guilty; yet we are willing to allow it the offspring of warm genius; and freely ſubſcribe to the praiſe of its being a moral, fanciful and affluent dramatic poem, which probably may improve the head, and can never taint the heart.

CON-

The CONSCIOUS LOVERS.

A COMEDY.   By Sir RICHARD STEELE.

A Conversation between Sir John Bevil and his
old servant Humphry, opens this comedy; the baronet seems full of concern about his son, and relates
an incident which happened at a masquerade, from
whence he draws apprehension, that young Bevil is
married to, or reproachably connected with a young
lady, who was at the forementioned public meeting.

From an observation that Humphry makes, we
find that one Mr. Sealand, whose daughter was in
treaty of marriage with young Bevil, has taken an
alarm, and postponed the match. Sir John, upon
this declares, that to clear up matters he will
insist upon his son's pursuing the contract with Sealand; and orders Humphry to pump his valet, as
possibly from him they may learn if his master is
engaged in any private amour. The prince of poor
coxcombs, as the old domestic calls him, enters in
a full flow of spirits, and rallies honest Humphry,
exulting in his own gayer and more unlimited state
of servitude; the volubility of his expression, the
vivacity of his remarks, and the humour of his
ideas, are a very entertaining combination of plea-
santries. The remark he makes of having never
taken a mug of beer for his vote---would every senator could say as much with truth---is satirical and
laughable.

Upon Tom's mentioning that he has a letter from his mafter to Lucinda, Humphry afks why he does not haften to deliver it ; this queftion brings about an explanation that it is not eafy to obtain ac-cefs to her, Mrs. Sealand, the young lady's mother, being averfe to her daughter's match with Mr. Be-vil, through a defire the old lady has of matching Lucinda to a relation of her own ; this intelligence, it appears, the loquacious valet has received from one Mrs. Phillis, a chambermaid, who, as he infi-nuates, looks on him with a very tender eye, and therefore lets him into the fecrets of the family. Upon the appearance of this fecond-hand lady of fafhion, Humphry retires, naufeated with the party-coloured beau's intolerable vanity.

A fcene of very peculiar fpirit here enfues between the valet and waiting-woman ; their affected polite-nefs, their jealoufy, and reconciliation, make up a juft and amufing picture of their fphere in life, fo diftinguifhed for mimic gentility. When their own concerns have been difcuffed, Tom recommends his mafter's letter for delivery to Phillis's care ; encou-raged thereto by a handfome bribe, fhe undertakes the matter, and concludes the fcene with two lines which have more of plaufibility than ftrict truth to recommend them.

They may be falfe who languifh and complain,
But they who part with money never feign.

A multitude of melancholy inftances prove, that in affairs of gallantry, money is often freely parted with to promote the moft culpable, vileft purpofes, of which deceit and treachery are the bafe founda-tion ;

tion ; however, the maxim is natural enough for a chamber-maid, who wishes fees at any rate.

We next meet young Bevil in his study alone, meditating on the difficulties his proposed marriage throws him into, and remarking, that his only hope is Lucinda's refusal of the match. This pleasing expectation he entertains for two reasons ; first, because she is pre-engaged to Myrtle ; and next, because he has by letter acquainted her with his inclination towards another : collecting resolution from this favourable view of matters, he determines to declare a readiness of consummating the nuptial rites, according to his father's earnest desire. When he has thus prepared himself for an interview, Sir John approaches, and enters upon the matrimonial subject, expressing great satisfaction at his son's dutiful acquiescence ; the young man proposes immediately waiting on his bride, but the baronet waves that, as knowing Sealand is not in a favourable mood of mind to see his intended son-in-law ; therefore, he leaves Humphry as a spy upon his son, and hastens to put Sealand into better temper.

No sooner does Sir John disappear, than Humphry, with a faithful, ingenuous openness of temper, mentions to his young master a lady that gives the old man pain. This draws from Bevil a confidential confession, and in an extreme pretty, well conducted tale, he relates the distressful hazards Indiana, a lady whom he had seen and conceived a passion for on his travels, experienced from the loss of parents, friends, and the villainy of one who was left her guardian, but would have proved her destroyer.

The

Confcious Lovers.

The circumftance of Bevil's meeting her on the brink of imprifonment, his humane, generous deliverance by concealed bounty, and his conducting her fafe to England, on the moft honourable and difinterefted principles, place him in a very favourable point of view. Upon Humphry's afking whether it was the young lady's paffion for him, or his for her, that gave him an averfion to the match of his father's propofing, he gives him an anfwer that fhews him rather uncommonly refined in his notions, never having once hinted to her the warm intereft fhe claimed in his heart; and this referve he imputes to an inviolable filial refpect, which checks him from entering into any engagement that might prove difagreeable to Sir John.

Upon being informed that Mr. Myrtle is at the next door, and would be glad of a conference, he expreffes readinefs to receive him; then afks Tom for an anfwer to his letter, who informs his mafter he was defired to call again. Here Humphry withdraws, dropping the fatisfactory hint, that there is a fecret impediment which will check the dreaded marriage with Lucinda. Bevil agreeably feels for his friend Myrtle's uneafy fituation, judging of it from his own; and concludes the act with a rhiming couplet, which would have been much better turned into profe.

Myrtle being introduced by Tom at the beginning of the fecond act, addreffes himfelf with fome degree of refentment, on the fubject of rivalfhip to young Bevil, who endeavours, by proper degrees, to explain the ftate of affairs; however, Myrtle, fpurred by a kind of jealoufy, rather warms, from a mifapprehenfion of Bevil's meaning. At length they

they come to understand one another, and a third
person is mentioned as a formidable rival, who
though old and an egregious coxcomb, stands a fair
chance of success.   After some doubts arising, as
counsel are to be consulted, it is resolved, that Myrtle
and Tom shall assume the appearance of the lawyers employed, and thereby delay matters at least.
This point settled, Myrtle goes off, and leaves
Bevil to his just and friendly reflections upon the
perplexed state of Indiana, whom he resolves to vifit; generously, as well as sensibly remarking, that
though filial duty will prevent him from ever marrying contrary to his father's inclination, yet that
duty does not deter him from the innocent company
of a virtuous woman, who is particularly agreeable
to him.

The scene changing to Indiana's lodgings, she and
her aunt Isabella come forward, conversing upon the
behaviour of Bevil, which appears interested and designing to the former, totally generous and honourable to the latter.   Isabella speaks with more precaution and knowledge than her neice, but Indiana
expresses the genuine gratitude and delicacy of a
good and susceptible mind ; in the full flow of
which, she produces a fresh instance of his benevolence, two hundred and fifty pounds in bank notes,
to pay for a new set of dressing-plate.

After an altercation of considerable length, in
which Indiana defends her admirer with reason, affection and delicacy, her aunt still perseveres in a
suspicion of danger, and, even continues her doubts
till Indiana's resentment is rather wrought up, and
leaves

leaves her to make fome old maidifh reflections upon
the perils waiting unfufpecting innocence.

Indiana immediately re-enters, and having been
informed of Mr. Bevil's approach, orders his admiffion, previous to which fhe reflects upon an
alteration in behaviour, a referve affumed fince the
report of his marriage ; however, love at his appearance banifhes all doubts, he appears inno-
cently amiable in her eyes, and their encounter is
fuch as may be properly expected from perfons of
fenfe and true politenefs. The converfation at firft
is employed upon matters merely indifferent ; at
length, the fubject turns upon the effential difference of love and efteem, upon which topic fome
agreeable remarks occur.

At length an opportunity offers for Bevil to fhew
a feeling of heart extremely recommendatory, that
of not being content with barely recompenfing
merit, but treating it with refpect alfo ; this introduces for Bevil's opinion the difpute Indiana has had
with her aunt, whether a man who confers favours
on a woman he is no way allied to muft not be in-
terefted ; Bevil's anfwer in the affirmative, rather
puzzles the young lady, who is evidently endeavouring to work out fome explanation relative to
herfelf; however, this is evaded on his fide, till,
at length, probably from an apprehenfion of what
her drift is, he retires fomewhat abruptly.

At this juncture Ifabella returns, and foftens
her neice's doubts concerning the real bent of Bevil's heart, but declares it neceffary for further fatisfaction and fafety, to find out whether Mr. Bevil
and Mr. Myrtle are really friends or rivals ; Indiana,

na, wrapping her heart in confidence of her lover's faith, concludes this act, as every act of this piece censurably does, with rhime; and that, to say truth, neither very significant nor poetical.

Tom and the volatile ludicrous object of his admiration meet and open the third act; but notwithstanding a free, kind salutation from him, the coquettish jade tosses up her nose, and passes him with an air of quality disdain; stung with this treatment, and knowing her disposition, he determines upon assuming airs also, and the repartee of flirtation is bandied about for some time with equal dexterity on both sides; at length, the swain softens, and relates with much natural whim, the important day and hour, and manner of his falling in love; this, after a few taunts and consequential airs, softens the nympth into an acknowledgement, that her lover's eloquence is very forceable; and she then acquaints him with the effect of his master's letter; how happy it has made Lucinda, giving him also one in return.

Tom applauds their negotiation, as something may be derived from it for their mutual advantage and settlement; here the interview takes a very soft, amorous turn, and some kisses are seemingly ravished by Tom, for which his mistress gives a faint repulse, acquainting him with the different views of Mr. and Mrs. Sealand, respecting Lucinda's wedding, then archly desires him to give her but one kiss more; after which they take leave of each other with great and laughable ceremony.

Lucinda, upon her entrance, enquires of Phillis who she has been hurrying off, and receives for an-

- swer,

fwer, a fweetheart; here the young lady, we apprehend, defcends a little out of her fphere, by obferving, that fhe has heard fomething like kiffing; to which Phillis makes a facetious and ingenuous reply; this draws on mention of Cimberton, and the fpirited chambermaid afferts, that he is as much married to Lucinda as quality generally are, that is, by confent of friends, fettlements and other pecuniary agreements. In the progrefs of this converfation, we difcover that Myrtle, whofe pretenfions were once favoured by the young lady's parents, has won her heart; the account fhe gives of her mother's referved peculiarity is pleafant enough; Phillis, who feems to be the friend of her young miftrefs's inclination's declares, that by liftening fhe has difcovered the whole of Mrs. Sealand's defign in favour of Cimberton; particularly the means ufed to gain confent from a rich uncle of his, ftiled Sir Geoffery. Upon the approach of Mr. Cimberton and her mother, Lucinda puts Phillis off the ftage; the old lady opens her own character by fome formal obfervations upon keeping family blood pure; to which her ftarched, antiquated kinfman replies in terms adequately ludicrous; fome of his remarks upon the matrimonial connection are grofs, and not a little heightened in that fenfe, both by Lucinda and her mother; the Lacedemonian inftitution and other points being difcuffed, they enter upon the main fubject. Mrs. Sealand pointing out her daughter to Cimberton as his intended wife; he with his fupercilious, philofophical mode of delivery, fpeaks of her fhape and motions, according to her own phrafe, as if fhe was a fteed at

2   fale;

fale; another of his remarks of not allowing her a
fallow feafon when married, though characteristic, is
fulfome.

Mrs. Sealand being informed that the lawyers
are come, orders them to be fhewn in; here Myrtle as ferjeant Bramble, and Tom as councellor Tar-
get appear; being feated, they enter immediately
on the debate; and while the former puzzles the
fubject with a verbofe, voluble introduction, the
other ftammers out impatient interruption till the
fcene grows very laughable; at length, Cimberton
naturally afks, as not underftanding the purport of
their pleading, to have a copy of it in Englifh, this
offends Bramble; a very good and fatirical ftroke
againft tedious letigation occurs by Bramble's reply, when Cimberton defires to have their opinions
without delay, " that the law will not admit of"
there is confiderable humour in the remark of Tar-
get after his opponent is gone; though he has not
uttered one perfect word, yet he fays " I touched
him to the quick upon Grimgribber. This fcene
has a great deal of fpirit and humour, but the incident is rather forced and improbable.

Sealand obferving that men of learned profeffions fhould talk as intelligibly as poffible, which
render what they fay of more eftimation, Cimberton makes this very fenfible reply.

" They might perhaps, madam, (gain by it)
with people of your good fenfe; but with the gene-
rality it will never do: the vulgar would have no
refpect for truth and knowledge, if they were ex-
pofed to naked view.

Truth is too fimple of all art bereaved,
Since the world will—why let it be deceiv'd.

At the beginning of the fourth act we find Tom in confusion, and his master chagrined at a kind of a blunder he has made, by letting Myrtle fish out of him Bevil's having received a letter from Lucinda; this, we learn, has produced a challenge from Myrtle to Bevil, for supposed double dealing. When Tom, according to order, retires, his master meditates with some warmth on his friend's precipitation; then reads Lucinda's letter, thanking him for declining the marriage, and making him even a confidant of her attention to Myrtle.

Bevil here kindly considers that some steps should be taken to cure the impatience and jealousy of his friend, for which reason he thinks it prudent to keep the forementioned letter sometime from his knowledge; having read Myrtle's challenge also, which is couched in brief and significant terms, that gentleman appears, and with a peremptory stile, requires that notice may be taken of his message.

Bevil's reply to this abrupt address is sensible and cool, desiring an explanation face to face; the subject, as is usual in such cases, rises fast, and Myrtle throws out an intimation of timidity, which draws from young Bevil these truly excellent and moral remarks, worthy a brave man, and which ought to be stamped upon every forward mind. " Sir, you know I have often dared to disapprove a decision the tyrant custom has introduced, to the breach of all laws divine and human : I have often told you, in the confidence of heart, I abhorred daring to offend the author of life, and rushing into his presence.---I say, by the same act, to commit the crime against him, and immediately urge on to his tribunal."--- Read, read, and treasure up in memory's securest cell,

Conscious Lovers.

cell, this salutary inftruction, ye favage, vindictive duellifts.

As there is a bound in every breaft beyond which patience cannot reach, fo Bevil, hearing the' modeft woman of his heart mentioned lightly, takes fire, and accepts the hoftile invitation ; here we tremble for good fenfe, virtue and friendfhip, tottering on the verge of deftruction ; however, the author, by a moft mafterly ftroke, the intervention of Tom, gives Bevil a paufe of reafon, which pleafingly and reputably brings him to the proper way of thinking. He fhews his rafh antagonift Lucinda's letter ; fo convincing a proof of his friend's innocence, reduces Myrtle to a degree of pity as well as cenfure ; however, the delicate cordiality of Bevil, anticipates any mortifying condefcenfion from his repentant challenger, and Myrtle is left, inftead of fervile acknowledgments, to make fome very inftructive obfervations upon the precipiece they have both efcaped, by Bevil's fuperior conduct. We contemplate this fcene with great pleafure, and affert, that it is as happily conceived, as judicioufly conducted, and as finely written as any other in the Englifh drama.

Sir John Bevil and Mr. Sealand fucceed the young gentlemen: at the beginning of their converfation, the baronet feems to plume himfelf on genealogy, which the refpectable merchant holds in a cheap light, and rallies Sir John upon it with fome degree of cynical humour. Sealand, in refpect to his daughter's marriage, objects his keeping a miftrefs ; this charge, the baronet, like a kind father, endeavours to exculpate his fon of ; however, the cit puts the matter to this iffue, vifiting the unknown lady

U 2   himfelf ;

himself; and if, upon the interview, he finds nothing to confirm his apprehensions, then there can be no impediment to the match Sir John so much urges, upon this proposal they separate.

From what passes between Humphry and his old master, after the Cit is gone, it appears, that Sir John's anxiety is chiefly about Lucinda's large fortune, which at any rate he wishes his son to obtain, the baronet frets very naturally, however receives some satisfaction from hearing his son's declaration of never marrying without his consent; this scene brings about no determination, but leaves matters in a proper state of doubt,

Phillis in the next scene, acquaints Myrtle that he is in the utmost hazard of losing his mistress, Sir Geoffry being hourly expected to compleat the marriage settlements; this perplexes the lover, when our chambermaid, with the true spirit of intrigue, advises him to personate the old gentleman, this wears so good a face, that he rewards her for so happy a thought, both with money and kisses, concluding the fourth act with a resolution to put her scheme in practice, as well as his disturbed state of mind will admit.

At the beginning of the fifth act Myrtle, metamorphosed into the shape of Sir Geoffry, is brought forward by Mrs. Sealand, Lucinda and Cimberton; he assumes the old knights peculiarity of expression, as well as his antiquity of shape; Mrs. Sealand, after seeing him seated, goes off to give necessary directions; and is followed by Phillis, that she may give the disguised lover an opportunity of being alone with his mistress; after some ludicrous marks

in the Cimberton ftile have been made, Phillis effects her purpofe in favour of Myrtle, by delivering a meffage to Cimberton from Mrs. Sealand;
this removes him, and the ftage is left clear for
the lover to difclofe himfelf, which he does with
fuch rapturous precipitation, that through furprize Lucinda fcreams out, which brings back the
company; here, upon apprehenfion of a difcovery,
Myrtle, with very quick addrefs, feigns himfelf in
a fit, which ferves as a good apology for Lucinda's furprize and confufion; the matter being
thus fettled, the fuppofed old gentleman is conducted off. The circumftance of pulling his nephew's
ear is farcial to the laft degree, therefore much
below the dignity of this piece.

Mr. Sealand, conducted by Humphry to Indiana's houfe, next appears, knocks at the door,
when Daniel, a high finifhed picture of ruftic fimplicity, furnifhed with fome degree of urbanic cunning and evafion, is produced; his anfwers to the
merchant's enquiry for his miftrefs are replete with
humour, and never fail of having a powerful effect; at length, by the help of that argument
which feldom fails to influence both the fimple and
wife, a bribe, Sealand gains admittance; firft obtains a fhort audience of Ifabella, who reeollects
him, but does not make herfelf known, and then
is introduced to Indiana; he addreffes her with refpect, as having fome money to pay her, which circumftance brings on the main fubject, Mr. Bevil's connection with her; the citizen reproaches
that young gentleman with deceiving fo deferving a
perfon, while fhe, with generous gratitude, vindi-
cates

cates his honourable conduct; at length, judging
Sealand to be his intended father-in-law, her paſſion
works up into a ſwell of grief.

In the flow of anxiety for loſing a man ſo dear to
to her, ſhe indulges her painful feelings with tears,
and very naturally recapitulates a ſucceſſion of misfortunes which have fallen upon her, even from ear-
lieſt infancy; ſome of the circumſtances ſtrike Sealand, who, at length by the circumſtance of a bracelet ſhe throws from her, and an enquiry into the real
name, he perceives her to be his own daughter; her
identity is verified by Iſabella, and the ſcene, which
is beautifully wrought up, here cauſes the moſt pleaſing ſenſations. The other characters now enter, having been told the wonderful diſcovery by Iſabella, Sir
John congratulates the happy father and daughter;
by the by, it is a little odd how they ſhould meet ſo
ſuddenly at Indiana's houſe, and how Sir John ſhould
know that Sealand intended to give her a fortune
equal to his wiſhes: however, the author wanted to
bring about his cataſtrophe, ſo claps Bevil and Indiana together as expeditiouſly as poſſible. This
circumſtance depriving Lucinda of half her fortune,
Cimberton, whoſe views were founded more upon
intereſt than love, gives up his claim, and thereby
affords Myrtle an opportunity of throwing off his
diſguiſe, and propoſing his own generous paſſion,
which Sealand immediately ratifies with his conſent.
Matters thus agreeably ſettled, Sir John briefly deduces from paſt tranſactions this excellent moral,
That providence ſuperintends and rewards the per-
ſeverance of virtue.

Having

Confcious Lovers.

Having paffed through this comedy with great pleafure to ourfelves, and we hope fatisfaction to the reader, we muft give its author great praife, both for his defign and execution. The plot is regular; intricate, yet obvious; the fentiments moral; the language eafy and genteel; there is fpirit without licentioufnefs, and furprize without improbability; the characters exhibit nature and variety.

Sir John Bevil, as a fond father, deferves refpect; but there is a felfifh, narrow-minded principle, capable of facrificing even the fon he loves to intereft, that greatly lowers our opinion of him; he has nothing to fay but what the mediocrity of Meffrs. GIBSON and BURTON may utter decently enough; we have feen feveral others exhibit the old knight, but fo little worth notice that we cannot recollect them.

Mr. Sealand is a plain, unaffected, generous citizen; a man of liberal principles without oftentation, and found fenfe without pedantry, bred in the fchool of adverfity. This honeft citizen was extremely well figured, and fuitably performed by Mr. SPARKS; his anxiety, furprize, tendernefs and joy, in the fcene where Indiana is difcovered to be his long loft daughter, were well expreffed, and he ftruck out many judicious beauties. Mr. BERRY, as was ufual with him, mouthed the converfation, and blubbered the pathetic; and, as to his perfonal appearance, it was very ungentleman-like, both in figure and deportment. At prefent, we know not any performer, at either houfe, however ftrange the affertion may feem, calculated to do the merchant juftice; who, though he requires no capital powers, yet calls for judgment and expreffion not eafily found. We are by no means fond of Mr. AICKIN's paternal feeling;

ings ; nor do thofe of Mr. CLARKE give us much
pleafure. Mr. HULL, we apprehend, muft come
neareft him, unlefs Mr. BARRY would vouchfafe to
perform the part.

Young Bevil is drawn a fine pattern for young
gentlemen of fortune ; virtuoufly generous, coolly
brave ; a difinterefted lover, a dutiful fon, and a
fincere friend. He has been ftiled " a faultlefs
monfter, which the world ne'er faw ;" but we cannot find any reafon for fuppofing that an author,
though he ornaments a charaƈter with many valuable qualifications, prefents him to view as perfeƈt ;
and fuch a man as young Bevil might have not only
fome weaknefs, nay fome vice about him, though the
circumftances of this play don't call either into
aƈtion.

To carry recolleƈtion back as far as we are able,
with any degree of precifion, we remember Mr.
QUIN, when he was big enough to do Falftaff without ftuffing, rumbling forth this part with very
near as great pompofity as he founded Cato with ;
a major wig, as in the *young* Chamont, graced his
large head ; and though young Bevil mentions
gaiety of drefs, by calling his cloaths the fplendid
covering of forrow, yet this *great* aƈtor once, perhaps oftner, ornamented the part with the very
cloaths which he played the Old Batchelor in.

Mr. SHERIDAN barked out young Bevil feveral
years in DUBLIN with great applaufe---a notable
proof of critical judgment in the audience there---
for, beyond every degree of difpute, he was not furnifhed with any one requifite ; the fnap of his expreffion, the ftiffnefs of his deportment, with the
natural alternate fqueaks and croaks of his unhappy
voice,

Confcious Lovers.

voice, were fuch a group of impediments, as never before incumbered an audience, or lowered an actor of any efteem.

Mr. Ross, when firft he played the character at Drury Lane, was as correct, eafy, fpirited and genteel, as criticifm could wifh; he looked, moved, and fpoke like a gentleman. From what we have feen of him lately, he is grown too corpulent for the requifite freedom, and too carelefs for the effential fpirit; performance feems rather a fatigue to him, and any trace of that muft be injurious to fuch a part as young Bevil. Mr. FLEETWOOD, who has left the ftage fome few years paft, had a great deal of merit in this character; his figure, manner, and delivery, all correfponded to place him in a very favourable light.

Mr. REDDISH is much the moft capable at prefent, as Mr. BARRY's age deftroys the merit he once had.

Myrtle has no particular characteriftical diftinction, his principles appear generally good, his temper fomewhat warm; he requires more acting than Bevil, as he affumes different fhapes, a volubility is wanting for Bramble, a low comedy feeblenefs for Sir.Geoffry. Mr. RYAN, allowing for age and oddity, was not at all amifs in perfonating of him: Mr. SMITH is no way difpleafing, nor in any fhape capital: Mr. JEFFERSON is faint indeed: Mr. LEE through the whole chaftely excellent.

Cimberton is a coxcomb of peculiar mold, facetioufly confequential, ludicroufly fententious; his vein of humour is not hard to hit, and his words fpeak for themfelves; however, we have feen him confiderably flattened in performance. Mr. SHU-

TER is too luxuriant, Mr. LOVE too dry, yet both have conſiderable merit ; there was a medium between theſe two gentlemen which Mr. TASWELL exhibited, thereby irreſiſtably working upon the comic feelings.

There never was a better drawn coxcomb of the party-coloured corps than Tom ; the outlines are highly natural, and the finiſhing exquiſite. If an actor has any merit in the fop caſt, he muſt give pleaſure in this part, there is a pert *jen ſe quoy* about him truly diverting : it is ſaid this part and Phillis were added to the piece by Mr. CIBBER ; if ſo, it is indebted to him for a very happy addition of vivacity ; we have ſeen his ſon perform it with conſiderable pleaſure, but think he rather grimaced it too much ; the ſame fault we find with Mr. WOODWARD, yet allow his ſtudied deportment more juſtifiable in this than many other parts, becauſe affected gentility will plan attitudes, while real grace of figure and motion proceeds from what Dr. JOHNSON calls ſpontaniety. Mr. DYER, by help of a ſong, has ſkipped through the valet agreeably enough ; but for the author's meaning, and nature without any trick, we muſt appeal to the animated critical execution of Mr. KING.

Daniel, as we have already intimated, is a moſt pleaſing ſimpleton, as well written for the length of him as any part in the piece, and though ſo ſhort a time in ſight, is by many of an audience longeſt remembered. Mr. HAMILTON well deſerves applauſe for the *navité* of his expreſſion, but nature's own comedian, Mr. WESTON, is droll beyond every degree of conception ; thoſe who have not ſeen or heard him muſt fail of an adequate idea. Mr. WALDRON has lately ſlipped into his ſhoes, but hobbles moſt horribly ſlip-ſhod.

KING JOHN.

A TRAGEDY: By SHAKESPEARE.

THIS Play opens with peculiar dignity, being the royal audience of a French ambaſſador, whoſe very inſolent addreſs and arrogant demands, are replied to with ſuch ſpirit as we wiſh Britiſh monarchs upon ſuch an occaſion may ever ſhew. From an obſervation made by the queen mother, upon Chatillion's departure, it appears, that the kindling flame of war has been lighted by Lady Conſtance, in favour of her ſon Prince Arthur, whoſe juſt title the queen ſeems to admit.

Robert Falconbridge, and his brother Philip, are introduced for King John's deciſion concerning a plea of birth-right, Robert urging baſtardy againſt his brother. Philip's blunt, ſportive method of expreſſion, tainted too with licentiouſneſs, is abominable ſtuff for the ears and reſpectful decorum of royalty to be violated with ; however, from tracing ſome marks in his viſage of that corrupt deſcent he ſeems to boaſt, after a ſlight altercation, the matter is ſettled thus ; heritage of the paternal eſtate is granted to the legitimate brother, and Philip, with an invitation to join the warlike preparation, is knighted and confirmed in baſtardy, by being ordered to take the royal name of Plantagenet.

After King John goes off, declaring his immediate intentions of invading France, our new made

X 2

knight

knight ftays behind to meditate upon the change of his fituation, which he does in a foliloquy of very quaint conceit; burthenfome to an audience, becaufe three-fourths of it is unintelligible to the general ear; and indeed, if not, is of very immaterial tendency. What enfues between this flighty blade and his mother, only ferves to confirm what the king and queen took as fact, merely from apprehenfion.

We cannot think our author had any kind of reafon for bringing Lady Falconbridge before an audience to confefs her fhame with fuch effrontery, therefore cenfure this fcene highly; and are of opinion, that the laft feven lines of this Act, fpoken by the Baftard, are much more fuitable to the bully of a brothel, than a perfon of good fenfe, good breeding, and real fpirit. This character might have been marked with oddity, as is evidently intended, without fo much offence.

At the beginning of the fecond act, by poetical conveyance, we meet the French king and his powers before the walls of Angiers, where Conftance and her fon Arthur, yield him thanks for efpoufing their diftrefsful caufe. Upon the arrival of Chatillion, his mafter is informed not only of King John's warlike refolution, but that he has courfed him at the heels with fuch unaccountable expedition, as to be within the found of beaten drums. We apprehend the play would have begun with much more propriety at this period, and there is not a fingle paffage in the firft act, fave King John's reply to Chatillion, that could caufe tafte or judgment to lament the omiffion of it.

Upon

Upon meeting his brother of France, King John first utters peace, and then, on refusal, denounces war, To this the French monarch replies by arguments, in favour of Arthur's right ; an altercation ensues, in which the ladies join, without seeming to have the least regard for essential delicacy : what passes between Austria and the Bastard also, is fitter for coalheavers than men of rank and education.

Upon a proposition of surrendering all his dominions in right of Arthur, John treats King Philip with contempt, but offers protection to the young prince ; this brings on a fresh brawl between the ladies ; at length, the citizens of Angiers being summoned to their walls by sound of trumpet, the two kings severally address them, denouncing threats on each side. Thus embarrassed, and equally endangered, the citizens very prudently intimate, that whoever proves strongest will prevail with them. This occasions immediate determination of a battle, for which purpose both kings go off. Here a scene of tumult, and what we may justly stile theatrical confusion, ensues, alarms ! heralds ! and a victory ; after which the kings again meet, again debate, and still talk in a high strain, while Falconbridge flames between them with the spirit of Até.

After much controversy, to very little purpose, more than to gratify a disposition for talking, they agree to unite their powers against the resisting town ; this sharpens the wits of the citizens, who, by way of palliating matters, propose a match between the Dauphin and Lady Blanche, a Spanish princess, nearly related to England ; which matter being, like all other state marriages, concluded by sudden consent of parties, without any appeal to

love,

love, the gates of Angiers are thrown open, and our two kings enter in friendly terms. John promising to alleviate the pain such a coalition must give Conftance, by creating young Arthur Duke of Bretagny, and giving him the Town of Angiers.

Here Falconbridge is again left alone to defcant upon the late tranfactions, which he does with keen and juft fatire; there is a fort of word-catching in this foliloquy, fome of the ideas are incumbered with fuperfluous expreffion, and the auditor's conception is fatigued with blameable obfcurity; notwithftanding which faults, we allow it to contain ufeful thoughts and lamentable truths, refpecting the influence intereft has upon the higheft as well as loweft characters of life.

In the firft fcene of the third act, as it has been rightly fettled by the ableft editors, Conftance appears, poffeffed of ftrong and natural refentment againft the French monarch, for entering into pacific connections with her enemy King John; fhe rather rates Lord Salifbury for bringing her the news, and when he propofes her going into the royal prefence, fhe replies with difdainful refufal, proftrating herfelf, and making the ground her throne, as fhe phrafes it.

Juft returned from the Dauphin's nuptials, the two kings encounter this monument of grief. Upon Philip's mention that fo happy a day fhall each annual return be kept a holy one, fhe rifes, and vents her paffion with much bitternefs of expreffion; her widow's curfe in the following terms is awfully nervous, and judicioufly introduced by the author, as prophetic of what follows.

Arm,

Arm, arm, ye heav'ns, againſt theſe perjur'd kings,
A widow cries, be huſband to me heav'n :
Let not the hours of this ungodly day
Wear out the day in peace, but ere ſun ſet
Set armed diſcord 'twixt theſe perjur'd kings.

Her reproaches to boaſting Auſtria are of a very
ſtinging nature, and the Baſtard's continuation of
them ſharpens their pointedneſs exceedingly.   Mr.
Pope, and other commentators, have added ſome
lines to make the Baſtard's behaviour more juſtifiable ; but, if we conſider what paſſes in the ſecond
Act, we find that Falconbridge indulges a general
blunt oddity, that even treads cloſe upon the heels
of majeſty ; indeed, mention of Auſtria's having
killed his father, is very proper to lay the foundation
of hearted reſentment.

Pandulph, legate from the Pope, conſequently in
thoſe days a miſchief-making prieſt, here enters ;
and, in terms of peremptory demand, enquires why
the then Archbiſhop of Canterbury was deprived of
his ſee : to this King John replies with very becoming independency of ſpirit, but we think in rather too harſh terms ; dignity never ſits with grace
upon abuſe.   The thunderbolt of papal authority,
excommunication, here iſſues from the enraged cardinal, who urges King Philip to ſupport the church's
quarrel againſt John ; which, after ſome tolerable
reſiſtance, and ſome well principled arguments, he
is at laſt perſuaded to by the churchman's able ſo-
phiſtry.   This occaſions inſtantaneous declarations
of hoſtility, and ſo very conveniently are both armies ſituated, that without a ſingle line to give time
for preparation, the battle joins.   We apprehend
that

that the cardinal and Conftance might have been furnished with fomething to fay, that would have been not only interefting but of ufe, to give fome trace of probability to the time of action.

After fome martial flourifhes, Falconbridge enters, as conqueror of Auftria ; we think the lion's fkin as a trophy of honour worn by his father, fhould be worn by the Baftard through the remainder of the play. . King John having taken Prince Arthur prifoner, commits him to the care of Hubert ; here a few more alarms fucceed, and the English monarch beats the French behind the fcenes ; after which he comes on with the Queen Mother, &c. orders Falconbridge to hafte for England, there to raife againft his coming taxes or contributions from the feveral orders of clergy.

We do not know any paffage, in any piece, that can boaft merit fuperior to the method King John takes of working Hubert to the deftruction of Arthur. His diffidence, his, foothing, his breaks, paufes, and diftant hints, are moft defcriptive lines of nature in fuch a depraved ftate of agitation. What follows we think fo rich a regale for poetical tafte, that we fhould deem ourfelves very blameable not to offer it to the reader's palate.

> The fun is in the heav'n, and the proud day
> Attended with the pleafures of the world,
> Is all too wanton and too full of gawds
> To grant me audience——if the *midnight* bell
> Did with his iron tongue and brazen mouth,
> Sound one unto the drowfy race of night :
> If this fame were a church-yard where we ftand,
> And thou poffeffed with a thoufand wrongs :
> Or if that furly fpirit melancholly

2   **Had**

King John.

> Had *baked* thy blood, and made it heavy, thick ;
> Which elfe runs tickling up and down the veins,
> Making that ideot laughter keep men's eyes,
> And ftrain their cheeks to idle merriment ;
> A paffion hateful to my purpofes :
> Or if that thou couldft fee me without eyes,
> Hear me without ears and make reply,
> Without a tongue——ufing conceit alone——
> Then in defpight of broad-ey'd watchful day
> I would into thy bofom pour my thoughts.

Notwithftanding the approbation we allow to that general excellence which diftinguifhes this fpeech, yet we cannot avoid remarking the two words diftinguifhed by Italics. One o'clock in the *morning*, cannot with propriety be ftiled the *midnight* bell——The word *folemn* would remove this objection——*Had baked thy blood*; to us it appears that melancholy is a cold, chilling difpofition of mind ; *baked* furnifhes an idea of heat, therefore we would fubftitute *caked*, as more confonant to the meaning.

After King John has wrought up Hubert to his murderous purpofe, and goes for England, the audience ftill remain in France, to hear Philip lament the effects of his late defeat ; and Conftance breath deep lamentation for the captivity of her fon. The unhappy mother's plaints are extremely forceable and tender ; yet, amongft many beauties, we muft object to that fpeech wherein fhe fpeaks of the courtfhip of death, in fuch figurative extravagance. When Conftance and the French king retire, Pandulph works on the Dauphin by fome arguments of deep and probable policy, to retrieve his own honour and that of France, by undertaking the invafion of England ; furnifhing warm hopes of fuccefs from the internal difquiets of King John's government, efpecially thofe of the enraged clergy, plundered by that monarch's order---A moft alarming circumftance to churchmen, who, notwith-ftanding they preach up contempt of this world, are peculiarly remarkable for coveting and holding faft its riches.

At the beginning of the fourth act, humanity encounters the painful circumftance of Hubert's commiffion to burn out Arthur's eyes, to prevent, by the Ottoman method, his fucceffion or advancement to the throne; this fcene, with refpect to the young prince's part of it, does our author great credit; he has moft happily traced nature, and has touched the tender feelings in a powerful manner, without ftraining them too much. Hubert's reluctance and pity are well defcribed, the two characters imprefs an audience with compaffion and efteem, infomuch, that tears of concern and fatisfaction alternately flow.

When King John acquaints his peers with his fecond coronation, the Lords Salifbury and Pembroke exprefs themfelves in very free terms concerning that meafure : the latter complains of Arthur's imprifonment, and claims his enlargement, which the monarch confents to, as fuppofing him difpatched. Here Hubert enters, and tells the king that his order has been fulfilled : when Salifbury and Pembroke are told of Arthur's death, they utter fome expreffions of vindictive difcontent, and leave the king to confider his perturbed, ticklifh fituation. At this point of time a meffenger enters, and increafes his embarraffment, by an account of the French invafion, and his mother's death. The warlike operations of this play are conducted with

2   aftonifhing

aftonifhing rapidity, for King John, between the
firft and fecond acts, carried an army to France,
which he landed before the French king heard
of it ; and between the third and fourth, the
Dauphin lands a formidable power before the Englifh know any thing of his approach. After Falconbridge is difpatched to footh the difcontented
lords, Hubert re-enters, to acquaint the king of fome
prodigies which have appeared, and the popular
confufion occafioned by Arthur's death; his defcription, particularly in the latter part, has fingular
merit. The guilty monarch's recriminating upon
one he fuppofes a ready agent to his fanguine orders, is highly natural ; the wicked always endeavour to lighten the oppreffive load of a bad confcience, by throwing part of it upon another: Hubert's exculpation of himfelf comes favourably from
the actor, but has more plaufibility than truth ; for
his affertion of a mind free from the taint of any
murderous thought, is contradicted by the readinefs
with which he underftood and coincided with John's
meaning ; to have rendered him truly amiable, fome
paffages might have been added to fignify, that he
only undertook the horrid charge to fave young
Arthur; at prefent he is left a very dubious or rather culpable character.

The unhappy young prince, raifed to a ftate of
defparation by his captivity, and other painful circumftances, appears on the battlements of his prifon, and refolves upon attempting an efcape ; but
by the fall puts an end to his life. The difcontented Englifh peers going to meet the Dauphin
now enter, and are accofted by Falconbridge with
meffage from the king, which they receive with

haughty

haughty terms. Upon feeing Arthur's body, their
wrath grows more enflamed, and a folemn vow of
vengeance is entered into.

Hubert, with a fecond meffage from the king,
and intelligence that the prince is alive, comes in,
when a warm altercation enfues ; being fhewn the
corpfe of Arthur, Hubert pathetically afferts his
own innocence, yet cannot gain credit from the
lords, who openly avouch their defign of joining
the Dauphin : even Falconbridge feems ftruck with
Arthur's fate, and fpeaks his doubts of Hubert.
The picture he draws of the reigning political confufion, is nervous and ftriking, and merits being offered to the reader, but that we have already exceeded in this play the propofed limits of quotation.

At the beginning of the fifth act, we meet an incident utterly difgraceful to Englifh annals, King
John's refignation of his crown, and receiving it
from Pandulph, as a mean dependancy on the Pope.
His fituation might politically require fuch a conceffion, but any man of even tolerable fpirit would
rather have died than fhame an exalted ftation fo
bafely ; in return for the Englifh monarch's fubmiffion, the cardinal goes to ftop the Dauphin's
hoftile operations. Here the Baftard enters with
intelligence that feems to ftagger John, whofe embarraffment gives Falconbridge an opportunity of
remonftrating with great fpirit and fire, efpecially
againft Pandulph's palliative commiffion ; his arguments fo far prevail, that he receives the royal
authority to repel force by force.

In the next fcene a folemn compact is entered into
between the Dauphin and the Englifh lords. Upon

on the cardinal's appearance, and the communication of his pacific difposition, the prince, with very
becoming judgment and fpirit, declines being pro-
pertied by the churchman ; who confiders no ¦fur-
ther than as circumftances relate to his mafter the
Pope. During this parley, Falconbridge demands
conference, in which he fupports with foldierly de-
meanour, the dignity of his king and native land ;
however, he lofes the gentleman in fome of his remarks, particularly where he poorly and indelicate-
ly puns upon the beating of drums ; bluntnefs and
rudenefs are very diftinct operations of temper ;
good fenfe approves the firft, but condemns the laft.

A battle here enfues, during which King John
appears, labouring under a heavy indifpofition.
Some tidings of great importance are brought by a
meffenger, but though of the favourable kind, the
fick monarch cannot relifh them, but defires to be
conveyed to Swinftead Abbey.

We are now conveyed to the French camp, where
we meet Salifbury, Pembroke, &c. in a ftate of furprize, at the ftrength, number, and fuccefs of King
John's arms ; to fill them with more aftonifhment
and confufion, Melun,ᶜ a French count, who has
received his death's wound, acquaints them with the
Dauphin's defign of cutting off all the revolters
who have joined him, in cafe of victory ; this determines them upon an immediate return to their
allegiance, of which the Dauphin is informed, as
well as of the fate his expected fupplies have met,
of being wrecked upon the Goodwin Sands ; however, he bears up with refolution, and determines to
ftand the iffue of another battle.

A fcene

A scene merely expletive, occurs between Falconbridge and Hubert, which is, and we think with justice, generally omitted in representation ; however, Hubert's account of the king's being poisoned, should be retained, and might come well enough from Salisbury or Pembroke, just before John's entrance.

We have now brought royalty to the last thread of life, and are sorry to be under the necessity of observing, that our author has not displayed his usual force of genius in what the expiring monarch says ; his speeches are too figurative for one in great pain, and are otherwise far short of the circumstances ; he resigns his breath too in a manner very unfavourable for stage action ; though a most abandoned politician, not one pang of a guilty conscience is mentioned, which even in the midst of distraction, seldom fails to shew itself.

The king no more, Falconbridge, with commendable spirit, urges union of forces, to expel the Dauphin and his invading powers ; however, it appears, that losses and disappointments have obliged that prince to concur in Pandulph's pacific plan, which the English lords and prince Henry seem ready to admit.   This draws our piece to a conclusion, and the whole is summed up with this excellent and truly British remark, uttered by Falconbridge.

> Come, the three corners of the world in arms,
> And we shall shock them !—nought shall make us rue
> If England to itself do prove but true.

In

In writing this play, SHAKESPEARE difclaimed every idea of regularity, and has huddled fuch a feries of hiftorical events on the back of one another, as fhame the utmoft ftretch of probability ; his mufe travels lightning winged, being here, there, and every where, in the fpace of a few minutes. We are by no means advocates for that pinching limitation which fo difadvantageoufly fetters modern compofition ; imagination will indulge feveral trefpaffes of liberty, but muft be offended when all the bounds of conception are arbitrarily trodden under foot.

In point of charaƈters King John is a very difagreeable piƈture of royalty ; ambitious and cruel ; not void of fpirit in the field, yet irrefolute and mean in adverfity ; covetous, overbearing and impolitic ; from what we can obferve, totally unprincipled ; ftrongly tainted with the oppofite appellations which often meet, fool and knave ; during his life we have nothing to admire, at his fall nothing to pity.

There is no capital charaƈter within our knowledge of more inequality ; the greater part of what he has to fay is a heavy yoke on the fhoulders of an aƈtor. His two fcenes with Hubert are indeed mafterly, and do the author credit ; like charity they may ferve to cover a multitude of fins ; the dying fcene is not favourable to aƈtion.

Mr. QUIN was the firft we remember to fee figure away in royal John ; and, as in moft of his tragedy undertakings, he lumbered through the part in a painful manner ; growled fome paffages, bellowed others, and chaunted the reft. Mr. CHURCHILL has fneered at Mr. MOSSOP for brow-beating the French

king ;

king; had he feen and remembered the gentleman under confideration, he would have thought the poor tame monarch in danger of being fwallowed up alive by his voracious brother of England. Mr. SHERIDAN has, no doubt, impaired as his faculties are at prefent, very ftriking merit, where he is working Hubert to the murder of the prince; his utterance and attendant looks are highly picturefque. We allow him to be alfo deferving of praife where he upbraids Hubert with fo readily obeying his bloody orders; but in the other fcenes of the four firft acts, low as they are, he finks beneath them; in dying, he overacts to a degree of particular offence.

Mr. MOSSOP, whom we have been obliged to find fault with upon feveral occafions, here deferves our warmeft praife, and we are happy to give it him. That ftiffnefs and premeditate method which, in other characters, took off from his great powers and good conception, being lefs vifible in his King John. The rays of glowing merit here broke upon us unclouded and dazzling; where the author's genius foared aloft, he kept pace with equal wing; where Shakefpeare flagged, he bore him up; wherefore, we are venturous enough to affirm, that no performer ever made more of good and bad materials mingled together, than Mr. MOSSOP did in this play. Mr. POWELL was too boyifh, he wanted weight and depth of expreffion to excel in John.

Of the chip-in-pottage French king, we fhall fay nothing, as no actor can make any thing of him; nor can his fon, for the like reafon, deferve much notice. However, we remember two performers that are worth mention, one Mr. LACY, who did

in

in the Dauphin than criticifm had any right to expect; and Mr. The. Cibber, who was undoubtedly the verieft bantam-cock of tragedy that ever crowed, ftrutted, and flapped its wings on a ftage.

The Cardinal is a very well drawn churchman of thofe times, fubtle, proud, irafcible; rather prone to promote than prevent public calamities, where his mafter's intereft feems concerned; a mere politician, not incumbered with delicacy of principle, or the feelings of humanity; he is not in favour of the actor, yet appeared very refpectable in Mr. Havard's performance of him, no other perfon ftrikes our recollection.

The Baftard is a character of great peculiarity, bold, fpirited, free---indeed too free fpoken; he utters many noble fentiments, and performs brave actions; but in feveral places defcends to keep attention from drowfing, at the expence of all due decorum; and what is very difgraceful to ferious compofition, caufes the weaker part of an audience to laugh at fome very weak, punning conceits.

Mr. Ryan had fome merit in this part, by no means equal to what he fhewed in many others. The unhappy impediment of his utterance being more confpicuous in it than ufual.

Mr. Sheridan has apologized for it, but from what we have already faid concerning his executive abilities, the reader may eafily judge how very unlike the character he muft be. Mr. Holland was too ftiff, and made too much ufe of his ftrong lungs. Mr. Smith is pretty and fpirited, but wants weight and bluntnefs. We have feen one Mr. Fleetwood appear in it this feafon, at the Haymarket, with eve-

ry fault of Mr. HOLLAND improved, and all his
strokes of merit diminished.

If ever Mr. GARRICK's figure made against him,
it was in this part; he struck out some lights and
beauties which we never discovered in the performance of any other person, but there was a certain petitness which rather shrunk the character,
and cut short the usual excellence of this truly great
actor. Upon the whole, we are obliged to declare,
that our idea of the Bastard and SHAKESPEARE's
meaning, to our knowledge, has never been properly filled. Mr. BARRY, for external appearance
and general execution, comes nearest the point.
This remark may serve to shew, that though we
greatly admire, and have hitherto warmly praised
our English Roscius, we are not so idolatrously fond
of his extensive merit, as to think him always foremost in the race of fame.

Hubert, though upon the whole an agreeable
agent, is by no means an estimable personage; he
appears in a very recommendatory light, and favours representation where there are any tolerable
feelings. Messrs. SPARKS and BERRY did him very
considerable justice, and Mr. BENSLEY has exhibited
him with deserved approbation; we cannot say so
much for Mr. GIBSON. At the Haymarket, Mr.
GENTLEMAN has passed muster, as not having mis-
conceived or ill expressed the part; but we cannot,
as a public performer, congratulate him much on
the happiness of his figure or features.

Prince Arthur is a very amiable and interesting
character of the drama; we have seen it done af-
fectingly by several children, whose names we forget; however recollect being particularly pleased
with

with Miss REYNOLDS, now Mrs. SAUNDERS, some twenty years since.

Who did the revolting lords has entirely escaped our memory, except at Mr. FOOTE's, this summer, and those gentlemen who personated them there may wish to be forgot also.

Every one of the female characters are too contemptible for notice except Constance; she indeed seems to have been an object of great concern with the author, and very seldom fails to make a deep impression upon the audience; her circumstances are peculiarly calculated to strike the feeling heart; dull, very dull must that sensation be which is not affected with the distress of a tender parent, expressed in such pathetic, forceable terms; even Mrs. WOFFINGTON, who, from dissonance of tones might be called the screech-owl of tragedy, drew many tears in this part; to which her elegant figure and adequate deportment did not a little contribute. A fine woman robed with grief, is a leading object of pity.

Mrs. CIBBER, in the whole scope of her great excellence, never shewed her tragic feelings and expression to more advantage than in Constance; there was a natural tendency to melancholly in her features, which heightened in action, and became so true an index of a woe-fraught mind, that with the assistance of her nightingale voice, she became irresistable; and almost obliged us to forget every other character in raptured contemplation of her merit.

Mrs. BELLAMY fell far, very far short of the forementioned lady, and cathedralized the unhappy princess offensively. Mrs. YATES and Mrs. BARRY,

have

have both powerful capabilities for the part, but can never juftly hope to equal their great predeceffor Mrs. CIBBER, who muft be always remembered with pleafure and regret by all perfons of tafte, who had the happinefs to fhed the facrifice of tears at the fhrine of her melting powers. Mrs. PHIL-LIPPINA BURTON was indifcribably deplorable.

The fhameful irregularity of plot we have already remarked; in the characters there is variety. The Baftard is an original and pleafing oddity, though fomewhat upon the extravaganza; the language is bold, flowing, and, where it ought to be, pathetic; yet in many places too figurative, obfcure and turgid. As to moral, there feems to be no other deduction but this; that King John's crimes having merited his fate, the juftice of providential·difpenfation is thereby vindicated. This play wants much alteration to make it quite agreeable on the ftage, and is at prefent we think a better reading than acting piece.

Before we difmifs this tragedy, permit us to offer a fhort anecdote related by a gentleman who faw it performed at Portfmouth laft war. The French party coming on with white cockades, a zealous tar fhouts from the gallery, Harkee, you Mr. Moun-feers, ftrike the white flags out of your nabs, or b--- my eyes, but I'll bombard you. A general laugh went through the houfe, but the actors deeming it merely a tranfient joke, took no notice; upon which, our enraged fon of Neptune gave the word fire, and immediately half a dozen apples flew, which worked the defired effect; three cheers enfued, and this incident diffufed fuch a fpirit through the houfe, that during the reft of the play loud huzza's attended the exits and entrances of King John's

2   party,

party, while King Philip and the Dauphin, notwithftanding the polite removal of their cockades, fuf-
tained many rough ftrokes of fea wit.

❋❋❋❋❋❋❋❋❋❋❋❋❋❋❋❋❋❋❋❋❋❋❋❋❋❋❋

The H Y P O C R I T E.

A COMEDY altered from CIBBER:

By Mr. BICKERSTAFF.

NOtwithftanding the NON JUROR did its author
great credit in its original ftate, yet we muft cordially applaud the defign of turning it into the prefent form.   The laureat's fatire was political, the
objects of which being now almoft forgotten, it became obfolete ; befides, we always looked on the
old piece as heavy for want of fuch feafoning as is
mingled with this alteration, which we are now a-
bout to confider.

It opens with a fcene between Sir John Lambert
and the Colonel, his fon, who is expoftulating warmly againft the influence allowed to Dr. Cantwell :
Sir John, the weak profelyte of enthufiafm, backs
his own opinion with fome paffion, and much prejudice.   The converfation turning upon Mr. Darnley's addreffes to Charlotte, the baronet objects to
· that gentleman, as not being pious enough for a
fon-in-law ; and being told of his coming to obtain
final confent, the father determines to go out that he
                                                    may

may avoid feeing him; declaring, at the fame time, that he has another man in view to marry his daughter. Colonel Lambert is ftartled at this information, and feems to apprehend it may be fome favourite of the Doctor's. Charlotte appearing, he opens the fubject; from her natural vivacity fhe fports with his grave beginning, till he calls her a giddy *devil*; we wifh the laft word had been changed for a politer one; a lady may, by an extravagant admirer, be called a *faint*, and that's fufficiently ridiculous, but in pleafantry to ftile one a *fiend*, is not a mark of good breeding; we know there are precedents, but they don't invalidate our objection, which lies as much againft lack of meaning as indelicacy.

On being told that her father is violently againft the match with Darnley, the young lady expreffes fatisfaction, as fhe feems to think that difficulties render an amour more engaging: her contempt of the addition her fortune may receive from Sir John's confent, is fpirited, and declaring herfelf a fine woman, pleafant. When the Colonel mentions that Sir John has a perfon in his eye for her, fhe, with the true feelings of coquetry, enquires who it is, and appears to find great pleafure from the idea of an additional lover. We have a ftrong objection to what this lady fays when preffed to a fingle attachment in Darnley's favour, notwithftanding the paffage always creates a laugh; the comparifon of herfelf to an *empty houfe to let*, is at leaft vulgar and trite, if not licentious; it is mere gallery wit.

Charlotte, by flipping out an obfervation of Darnley's being rather jealous in his temper, fhews that he claims fome degree of her notice, which the Colonel
remarks:

remarks : her lover enters, and for fome time fhe
pretends not to perceive him, but repeats, as if in
foliloquy, fome poetical lines ; the lover preffes to
gain her attention. At laft, he makes rather a
peevifh remark, and draws upon himfelf fome fpirited raillery ; this gives him a turn, which we think
of an ungracious caft. Mention of a rival agitates
Darnley very much, and he makes eager enquiry
concerning who the perfon is ; the Colonel fuggefting that it is probably fomebody of Cantwell's
recommendation, the lover feems to think the
Doctor is his friend ; Charlotte here takes an odd
turn, and makes a whimfical exit, very advantageous
to a capable actrefs.

After his fifter is gone, the Colonel affures Darnley of being in his miftrefs's favour ; and hints, that
if Sir John's confent can be obtained, the Doctor
may be brought over by young Lady Lambert,
who apparently has great intereft over him, and as
fuppofed from amorous motives ; this inclination of
the Hypocrite for his patron's wife, is going to be
accounted for, when the explanation is ftopped by
the appearance of Lady Lambert, Seyward, and the
Doctor. Cantwell fets off in the true methodiftical
ftile of felf accufation ; and obferving, that he is
maintained too luxurioufly for his fpiritual welfare,
declares his intention of quitting the family for a
lefs fenfual fituation : fuch an irreparable lofs fhocks
her ladyfhip, who reprobates herfelf alfo, and therefore intreats his ftay upon the tendereft terms of
perfuafion, to promote her thorough reformation.

The Colonel returns with Darnley, when, after
reciprocal falutation, the wickednefs of going to
plays is brought in view, and the old lady warmly
                                                    feconds

seconds her ghoftly guide. Some words arifing between the Colonel and Cantwell, the former reproves
the latter's infolence with becoming fpirit, which
facrilegious violence drives off her ladyfhip, filled
with apprehenfions of fome extraordinary punifhment for fuch violence to fo pious a character; and
the Doctor himfelf retires, with threatning to acquaint Sir John. A few fpeeches intervene, refpecting the manner of his getting into the family;
when he returns, following Charlotte, who feems to
be much offended at his intrufion upon her; the
Colonel and her lover alfo, both exprefs refentment
at his bolting into her room, without any previous
notice; the Doctor pleads Sir John's authority for
what he has done, and deports himfelf with much
haughtinefs; Charlotte being queftioned as to the
particular offence fhe has received, gives a pleafant,
but we think reprehenfible account of it.

In the following part of this fcene, Charlotte a-
gain indulges her fportive humour with Darnley,
whofe patience is put to fevere trial; however, at
laft, fhe gives him leave to hope. They are interrupted and furprized by the entrance of Sir John,
who, without uttering one fyllable, takes his daughter off the ftage in a very abrupt manner: this Colonel Lambert imputes to the Doctor, and laments
the weaknefs of a father, whofe difpofition and underftanding are naturally good; however, he hints
having a thought that may prevent the Hypocrite's
bringing ruin on the family: fo ends the firft act.

By a foliloquy of Seyward's, at the beginning of
the fecond, we find he is deeply in Cantwell's
fecret tranfactions; and he mentions one of his
villainous defigns, which appears to be no other
than

than cutting off Charlotte, by a deed of settlement, with a shilling, unless she marries him. It appears, that Seyward is shocked at this knavery, and stimulated by a passion he has conceived for the young lady, determines upon using his power to prevent the pernicious settlement from being perfected. Sir John enters, and sends Seyward off to transcribe hymns for his supposed uncle, the pious Doctor.

Upon Charlotte's speaking in favourable terms of Seyward's good breeding and neatness, her father upbraids her with not considering a man's real merit; from whence, after some grave, preparatory speeches, he explains his intention, and proposes the Doctor, not by name, but descriptively; the young lady rallies, her father's notions of life and matrimony in a sensible and agreeable manner. At length, when he orders her to think no more of Darnley, and plumply names Cantwell, she bursts into a horse-laugh; then growing serious, suggests an objection which, as she rightly observes, is with fathers in general a weighty one, the Doctor's want of fortune; however, Sir John intimates a design of giving him one. The baronet being called by a message from his spiritual guide, Charlotte confesses to her step-mother, young Lady Lambert, painful apprehension of her father's doing any thing that may impair the fortune of her brother, the Colonel, who, upon being informed that his sister is destined for Cantwell, is so enraged, that he hints to Lady Lambert the Doctor's passion for her, which, upon being pressed, she acknowledges to have perceived. What Colonel Lambert says about the Turkey-cocks, might as well have been omitted; the characters

are too ferious for joking here; befides, the idea conveyed is not very fuitable to modeft ladies.

When the Colonel hears of his father's intention
of fettling a fortune on his chaplain, he thinks it
time to lay fome plan for the Hypocrite's deftruction, and this he throws upon Lady Lambert, requefting her to encourage the Doctor's addreffes,
from which he will devife the means of overturning
all his fchemes and influence ; this fhe promifes to
confider of. The Colonel then goes off upon an
appointment to meet Darnley.

Old Lady Lambert enters, and complains of
Charlotte's wearing thin lace over her breaft, as Dr.
Cantwell deems it indecent ; Charlotte gives her
opinion of the fuppofed faint in pretty tart terms,
yet the old lady perfeveres, and makes the following
truly characteriftical remark : " How has he weaned me from temporal connections ; my heart is
now fet upon nothing fublunary, and I thank heaven, I am now fo infenfible to every thing in this
limbo of vanity, that I could fee you, my fon, my
daughters, my brothers, my grand children, all ex-
pire before me, and mind it no more than the going
out of fo many fnuffs of candle." There never
was a better picture of methodiftical philofophy,
which annihilates every trace of focial feelings to a
miftaken, ridiculous fpirituality.

Sir John and Cantwell join the old lady, when the
baronet, with much feeming anxiety of mind, begs
of his mother to join in foliciting the Doctor to ftay
in his family, from whence the dear creature pretends to go, as thinking himfelf obnoxious to Sir
John's children, confequently the caufe of animofi-
ties and difturbances amongft the family : this
plaufible

Hypocrite.

plaufible humiliation of mind, plays a deep game of
policy, efpecially where he propofes to return Sir
John his deed of fettlement, and feems to lament
the Colonel's perilous, reprobate fituation. Charlotte being mentioned, Cantwell imputes her refufal
to female modefty, and thinks fhe may be wrought
upon, but advifes that the matter may reft awhile.

Maw-worm, a new character, and one of the felect,
is introduced; as laughable and well-drawn a perfonage as we know. This ignorant, melancholly
fprig of enthufiafm, is moft exquifitely delineated,
and calls powerfully on the rifible faculties; if it
was not too great an infringement upon our due
bounds, we would tranfcribe the whole of this excellent fcene; to give only a part would be injurious, for there is an admirable connection of plea-
fantries, the jokes and blunders happily arifing out
of each other. It is much to be lamented that there
are fo many Maw-worms in real life.

After old Lady Lambert departs, Cantwell gives
Seyward fome papers, with an obfervation to lay
them where they may be foon found, as he fhall
have occafion for them in the afternoon. This furnifhes Seyward with an idea that matters are ripening faft, fo he determines to acquaint Charlotte;
fhe appears, reading Pope's Homer, and afks fome
queftions concerning the original, of which fhe
knows two words. Upon repeating them, and defiring an explanation, Seyward applies them to his
own purpofe, fpeaking both the original and tran-
flation with fuch a glow of amorous emphafis, that
Charlotte takes notice of it. In what follows, he
difcovers to her, that Cantwell, though fuppofed his
uncle, is not really fo; then pathetically tells his

A a 2   fituation,

fituation, lamenting that he has joined in any of the Doctor's vile fchemes, even by connivance. Charlotte perceives in the progrefs of their interview, that Seyward loves her : when he has acquainted her with the deed of fettlement, containing a provifo of four thoufand pounds for her in cafe fhe marries the Doctor, and a total difinheritance of her brother, her volatility vanifhes ; fhe feels ferioufly, and requeft-ing the deed from Seyward, fhe concludes the act, with defiring him to meet her at a lawyer's in the Temple.

At the beginning of the third act we are introduced into Charlotte's dreffing-room, where fhe is acquainted by Betty, her maid, that Mr. Darnley had been to enquire for her, and feemed uneafy at her not being at home, which fhe interprets into jealoufy, and refolves to teize him. At this unlucky moment he comes, and meets with fo whimfical a reception, that he remarks upon it ; the collifion of converfation of two lovers is defcribed here with fpirit, a good deal of acid, as Lady Townly calls it, is mingled, and Charlotte very juftly mortifies the impatience of her gallant. At length the fubject is waved, and Darnley informs his miftrefs that he has heard from Colonel Lambert, Sir John's defign of efpoufing her to the Doctor; here the amantium iræ breaks out again, and poor Darnley is wound up to a pitiable pitch of uneafinefs ; he makes an effort to fhake off her power, but fhe plays him fo very judicioufly, that he turns foft, and almoft melts her.

When brought to a very critical point of feeling, Seyward's entrance gives Charlotte a very feafonable paufe : what fhe fays to that young man again a-larms Darnley's jealoufy, who queftions him what bufinefs he has with the lady. Colonel Lambert

I   enters,

enters, and finding his friend ſtrongly agitated, kindly endeavours to talk him into a calm, promiſes his aſſiſtance, and appoints a meeting in the Park: Charlotte re-enters, and the Colonel aſſumes his friend's buſineſs directly, but cannot bring his ſiſter to any ſatisfactory explanation.

Young Lady Lambert appears, ſays ſhe has deſired a conference with Cantwell, and mentions her determination to give a good account of him. At ſight of the Doctor, Charlotte and her brother retire: after a well conducted tete-a-tete with the lady, wherein the lamblike wolf plainly ſhews his iniquitous deſign upon his patron's wife, the Colonel ruſhes precipitately in, and menaces diſcovery to his father; Cantwell, with quick policy, turns his meaning to the love he has for Charlotte. During this confuſion Sir John enters, and is told by his ſon of the Doctor's paying addreſſes to Lady Lambert; this gives the ſactified knave an opportunity of working upon the baronet's credulity, with all the plauſible addreſs of hypocriſy, and ſo far triumphs, that Sir John in rage forbids the Colonel his houſe. Here Cantwell's Chriſtian charity artfully interpoſes in favour of his enemy, and he propoſes a reconciliation, which the Colonel very properly declines; this confirms Sir John in reſpect of the ſettlement, and gives the Doctor a plea for accepting it, which he declares is only as a truſtee.

Seyward and Charlotte begin the fourth act; by their converſation we are informed that a deed has been ſigned in preſence of the former, who, for his friendly interpoſition, is promiſed favour with regard to his own circumſtances; however, he hints that intereſt was not his motive ſo much as love:
the

the young lady's treatment of him here shews a good understanding, and a candid mind; she commends his modesty, avows a previous passion, and recommends avoiding to play, moth like, about a flame which may be fatal.

After a very characteristic soliloquy, Lady Lambert informs Charlotte that the Doctor, by Sir John's express desire, is coming to be his own advocate for her favour: being introduced by Betty, the chambermaid, Cantwell opens the interview with observing, that he considers himself as a person not very agreeable to Charlotte, which opinion she most cordially confirms; after receiving her contemptuous treatment of him with much composure, he acquaints her that she must not marry without his consent; then causes her to confess an inclination for Darnley, and modestly offers to favour that proposal, in case she gives up half the four thousand pounds allotted for her by Sir John; this she comes into, and receives warning from Cantwell not to attempt any prejudice against him, as any thing of that nature must retort upon herself. When he is gone off, a short scene occurs, wherein the Colonel informs his sister of having laid the foundation of Cantwell's overthrow. Darnley appears; after some strokes of amorous dalliance, he relates what has been done in Seyward's affair, and how far the Doctor's villainy is detected. The young lady, with much good nature, recommends Seyward to her lover's patronage, and he with great gentility promises it. The Colonel returning unseen, hears his sister still trifling with her gallant, and interposes, going so far as even to fix a wedding-day for her; and, at length, he so far prevails, that she gives her

hand

Hypocrite.

hand to Darnley, and taking the gallant into another chamber, the fourth act is concluded.

We meet the lady and her fwain at the beginning of the fifth act, conversing upon the bargain she has provisionally made with Cantwell for his consent, which Darnley seems willing to fulfil. Sir John joins them, and after apologizing for his abrupt behaviour, enters upon the topic of his daughter's marriage; he acknowledges the Doctor has quitted his claim, yet still seems determined to have him for a son-in-law. Charlotte, warmed with indignation, lays a heavy charge against the Doctor, and being provoked by her father's obstinate credulity, declares her resolution to marry Darnley at all events. Charlotte's earnestness, and his lady's proposition of giving him occular demonstration, make him consent to stand behind a screen, while Lady Lambert gives his hypocritical favourite an audience.

When the fair spoken son of impiety appears, her ladyship, with powerful artifice, seems apprehensive of another surprize, and cautions him to fasten the doors; then enters upon the declaration of love he has made, and plainly intimates, that it was not only acceptable, but very agreeable to her. Thus she lures him on till he comes to the point, and goes so far as to say openly, that he can lead Sir John by the nose; here the enraged baronet rushes forwards, and loads him with just accusations, which Cantwell strives for some time to throw off by calm evasion; but, being pressed, fires into resentment, and adverting to the deed of settlement, desires Sir John to walk out of his house. While matters are in this state, Maw-worm and old Lady Lambert enter; upon the baronet's telling his mother that the

Doctor

Doctor is a villain, fome very ludicrous remarks drop from his difciple, who wont believe any thing to his prejudice. Charlotte, in a fright, acquaints her father that fhe apprehends murder, as the Doctor was heard at high words with Seyward, and immediately after a piftol went off. This matter is foon cleared up by Seyward ; after which Cantwell is going off, but Colonel Lambert meets him with a tipftaff, properly attended, and delivers him into cuftody. Even in this fituation of conviction and dilemma, his infolence continues, and he boafts of being mafter of the houfe: in this, however, he is defeated, by having a deed quite the reverfe of what he imagines ; here he is carried off, we think with too much tamenefs on his fide : the old lady and Maw-worm go off, not convinced.

After the hero is thus difpofed of, the piece is brought to an excellent conclufion by the following fpeech, delivered by Charlotte, when Sir John, in the heat of his vexation fays, that henceforth he fhall hold in abhorrence every thing which bears the appearance of piety : " Nay now, dear fir, I muft take the liberty to tell you, you carry things too far, and go from one extreme to another---What ? becaufe a worthlefs wretch has impofed upon you, under the fallacious fhew of auftere grimace, will you needs have it every body is like him, confound the good with the bad, and conclude there are no truly religious in the world ? Leave, my dear fir, fuch rafh conclufions to fools and libertines ; let us be careful to diftinguifh between virtue and the appearance of it ; guard, if poffible, againft doing honour to hypocrify ; but, at the fame time, let us allow there is no character in life greater or more valuable, than

that

Hypocrite.

that of the truly devout ; nor any thing more noble or more beautiful, than the fervour of a sincere
piety."

The plot of this play is regular, and sufficiently
intricate without being improbable or obscure ; the
incidents are well ranged, an agreeable suspence is
properly kept up, and the catastrophe gratifies every
liberal mind ; the characters, which exhibit variety
within natural bounds, we shall, according to the
rule of this work, consider separately.

Sir John Lambert is possessed of that kind of
weakness which designing men work on at pleasure : enthusiasm flourishes, and indeed can only
exist in flexible understandings ; it is a weed that
like thistles among corn, destroys the noblest har-
vest of the mind. The baronet appears to be a very
well-meaning man, a good husband, and a tender
father ; yet, under the abominable influence of a
canting knave, seems ready to violate every principle of those two leading characters in the social compact. In representation this baronet is neither for
nor against the actor, and we presume ourselves right
when we think as well of Mr. PACKER, as of any
body else that could be put into the part.

Darnley appears to be possessed of good qualities,
but has a taint of suspicion and impatience in his
temper by no means agreeable. Charlotte's method
of making him feel his failing is sensible, and occasions much pleasantry. The circumstances he is
placed in are not very desirable to a performer, and
therefore we could wish that so estimable an actor
as Mr. REDDISH was eased of him : that gentleman,
by being a little spared, would rise faster in public
estimation ; besides, we dont conceive Darnley to

be in his ftile of acting. It is no doubt a compliment and advantage to an author to have as many capital performers in his drama as poffible, but it is rather fevere upon one who ftands in the firft light, to be either put out of or below his fphere.

Colonel Lambert is a free, fenfible, fpirited gentleman, who has fo little perfonal concern with the piece, that he might eafily be cut out and not be much miffed ; however, he is not at all a difagreeable object, and we wifh he was in the hands of fome perfon poffeffing more vivacity than Mr. JEFFERSON,

Seyward is a very amiable young perfon, whofe fentiments we approve, and whofe fituation we pity ; the circumftance of his love is at beft but trifling, and vanifhes we know not how ; it might have been omitted, and then the part he acts againft Cantwell, coming from difinterefted honefty, would place him in a fairer degree of praife. We remember to have feen Mr. PALMER do this part in the original play, with much more feeling and propriety than Mr. CAUTHERLY manifefts in it at prefent, not but we allow the latter to be very tolerable, as acting goes at prefent ; Mr. Rofs was much the beft.

Doctor Cantwell, much more emphatically called Wolf, by CIBBER, is a very high finifhed piece of villainy ; proud, avaricious, fenfual, ungrateful and hypocritical ; one who facrifices confcience, honefty and religion, to the bafeft, underhand purpofes ; a monfter in nature, and a difgrace to the human race. We remember to have heard a very fenfible remark from a liberal, moral judge of mankind, that chaplains in general, of every religion, have oftener promoted domeftic confufion than piety ; and we cannot help highly approving the expreffion of a Roman

Hypocrite.

man Catholic nobleman, who, during the rebellion of forty-five, shewed himself zealous in the Protestant cause ; upon being asked his reason, he said he liked the present form of government, and wished Popery to be kept out of the kingdom ; for if that prevailed, his chaplains, who now would bear a message for him, would turn the tables, and make him their message carrier. Cantwell is placed in very judicious points of view, to shew the danger of such sanctified vermin, who creep, snake-like, into your bosom, to sting you mortally. His villainy is revealed by just degrees, and his fate is well suited to his deserts.

There is more difficulty in doing this character justice than is commonly imagined, much and strong expression of countenance is requisite, as well as smooth and nervous utterance. We have seen the Doctor personated with great ability and much applause, by both Mr. THE. CIBBER, and Mr. SPARKS; however, they were both too mechanical, wanting that essential ease and plausibility which makes us give Mr. KING the preference.

Maw-worm we owe to the alterer of this piece, and are highly obliged to him for so rich an improvement of the laureat's production. We are equally obliged to Mr. WESTON for his inimitable support of it : Mr. MOODY once exhibited this risible piece of religious insanity, but we hope never will again ; and Mr. WALDRON was so much out of his depth, when the managers *popped* him, like Mr. FOOTE's Lindamira on for it, that we are amazed the young man was not overwhelmed by the tide of popular displeasure ; if he is held forth as the turtle of low comedy, we beg leave to borrow an

idea

idea from Mr. COLMAN, and affert, he has not one bit of the green fat about him.

We hear Mr. WESTON is gone to Scotland; is it not amazing and vexatious to all lovers of the drama, that when there is fuch a lamentable, unparalelled lack of merit, at both houfes, two fuch intrinfic performers as Meffrs. WOODWARD and WESTON, fhould be driven to a northern migration. Is this gratitude to the public? oh fhame!

Old Lady Lambert is alfo an additional character, of no great confequence, yet well conceived; as by her we perceive that perfons of rank and education are liable to catch the infection of enthufiafm, as well as thofe of the lower and more uncultivated clafs. Her ideas of religious purity are diverting, and we have no objection to Mrs. BRADSHAW's method of delivering them; fhe maintains the fanctified formality in a very fuitable manner.

Her daughter-in-law is a very good, conformable young wife, to an odd kind of an elderly hufband; fhe feems defirous to promote his happinefs and the welfare of his family, but has nothing to fay worth notice, and at beft can only be confidered as an agreeable daudle: Mrs. W. BARRY deferves a better part, and does what fhe can with this.

Charlotte is undoubtedly the beft drawn coquette, and the moft defenfible one on the ftage; fhe likes adulation, yet has fincerity enough to own it; fhe loves a man, yet has difcernment to fee his particular failing, and refolution to laugh him pleafantly out of it; fhe is ornamented with generofity, fprightlinefs and wit, nor is her vanity any way offenfive. Mrs. WOFFINGTON, in the NON JUROR, obtained fingular applaufe, not without great merit;

2   however,

Hypocrite.

however, there was fuch an uncharacteriftic affectation about her, that fome degree of difguft muft attend it; and fhe marked thofe paffages which had
any relifh of licentioufnefs very offenfively. Mrs.
PRITCHARD had much more eafe, and equal fpirit
of expreffion; but was, from corpulence, fo very
abfurd an appearance, that however our ears might
be pleafed, our eyes were offended. Mrs. ABING-
TON being a very agreeable mixture of thefe ladies,
much freer than the former, and more delicate than
the latter, fills our idea of Charlotte to every degree
of fatisfaction. Mr. BICKERSTAFF, in his preface,
has paid this accomplifhed actrefs a very genteel and
juft compliment.

As we have obferved at the beginning of our cri-
ticifms on this piece, the NON JUROR was growing
obfolete, it was therefore highly judicious to give
the fatire a new and more intelligible form: CIB-
BER's dialogue, though not remarkably correct, is
natural, eafy, and fpirited; the additions in no fhape
difgrace him, and there are fome omiffions which
do him credit. Upon the whole, we heartily wifh
the HYPOCRITE encouragement on the ftage, and
attention in the clofet.

THEODOSIUS.

A TRAGEDY: By LEE.

THE tragedy of THEODOSIUS opens with all
the pomp of religious pageantry ; a decorated altar, the figure of Conftantine kneeling to an air fuf-
pended crofs, priefts, chorifters and mufic : after a
preparatory hymn and chorus, Atticus, the high
prieft, enters into conference with Leontine, a philofopher. By what paffes between them, we find
that Theodofius, from a fixed melancholly on his
mind, has determined to lay afide the reins of government for holy retirement : Leontine, who had
been tutor to him and a Perfian prince, called Varanes, delineates thefe royal characters, and fignifies,
that the latter, attended by his daughter, is coming
on a vifit to the former.

Varanes approaching with Athenais they retire ;
the fhort fcene which occurs between thefe lovers,
means no more than to declare his warmth of paffion and her diffidence, arifing from difparity of
rank between the heir of empire and a poor philofopher's daughter. The prince's declarations manifeft rather an impetuous than a prudent paffion.
The approach of Theodofius being announced by
found of inftruments they retire, and make way for
the Emperor, attended by his two fifters, Marina
and Flavilla, who have determined to take the veil.

Previous to his fpiritual admiffion, the Imperial
devotee confeffes to Atticus, in a very pleafing defcriptive

Theodosius.

scriptive narration, that love, to an incurable degree, is the cause of that anxiety which exiles him from public life. Leontine pronounces the approach of Varanes, who immediately enters, warmed with the glow of early and sincere friendship; their adverting to the sports of former days, the theatre and the field, is very natural for juvenile, as well as aged minds; what Varanes says of hunting, is poetically imagined and well expressed: the prince uses his endeavours to persuade Theodosius from his purpose; however, seems struck with the awful ceremony of admitting nuns, and by the conclusive speech of the first act, shews as if he was half won over to retirement; the sentiments he utters, and his remark upon the weight that royalty lays on mental freedom, are pretty, but horridly disgraced by rhime.

At the beginning of the second act, Pulcheria, Theodosius's sister, who is invested with imperial authority, hears the clash of swords, and soon after is accosted by Marcian, a Roman general, who apologizes for quarrelling in the palace, by reciting the particulars of his provocation; in doing of which he throws out many low and indecent observations; these, we presume, the author meant as proofs of martial bluntness, but are in reality absolute breaches of decorum, censurable to the last degree, and the more so as being quite unnecessary; his reflections upon court effeminacy are, no doubt, very natural effusions of an honest mind, irritated by the buzzing, gaudy insects of court sun-shine, and this part of the scene we highly approve.

Openness of expression becomes an honest and brave character, but to bully a lady of exalted station,

tion, as this militarian does, is beyond all bearing, and we think she fuftains his abufe too long; however, at length, becoming fpirit breaks forth, and she reproves him in fevere terms, at the fame time banifhing him after three days; there is fomething whimfical enough in Pulcheria's intimation afide, that he is once to lord it over her. Lucius, upon feeing his friend, the general, droop, at receiving fo harfh and fudden a fentence, propofes to affert his caufe by force, which Marcian declines, accepting exile and retirement in the following well fancied, well expreffed lines.

> We'll fly to fome far diftant lonely village,
> Forget our former ftate, and breed with flaves;
> Sweat in the eye of day, and when night comes,
> With bodies coarfely filled and vacant fouls,
> Sleep like the labour'd hinds and never think.

Athenais and Leontine prefent themfelves, the latter obferving, that they have paid the compliment Varanes defired, of attending him to Theodofius's court, propofes returning to Athens; this affects the love-ftricken maid, who confeffes her uneafinefs, and draws from Leontine a doubt of the prince's fincerity, which Athenais cannot admit; however, upon her father's ftarting the idea of a difhonourable connection, with the juft feelings of a chafte referve, she declares that no confideration, however interefting, not a parent's life in danger, shall impair her virtue; this fatisfies the old man, who, upon feeing the prince approach, retires.

By what Varanes fays to his friend Aranthes at entrance, it appears, that the latter has been advifing him againft a matrimonial connection, as difgraceful,

Theodosius.

ful, which he feems to admit in very ungenerous terms; yet, upon feeing Athenais, he renews his vows with great fervour, and in a very bombaftic flow of expreffion declares, that he prefers her to all the Perfian greatnefs. Upon mention of his father's difpleafure if he fhould know of his fon's attachment to fo inadequate a character, he utters the following beautiful effufion of a fond mind.

No more of this, no more, for I difdain
All pomp when thou art by : far be the noife
Of kings and courts from us ; whofe gentle fouls
Our kinder ftars have fteer'd another courfe;
Free as the foreft birds we'll pair together,
Without remembring who our father's were ;
Fly to the arbours, grots, and flow'ry meads,
And in foft murmurs interchange our fouls ;
Together drink the chryftal of the ftream,
Or tafte the yellow fruit which autumn yields;
And when the golden evening calls us home,
Wing to our downy neft and fleep till morn.

When Athenais mentions a neceffity of parting, Varanes takes alarm, which caufes her to refer him to Leontine for explanation ; the philofopher ingenuoufly queftions the real meaning of his paffion, which throws the prince into confufion ; and being urged to the critical point of marriage, his illiberal pride, getting the better of generofity and truth, occafions him to treat the woman of his heart, and his venerable good old tutor, in a moft brutal, contemptuous manner ; Leontine warms into a noble refentment, which forces the hot-brained Perfian off in a very difgraceful manner.

Vol. II. C c Every

Every heart, susceptible of tender feelings, must here sympathize in that painful concern which overwhelms the injured father and slighted maid; the latter of whom acknowledges at large her ardent affection, but nobly resolves to sacrifice it at the shrine of just resentment, and gives her approving fire the most solemn, comfortable assurance, of inviolable virtue; this scene takes strong possession of the tender passions, but concludes with some very enervate, pitiful rhimes.

Varanes, totally repenting his treatment of Athenais, meets Aranthes at the beginning of the third act, and communicates his readiness to make her any reparation: being informed that she and her father have left the court, without any trace by which they might be followed, with the utmost violence of anxiety, the hair-brained lover determines upon a personal pursuit, ordering his chariots to meet him in the Hippodrome. In the next scene we are surprized with the conversion of Athenais to Christianity, for which we have been no way prepared; nor do we know whether it is Leontine's choice that his daughter should go one road into futurity, while he himself pursues another. The matter is very soon brought about, and is not sufficiently probable; however, we find it so, and that Pulcheria has wrought the change, for which her proselyte returns thanks in grateful terms: the imperial princess vows strict friendship, and proposes a mutual participation of joys and griefs. Touching upon the master-string of her heart, Athenais, who, but a few lines since says, that conversion has eased her of the *lumber of passion*---a kind of methodistical thodiftical figure---here gives a loofe to grief, and vents bitter reproaches againft the fallacy of man.

Theodofius coming in, his fifter prefents her fair convert, when lo ! it appears, that fhe is the identical unknown beauty who had infpired him with love, and for whofe fake he meant to leave the world. This incident tells well in action ; his immediate proffer of marriage is violently fudden, yet no harfh violation of nature. Leontine's approbation of the honourable choice is fuitable, and the author has furnifhed Athenais with a proper degree of diffident fubmiffion in her reply ; the new appointed Emprefs, Pulcheria, &c. being retired, Varanes, who comes to take his leave of Theodofius, is acquainted with the unexpected change in favour of that monarch's happinefs ; the Perfian prince, though deeply wounded in mind himfelf, congratulates his friend's joy, and laments that his own painful fituation wont let him ftay to fhare it.

This naturally damps Theodofius's fatisfaction ; however, he requefts Varanes to fee his bride before he goes, which the latter feems willing to decline. There is fomething odd in the Emperor's behaviour, not to afk the caufe of his friend's melancholly and fudden departure ; the plot has here intruded much upon friendfhip ; Athenais is brought on, and prefented by her imperial lover to the Perfian, whofe aftonifhment and confufion may be much more eafily imagined than expreffed. To increafe the fwell and agitation of his heart, fhe treats him as the provocation he gave her merited, and leaves him to vent his paffion with Theodofius. What paffes between thefe royal perfonages is again very odd, for though the half-headed Emperor fees his friend

eaten

eaten up with paffion, and fuffers himfelf to be cate-
chized for taking the woman he likes, yet he never
enquires into the reafon of all this ; indeed, when
Varanes clears up the matter, by avowing his paffion, he fhews fome generous fenfibility, by offering
to fubmit his claim to the lady's choice. This
caufes Varanes to whimper like a whipped fchool-
boy ; and Theodofius, pioufly leaving the iffue to
heaven, goes to prepare Athenais for an interview
with his diftreffed rival. Aranthes, by offering to
comfort his mafter, inflames his rage more, and is
charged with being the author of his misfortune ;
notwithftanding the prince is half mad, our author
has put into his mouth a poetical defcription of the
tranquility of rural obfcurity ; yet this we could
have borne tolerably well, as the thought is pretty,
and the lines flowing, had not jingle been introduced.

At the beginning of the fourth act, we meet
Marcian lamenting his fallen ftate ; he is foon joined by that other unentertaining fuperfluity, Pulcheria, who, as it would feem, has fneaked after him.
The laft time they parted fhe pronounced his ba-
nifhment, yet now fhe fo far forgets herfelf, as to
truft him with a very fignal inftance of her imperial
brother's folly ; andd then as ftrangely difcovers,
without any hint to ftir recollection, that fhe has
been talking with a profcribed traitor. This draws
on three or four lines of frefh reproach, then fhe
foftens, taking a very dubious leave.

When Lucius concludes fhe is in love with the
general, and tells him fo, Marcian very juftly replies, that they neither of them know any thing of
her, and that it is out of the power of human nature

to

to scan her. We most heartily concur in the soldier's opinion, for, as the author has drawn her, she is equally unintelligible and infignificant : an unprincipled excrefcence of a poetical brain.

The token of Theodofius's weaknefs, which she has put into Marcian's hand, he determines to make ufe of, for roufing the Emperor from his lethargic effeminacy. This the author has made him put in practice, but the fcene is generally omitted, and we think blameably ; for though it wants much foftning on Marcian's fide, yet a fubject forcing bold, honeft truths, into a weak monarch's ear, is a very pleafing and inftructive picture for a Britifh ftage ; though perhaps fuch a one, in a new piece, might not now be licenced ; poffibly it is from a fimilar principle omitted by courtly managers. We remember the fcene once done in Dublin, with very pleafing and proper effect.

The fhort fcene between Theodofius and Athenais, preparatory to feeing Varanes, fhews the Emperor to be a moft condefcending rival ; and the lady obferves, with great good fenfe, that it is a fevere and dangerous trial, to throw her in the way of one who had once infpired her with fo tender a paffion ; he notwithftanding, leaves her to the violent ftruggle of love and glory. No fooner is he gone off, than Varanes appears, a picture of defpair ; fhe is ftruck with the fettled melancholly that clouds him, yet refolves to withftand the fofter feelings : her taunts are remarkably fevere, particularly where fhe mentions hearing him in obedience to the Emperor's command. In fhort, fhe reduces the prince to fuch an exquifite degree of pain, that though fome of his conduct merits contempt, we are obliged to pity him.

him. Where he mentions his death, and begs that compaffion which he cannot obtain in life, the fcene grows truly pathetic, and the audience muft melt with Athenais ; who, fhocked at the found of an everlafting farewell from the idol of her heart, calls him back, and candidly, with warmth, expreffes her love, yet leaves him with the idea, that their inclinations cannot be fulfilled. What the reafon of this infuperable perplexity is, we dont fee ; having forgiven the infult fhe received, and Theodofius being difpofed to confirm her choice, what happens appears to be only the author's obftinate purfuit of a tragical cataftrophe. What Varanes fays after fhe is gone, appears to us very ftrained and bombaftical : comparing himfelf to a perfon buried alive, is ftraining idea horridly : it is worthy of remark, that in this fcene, Varanes fwears by, or appeals to the gods, no lefs than fix times ; indeed, through the whole piece, Marcian and he are bringing in the deities upon every occafion ; infomuch, that allowing the difference of plurality, it might be fuppofed they had been educated among the Englifh foot-guards, where fwearing is a capital accomplifhment, and conftant practice.

Athenais, ornamented with imperial robes for the nuptials, begins the fifth act, with her attendant Delia. She very juftly complains of being hurried to the Temple at the midnight hour, but is told that the defign is to keep her marriage as long as poffible from the knowledge of Varanes, in compaffion to his pains ; her confidante difmiffed, fhe determines upon taking poifon, and empties the deadly cup. Pulcheria, at entrance, takes notice of the Emprefs's diftrefsful and pallid looks : doubting the

effect

Theodosius.

effect of what she has done in futurity, Athenais asks what punishment awaits suicide, which is a very. natural question, as she has been so lately made a Christian, and heathen sects hold it a meritorious, action to seek refuge in voluntary death, rather than labour under excess of pain or disgrace. Leontine coming to conduct his daughter to the Temple, observes and reproves her melancholly, charging her to think no more of Varanes, who has used her ill; the unforgiving rigidity of unfeeling age is here well contrasted to the relenting softness of a female heart, impressed with a tender regard; the unhappy bride suffers herself to be led like a tame victim, yet pathetically declares Varanes can never be erased or banished from her mind.

The Persian prince, wholly a prey to despair, appears next, in soliloquy. Our author has drawn together, and furnished him with various striking images, well adapted to the gloom of melancholly; but what in the name of nature and common sense, could make him run it into rhime: we had some idea of relieving this speech from such shameful fetters, in the same manner we did that of the Fryar in Romeo and Juliet, but as the play wants alteration in many other respects, we have declined it.

Upon the entrance of Aranthes, who has been sent by the prince to Athenais's apartment, he acquaints his master that she is gone to be married; this determines Varanes on speedily putting a period to his intolerable life, and he claims holding the sword against his breast, as an action of friendship, from Aranthes; who proposes to attend his master in death, but is charged to survive, and bear his bleeding corse immediately to the Temple.

Things

Things so disposed, our broken-hearted hero puts his fatal resolution in practice, and breaths his last in a most miserable couplet, rather laughable than pathetic.

We are once again conducted to the Temple, where, after a nuptial benediction is given, Aranthes enters with the body of his deceased lord ; and in two speeches, interestingly descriptive, relates the manner of his death. Athenais, overwhelmed with the circumstance, quits the living bridegroom for the dead lover ; embraces his body, declares, to the astonishment of her husband, father, &c. that tho' she consented to marriage, her heart was always with Varanes ; wherefore, she took a poisonous draught, which soon takes effect, and sends her after the dear object of her first inclination. Theodosius, struck with this unexpected incident, renews his former intention of laying down the reins of government, and gives the empire to Pulcheria and Marcian, who have made up matters very strangely ; thus the piece hurries to a conclusion.

The tragedy of THEODOSIUS is regular in its plot, and has many scenes of peculiar tenderness ; yet is sadly incumbered by those disagreeable non-essentials, Marcian and Pulcheria, who have almost as little business in that piece, as they would have in Julius Cæsar. The play might easily be altered so as to leave them entirely out, by which means the other characters would necessarily be enriched, and the main action more properly attended to : the versification is flowing, and many of the sentiments brilliant, yet bombast frequently soars to a disagreeable, unintelligible height ; the author has

shewn

Theodosius.

shewn warmth of genius, but coldness and inactivity of judgment.

Theodosius---sure there never was such an insipid morsel of royalty, is scarce a character in any shape; he has nothing to mark him but a kind of boyish, amorous weakness. After his first scene, he has not a line to utter that is worth an actor's speaking, or a spectator's hearing : it is hardly reasonable, though he gives name to the piece, to mention the performance of such an unseasoned incumbrance upon action ; if we mistake not, Mr. SMITH made his first attempt in this unfavourable part, which he rendered in some measure bearable, and has continued to bear it up ever since till last season. Mr. DIGGES has been pushed on for it, but was much too manly in his person, and too declamatory in his expression ; the lover, at least of this class, sits uneasy upon him. Mr. REDDISH ! in the name of equity, if any such principle dwells within a theatre, why should such superior abilities be crammed into so disagreeable an undertaking ? especially when that *capital* actor, Mr. CAUTHERLY, might much more properly drudge through it, than Hamlet, Romeo, and a dreadful &c. which with most cruel kindness are imposed upon him.

Marcian, the tragical blunderbuss, who seems to have no idea of any difference between freedom and rudeness of speech, utters several sentiments which, well expressed, cannot fail of applause, and Mr. SPARKS used to give us singular pleasure in those passages : Mr. CLARKE is by no means displeasing, but Mr. AICKIN, mounted on LEE's fiery, hard-mouthed PEGASUS, sits in a very ticklish, tottering situation. Mr. MOSSOP did it one season in Dublin, and thinking it unworthy his powers, acquired, through negligence, an ease which he wanted in more important characters ; so became, by accident, much the most agreeable performer we ever saw in this part.

Leontine is a character of worth ; he may be rendered estimable without any capital requisites ; his solicitude for Athenais's virtue, and contempt of aggrandisement upon unworthy terms, speak him equally a tender father and a good man ; he must interest an audience, especially where he calls his pupil to an explanation. Mr. RIDOUT personated this amiable philosopher with ability : Mr. GIBSON has had the misfortune to follow him in the part, but never can succeed to his merit ; having either no feeling at all, or such a disgustful utterance of it, as is worse than none : Mr. HULL should certainly do it at Covent Garden.

Aranthes has but two speeches of any regard, they indeed should be taken care of ; wherefore, we cannot sufficiently express our surprize to think any manager should so far mistake his place and judgment, as to suffer the marring of them by that distinguished mutilator of sense, language and character, Mr. DAVIS : on the other hand, we cannot reconcile giving this attendant at Drury Lane, to Mr. PALMER, who frequently stands in a first light ; it is making both head and tail of a man. Certainly, amongst the number of young mutes, who serve only to prop up the side wings, and bow to every bashaw of three tails, some one might be found to do such a part as this with tolerable decency.

Varanes, who was most the object of our author's attention, is an odd medley of love and pride ;

now

Theodosius.

now he will, then will not; profuse in professions, irresolute in practice; tender, impatient; in short, a romantic madman; yet, notwithstanding inconsistencies of a glaring nature, he is as a dramatic personage, highly interesting. We have undergone the torture of hearing him preached by Mr. SHERIDAN, whose stage-love was the most grating that ever wounded a tender ear; yet we cannot justly avoid allowing him a very characteristical despondance of features in the last scene of the fourth act, and considerable merit in the midnight soliloquy. Mr. Ross is very bearable, but wants much of that fire necessary to keep pace with his author: when Mr. SMITH took leave of the Emperor, and formed an alliance with the Persian prince, he made a most lamentable mistake; and we wish, for old acquaintance sake, he may return to his original, disagreeable as it is, rather than shew himself to more conspicuous disadvantage.

Mr. BARRY must in imagination to those who are at all acquainted with his performance, fill up every idea of excellence in this character; his love was enchanting, his rage alarming, his grief melting; even now, though overtaken by time, and impaired in his constitution, he has not the shadow of a competitor. The rheumatic stiffness of his joints has been industriously trumpeted forth, and every mean art made use of to lower him in public opinion: yet true it is, that if he hobbled upon stilts, he would be better than any persons in his stile upon their best legs. A gentleman of acknowledged judgment lately made the following just and striking similitude, that Mr. BARRY was like the time-worn ruins of Palmira and Balbec; which, even in a fallen

state,

Theodosius.

ftate, fhew more dignity and real beauty, than the compleat productions of modern architecture. We heartily lament that this gentleman's caft is fo inconfiftent with his years, and wifh his prudence had laid up an independancy, that he might have retired ere envy and theatrical policy had fapped the foundation of his well-earned fame.

Pulcheria, as a character, we have already given our opinion of; what fhe fays is full as infignificant as what fhe does; and Mrs. VINCENT, whom no length of years can make old, if fhe had never been trufted with any fuperior undertaking in tragedy, might here have been bearable enough : but what dull head, or hard heart, could have put the agreeable Mrs. W. BARRY, of Drury Lane, upon fo irkfome an undertaking-- Come forth Mrs. HOPKINS, and feize this Roman princefs, more confonant to thy abilities, than the young and beauteous Zara, and as fuitable to thy delicate figure.

Athenais is much the moft eftimable character in this piece; for, laying afide the weaknefs of her fex, and refifting the temptation of a darling object, fhe maintains that exalted virtue practically, which her father only admires and recommends in fpeculation ; however, tho' we approve her general conduct, yet fhe manifefts a ftrong taint of romantic ideas : her felf-denial is carried to an extreme. As to the termination of her own life, we have already exculpated that, by remarking, that fhe had not been informed how abominable an action felf-murder is deemed in the Chriftian fyftem.

The part of Athenais, though well delivered from the author's pen, has none of thofe mafterly ftrokes of action, which gave Mrs. CIBBER an opportunity

of

Theodosius.

of displaying her exquisite abilities ; wherefore, we always thought that lady rather below herself in the fair Athenian, and allowed Mrs. BELLAMY to come nearer an equality in this, than any other character ; they both were singularly pleasing, but we must prefer Mrs. BARRY to either, as having equal force with more nature.

Miss MILLER has certainly given Mr. COLMAN some bitter provocation, that he pushes her on for this and several other characters equally unfit; indeed, she did it for her benefit, which is a season when many performers, to indulge vanity, kindly treat their friends with the barbarous and dreadful, though not bloody murder of a principle character ; this is like asking acquaintances to dinner, and giving a thin breast of mutton instead of a good sirloin of beef, which is equally ready.

This play has no moral, there is no vice to merit punishment, and what virtue there is falls a sacrifice to ill conducted passions : we are apt to think its tendency prejudicial to young minds, as it furnishes very extravagant notions of love; and therefore, though it always pleases in representation, cannot cordially recommend it.

The FOUNDLING.

A COMEDY, by Mr. MOORE.

IN the firſt ſcene we meet young Belmont rallying Colonel Raymond, for making love in a ſtile of gravity to his ſiſter, of whoſe volatile and coquettiſh diſpoſition he draws a very pleaſant picture, and alſo, by way of contraſt, ludicrouſly paints the Colonel to himſelf; after this, he enters upon an account of women, which we think extremely injurious, to the ſenſible part of the ſex at leaſt, and ſhews his notions to be unnatural; to ſuppoſe that good underſtanding will make any female more ready to encourage a fool, is ſtrange doctrine; pride may work ſuch an effect, but ſound ſenſe cannot: freedom, among friends, is the life of ſocial enjoyment, but, we think young Belmont places the Colonel in too ſevere and ridiculous a light; it ſeems as if the author had ſacrificed every other conſideration to that of enriching his favourite character. When Fidelia comes to be mentioned, Belmont goes on in the ſame rhapſodical ſtile concerning her, that he has made uſe of concerning his ſiſter, reſpecting the uncertainty of her birth; Belmont ſpeaks as a man of gallantry with very vague, undetermined principles; upon the Colonel's enquiry, whether Roſetta knows any thing of Fidelia's real ſtory, Belmont declares ſhe does not, but believes her to be the ſiſter of a fellow collegian of his, and in

that

that light recommends her as a wife to him; being asked his father's disposition towards the young lady, he says, there is nothing wanting of recommendation to the old gentleman but some certainty of a fortune; here he takes a most reprehensible method of removing a kind of dilemma he is in, and meanly says, as he has brought her into the family by one misrepresentation, he'll remove her by another; and what is that? forsooth, by scandalizing her virtue. Belmont favours action in this scene, but he is no more nor less than a despicable reptile, furnished with more words than meaning, more humour than sense.

In the succeeding conversation between Rosetta and Fidelia, we find that the former rattles away in the same stile and sentiment, concerning men, and the treatment of them in love affairs, that her brother, in the preceeding scene, used respecting her; Fidelia charges her with being in love with Colonel Raymond, though she makes him wear such painful chains. The gay coquette sports with this circumstance a little, yet acknowledges he is not indifferent, and assigns a very generous motive for keeping him off at present; having held his solicitations at a distance, while his circumstances wore an unfavourable aspect, she justly thinks surrendering, when fortune smiles upon her lover, would seem mercenary.

By what she drops, we perceive, that Sir Charles, the Colonel's father, was attainted, as having joined the rebellion, but lately pardoned by royal clemency; Rosetta cautions Fidelia against the wildness of her brother, which draws from the latter a declaration, that let the danger be what it may,

I

he

he is the man of her choice; here Rofetta archly advifes her friend to marry Sir Charles, who, it appears, has fhewn a particular attachment for her; this, however, Fidelia thinks proceeds merely from his humanity, and is laughed at by the coquette for her grave ideas.

Juft as fhe is uttering thefe words, " What a fweet mama fhall I have when I marry the Colonel," young Belmont and that gentleman enter; the former repeats his fifter's words, which the Colonel calls lucky ones. She aims at giving them a different turn; but Fidelia counteracts the defign, and confirms them, by repeating what fhe has faid concerning Sir Charles; and having her for a mama, &c. thus the grave young lady indulges her mirth, while her gay companion is confiderably puzzled how to turn the tables. Belmont keeps up the fret, and even the Colonel feems to enjoy it; at length, a fervant brings a letter which relieves her; it appears to come from one Mr. Faddle, whom fhe fpeaks of with rapture; the Colonel feems much ftruck, and fhewing his uneafinefs, gives her an opportunity of triumphing in turn, which fhe does by reading the coxcomb's frothy epiftle, and afking her lover's opinion of it.

The firft act concludes with a foliloquy of very boyifh import, and the couplet is remarkably feeble; Sir Roger Belmont and Sir Charles Raymond begin the fecond act; complaints are uttered againft his fon's conduct by the former, which the latter endeavours to mitigate; it appears, that Sir Roger's uneafinefs arifes from being at the expence of keeping Fidelia, without knowing whether fhe has any fortune to repay, in cafe of marriage with his

fon;

Foundling.

fon; Sir Charles hints that a ferious connection is not much to be dreaded, and both the old gentlemen appear concerned for the prefervation of Fidelia's honour, whofe myfterious fituation is fo unaccountable: to clear up the doubts that naturally arife, Sir Charles advifes his friend to bring young Belmont, as foon as poffible, to an explanation of whom the young lady really is; Sir Roger feeing his fon approach, refolves to attack him on this point.

The young gentleman enters, repeating fome rapturous lines; the father, upon his mentioning that times are hard, obferves, that he ought, as her Guardian, to improve Fidelia's money, and that a good round fum may be thrown into the ftocks to advantage; this throws the young gentleman into confufion, and occafions a very laughable fcene of equivocation; after bearing a great deal, the old man feems to conceive matters in the right light, and gives, at his going off, an intimation which ftartles young Belmont; he thinks his fifter concerned in the affair, and refolves, by the aid of Faddle, to out-plot her; fhe joins him, and after playing agreeably through fome fpeeches upon patience, the definition of a coquette, and that of a rake occur, which are both pleafantly given; however, we think, as a brother, young Belmont explains himfelf too far.

Seeing the Colonel, he goes off, and leaves him to a tete-a-tete with the young lady; this ferious fon of Mars addreffing his miftrefs in the folemn way, fhe afks him if he is a rake; and demanding how he would behave to her if really fuch a character, the Colonel collects unufual fpirit; kiffes her hand,

and breaths a glow of rapture, which she receives ironically, and thereby draws him again into the serious mood, nay even works him into a degree of warm resentment, which also she treats lightly.

Just as the Colonel is fooled to the top of his bent, Faddle appears, and immediately feels some effect of the Colonel's choler, while the frighted Fop is in consternation at the rough treatment he has met, young Belmont and Fidelia join the company; this gives him a respite, and by degrees he is led on to a laughable account of himself and his companions; however, the author has certainly given him too much of this whip sillabub stuff. A servant whispering Rosetta that dinner is ready, she asks the gentlemen to partake, but Belmont having engaged Faddle to dine at a tavern, they remain while the other characters go off; when by themselves, Belmont gives Faddle a purse, by way of retaining fee, to assist him in getting Fidelia out of his father's house, as she is there too secure from his licentious designs; he owns himself to be only a fictitious guardian, and partly opens the manner in which he got possession of her; Faddle, who seems, as his employer observes, fit for any rascality, immediately suggests to himself a method of throwing the family into such confusion as may answer the purpose; pregnant with this hopeful design, they hasten off to dinner and conclude the second act.

At the beginning of the third, Rosetta and Fidelia present themselves, conversing upon the same subject that employed their first scene; the former insists that cruelty, or seeming cruelty to gallants, is the best treatment of them; Fidelia differing from

Foundling.

this opinion, a pretty and pertinent song is introduced ; a servant brings a letter, the contents of
which affect Rosetta so strongly, that she desires
him to go for her brother and Faddle to the tavern
where they dined. Fidelia requests to be a par-
taker of her friend's concern, which, after some
hesitation is granted, by shewing the letter.

Upon perusing it, and finding herself not only
represented as an imposter but a prostitute, Fidelia's
feelings rise to a tender pitch, and she confesses herself not what the scroll represents, nor what she has
been thought. Rosetta, though disagreeable doubts
arise, treats her with cordial gentility ; in consequence of the message Faddle comes in, and is taxed with his knowledge of the subject, or the writer of that letter ; his evasions are whimsical ; at
length, half owning the matter, and laying some
imputation on Fidelia, her resentment so far gets
the better of her delicacy, that she strikes him ;
Rosetta promises every kind of protection, if he can
make any discovery in which the honour of her family is concerned ; or wishes him poverty and contempt if he has himself any part in trumping up
so illiberal and base an accusation.

With the true effrontery of a villain, he treats
the matter lightly, and hurries off, leaving it totally
unexplained ; Rosetta, agitated with doubt, presses
Fidelia to open the affair as much as in her power ;
which however she declines, through delicacy of
a promise made to young Belmont that she does not
chuse to break. Coming in at this critical point of
conversation, his sister opens the matter, giving
him the letter ; which he represents as the offspring of
scandal, and threatens to revenge the matter on

Faddle ;

Faddle; as he makes this an excuse for getting off, Fidelia stops him, and mentions that she has owned herself a counterfeit, which he takes umbrage at; however, she begs of him to clear up her character from the vile and groundless imputation of prostitution; this he avoids in a very churlish and ungentlemanlike manner.

After his abrupt exit, Rosetta leaves her abused friend with a declaration, that she expects to have her doubts cleared, before she can afford continuance of that cordial esteem she has hitherto manifested; Fidelia, in a short soliloquy, laments her perplexed situation, and goes off to make way for her treacherous gallant, who meditates on his own rascality, and views it in the proper light, yet seems to think himself possessed of honour above lying, and honesty above deceit; at the same time, that he does not shew a gleam of contrition, but even resolves to pursue his scandalous purpose.

In a short conversation with his vicious agent, that rhapsodical fool hints, by way of getting a fresh bribe, qualms of conscience; after some threats, young Belmont promises another purse, if he will bring him word what passes between Sir Charles Raymond and Fidelia, who are gone into an adjoining chamber; this Faddle cheerfully undertakes, and his employer goes to the King's-arms to wait for his intelligence.

The old Baronet and young lady are next discovered, in conference upon the letter which has occasioned so much uneasiness; Sir Charles blames Fidelia for too much reserve with Rosetta; she apologizes for it by owning her regard for young Belmont, which seals her lips: Faddle, true to his trust,

I   appears

appears liftening, and when the old gentleman
humanley propofes taking Fidelia under his protection, if Rofetta's fufpicions fhould make the Belmont family uneafy to her; he catches the idea of
her being, as he phrafes it, a bit for Sir Charles,
and pofts away to the tavern with what he thinks
a rare bit of news.   Fidelia's tears draw a confola-
tory remark from the Baronet, that he hopes fomething may be foon done for her relief; and fhe
ends the act with a pretty thought relative to patience, if it had not been jingled into rhime.

 The Colonel and Rofetta commence the fourth
act, he renewing his addreffes, and fhe continuing
her coquettifh raillery : the Colonel, in compliance
with his miftrefs's defire, gives the following pretty
and juft defcription of matrimony.   " To fools,
madam, it is the jewel of Æfop's cock ; to the wife a
diamond of price in a fkilful hand to enrich life ; it
is happinefs or mifery, as minds are differently difpofed.   The neceffary requifites are love, good
fenfe, and good breeding ; the firft to unite, the
fecond to advife, and the third to comply ; if you
add to thefe neatnefs and a competency, beauty will
always pleafe, and family cares become agreeable a-
mufements."

 Rofetta animadverts pleafantly upon this picture
of the married life, and ftill dallies with the amorous
Colonel; at laft, fhe changes the difcourfe to Fidelia, of whom fhe fpeaks in a friendly manner ; and
tells her gallant, that if he hopes to make love fuccefsfully, it muft be by endeavouring to clear up
the perplexity of her fair friend, then propofes to
vifit her with him.

Young

Young Belmont and Faddle prefent themfelves, converfing upon the fuppofed defign of Sir Charles, in offering Fidelia apartments, which the latter declares to be with a vicious intention. Seeing the old baronet approach, young Belmont retires, and leaves his worthy affiftant to banter him ; for which purpofe he addreffes Sir Charles with all the familiarity of an unblufhing coxcomb, offers his fervice, but fneeringly obferves, that old poachers hunt fure; with other impertinent remarks, which the baronet feems not to underftand, till he draws Faddle into a repetition of his own words, concerning the apartments, and Fidelia's acknowledgment for the propofed favour. Roufed by his infolent ribaldry and fcandalous infinuation, Sir Charles fhuts the door ; this alarms the conficious fcoundrel, who, after two or three hearty fhakes by the collar, firft confeffes that he did liften, and next acknowledges his having forged, with young Belmont's connivance, the anonymous letter which has caufed fo much pain and confufion. Having thus made the difcovery he wanted, Sir Charles difmiffes the parafite, with a moft excellent lecture ; fo defcriptive of fuch reptiles, and fo pregnant with inftructive truth, that we beg leave to offer it our readers.

" Thy life is a difgrace to humanity ; a foolifh prodigality makes thee needy ; need makes thee vicious, and both make thee contemptible ; thy wit is proftituted to flander and buffoonery ; and thy judgment, if thou haft any, to meannefs and villainy. Thy betters, who laugh with thee, laugh at thee ; and who are they ? the fools of quality at court, and thofe who ape them in the city ; the varieties of thy life, are pitiful rewards and painful abufes ; for

the

Foundling.

the same trick that gets thee a guinea to-day, shall get thee beaten out of doors to-morrow ; those who caress thee are enemies to themselves, and when they know it will be enemies to thee ; in thy distresses they'll desert thee, and leave thee at last to sink in thy poverty, unregarded and unpitied ; if thou canst be wise, think of me, and be honest."

Faddle, thus severely catechised, feels himself in a fresh dilemma, upon the approach of young Belmont ; however, having cleared himself of one scrape by telling of truth, he determines to escape another, by means of lying heartily. To this end he tells young Belmont, that Sir Charles has made him a confidante, but the assertion is deemed apocryphal. Seeing Sir Charles returning he decamps, prudently resolving never to set his foot in the house again.

The baronet comes on with a servant, who has delivered him a letter, purporting, that if the interest of his family be dear to him, it is essentially necessary that he should attend the bearer of the letter ; this extraordinary summons startles him, but however important, he says there is another concern that must precede it. Here young Belmont asking what news, Sir Charles attacks him in an emphatic strain of spirited reproach, for his design upon Fidelia, which he only answers by recrimination ; and the baronet's noble, disinterested sentiments, place Belmont's equivocation and false fire in a contemptible light ; even his challenge is foiled with disgrace, by the old gentleman's unanswerable method of treating it. Being told of Faddle's discovery, he takes shame to himself with a tolerable grace, and appears ready to make any reparation. Sir Charles desires

him

him to undeceive his fifter, and then goes to the
bearer of the letter. When alone, Belmont takes a
juft view of his proceedings, which he finds as weak
as they have been defpicable ; and feels perplexity
rife fo faft, that he refolves to fly upon the wings of
penitence to injured Fidelia, and feek from her advice
that peace of mind he cannot ftrike out for himfelf.

At the beginning of the fifth act, Sir Roger Belmont enters, confiderably fluttered with a letter he
has received ; which letter, from a pretended guardian of Fidelia's, threatning a law-fuit for ftealing
her, he fhews to Sir Charles in great anxiety, and determines that fhe fhall be packed off immediately ;
but this hafty refolution his friend diffuades him
from, and they retire to confult upon the matter.

Young Belmont, in the next fcene, receives fome
very juft and keen reproaches from Fidelia, for the
bafe treatment fhe has received from him ; he pleads
hard to obtain forgivenefs, yet, though a violence
to her love, which fhe candidly acknowledges, fhe
holds him at a diftance. Thus preffed in his feelings, he offers marriage, but this alfo, on a generous
principle, fhe declines. Rofetta here joins them,
full of the intelligence that Fidelia has been ftolen
by her brother, and that her guardian is at hand to
demand fatisfaction. This, young Belmont receives
as a pleafing piece of information ; he is going to
explain the ftory of Fidelia, when Sir Roger, Sir
Charles, the Colonel, and Villiard enter, the latter
of whom is informed, that if he claims the lady, and
makes good his claim, fhe fhall be reftored without
any hefitation.

He afferts her to be his ward, and that fhe was
ftolen by violence from him by Belmont. His
proofs

proofs being demanded, he evades the point, and
says, they shall be produced in a court of law. Fidelia is then questioned, who, after his accusations
have been heard, draws a pathetic picture of Villiard's brutal attempt, which Mr. Belmont, by mere
accident, saved her from.

The circumstance of having relieved distressed
innocence, gives Sir Roger a generous feeling of
joy for his son's humane, gallant interposition. Villiard, finding no probability of success by staying,
goes off, with warm threats. Rosetta asking who
the anonymous scroll, written by Faddle, came from,
her brother frankly owns he had a hand in it ; and,
by way of reparation, offers to take the young lady
for life : here Sir Roger's love of money cuts off
his consent. This draws a most generous proposal
from Colonel Raymond, which is to take Rosetta
without a fortune, so her's may be bestowed on Fidelia. While matters remain dubious, and a good
deal of delicacy is manifested on all sides, Sir Charles
steps in, and declares, that he will make Fidelia e-
qual to Sir Roger's utmost wish, in point of property ; and, in a few lines after, with a melting flow
of paternal tenderness, declares her to be his daughter. The general astonishment arising from this
unexpected discovery, he removes by the following
explanation : That at the time of his banishment,
he left this daughter, an infant, to the care of a woman, who, to secure some jewels, made the child
believe she was a Foundling, and changed her name
of Harriet to Fidelia, that at twelve years old she
sold her to Villiard ; that being seized with sudden
illness, and having heard of Sir Charles's return, she
had sent for him, and from apprehensions of death,

confeſſed tne whole ; thereby proving the idendity
of a child, which, during his exile, ſhe ſent him
word was dead. Matters brought to this agreeable
criſis, all parties are made happy ; the two young
couple, by interchange of hands, and the old baro-
nets, by ſeeing their children united according to
mutual inclinations.

Young Belmont concludes the play with a very
apt deduction from his own miſconduct, and a ſenſible remark---would it had not been made in rhime--
that libertiniſm preys upon that beautiful, weak
part of the creation, which it is man's natural province to defend.

The piece now conſidered, has proved a very a-
greeable ſubject for criticiſm, having much to praiſe,
and little to cenſure ; for however perſons who feel,
and ſhrink at, the touch of our rod, may think we
tend to ſeverity, it is an undoubted fact, that we are
infinitely better pleaſed to point out merit than deficiencies, in both writing and performance.

It has been ſaid that this play was evidently borrowed from the Conscious Lovers, but we can
perceive no ſtriking ſimilitude to authoriſe that opinion ; the diſcovery of a daughter in each, is not
ſufficient to ſupport the remark ; there is indeed
ſome likeneſs between Fidelia and Indiana, but all
the other characters differ eſſentially.

In the Foundling, critical unities are well pre-
ſerved, and the plot lays proper hold of ſuſpence
and attention ; there are no make-ſhift ſcenes, nor
any that are tedious ; ſeveral excellent.

Sir Roger Belmont has nothing peculiar to mark
him, and may be called a good kind of an old fellow ; only a little tainted with the love of money.

If

Foundling.

If the author had done half as much in writing the part, as Mr. YATES did in acting it, Sir Roger would have been as conspicuous as any man in the piece. Mr. LOVE, to those who have not seen the forementioned gentleman, may pass very well.

Sir Charles Raymond is an object of great esteem, his tender concern for Fidelia, before he knows any more of her than that she is young, beautiful and in dangerous hands, recommends him much ; the manner of chastising both Faddle and Belmont, on her account, does equal honour to his justice, his humanity, his spirit, and his good sense. Tho' we never admired Mr. BARRY in prose dialogue, yet it would be very injurious not to allow, that where the part materially called upon him, he powerfully answered. In the fourth act, he supported the character with emphatic dignity ; in the last, with melting tenderness ; we dont recollect any body who could have been better. Mr. BERRY was heavy, ungraceful, and out of character : Mr. BANNISTER has no expression of soft feelings, but speaks the four first acts very well, and figures the part agreeably. Mr. POWELL had requisites to render Sir Charles Raymond very pleasing ; and Mr. REDDISH would do him more justice than any other part in the play.

Young Belmont is very censurable as a man ; he does the meanest things, even under self-conviction, with no other plea of excuse than the pitiful one, that his appetites drive him on ; had he rushed upon vice, without giving himself time to think, he would have been more bearable ; a speculative libertine is the most dangerous, and most incurable. His rescuing Fidelia must be considered as an action

F f 2

of

of spirit, and yet by his behaviour afterwards, it is little more than a lion saving a lamb from the wolf, that he may devour it himself.   As a character for action, the author most undoubtedly meant him capital; yet, excepting the first scene, and that with his father, which we allow truly pleasant ; and that with Sir Charles, where he is little better than a foil to the baronet, he has nothing to say worth notice ; and then he is placed in such a disgraceful light, that we cannot think him very desirable for an actor of merit ; however, Mr. GARRICK's peculiar qualifications, and happy use of them, added amazing spirit to the piece ; giving young Belmont much more consequence than can well be imagined.

Mr. LEE is very pleasing and characteristic in this part, though rendered worse within some late years by studied improvements, than he was when he took less pains.   Mr. Ross, and this gentleman, are a striking contraste ; the former, by negligence, impoverishes good natural talents, and the latter, by a laborious, theatrical mechanism, impairs very agreeable qualifications.   Mr. REDDISH appears to very great disadvantage in this part, he has nothing of the requisite volubility ; Mr. KING should certainly do it, if public satisfaction is in any shape worthy managerical consideration ; a point we have much reason to doubt of late.

Colonel Raymond is a butt of ridicule, a mere cypher in action ; Mr. HAVARD did him originally, as well as ever he has been done since, and there is nothing in him beyond the power of Mr. PACKER.

Faddle is a thorough-paced reptile, ready to transact any mean business for a bribe ; and, under the appearance of rhapsodical foppery, a designing knave.

knave. Several paſſages of this part were originally repulſed, and we think with great juſtice, for a
great deal of what he ſays in his firſt ſcene is frothy,
ſuperfluous and low; we think his getting off without any other chaſtiſement than what Sir Charles
gives him, is rather ſacrificing poetical juſtice.

Mr. MACKLIN, who never had, in voice, figure,
or features, much capability for the fop caſt, yet
ſtruck out ſome things in Faddle, which we have
not ſeen any body equal; particularly marking the
obſequious knave all through. After allowing thus
much, we are willing to pronounce Mr. DODD better
than any other performer we remember.

Roſetta is a moſt agreeable coquette, ſenſible, and
full of vivacity; tinctured with harmleſs inconſtan-
cy and pardonable pride; her notions are conſonant
to gay life, florid youth, and a flighty imagination; if ſhe does not manifeſt abſolute wit, ſhe yet
may be allowed a brilliance of idea, and ſprightlineſs
of expreſſion. The part was undoubtedly conceived
for Mrs. WOFFINGTON, and ſhe did it particular
juſtice; nor ſhould we wonder, ſince the elegance,
the notions of love, and the vanity of admiration
from gallants, which are united in Roſetta, were
natural to that lady; ſo that here ſhe had the advantage of looking, walking, and ſpeaking her own
character. Notwithſtanding our general veneration
for Mrs. PRITCHARD, we cannot place her upon a
level with the *je ne ſe quey* of Mrs. WOFFINGTON, in
this part. Miſs POPE falls inconceivably below
both. Where, oh drowſy or partial managers! is
Mrs. ABINGTON, who has ſo much of the pleaſing
and elegant original about her.

Fidelia's circumſtances place her in a very particular degree of eſtimation; her principles are unexceptionable, and her conduct prudent; we pity her critical ſituation, and rejoice at the diſcovery which eſtabliſhes her happineſs. That delicate ſoftneſs and pathos which diſtinguiſh this character, ſat with much eaſe upon Mrs. CIBBER; at preſent, Mrs. BADDELEY ſupports it with very agreeable capability, and is by far the moſt adequate performer in the piece.

If this play muſt be compared with the CONSCIOUS LOVERS, we readily admit it to the ſecond place; but take it in a ſeparate view, and it deſerves conſiderable praiſe. It ſpeaks ſo feelingly to our paſſions, ſo chaſtely to our ideas, and ſo inſtructively to our ſenſe, that we wiſh it often well performed on the ſtage, and a cordial reception in the cloſet.

THE

The EARL of ESSEX.

A TRAGEDY, by Mr. JONES.

So interesting has the story of Essex been considered, at least so advantageous a light has BANKS, who first wrote upon the subject, placed it in, that there have been no less than three plays struck out upon his plan; we have chosen that by Mr. JONES, as being in possession of the stage, and, in many respects, the best composition; though produced by a man whose whole dependance was on natural genius, of which he gave several strong proofs, and might have furnished more, had his conduct any way coincided with his talents; but like many other unhappy sons of the muse, his life was a disgrace to his writings, and though his capacity gained him many friends, the turbulence and ingratitude of his temper, prevented him from ever keeping one; but his work being more properly the object of our concern, we'll proceed to that, without further comment on its imprudent author.

Burleigh, the leading and very able minister of Eliza's reign, begins this piece with acquainting Raleigh that a bill to clip the wings of Essex's ambition has passed; he asks for coroborating proofs, which Sir Walter says are arrived; such as his making a private treaty with Tyrone, and the Scots King, calculated to ruin Burleigh in his Mistress's opinion.

Wary

Wary Cecil defires that this pleafing piece of intelligence may be kept, like a battery concealed, to play upon the enemy by furprife ; a meffenger announcing the approach of Lady Nottingham, Burleigh confiders what her bufinefs may be, as knowing her to have a partial regard for Effex ; he prepares againft any artifice fhe may ufe in that peer's favour, and difpatches Raleigh to watch the motions of Southampton and his friends, obferving, that as a leader of faction, he muft be taken care of. After fome compliments from Nottingham, on his great abilities as a ftatefman, Cecil is acquainted by her that fhe has renounced Effex ; fhe acknowledges having heretofore joined with him in his defigns againft the minifter, but now determines to counteract thofe defigns, which a blind paffion for Effex made her promote ; as her refentment arifes from a flight thrown on her charms, Burleigh with great addrefs improves her indignation, by mentioning the preference given to Rutland, even fo far as their being united by a fecret marriage before the Earl's fetting off for Ireland.

This intelligence, like oil on flames, throws the Countefs's temper into a blaze, and fhe execrates them in terms which we think too grofs for her rank, though moved by jealoufy. Upon Burleigh's propofing to work him out of royal favour, the only bar to his ruin, fhe gladly accepts the office of imbittering his royal miftrefs againft him, and goes off fully determined to try every method for effecting, not only his fall but death. Here Raleigh enters, and fpeaks of Southampton's approach.

That

Earl of Essex.

That Earl, in the full glow of friendly resentment, accuses Burleigh of putting in practice iniquitous measures, for the destruction of a worthy
man and a good subject; the politician stands his
warm reproaches with very prudent coolness, and
asserts his own good intentions with confidence;
throwing out an insinuation that too violent an attachment to Essex's cause may involve the hardy
friend in his fall. This oblique threat Southampton treats with contempt, and mentions how inef-
fectually malice must labour to tear the wreaths
of honour from Essex's brow; this brings the
conference to an end, and Cecil goes off observing, that the queen shall judge of their debate;
Southampton, after a warm effusion of friendship, in soliloquy, follows him to the royal presence.

Queen Elizabeth, seated on her throne, expresses
displeasure at the bill of impeachment passed against
Essex, without her privity or consent; upon this
point she speaks warmly to Cecil, charging him
with it; this he evades, but confesses a concur-
rence of opinion with parliament. While her
Majesty is on the fret, Southampton enters, to
whom she shews what she calls the base portrait of
Essex; this gives him a fair opening for the defence of his friend, which he undertakes, by painting in nervous terms his innocence and loyalty.
After a general reproof concerning the bill, the
Queen dismisses all but Burleigh, to whom she
gives an order for suppressing it: he begs the
Queen to consider how unpopular such a step
would be, and mentions proofs; however, she
will hear nothing that way, and with an amiable

degree of generous juſtice, declares accuſation muſt ceaſe, till he can make a perſonal defence. After Burleigh goes off, Elizabeth expreſſes her good opinion of Eſſex, though ſhe knows his weakneſs : a hint is dropped of the place he has in her heart ; ſhe ſeems to view Burleigh in the right light, and concludes the firſt act, with determining to ſhield Eſſex againſt his fraudful machinations.

Cecil, at the beginning of the ſecond act, confeſſes to Raleigh, that the unexpected return of Eſſex rather confuſes him ; however, he ſends for Nottingham, and determines to alarm the Queen as much as poſſible ; finding affairs, brought to this critical ſituation, that Eſſex or he muſt be ſacrificed. The queen upon her entrance, expreſſes much ſurpriſe, that her favourite ſhould return from his command in Ireland without leave ; finding her temper warmed, and therefore in ſome meaſure fitted to receive an unfavourable impreſſion of Eſſex, Burleigh mentions the ſecret treaty with Tyrone and the Scots King, tending, through the aſſiſtance of Eſſex and his friends, to attack even her native Iſle ; at firſt, ſhe doubts this ſtrange aſſertion, but upon conſidering ſo great a breach of duty in her general, as to leave his command without any authority but his own will ; ſhe collects all the dignity of ſtation, and orders the culprit into her preſence.

After an introductory addreſs of Southampton's, the Earl of Eſſex appears, and, with a becoming degree of humiliation, addreſſes his ſovereign, and apologizes for his conduct, by alledging, that he thought it proper, in perſon, to oppoſe ſcandal and the undermining efforts of envy ; the Queen

does

Earl of Essex.

does not seem to confider this exculpation as he could wish, and justly obferves, that the glow of language is, in his cafe, but of little ufe; that having appealed from her to the laws, he muft abide by the laws.

After Elizabeth and her courtiers are retired, Effex ruminates, in foliloquy, upon the ill return his martial dangers and fatigues meets; he determines to ftand the fhock of adverfity with refolution, feeming to think his ruin inevitable. Southampton returns, and tells his friend, that the Queen's difpleafure, cherifhed by Lord Burleigh, increafes; the ficklenefs of courts Effex feems to defpife, and defires, as a more material concern than his political affairs, to be led where he may fee his mourning lady; this he is warned againft, as a dangerous ftep, it being neceffary that their marriage at this particular juncture, fhould be concealed. Burleigh, by the Queen's command, demands Effex's ftaff of office; this inflames him to utter harfh terms againft his undermining foe, and he declares, that having from her own hand received it, to her alone he will refign it. Southampton goes once again upon the bufinefs of interceffion to foften the Queen, and leaves his friend ftill further to confider the inftability of human greatnefs; this foliloquy has confiderable merit, the imagery is agreeable and ftriking, without any ftrain of conception.

Rutland, with all the joy and tendernefs of an affectionate wife, here flies into her hufband's arms, who, for a moment, forgets his fallen ftate; and, when he recollects it, refolves to fly from courtly ingratitude to the fweets of retirement, with his be-

loved

loved object. Rutland obferving the danger they
ftand in of a difcovery, being in one of the Queen's
apartments, Effex leads her off, with the pleafing idea
of calm content, when feparated from the houfe of
greatnefs, where honefty and plain dealing are for-
bidden fhelter.

At the beginning of the third act, Nottingham
meets Burleigh, and enquires what occurred, after
the Earl's audience of the Queen: this Burleigh
relates, fignifying, that her majefty was highly difpleafed at his refufal to return the ftaff of office, in
compliance with her pofitive mandate; that her paffion went fo far as to threaten him with death; then
foftened into a recollection of his many fhining qualities, and turned reproach on Cecil, for driving him,
as fhe fuppofed, to fuch extremes; however, that
after many changes for and againft, fhe had ordered
Effex to the Tower; but, in conclufion, commanded him to be brought into her prefence. A meffage
coming to Nottingham from the Queen, defiring
her attendance in the royal clofet, Burleigh fuggefts,
that it is to confult her concerning Effex, and urges
her to make the moft of fo favourable an opportunity, of ftirring majefty to more effential refentment.

The Queen, difcovered in foliloquy, feems deeply concerned for Effex's weaknefs of temper; which,
with the artifice of his foes, places him in fuch a perilous, and pitiable fituation; her pride appears
hurt at his refiftance, but love foftens that pride into compaffion. Here Nottingham, pregnant with
all the fatal malevolence of jealoufy, approaches
Elizabeth, who tells her of Effex's contemptuous
behaviour; at which, to cover her purpofe the better, fhe feems furprized; but, as the conference
proceeds,

proceeds, ftirs up the flame againft him fo far, that the Queen perceives a defign of urging feverity, which fhe checks, and defires Nottingham to fend Rutland; then ruminates on the painful ftate of folitary grandeur, which, wanting the free, comfortable communication of focial equality, is forced to bear its griefs and anxieties alone.

When Rutland appears, Elizabeth afks her opinion and counfel, refpecting Effex: the Countefs afferts, that his faults are created by envy, that they have no real exiftence; and fpeaks of Effex in fuch terms, that the Queen, with eagle-eyed jealoufy, which however fhe conceals for fome time, perceives her partial regard for the Earl: at length, Rutland's zeal goes fo far, that her royal miftrefs difmiffes her the prefence.

Effex, conducted by Burleigh and others, prefents himfelf, while the Queen is agitated: fhe demands why he refufed to yield his ftaff; to this he replies, that it was his wifh to lay his honours at the feet of her who had conferred them: on being charged with a felf-fufficiency of fpeech, he pays himfelf fome compliments, which no degree of provocation would draw from a man of real fenfe. At the charge of making a fhameful compromife with rebels, Effex feems to think his life levelled at; however, as an exculpation, he afferts having been invefted with difcretionary power, and obferves, that the circumftance of affairs obliged him to ufe that power as he had done. This defence he makes in terms that we think highly provocative, and therefore applaud the Queen's refentment, till fhe degrades her rank and fex, by ftriking him. This, we naturally fuppofe, roufes his impetuous temper ftill more; however,

his

his fury vents itſelf only againſt the court tools, whom he violently threatens. After the Queen's departure, he gives an enlarged ſcope to rage ; and, notwithſtanding Southampton's palliative advice, vehemently, at all hazards, determines upon revenge.

At the beginning of the fourth act, we find, by Elizabeth's enquiry and Nottingham's anſwer, that Eſſex has been guilty of ſome outrage againſt the peace and dignity of government ; that force has obliged him to an eſcape, and that he is fled to a place near the Thames, where reſiſtance on his part is reſolved. This behaviour, ſo unpardonable in its nature, wounds the Queen's regard for him deeply, and ſhe expreſſes her concern pathetically, but recollecting her ſtation, calls up becoming ſpirit.

Burleigh acquaints the Queen that Eſſex, Southampton, and all their factious adherents are ſecured; that their deſign, could they have gained over the citizens to aſſiſt them, was no leſs than attacking her royal perſon ; that all the characters of leſſer note concerned in this traiterous attempt have been ſecured, but that the two Earls, and others of diſtinguiſhed rank, are left to her majeſty's diſpoſal : this account draws from Elizabeth ſome pertinent and affecting remarks on the ingratitude of ſubjects, ready to riſe againſt a monarch, who has always ſtudied their advantage, collectively and individually.

She orders Eſſex to a private audience, and when he appears, addreſſes herſelf to him in very ſtinging terms, which he receives with all the anguiſh of remorſe and ſelf-conviction ; with this ſhe ſeems touched,

Earl of Essex.

touched, and coolly expostulates with him on the
ungrateful return he has made her bounty, so peculiarly manifested to him ; then observes with cordial concern, that she fears the public voice will
force him to the peril of his life ; but to palliate the
pain of his suspence declares, that she, as an individual, is willing to forgive his errors freely and
fully. The apology he makes for his conduct is
plausible, but no way conclusive; however it
touches Elizabeth's heart, already so prejudiced in
his favour, and she condoles with him most humanely: at length, being wrought up to a particular
pitch of tenderness, she gives him a ring, with her
royal promise, that if public justice should sentence his life, upon returning that token of her
favour, he may be sure of finding clemency.

Thus secured from public and private foes,
Essex retires, with expressions of fervent gratitude ;
after she delivers him to custody, a foreboding sits
heavy on her heart, but she determines to stand
between him and danger, however popular clamour
may censure her protection.

Rutland, naturally afflicted, and urged on by
her husband's situation, not knowing the degree of
favour in which he stands, notwithstanding his misconduct, pleads to the Queen for his life and unhappily lets fall that he is her husband. This unexpected intelligence fixes a dagger in Elizabeth's
heart ; she orders the Countess, whose grief borders on distraction, to be taken from her presence,
and after that order is fulfilled, concludes the
fourth act, with painting in strong, and expressive
colours, the melancholly state of her own mind ;

we

we look upon her at this period as an object of great pity, agitated between public duty, private affection, and confirmed jealousy.

Raleigh, with the lieutenant of the tower, begin the fifth act, and we are informed, that the two Earls, after a very candid trial by the peers, have been condemned; Nottingham enters, and demands admittance to Essex, which is granted; this revengeful lady comes with design to effect a confummation of vengance, therefore wears the semblance of friendship, and pretends that the Queen had sent her to know if the Earl has no plea to avert his sentence.

Essex, not suspecting any sinister design, after some thankful compliments for the lady's humane interposition, gives her the important pledge; and with it a generous follicitation for his friends life, without any mention of his own: poffessed of this mark of royal regard, the Countess hurries off, exulting in the prospect of accomplishing her vindictive purpose; the Queen impatient for Nottingham's return, appears next; upon seeing her messenger, she afks what Essex has said, Nottingham, with singular art, works her up gradually, and seems to lament the Earl's sullen, unrelenting obstinacy; and says that even with death in view, he disdained making any conceffion to injured majesty. The Queen, at length, enquires particularly if he made any mention of a ring, which is denied; this circumstance is so striking, that Nottingham seldom fails of getting very rough language from one or more of an audience.

After

After every aggravation against the man she wishes to save, Elizabeth gratifies Nottingham with an order that he may be led to the block; nay, her resentment is wrought up to such a pitch, that she even determines upon going to the Tower, that his fate may be imbittered by her presence.

Essex and Southampton, habited for the scaffold, next appear; the former, giving his friend hopes of life, the latter, with philosophic resolution, casting aside such flattering ideas. Some of the lines he speaks, we think worthy quotation.

> Life! what is life? a shadow,
> Its date is but th' immediate breath we draw,
> Nor have we surety for a second gale;
> Ten thousand accidents in ambush lie,
> For th' embodied dream————
> A frail and fickle tenement it is,
> Which like the brittle glass that measures time,
> Is often broke ere half its sands are run.

The whole of this scene shews warm friendship in one, noble resolution in the other. When the Lieutenant of the Tower comes on to signify that a warrant is arrived for both Earls to suffer, Essex emphatically laments the fate of his friend, and Southampton meets it with a determined, vigorous resolution; but when unexpectedly a pardon comes to the last mentioned nobleman, he melts into softness at the fate of his friend Essex, and parts from him in terms of noble, unshakeable friendship.

After this separation, Rutland comes to give her husband yet a severer trial of affliction; she clings about his heart, and melts him almost to a disgraceful degree of tenderness: at last, after many expreſſions of mutual endearment, the Lieutenant ſignifies, that time calls ſo preſſingly, he muſt require the Earl's departure ; this throws both Eſſex and Rutland into an exceſs of tenderneſs, which occaſions very ſtrong feelings amongſt an audience. At length they are ſeparated, he goes to his fate, and ſhe is left diſtractedly to lament it.

Here the Queen enters, we think much too ſoon ; for, according to her forbiddance of the execution immediately, it is improbable, nay impoſſible, the place conſidered, that his head could be taken off before her mercy is known ; however, ſo the plot takes its courſe, and Rutland, being diſappointed of a hope ſhe had conceived from the Queen's clemency, falls into a ſtate of abſolute madneſs, in which Elizabeth humanely offers to comfort her. Burleigh, who brings tidings of the execution, relates Nottingham's treachery, which ſtrikes the Queen with freſh concern, as conſidering that not only her regard for the man is violated, but even her fame ſtigmatized ; her concluſive lines have a good moral tendency, had it not been enervated with unnatural and unneceſſary rhime.

This tragedy, being founded on hiſtorical fact, and that domeſtic alſo, has particular influence upon a Britiſh audience ; the plot is regular, the ſcenes well ranged, and the characters naturally drawn ; the language is chaſte, the verſification harmonious and expreſſive ; and the ſentiments inſtructive ; it is leſs bombaſtic, and more natural than Banks's ; not ſo nervous or ſentimental as Brooks's play, on the ſame ſubject, but more conſonant to general apprehenſion and taſte ; it moſt certainly does not deſerve the ſtile of a capital performance, but, as

we

Earl of Essex.

we think, may very properly stand the test of perusal and performance.

In the EARL of ESSEX, there are but few characters, consequently most of them have some degree of importance. We find the hero brave, loyal, loving and friendly ; strongly tinctured with
pride and violence of temper ; too open and bold
in speech for the ambiguity and finesse of court
sophistry.

Mr. BARRY had every requisite to render this
character agreeable ; a fine figure to apologize for
all the ladies, even majesty itself to be in love with
him ; a most harmonious utterance for the amorous
passages, fine breaks for the grief, and natural spirit
for the rage ; he was, through the whole, every
thing a critical spectator could wish, and must have
pleased the most unfeeling. Mr. Ross, though
greatly inferior to the original, has considerable merit in the part, and supports it much better than
most capital characters are now supported.

Southampton appears only in the light of a generous friend, warm and steady in his attachment :
Mr. SMITH gave us much pleasure in personating of
him, and we may venture to say it sat easier on him
than any other tragic character he ever played ; why
then give it to Mr. BENSLEY, who looks and plays
it more in the stile of Bajazet, than that of an accomplished nobleman ? Mr. REDDISH fills our idea
best. Burleigh, as presented on the stage, is cool,
politic and resolute ; an excellent judge of character, and equal to any task of state. In just veneration
of that great statesman's name, we could wish he
had not been drawn on the stage so unfavourably ;
for his plotting against Essex, merely as a check to

his

his ambition, and a rival in the Queen's favour, is a heavy imputation on Cecil's fame.

Mr. Sparks reprefented him with becoming dignity, and gained that attention we have never perceived any other performer obtain, or in the leaft deferve. Mr. Gibson is horrid to a degree of pain ; he does not lay the leaden mace of flumber on his audience, but buffets their ears with founds more diffonant than the hum-ftrum of a hurdy-gurdy. Mr. Gardner, who played the part in Brooks's Essex at the Haymarket with merit, fhould do this part at Covent Garden.

Queen Elizabeth is a charaĉter of importance, though we think underwritten. She has fome weaknefs as a woman, none as a monarch ; however female inclinations arife, royalty maintains preeminence, and fhe will be Queen even over the man fhe loves. Mrs. Hamilton, by an abundance of teaching, for fhe could never get out of leading-ftrings, made a very refpeĉtable figure in the charaĉter, and did the author more juftice than could be expeĉted from her, efpecially in the tragic ftile ; her perfon, deportment and aĉtion, were well adapted. Notwithftanding we have faid thus much in favour of the original, our regard for merit obliges us to fay, that no part was ever fpoke or felt more properly, than Queen Elizabeth was by Mifs Ibbot, who played it as we remember one night, and no more, at Covent Garden, becaufe Mr. Rich, who delighted in oppofing the opinion of the public, did not concur in the approbation fhe received. Even at this diftance of time, we remember to have been peculiarly ftruck with her expreffion in that fcene where fhe gives Effex the ring as a pledge of fafety

from.

Earl of Essex.

from his foes; the whole interview was interesting, but these lines she uttered inimitably; by reading the passage we can scarce conceive the additional force she gave it.

> With prudence make your best defence; but should
> Severity her iron jurisdiction
> Extend too far, and give thee up condemned
> To angry laws, thy Queen will not forget thee.

Mrs. WARD, who once had considerable merit, is now so mutilated by time, that she has hardly a trace of her former self; therefore, we need not be surprized that she makes such a wretched figure in the Queen, and more especially as the part never came within her compass; but however we may pity her, as being commanded upon such a forlorn hope, what apology can we make for the managers, indeed, what can they say for themselves, to obtrude performance in a capital light, so very inadequate and disgraceful to a London theatre. Mrs. HOPKINS does not trespass upon the bounds of decency, but merits no other applause than silent sufferance.

Rutland is so circumstanced as to claim our concern; her anxious love, her perplexed state, and her distracted grief for the loss of her husband, all concur to touch the melting heart; the character took happy possession of Mrs. CIBBER, and she of the audience. Her merit never shone more conspicuously than in the last act of this play, when abounding sighs and tears gave her just tribute of the truest applause. Mrs. BARRY, though without power to equal this great original, gives very irresistible sensation in this part. Miss MILLER, who rubbed through it lately at Covent Garden, was shamefully imperfect

imperfect ; shamefully we say, because no doubt
she had due time for preparation. It is the duty of
those who have the greatest abilities to know the
author, how much more incumbent upon them who
possess such slender talents as this lady, of whose
executive powers we will venture to say, that had
she been minutely acquainted with every syllable of
Rutland, it is not in her power to do one tenth of
the part justice.

Nottingham is a very disagreeable, yet we believe
a natural character, for where jealousy taints the
mind of either sex, all moral and social concerns are
rooted up. She requires a good actress, and is a
painful task for such a one, being all up hill performance : Mrs. VINCENT was very improperly
chosen for the original, seventeen years ago, and we
suppose is to retain it for life ; this is rather more
absurd than Mr. RYAN's doing the part of Marcus
in CATO, when he was seventy, because he had done
it when he was five and twenty---For heaven's sake,
Mr. COLMAN, without diminishing a worthy woman's salary, have some pity upon criticism, dont
compel it to sting through public misapplication,
so excellent a private character. Where is Mrs.
MATTOCKS ? She sometimes plays tragedy, though
not her fort, and must, at least in stage appearance,
give tolerable grace to what Burleigh hints of
charms. Mrs. STEPHENS, though her powers were
not equal to the part, yet was capable of giving
much satisfaction in this Countess.

At the Haymarket, last summer, the ESSEX of
BROOKES was exhibited ; though not strictly within our plan, being a different piece, perhaps our readers may not be displeased with some strictures on

the

the performance. Mr. SHERIDAN was bombaftic
in the paffages of paffion, and difcordant in the tender ones; hurtful through extravagance of action
to eyes, and painful through falfe modulation of
vile tones to ears. Mr. J. AICKIN's Southampton
was modeft, fenfible, feeling, and within the lines
of nature, but rather faint for a large audience: if
this gentleman could rouze up a little more expreffion, there is a degree of propriety about him
which few reach; why he is placed in fuch an obfcure, difadvantageous light at Drury Lane, none
but thofe who fteer that ftate can poffibly fay.
There are feveral parts which Mr. PACKER is injudicioufly, or partially packed on for, which would
fit much eafier upon him. Mr. GARDNER, whom
we have already mentioned as fit to take Mr. GIB-
SON's poft, fhewed, in his playing of Burleigh, capability for fupporting a fimilar caft.

Mrs. BURTON! Mrs. PHILLIPPINA BURTON!
was the moft mouthing, ftrutting, ftaring, Wapping
landlady reprefentative of poor Elizabeth, that ever
tortured the two delicate fenfes of fight and hearing. It is impoffible to fay, amidft fuch a compli-
cation of wretchednefs, whether her ungracious
countenance, her lumbering figure, aukward action,
wild modulation, or barbarous dialect, gave moft
difguft; let us advife this poetical adventurer to
change her pen and tragedy fceptre for the rolling-
pin or mop, and then fhe may become a ufeful member of fociety.

Mifs HAYWARD, for fo inexperienced a performer, fhewed great merit in Rutland; her laft act was
truly affecting; a few vulgarifms, and fome Shere-
donian oddities of expreffion, clouded her abilities;

but

but we think ſhe has the materials about her, with proper aſſiſtance and diligence, to make in a ſeaſon or two the third tragic actreſs in our London theatres; we wiſh the managers impartiality to make the beſt uſe of her capacity, and her the happy prudence to make the beſt uſe of herſelf. Mrs. JEFFERIES is conſiderably the beſt Nottingham we have ſeen. It is remarkable, that the two principal parts in this exhibition, Eſſex and Elizabeth, were notoriouſly the worſt.

From this tragedy ariſes the uſeful obſervation of that danger and mutability which attends court favour. In a compariſon of BANKS's, JONES's, and BROOKES's, the former muſt be pronounced replete with offenſive bombaſt, forced figures, unnatural ideas, and pitiful expreſſion; the ſecond, regular, chaſte and affecting; the third, leſs turgid than BANKS, more laboured than JONES; nervous, but ſtiff; wherefore, we recommend that play which has paſſed review both for action and peruſal.

THE

The PLAIN DEALER.

A COMEDY, altered from WYCHERLY:

By Mr. BICKERSTAFF.

THE comedies of CHARLES the SECOND's time were animated with wit, humour and a character ftrongly marked; but had in general a vicious tendency; our public tafte being moralized; though private vices are as enormous as ever, the dramatifts of our days make an adherence to decency apologize for all the other effentials.

To refcue from oblivion the fterling ore of antiquity; to purge it of grofs alloy is an undertaking worthy of praife; it is like recovering a picture highly finifhed from obfcuring filth; when this is done, without impairing the mafter's beauties, it fhews judgment, and if any retouching is neceffary, to blend the addition with an able hand manifefts genius; Mr. BICKERSTAFF found the Plain Dealer a good, but an immoral play; this may feem a folecifm in expreffion, but we mean good as to the leading dramatic qualifications; what he has done by refitting it for public infpection we are now to examine, after premifing that he has dealt candidly with his original and readers, by marking the additions he chofe to make; thus whatever cenfure or praife they may deferve, becomes directly and fairly his own.

VOL. II.   I i   Manly

Manly begins this piece, with opening his own character in a conference with Lord Plausible, who seems a very disagreeable visitant. In the course of their short conversation, they appear strong contrasts ; one seems churlishly fond of viewing and describing human nature in the worst light, while the other pleases himself with being the white-washer of frailty ; the wide difference of opinion, makes Manly cut short the thread of discourse in a very unhospitable, uncivilized manner ; however, the roughness of one and pliancy of the other, have a pleasing effect.

Oakham, a sea domestic of Manly's, seeing the peer treated so roughly, soliloquizes, with marine pleasantry, upon the incident; gives us to understand, that the Plain Dealer is a captain in the navy, that he is just landed from an unsuccessful cruize, and that he had sunk his ship to prevent her falling into the hands of the French : we think this speech of the honest tar's well introduced.

Manly returning with Freeman, is asked how he could treat a peer so roughly, when he makes a reply which we must transcribe as excellent. " You are one of those who esteem men only by the value and marks which fortune has set upon them, and never consider intrinsic worth ; but counterfeit honours will not pass current with me, I weigh the man, not his title. It is not the king's inscription which can make the metal better or heavier, your lord is a leaden shilling, which you bend every way, and debases the stamp he bears, instead of being raised by it." After some humorous reproofs to Oakham for admitting a visitor without leave, Manly

Manly forbids the admiffion of any more, male or female,

In continuation of the conference between Manly and Freeman, we find the latter kindly endeavouring to foften the rigidity which characterifes the former. One is for ftrict truth and open fpeaking upon all occafions ; the other, for giving way reafonably to fome cuftoms and prejudices of life, that he may not be in a ftate of continual warfare with his fellow-creatures. Juft as Freeman is making a tender of cordial friendfhip, Fidelia, difguifed in men's cloths, enters, and torments Manly's patience with fimilar profeffions ; he charges his female volunteer with cowardice, and upon that principle difmiffes her ; fhe remonftrates againft this feverity, but in vain.

Here Oakham fignifies the boifterous approach of a clamorous old lady, widow Blackacre, who, by defcription, we find to be the effence of litigation ; fo fond of a law fuit, that fhe prefers it to any other enjoyment. Upon her entrance fhe complains of being kept fo long in waiting, to which Manly replies, by afking for her niece Olivia, regardlefs of the queftion, fhe proceeds to the ftating of a caufe fhe has in hand ; Jerry, her fon, is ordered to put the cafe, which, after many interruptions, he attempts, but blunders fo, that the impatient mother proceeds herfelf ; till Manly, driven beyond patience, damns the caufe, and all the parties concerned. Upon being offered a fubpœna, he flounces out of the room, and leaves the widow to lament his Gothic behaviour.

After he is gone, Freeman makes a kind of matrimonial attack upon Mrs. Blackacre, which, for the prefent, is cut fhort, under the idea of affection

for

for her fon. By the next fcene, which is an added
one, we learn that Manly has fixed his undivided
friendfhip upon a man called Varnifh, and his love
upon a woman called Olivia, not remarkable either
for beauty or fortune ; however, it appears, that this
odd fon of Neptune, upon going to fea, had pro-
vifionally left this object of his affection poffeffed
of no lefs than ten or twelve thoufand pounds ;
from a partial opinion of her being, what he thinks
rare, a faithful woman.   Freeman goes off to plead
in Fidelia's favour, and leaves that female to inform
us that fhe is in love with Manly, that fhe has taken
a difguife to watch an opportunity of gaining his
affections, though fhe knows them to be previoufly
engaged.

The Plain Dealer appears dreffed, and fignifies to
Freeman that he is going out ; on being told that
it is on a vifit to his miftrefs, with an obfervation
that fhe muft be in the phenomenon ftile to engage
fuch a difpofition as his, he launches out violently in
her praife, becaufe fhe is confonant in temper, as he
imagines, to him.   A glaring inftance of weaknefs
drops from the blunt captain here, which is giving
her unlimited credit for requefting to fwear fhe
would not hear the addreffes of any perfon while he
was at fea : as a proof of her valuable and amiable
qualifications, he defires Freeman to call on him at
her lodgings in an hour, obferving, that the young
volunteer can fhew him where fhe lives.

Olivia and Eliza begin the fecond act : from what
paffes between them we find, that the former,
though fhe difclaims all liking for gay life and elegance of drefs, is warmly attached to both : through
the whole of this fcene, fhe difplays contempt of
every

every thing that is pleasing to her, especially any
concern with the male sex: her character opens itself, and shews a very palpable mixture of pride,
peevishness, and prudery.

A foot-boy bringing in word that a gentleman,
who frequently comes, desires admittance, she pro-
tests against the knowledge of any visitors: on being told the person's name, she is rather confused,
and wants to make Eliza the cause of his visit; then
gives a character that shews she is intimately acquainted with him. With admirable effrontery she
calls up Novel, as if to please her cousin: this alert
sprig of fashion no sooner appears, than he enters
upon a subject very common in modish life, that is,
delineating the characters he dined with the day before; however, Olivia, who professed herself a foe
to detraction but a few lines since, outstrips Novel
so much in the dissection of Lady Autumn and her
daughter, that he attempts to march off, but is detained.

Lord Plausible being mentioned, the tender Olivia cuts him up too; and Novel is speaking of him
in very harsh terms at the moment he appears.
This turns the scales, all immediately becoming
complaisance and cordiality. His lordship observing that he met two worthy characters at Olivia's
door, Count Levant and Lord Court-title, there is
a fresh field for scandal opened, and every one whose
name happens to fall in is sacrificed; till Eliza,
wearied with such stuff, goes off, and Manly is heard
squabbling at the door with the foot-boy: he enters, and is astonished to see Olivia in such company; his vexation and surprize are expressed in pretty
rough

rough terms, and she replies rather with upbraiding than conceffion.

While Novel and Plaufible are on, he is much agitated, and treats the *things,* as he juftly calls them, with becoming fpirit : at length they retire, rather intimidated, to another room.

Olivia's aggravation, when by themfelves, rifes fo high, that he renounces her ; she coolly goes off, and fays she shall return foon. Fidelia and Freeman, who have overheard the fquabble, join the captain, and feel fome rubs from his rouzed fury ; however, Freeman urges him to demand a reftitution of the money and jewels he had placed in fo unworthy a miftrefs's hands. When Olivia appears, Fidelia unites with Freeman in this demand ; to which she replies, that what they afk have been delivered to another perfon. This awakes the captain, he demands who, she returns, her hufband ; and that she dare not hint at their being given back, leaft he should think she had received them upon unworthy terms.

This affirmative confeffion of deceit provokes Manly fo much, that he bids her go off to avoid fomething worfe than rough words ; she complies, with moft provoking indifference.

Mrs. Blackacre, Jerry, and Major Oldfox, are introduced : Freeman addreffes the widow in very plain and pofitive terms, which makes her retort sharply : this encourages Oldfox to mention his claim, which the choleric old dame repulfes with fevere warmth, and is humoroufly fatirical ; her abufe of Freeman goes too far, when she calls him a *lath*-backed fellow : full of law she leaves both
her

her old and young gallant, to try if Olivia can influence any of the jury in a depending caufe.

At the beginning of the third act, Manly prefents himfelf, folus, violently difturbed in thought at Olivia's perfidious, unexpected behaviour, and lamenting that the injury he fuftains fo hardly, was not done by a man, that he might have demanded and compelled adequate fatisfaction; however, he confeffes love for her, in fpite of fuch peculiar provocation to wean his mifled affection; while he is wrapped in this painful reverie, Fidelia enters and defires to be heard a few words, which requeft Manly is loth to comply with, however, being preffed, and mention of Olivia occurring, he joins converfation.

When the fuppofed volunteer utters harfh terms againft his captain's miftrefs, love gets the better of ill ufage, and caufes Manly to threaten Fidelia; after this, with great precaution, he acknowledges his paffion for Olivia, but confeffes it as a great fecret; interprets her culpable behaviour in many favourable lights; infifts upon Fidelia's going to her houfe, fuppofing fhe may have repented her difdainful behaviour, and may be willing to make fome acknowledgment.

The female volunteer undertakes this commiffion, in hopes of getting the money and jewels returned, but Manly forbids any idea of that kind, and fays he is going to Weftminfter Hall; here the fcene concludes, and that which fucceeds, places us in view of the law market; where Mrs. Blackacre appears, furrounded with long robed harpies, railing at a follicitor who has pacifically recommended a reference.

Major

Plain Dealer.

Major Oldfox coming on, a very immaterial, unentertaining scene ensues at a bookseller's stall, between him and the litigious widow ; at length, she is called off by seeing a person who has proposed selling her a chancery suit, upon what she thinks moderate terms. Seeing Freeman, his rival, the Major becomes very crusty, and hobbles after his mistress. Jerry wanting to buy Rochester's jests, but not having money to pay for the book, Freeman lays down the price, and laments that a young gentleman, of large expectations, should be kept so bare ; then asks, why he wont give consent to his marrying the widow. This draws from Jerry an explanation of his mother's character, her penury, and spirit of litigation.

Freeman, finding Jerry a good subject to work upon, puts two guineas into his hand, and they form an alliance against the old lady. The squire, being possessed of such an immense sum, goes off with a pleasing remark, that he'll go and pay two shillings he owes, because he believes the man wants it. Manly, harrassed by Mrs. Blackacre, about her cause, enters, declaring he'll be plagued no more with it ; when the widow misses her hopeful son, she hurries off with the Major, to search for him. Freeman observing to his captain, that his patience must be pretty well tried, the enraged Plain Dealer replies, that since his coming into the Hall, he has incurred a challenge and two law-suits.

Seeing Novel approach, he wants to sheer off, but being hailed by the beau, brings too. The talkative sprite proposes some insignificant questions, which are replied to with a mixture of roughness and contempt. We cannot help thinking this
scene

scene a very weak and unneceffary addition, it means little to the plot, has but very faint humour to recommend it, and confequently hangs heavy on attention. What paffes between Freeman and Novel, might alfo be very well fpared; when the latter, having made a flip concerning Manly's courage, fneaks off, Jerry Blackacre, full of refentment againft his mother, enters, claiming the promifed affiftance of his friend Freeman.

Seeing her approach, they go off: the widow here prefents herfelf, fuming with paffion at the infolence of Jerry, who has threatened to go on board Manly's fhip; her concern feems not for the fon, but the writings he has got with him, on which her jointure and law-fuits depend. She goes off, threatening Manly, as an accomplice in the boy's elopement. Fidelia joins the Plain Dealer, and informs him of Olivia's confirmed infidelity; he doubts for fome time, but when the young volunteer fays, that Olivia has not only made love to him in direct terms, but that he is to be admitted to her bedchamber at midnight, Manly infifts on his going, which Fidelia declines. Manly then refolves himfelf to make ufe of a garden key fhe has given him. Freeman's appearance cuts fhort their difcourfe; the lieutenant informs his captain of Jerry's revolt from maternal authority, and that he intends to make a proper ufe of that event.

Manly begins the fourth act with Fidelia: after obferving, that he has been out all night, and that he now confiders Olivia as the vileft of her fex, he difcovers diforder in Fidelia's countenance, which fhews fhe has been in tears; he fpeaks in friendly terms, promifing protection: he explains

the method of confirming Olivia's treachery, which
was by paffing in the dark for her expected young
volunteer ; and defires that Fidelia, in that character, to favour his defigns, will write a tender
letter to the falfe fair : her objecting to this, fuggefts an idea of jealoufy to Manly.   Upon faying
he muft either give up Olivia or her, he fternly afks
what they have to do with each other : at length,
upon an explanation that he only wants through
this fecond appointment, to confront Olivia with irrefiftable conviction, fhe goes off to write the propofed letter.

Major Oldfox, though they parted upon fuch ungentleman-like terms in Weftminfter Hall, is here
introduced by Freeman to the Captain, both as a
foldier and an author.   The old militarian propofes employing his pen in a relation of Manly's
lofing his fhip, which the tar treats with contempt.
Oldfox's remarks upon his own abilities, and Freeman's mode of humouring his abfurdity, are agreeably imagined ; but this, like feveral other fcenes,
has no kind of connexion with the plot, and feems
more calculated to make Oldfox a tolerable part,
than to enrich the piece.   It appears to us, that the
fcene which now ftands third, would have been
more properly placed as fecond.

The circumftance of Freeman's wanting fpirit to
quarrel with one who had called him an impertinent,
infignificant, ignorant fellow, is fomewhat odd for
the character of an officer : after the Major retires,
we are informed by the Lieutenant, that he has new
rigged his charge. Hearing a knock, which is
known to be Mrs. Blackacre's, they retire.

The

The scene changes to Covent Garden Piazza, where we perceive the widow, who declares she won't set foot in Manly's house without her lawyer. We wish Mr. BICKERSTAFF had placed Quillet's chambers in any other than *Coney* Court, especially as it was to come from a female mouth. Upon Jerry's coming forth in his new habiliments, Mrs. Blackacre takes notice of the change, and being told that he has chosen Freeman for a guardian, she softens, desiring he will go home with her. An altercation here arises, in which the characters are extremely well and homorously supported: being hard pushed, and much enraged, the widow sacrifices her own reputation at the shrine of resentment; declaring, that Jerry is base born : wherefore, his claim to the family estate, or choice of a guardian, can have no validity. With this very creditable subterfuge, she hastens to Doctor's Commons. Jerry, and his new guardian being alarmed with this unexpected declaration, they go off to fight her in her own way, by engaging a considerable detachment of pettifoggers.

We are now conducted to Olivia's lodgings, where we meet that lady bringing on Vernish, her husband : the remarkable palpitation she appears in alarms suspicion, which she takes endearing methods to cast aside; and tells him not only of Manly's return from sea, but of her manner of treating him : here Vernish opens his own character, and shews that he is linked with the woman to impose on an easy, unsuspecting temper. We perceive this rascal to be the *one* friend mentioned by our Plain Dealer in the first act, with such cordiality and confidence.

Olivia mentioning the necessity of taking means to secure the money placed in her hands by Manly,

Vernish

Vernifh goes off for that purpofe, and fhe gets breathing time. By her foliloquy, it appears, that fhe repents her marriage, and is very apprehenfive of danger to her young favourite, the volunteer, fhould fo dark and dangerous a temper difcover her attachment. Here Fidelia prefents herfelf : a converfation enfues, which fhews Olivia much enamoured and very forward. She propofes flying from her hufband ; then invites her gallant to a collation in the next room, which we think not very probable, under fear of Vernifh's return. Being perplexed with folicitation, Fidelia feigns the approach of a fit ; Olivia goes into another chamber for fome fpirits, and immediately returns in great confufion, announcing her hufband's approach : it appears, that while the fervant went for a coach, he had changed his riding drefs. On feeing Fidelia, he accofts her in very rough terms, indeed very vulgar ones : why would our alterer furnifh fuch paffages as thefe ? " By the *Lord*, you fhant flip by me---*Damn* you, firrah"---Fear of death caufes Fidelia to own fhe is a woman ; of this the brute takes an advantage, and preffes his licentious fuit with violence. Her fituation here claims pity, and the audience are judicioufly left at the end of the fourth act, in a ftate of anxious concern for her honour and fafety.

Olivia, concerned for her rotten reputation, begins the fifth act with Eliza, who comforts her on that point, with obferving, that her character was fo bad before any late incident, it is paft the attack of any frefh injury. Vernifh enters, Olivia, confcious of guilt, craves pardon. This draws from him an explanation that the volunteer was a woman, in man's cloaths,

cloaths, a difcovery made by his pretending to be rude
with her. When his wife finds the lover, male or female, has efcaped, fhe turns the tables upon him, and
charges Vernifh with criminality, where fhe herfelf
was guilty. Her hypocrify is very well defcribed ;
he fooths her paffion, and begs Eliza to work a reconciliation.

When he is gone, Olivia, true to vice and effrontery, difclaims any knowledge of a gallant, though
clofely preffed thereto by her coufin : in fhort, her
hardened, negative infolence here, is very characteriftic of a mind fteeled againft every juft and delicate
feeling. Her unblufhing confidence warms Eliza,
and they part with angry terms.

In the next fcene we meet Freeman and Manly ;
the latter mentions Fidelia's efcape from Olivia's
lodgings, and makes an appointment with Freeman,
for him, Oakham, and as many more as he chufes,
to meet at half an hour after feven in her chamber.
Freeman gone off, Vernifh appears, to whom the
Captain gives a moft friendly welcome. This fcene
produces natural and pleafing perplexity, by Manly's boafting of the laft favour from his fuppofed
friend's wife. The exultation of the one, and anxiety of the other, are entertaining : the Captain, in
rapture, mentions a fecond appointment of amorous nature, and makes his exit, defiring they may
meet at fupper. In a fucceeding foliloquy, we find,
that Vernifh, in order to convict his wife, determines upon making her believe he is under a neceffity of going immediately to Oxford ; by which
means he imagines her guilt or innocence will certainly be brought to light.

Major

Major Oldfox, Mrs. Blackacre, and Counsellor Quillet, present themselves in the next scene : their conversation amounts to no more than making the widow's litigious character more strongly apparent, and having no further connexion with the piece, may be deemed an excrescence, obtruded upon the original by Mr. BICKERSTAFF : if the scene which now stands eighth, immediately succeeded Vernish's soliloquy, it would have been better. Upon being arrested at the suit of Freeman, as guardian to her son, the old lady bends her high spirit into supplication ; however, mercy lies open but one way, which is by marrying the Lieutenant.

Frighted at the loss of her authority by such a union, she offers Freeman an annuity of three hundred pounds a year, and payment of his debts ; justly surmising, that his view upon her is merely pecuniary advantage. He intimates, that her family has cheated him of four hundred a year, landed estate, and proposes, upon a surrender of that property, to give up the guardianship of Jerry ; this, and a stipulation that she shall allow the young gentleman one hundred pounds a year, is agreed to, and they go off to ratify the agreement.

Olivia is brought forward in fresh expectation of her young volunteer ; Fidelia enters, and in her masculine capacity sustains a very warm attack, with strong solicitation to make an elopement : upon hearing a noise, and discovering that it is her husband returned, Olivia gives a casket, containing jewels and bank notes to a considerable amount, to Fidelia ; who, upon Manly's entrance, gives them to him. Vernish forces a door open, and attacks

Manly

Manly and Fidelia; while they are scuffling by the faint glimmers of a dark lanthorn, Freeman, Plausible and Novel enter; when lights appear, the Plain Dealer perceives that Olivia's husband is the identical friend he had selected from mankind. The play now hastens to a conclusion, Manly finding that his volunteer is a woman---we wish this point had been explained more satisfactory---he presents her with a casket, and offers his heart; Fidelia gladly accepts the latter, which she has toiled hard to gain; and makes him acquainted that she is possessed of two thousand pounds a year. We think the catastrophe of this piece very defective, as neither Olivia, Vernish, nor widow Blackacre, are sufficiently punished for the bad principles they manifest upon every occasion.

Take this comedy as it is now offered to the public, we find many scenes of powerful humour, several very languid: for most of the former we are indebted to WYCHERLY, for the latter in general to Mr. BIKERSTAFF, whose alteration has rendered the play more chaste, but not more entertaining. We should have been happy to allow the same degree of praise here we have given the HYPOCRITE, but it is by no means deserved; however, the unities' are well preserved, the plot judiciously conducted, the characters, such as they are, properly maintained, and the dialogue easy.

Manly is an uncommon, yet not an unnatural character, his spirit of speaking what he thinks upon every occasion, leads him often to the verge of rudeness, and gives his conversation a very saturnine cast; however, plain dealing in one sense may be a jewel, yet in such a latitude as the Captain uses it, social communication becomes hurt by unneceffary, ill-timed truths : if it was commonly practifed, according to the known feelings of mankind in general, we might expect nothing but conftant bickerings amongft neighbours : indeed, it is not every man that enjoys fufficient judgment to diftinguifh what are really errors and vices, where, as fools are moft apt to give their opinion, the reftraint of cuftom and civility becomes effential.

Manly's fingularity pleafes in action, but would be difguftful in private life ; he feems to have an honeft, unfufpecting heart, but a wretched weak head ; we remember to have feen Mr. QUIN exhibit the Plain Dealer with fingular merit ; the cynical roughnefs being in a great meafure his own difpofition, became him well ; yet, as being more fpirited, we are apt to conclude Mr. HOLLAND better---Mr. AICKIN is indeed a lamentable falling off from both.

Freeman has very little to recommend an actor, the prefent Mr. PALMER deferves as much praife as can be merited by fuch an infipid undertaking. Lord Plaufible is very little more than a name, he is a very poor contraft to Manly, has nothing to do with the piece, and fcarce any thing to fay worth attention ; he is totally unworthy of fuch pleafing talents as both Mr. PARSONS and Mr. DODD poffefs. Novel is equally an excrefence, and ftill more below the happy execution of Mr. KING ; however, there is fome policy and a compliment to the public in putting good performers on fuch ungracious undertakings.

Vernifh is a confummate knave, a dead weight to drag, and will never be fo well fupported as by Mr. LEE.

Lee. Major Oldfox is meant as a humourift, but his influence upon the rifible faculties is very weak; Mr. Love fupports this opiniated, caroethes fcribendi coxcomb, better in action than the author has in delineation. Jerry Blackacre we find a very laughable ninny-hammer, placed in feveral diverting points of view; Mr. Yates no doubt fhewed himfelf a very good actor in the performance of this part; but for true character and powerful fimplicity, Mr. Weston goes far beyond him; nor do we think it too indulgent for criticifm to place Mr. W. Palmer fecond; who with diligence and countenance from the managers, may make a firft rate low comedian.

In the character of Olivia, we find an entire want of every amiable qualification; fhe is proud, flanderous, deceitful, falfe to a lover who has conferred great obligations upon her, and equally difpofed to abufe her hufband, for fake of a third perfon; fhe is fo hateful in principles that a good actrefs is requifite to make her fufferable, and fuch we admit Mifs Pope fhews herfelf in this part, though both authors have left it very unfinifhed for reprefentation.

Fidelia is a lady of the romantic caft, refolved to have a man at any rate; if love is an excufe for grofs breaches of decorum fhe may ftand excufed; however, we cannot help confidering her as a reprehenfible object. Mrs. Yates gave very adequate fatisfaction in perfonating this adventurous fair one, yet notwithftanding her great merit and greater name, we are not afraid to declare that Mrs. Baddely pleafes us better. Mrs. Blackacre, who gallops on the hobby horfe of law, retir-

Plain Dealer.

ed with Mrs. CLIVE to the neighbourhood of Strawberry-hill, and will not in our judgment return, unless Mrs. GREEN takes her by the hand; Mrs. STEPHENS made some very unsuccessful attempts upon her last winter, and Mrs. HOPKINS worse this. In short we are surprized that the last mentioned lady, who has as little humour as pathos about her, should be bundled into so many characters of importance both tragic and comic. Miss PLYM, and Mrs. W. BARRY may both be justly stiled pretty Elizas.

The comedy, whatever praise it might receive in its original state from the wits and connoissures of the last age, or however it may be improved by the present alteration, has yet many very weak parts, and the remarkable fault of having three characters Plausible, Novel and Eliza, very near superfluous. Mr. BICKERSTAFF has softened some roughness of character, and omitted many exceptionable passages, for which he deserved both the praise and profit that attended the undertaking; yet we cannot wish to see the play often, nor can we, as its moral is at best very vague, urge the perusal of it.

TAMER-

TAMERLANE.

A TRAGEDY: By ROWE.

THIS tragedy opens in the camp of Tamerlane : the Prince of Tanais, and two other chiefs, make us acquainted with the character of their illuftrious mafter ; and point out alfo that of his brutal antagonift ; whofe repeated breaches of faith, in contempt of folemn treaties, has brought them to the eve of a decifive battle. Tamerlane approaches, meditating beautifully on the devaftation of war. Axalla, with Monefes and Selima prifoners, prefents himfelf at the Emperor's feet, introducing his fair captive, who proves to be the Sultan's daughter. She fues for protection, which is promifed in the kindeft terms, and fhe is given, with an infinuation of its being a pleafing tafk, to Axalla's care.

Tamerlane enquiring whether there is any other prifoner of confideration, Monefes is brought forward : touched with Tamerlane's benevolent reception, he difclofes the royalty of his lineage, derived from the Greek emperors ; then mentions being made, together with a female he calls a fifter, captives by Bajazet.

It appears, by his narration, that the Turk had compelled him to take arms ; that being fent to guard the Princefs Selima to her father's camp, he had left Arpafia behind as a pledge of faith ; and that by Axalla's fuperior fortune, he had fallen into new captivity. Tamerlane, though he entertains a

high

high opinion of the honour and intrepidity of Monefes, yet, from a very delicate principle, defires his fword may reft neuter during the impending battle. Tamerlane goes off with a pious addrefs to the great difpofer of all things, for affiftance. When left alone with Selima, Axalla, who had contracted a paffion for her during his embaffy at the Sultan's court, prefers his addreffes, which from the idea of being brought into a ftate of bondage by him, fhe at firft treats with feverity; but foftens fo far as to acknowledge fhe entertained tender thoughts of him, till the duty of a child obliged her to confider him as her father's foe.

She requefts being delivered to the Sultan, but this the general obferves is impracticable, confidering the fituation of the armies. Being fummoned to the field, Selima, yielding to the impulfe of love, forms ideas of his falling in battle, and gives him every confiftent mark of tender regard, which animates and fills him with happy prefages of fuccefs. The fimile with which he takes his leave is fuperfluous, and every one of the rhimes, in the two laft fpeeches of the firft act, would be better omitted.

Our author having very judicioufly left the battle entirely to imagination, begins his fecond act with Monefes, who mentions the glorious victory Tamerlane has obtained. Stratocles, the Grecian, brings an account that Bajazet is taken; but being queftioned concerning the fate of Arpafia, he can fay no more than that there are fome women amongft the prifoners. This fends Monefes off, with a damp on that pleafure which he received from Tamerlane's triumph.

The

Tamerlane.

The conqueror, feated in his pavillion, receives, with fenfible referve, the compliments of his generals, wifely confidering himfelf and his army, but as fecondary caufes of the fuccefs they have been crowned with. The following addrefs to Axalla, ought to be imprinted upon every royal, indeed every fubject heart:

> Oh Axalla,
> Could I forget I am a man as thou art,
> Would not the winter's cold, or fummer's heat,
> Sicknefs, or thirft and hunger, all the train
> Of nature's clamorous appetites, afferting
> An equal right in kings and common men,
> Reprove me daily?---No, if I boaft of ought,
> Be it to have been heav'ns happy inftrument,
> The means of good to all my fellow-creatures.
> This is a king's beft praife.

Bajazet is here introduced, fwelled with difappointment, rage, and horror. Upon the victor's mentioning that he has a right to demand attonement for the torrents of blood fhed by and through the Sultan's ambition, a reply of great fpirit is made, and even defiance hurled in the victorious monarch's face. Through the whole of this interview, Tamerlane contrafts a fpirit of philofophic dignity, to a kind of favage fury ; indeed majefty, in feveral paffages, cafts afide every idea of royalty, to become abfolutely fcurrilous : he rails, curfes, fwears, and gives the lie moft grofsly. The manner in which his life is given him, the affignment of a royal tent for his accommodation, and the propofition of moderate terms, reflect great honour upon his humane, generous conqueror ; while his churlifh refufal of every favour ftamps him a brute.

I

Tamer-

Tamerlane's remark of virtuous delicacy, which does not administer benefits through mercenary hopes of reward, would have been much better if it had been expressed without jingle. Upon the entrance of Arpasia, Bajazet makes a fine picturesque assimilation of his own feelings, at sight of the woman he loves, in such a fallen state. When Haly presents her to him, he comments nervously on her disdainful looks, which she returns with bitter reproaches, for causing the wrongs she has suffered.

The appearance of Moneses kindles Bajazet's indignation, which rises higher on the Prince's presuming to approach Arpasia. Being accused by the Sultan of wanting courage and faith, he offers a spirited vindication, which puts the tyrant past all patience, and causes him to hurry off in a frantic fit of passion, leaving the two lovers to a mournful interview; mournful, as Arpasia pathetically informs Moneses, that in his absence, though she had confessed herself his wife, yet Bajazet, deaf to tears and intreaties, had forced her into the ceremony and consummation of a marriage. This scene is wrought up to a degree of melting tenderness, and the act concludes with an affecting separation.

It is a misfortune that the third act should begin with another love scene, so much inferior to that we have just looked over. Axalla, as we find, has with painful struggles, determined to yield up Selima to her father: when the Emperor comes on, murmuring at the thoughts of obligations received, she presents herself, and for a moment he feels paternal softness; but, being told by the Prince that he must receive her as a fresh mark of Tamerlane's indulgence, the monster of pride and ingratitude breaks

breaks out, and he goes near giving his benefactor that polite title given the electors of Middlesex---*scum of the earth*---When Selima speaks favourably of Axalla, she comes in for her share: the Prince afferts his own dignity in so becoming a manner, that he puts the imperial scold into a corner. Upon promising to restore him his crown and empire, the savage fixes Tamerlane's head as the only price that can purchase his daughter.

Seeing Axalla shrink, like a man of honour and loyalty, from so base a proposition, he again puts on the bully, drags off Selima, and leaves Axalla without any comfort but that conscious integrity which prevents even the strong impulse of ardent love, from making him undertake a base action.

We next meet Monefes, soliciting an audience of Tamerlane; but being told by the Prince of Ta-nais that the Emperor is in private conference with a Dervise, he goes off to make way for the two last mentioned characters, who enter conferring on a religious subject. The priest, like a true sanguine bigot, rates Tamerlane for giving protection and countenance to Christians. The narrowness of thought, the uncharitable, exclusive opinion of sectarists, which devote to temporal and spiritual destruction all who are not of their own class, are set in a light of just contempt by the following very moral, argumentative, conclusive and beautiful lines:

> ———No law divine condemns the virtuous
> For differing from the rules your schools devise;
> Look round how providence bestows alike,
> Sunshine and rain, to bless the fruitful year,
> On different nations all of different faiths;

And

And though by different names and titles worſhipp'd,
Heav'n takes the various tribute of their praiſe,
Since all agree to own, at leaſt to mean,
One great, one good, one only Lord of all.

We are bold to aſſert, that no pulpit ever advanced a more uſeful, liberal piece of inſtruction, which wiſely conſiders human nature whether in the torrid, frigid, or temperate zone ; whether of complexion black or white, brown or copper colour, as children of one univerſal, impartial parent.

Being foiled in all his arguments by the nobleſt principles of reaſon and humanity, the hot-brained prieſt tries what a dagger will do, but is there too prevented, by the magnanimous monarch, who diſarms, and mercifully, we think too mercifully, diſmiſſes him without any other puniſhment than reproof. The holy Aſſaſſin being departed, Moneſes, oppreſſed with griefs, proſtrates himſelf at the Emperor's feet, confeſſes the falſhood he had been guilty of, in calling Arpaſia his ſiſter, and ſollicits having her reſtored as his contracted bride. Tamerlane, knowing her to be Bajazet's queen, juſtly declines any interpoſition, and prudently recommends the weaning his affection by martial activity, from the ſoft bands of love to the thirſt of glory.

A very pleaſing, and poetical picture of the mind under theſe different influences cloſes the third act ; the Derviſe, who conſiders Tamerlane's clemency as folly, begins the fourth act, acquainting Haly that he has ſtruck out another ſcheme for Bajazet's ſervice ; by inflaming the diſcontent of Omar, a powerful chief, who having claimed Selima from

the

Tamerlane.

the Emperor, is refused on account of a preference given to Axalla.

By what Omar says at his entrance, we find, that he considers Tamerlane as under peculiar obligations to him, and ungrateful in refusing his request. The Dervise resumes his inflammatory insinuations, and Haly, mentioning that Selima may be had at her father's hands, the Tartar determines to join Bajazet's cause : hearing, by sound of trumpet, the Emperor's approach, they retire.

A song, suited to the distress of Arpasia, and much better written than songs in general, occurs here. The music ended, she meditates on death, as a desirable refuge from sorrow ; but, as a Christian, nobly resists some great examples of self-destruction. Tamerlane, upon the humane principle of consolation appears, and endeavours to balm the fair one's wounded mind. Bajazet entering while they are in conference, takes a jealous alarm, and bursts into fury like a sprung mine. His vulgarity in the first scene we have been severe upon, but that we find in the scene before us, no lash of criticism is any way equal to.

After bearing more than is possible to imagine, Tamerlane warms so far into resentment, that he delivers Bajazet to the guards, and orders him to be executed : this, by Arpasia's interposition, with the Emperor's lenity, is set aside, and Tamerlane prudently retreats, lest he should be kindled into rage again. What pity it is that Mr. ROWE has made him speak a sort of epilogue to every scene.

The irascible Turk, whose barbarous mind no weight of obligation can impress, goes off, storming at Arpasia for having saved his life; and disclaiming paradise, because *woman* is placed there. This thought admits of an objection, if we consider the Mahometan opinion, that all the females of this life are, after death, annihilated; 'tis true, the prophet has furnished the future world with black-eyed girls, but we know not whether this justifies Bajazet's extravagant idea. Arpasia, almost sunk with accumulating sorrows, so much increased by the tyrant's vile insinuation of criminality with Tamerlane, is joined by Moneses; their mutual plaints are extremely pathetic, the interchange of affection highly interesting, but the scene concludes with two triplets which we can by no means approve; they are, if we may be allowed the similitude, like yellow fringe upon the border of a mourning gown.

Bajazet now comes forward, making large promises to his new ally Omar, by whose assistance there are favourable appearances of his gaining ample revenge upon Tamerlane. There is something odd here, that Axalla should be made and detained a prisoner in his master's camp; however, he is brought on by Omar in that state. The Sultan proposes to the prince, either joining with him or death; Axalla, with noble firmness, prefers the latter, which, but for Selima's solicitation is resolved on : at his daughter's request, the Sultan defers his sentence, and Selima takes him off to try the power of her persuasion.

Affairs being thus seemingly well disposed for Bajazet's grand design of recovering empire, he concludes the fourth act with a most noble assimulation of himself to Jove engaged with the Titans. Arpasia, again in soliloquy, commences the fifth act :

I

we

we think there is a famenefs in this lady's lonely meditations, which rather palls : fhe informs us of what we already know, that Monefes is made a prifoner. While fhe is indulging gloomy thought, Bajazet enters, confeffing what influence fhe has over his mind, even in the midft of moft important concerns ; that even empire and revenge hold but the fecond place in his heart. He determines, either by gentle means or force, to take her with him ; the former he tries in terms, for him, unufually fmooth ; her difdainful treatment of his folicitation, again kindles up the flames of paffion, and he threatens her with death ; but fuppofing that the execution of Monefes will wound deeper than the lofs of her own life, he orders the unhappy prince to be ftrangled in her fight.

The parting of thefe lovers is particularly pathetic, though we think there is fomething very difagreeable in the mode of Monefes's cataftrophe. Arpafia's end is not totally unnatural, but bears rather too hard upon probability ; the word *blaft*, twice ufed in her laft fpeech, is much more becoming a lady of eafy virtue than a tragedy heroine, however agitated : the confufion of Bajazet, at lofing the woman he loves fo ftrangely, is interrupted by the Dervife, who brings intelligence, that as there are apparent movements in the camp, it becomes neceffary to haften flight : fcarce has he finifhed his meffage, when Omar declares that they are furrounded, and imputes the difcovery of their defigns to a prifoner, who, by the Princefs's order, was fuffered to efcape. Bajazet, ftruck with his daughter's treachery, refolves to take revenge upon Axalla.

Being

Tamerlane.

Being told he was the perfon that had efcaped, his fury rages againft her, and he makes feveral attempts to kill her, but fome feelings of the father prevent his fatal purpofe ; at length, hearing the approach of Tamerlane, he configns her fate to the mutes, from whom fhe is refcued by Axalla, while the tyrant is once more taken into cuftody.

After fuch repeated and capital provocations, we are not to be furprized that the Emperor's lenity gives way to his juftice ; further forgivenefs would have been a proftitution of mercy : the fentence he paffes upon Bajazet of being caged, is feverer than death, by fo much as pain of mind is more infufferable than that of the body. The Sultan's departure is ftrictly confonant to his behaviour all through the piece, which concludes with a very noble remark upon that impious pride, which forgets the dependant ftate of human nature, and arrogates to itfelf the advantages and grandeur of life.

Notwithftanding this play is merely ufed as an anniverfary one, yet, we think, when actors capable of fupporting it can be found, that it fhould ftand more forward in the rank of living tragedies. The incidents are various and affecting, the unities tolerably well preferved, the fentiments elevated, and the language adequate without bombaft. It is in fome places rather too flowery, and the verfification fo flowing, fo feldom broke, that it requires great judgment in feveral of the parts to avoid monotony.

Tamerlane is a character worth every monarch's imitation, active and intrepid as a foldier ; wife, juft and merciful, as a fovereign ; affable, friendly, and benevolent, as a man : he reflects that credit upon his ftation, which no ftation nor dignity can give an
unworthy

unworthy poffeffor. No higher compliment could be paid King William than marking him out as the original of this pleafing picture.

Mr. Quin fupported Tamerlane with great dignity, but offended by his unnatural fwell of utterance. Mr. Havard had all the effential placidity, but wanted confequence both of figure and deportment. Mr. Sheridan fhewed more propriety than either, as to expreffion, but in appearance and deportment fell very fhort of the firft mentioned gentleman. We have feen Mr. Sowdon do the part refpectably. The two prefent Tamerlanes are not worth mention, they want both internal and external requifites. Omar would do much better for Meffrs. Bensley and Aickin; the former of thefe gentlemen has been placed in fuch a variety of acting, though always the fame, as was fcarce ever known; fops, lovers, declaimers, tyrants. Who, but Mr. Colman, could have allotted Sir Brilliant Fafhion and Barbaroffa to the fame performer? efpecially one who has no variation.

Bajazet, though a hateful, and indeed vulgar character, always claims particular notice from an audience; there is a refiftive fpirit about him which gives pleafure, notwithftanding it is founded upon the worft principles. His pride, ambition, ingratitude and cruelty, are deteftable, yet greatly counterballanced by his noble ideas of independance; he is the moft agreeable monfter we know, and very great powers are wanted to do the author juftice.

Mr. Quin, in the brutal part, excelled all the Bajazets we have feen, but had no part of the requifite fpirit. Mr. Barry, though better in the latter, had too much harmony of voice and feature to

mark

mark the former properly ; for though a foft fpoken or fair looking man may be a brute, yet fuch being a deceptive character, does not fill our idea on the ftage. In the laft fcene with Selima, Mr. BARRY's excellence furpaffes our praife. Mr. BERRY laboured through the part abominably, and. Mr. SMITH has made lamentable attempts upon it : for effential fire, contemptuous afpect, extent and variety of voice, we place Mr. MOSSOP firft, at the fame time that we allow Mr. HOLLAND great merit ; as the chains and Turkifh habit rendered his mechanical movements lefs offenfive than they were in modern cloaths.

Monefes is diftinguifhed by nothing but his love and misfortunes, which reduce him to a moft whining ftate : he is generally given to fecond-rate actors, though he certainly was drawn for, and deferves capital ones. We have had pleafure from feeing Mr. RYAN exhibit this prince, and pain from Mr. HULL. It hurries us beyond all patience, to think that any degree of managerical authority, whether ignorant or malicious, fhould force fo refpectable a performer totally out of his way.

Mr. REDDISH is extremely pleafing and characteriftic ; he neither rifes above, nor falls below his author, and has more merit than all the other men put together, as it is now played at Drury Lane : why does not Mr. Ross do it at Covent Garden, where, without any great degree of eminence, he muft ftand foremoft.

Axalla, we thought, could fcarcely be worfe than in the late Mr. PALMER's hands, but Mr. PACKER and Mr. PERRY, are ftrong proofs of our miftake ; fuch a brace of heroic lovers---hoh ! hoh ! hoh !

were

were furely never feen before. Omar, when performed by Mr. SPARKS, made a very confpicuous
figure; at prefent, he falls off confiderably in the
hands of Mr. HURST, though he is fecond beft in
the play, for we have fpoken of Mr. BARRY in the
Sultan as he *was*, not as he *is*. The remaining male
characters are too inconfiderable for notice, being
generally given to the tag-rag and bob-tail of a
theatre.

Arpafia's painful fituation touches fenfibility; we
fympathize with her tears, while we are pleafed with
her fpirit and conftancy. We could never admire
Mrs. WOFFINGTON's croaking of this part; 'tis
true, fhe figured it fo elegantly, that her firft appearance prejudiced fpectators in her favour; but
harmony of perfon was greatly injured by diffonance
of voice. Mrs. PRITCHARD played the princefs
much better, but had not the neceffary foftnefs. Mrs.
BELLAMY had the proper degree of pathos, but
whined. Mifs MILLER has ftumbled upon the
part moft injudicioufly; while Mrs. BARRY looks,
moves, fpeaks, and feels up to the higheft degree of
criticifm.

Selima is a mere foil to Arpafia, of very little confequence, and therefore very little attended to, yet
we remember to have feen Mrs. ELMY give her uncommon graces. Mrs. W. BARRY and Mrs. MAT-
TOCKS are agreeable, but we beg leave to hint that
the laft mentioned lady has a ftrong taint of the
cathedral ftile.

We think the play of TAMERLANE has two confpicuous faults; firft, the double love plot, which
renders Axalla and Selima very unaffecting: next,
the author's neglect of giving Eaftern characters
                                        fomething

Tamerlane.

something of the Eastern stile ; this is a commendable propriety which the author of Zingis has adhered to. The frequent execrations we meet are also censurable, nor can we forgive so many repetitions of the word ALHA, the immediate title of the Supreme Being is not fit for stage expression ; however, this tragedy, well performed, must please in representation, and we cannot apprehend any prejudice from perusal of it : indeed, some scenes are highly instructive, and worthy recollection of the most serious mind.

ALL

ALL IN THE WRONG.

A COMEDY: By Mr. MURPHY.

SIR John Reftlefs begins this play, reflecting on himfelf for taking to wife an improper perfon; and enquires of Robin which door fhe went out, that towards the ftreet, or one to the Park; being anfwered through the latter, jealous fufpicions arife, which the domeftic honeftly and fenfibly endeavours to remove from his mafter's mind; but, like a true felf-tormenter, Sir John, though much in love with his lady, from which principle alone he married her, increafes fhadows into fubftances, for the ftrange purpofe of working his own perplexity. Robert obferves, that this ftrange mode of behaviour has tainted her ladyfhip alfo with jealoufy.

The baronet, on hearing that fhe bent her courfe towards the Horfe Guards, grows very warm; and fending off Robin, goes himfelf, fraught with ideas of cuckoldom, in purfuit of her. Belmont and Beverley meet; the purport of their converfation is a mutual confeffion of love, the former with Clariffa, and the latter with Belinda. From what paffes, it appears, that Beverley has a temper fomewhat fimilar to Sir John's, which is roufed into a ftate of confiderable folicitude, by mention that Belinda's father and Belmont's have determined upon uniting their children by marriage; however, to relieve his friend's pain, Belmont declares, that Clariffa and he have agreed matters fo as to counteract the old gen-

tlemen's defigns. This gives Beverley great fatisfaction, and to increafe his rapture Belinda appears,
whom he addreffes with much gallantry : he prefents her his picture, which fhe partly approves, but
thinks a better painter might have been found,
meaning Cupid, who forms the moft pleafing impreffions.

Clariffa and Belmont, who indeed fay nothing
worth ftaying on for, retire, and leave their friends
to a tete-a-tete. Beverley feems to think Belinda's
inclination is not totally his, and from this idea he
behaves to her in a ftrange manner, for which fhe
properly reproves him ; many trifling motives of
irritation ftart up, and the converfation is a kind of
fnip-fnap. At length, juftly irritated at his peevifh
fufpicions, fhe retorts upon him emphatically, and
he endeavours to reprefent the whims of his uneafy,
capricious mind, as delicacy. Lady Reftlefs croffing the ftage interrupts them, and they go off with
a promife from Belinda, that fhe will let him into
that lady's character. The baronet's perturbed con-
fort, upon not being immediately anfwered upon
ringing at her own door, fuppofes that fome bafe
tranfactions are going forward in the houfe, and fteps
afide to watch.

Having heard the bell tattle, the chambermaid
opens the door. Marmalet, a vifitor, after fome
reflections upon their different fervices, is going off ;
her ladyfhip coming again to the door, and feeing
this fecond-hand gentlewoman neatly decked out,
demands her bufinefs, intimating, that fhe fuppofes
it has been with Sir John ; the girl's natural confufion at fuch an imputation, ftrengthens fufpicion.
During Marmalet's vindication, obferving her to
have

have a frefh complexion, Lady Reftlefs, fuppofing
her to be painted, attempts rubbing off the unnatural ornament : finding it real, fuch a complexion
gives her frefh uneafinefs, and fhe orders the confounded waiting-woman to come no more near her
doors.   Marmalet's going off rather pettifhly, helps
to feed her jealoufy, as annexing fuch pertnefs to the
idea of a miftrefs ; and it grows to fuch a whimfical
pitch, that fhe fuppofes Sir John has given her the
handfome gown fhe wears.   She then enquires for
her fpoufe, and being told he is gone out, expofes
ftill more her own weaknefs, by rating of Tattle, her
maid.

Belinda and Beverley here enter, again refuming
the former fubject ; his uncertain temper, of which
the lady feems to have a very clear idea ; therefore,
brings him to expletive preliminaries, which he implicitly fubfcribes to.   Seeing Sir William and
Blandford, fhe hurries him off, and in three lines
obferves, that though the old gentlemen are laying
their heads together to counteract the fchemes of
love, yet they muft be difappointed.

The fathers, in a few lines, exprefs what we have
been previoufly acquainted with, their mutual intentions concerning their children.   Belinda being
fpoken to on the fubject, mentions Beverley, as having been once encouraged by her father ; but he
obferving that he has changed his mind, peremptorily infifts upon her obeying the dictates of his will :
this tyrannical obftinacy throws her into an over-
powering diftrefs of mind, fo that fhe faints, juft as
Sir John Reftlefs comes on, and in her fainting drops
Beverley's picture.   While the baronet is engaged
upon a principle of humanity in affifting the diftreffed

fair

fair one, his turbulent consort sees him from a window, and misinterprets his meaning into gallantry; upon his proposing to take Belinda into his house, her ladyship flies down to confront them.

The young lady chusing to go home, Sir John humanely and politely gives her personal conduct: Lady Restless entering upon their departure, is quite enraged that she missed them, but picks up the picture Belinda dropped, and hopes from thence to make some discovery.

At the beginning of the second act, we meet Sir John enquiring of Robert for his lady; seeing her approach with Tattle, he steps aside, to hear, if possible, any thing consonant to his suspicions. When Lady Restless enters, she blames Tattle for being in a conspiracy against her; then reflects upon the picture, which being that of a man, she supposes to be a former gallant of the unknown lady. At this point of time, while she is railing against husbands, her lord and master peeps in; during some remarks she makes upon the unequal restrictions of men and women in the married state, he swallows what she says as a proof of infidelity. Tattle being ordered down stairs, the jealous lady wishes she had never seen her husband's face, which kind compliment he returns aside: she contemplates the picture, admires its beauty, and feeling perfume puts it near her nose, this Sir John takes for kissing it. While she goes on to compliment the portrait, wishing that she had such a man, the baronet enters tip-toe, comes behind, looks over her shoulder, and seems to approve her choice of a gallant: at length, his patience being quite exhausted, he snatches the bauble; a squabble ensues, wherein mutual mistakes occur laughably; he

charges

charges her with guilt, and she warmly recriminates upon him; he upbraids her with the picture, and she him with the lady he was assisting, till the scene rises into a degree of peculiar pleasantry: at last he goes off to find some proofs against her, and she goes off to attain some against him.

Sir John re-enters soon with Robert, desiring him to look at the picture, and enquires if he can distinguish who it is, insisting at the same time that he can tell if he will, he tries every means to pump some intelligence out of him, but without a satisfactory answer. A Footman comes on and enquires for Sir John's; the Baronet asks his business, and takes a letter for Lady Restless from him; which upon perusal appears to be written by Lord Conquest in his Lady's absence, as an exculpation of the guilt with which Marmalet was charged in the first act; and which, by the tenor of his Lordship's letter, has since been enforced by Lady Restless.

Sir John, still in a state of egregious mistake, interprets all this to his wife's dishonour, employs Robert to go and enquire for Mrs. Marmalet, and seems more alarmed at being told she visits Tattle; he appoints a meeting too with the waiting-woman in the Bird-Cage-Walk, and cautions Robert to extreme secrecy, desiring at the same time that she may meet him masked. Matters thus settled, he goes to search for the original of that picture which he found in his wife's possession.

Belmont and Beverley succeed the discontented sprite conversing upon their amorous concerns; and it appears that Belmont's father, Sir William, has positively declared against his union with Clarissa; however he assures Beverley of never interfer-

ing

ing with his miſtreſs, Belinda ; notwithſtanding
which, that very odd mortal goes off in a ſtile that
we know not well whether he is pleaſed or diſpleaſ-
ed. Sir John enters, and by the introduction of
what's o'clock joins Belmont, in whom he can diſcover no likeneſs of the picture : Beverley re-entering accoſts Belmont, in phraſeology the author
ſeems fond of, my boy, dear rogue, &c. Sir John
cruiſes round for the purpoſe of diſcovery, conſiders Beverley very minutely, and draws concluſi-
ons of his being the original of that picture which
has given him ſo much uneaſineſs. The behaviour of
Sir John here has no doubt humour, but we think
the author has ſacrificed probable nature to catch
at laughter. Belmont and Beverley being very juſtly ſurpriſed at his behaviour, he thinks they laugh
at him ; indeed the exerciſe of a cane over his
ſhoulders would better ſuit his behaviour, but that
he eſcapes.

At length Beverley knowing the picture to be
that he gave Belinda, catches jealous feelings, eſpecially as Sir John puts it haſtily into his pocket,
and upon being aſked another ſight of it retires
precipitately into his houſe ; this ſets the tinder-
tempered lover into a blaze, as ſuppoſing his miſtreſs has given that token of regard to another
gallant ; the act concludes with a ſhort and unneceſſary ſoliloquy of Sir John's, intimating that he
muſt prove the identity of Beverley.

The two young ladies, Belinda and Clariſſa,
meet us at the beginning of the third act, ſtill con-
verſing upon their matrimonial projects ; the latter
ſeems to heſitate at ſome reſolves ſhe has taken,
while the former appears to laugh at her diffidence ;

the

the caprice of Beverley is mentioned again by Belinda, who, notwithstanding such a ticklish temper, cannot avoid loving the man : Clarissa very justly remarks that there is some reason to doubt her friend's temper, being rather like the man's she complains of; this Belinda denies, and Beverley is introduced to speak for himself; after a few lines, Belmont asks for the picture, which she cannot find, and charges one or other of them with having it, this nettles Beverley : Seeing the capricious lovers ready to squabble again, Belmont and his mistress very prudently retire from the approaching storm.

When they are gone the agitated swain upbraids his lady very severely, for having given, as he supposes, his picture to a more favoured gallant; his childish behaviour she only laughs at, and indeed it deserves no other treatment. She leaves him in a state of dissatisfaction; but returns soon with Clarissa, they pass him by, sneer at his uneasiness, and thereby increase it much; in soliloquy he expresses himself with vehemence, and determining to know the bottom of the matter he resolves, when they are out of sight, to visit Sir John, whose house he knows by having seen him go into it.

Lady Restless meeting Robert with some cloaths over his own, stops him to search the pockets for letters; not finding any, she renews her former accusation against the servant, that he is her enemy and in combination with his master; hearing a rap at the door she listens, and, Tattle coming on, enquires who is at the door, then upbraids her for going out without leave; on being informed that she went to bring Marmalet for their mutual justi-

fication, this is conftrued into a frefh crime by her
Ladyfhip, and fhe refolves upon vifiting Lady Conqueft, having had no anfwer to her letter; Tattle,
true to her name and ftation, throws out a fuppofition which gratifies Lady Reftlefs's fufpicions, by
telling that Robert was at Lord Conqueft's, defiring Marmalet to meet his mafter in the evening.

While the wretched wife is enjoying this piece of
information, a fervant acquaints her that a gentleman below wants to fpeak to Sir John about a picture; hoping fome difcovery from this interview,
fhe orders him to be fhewn up ftairs; Tattle's intelligence, which fhe feems willing to enrich with
all the ornaments of fcandal, is interrupted by Beverley's approach. After mutual falutation they
enter upon the fubject of his vifit, when they plant
thorns in each other's breaft by a chain of mifin-
terpretations; he looks upon it as certain that
Belinda gave Sir John the picture, and to confirm
the matter her Ladyfhip feelingly defcribes the fituation fhe faw them in during the fainting fit;
adding, that fhe believes her hufband capable of
any vile action.

This fcene is admirably well wrought up, as the
confufion of miftakes arife from very probable appearances, and the characters part under conviction
that their fears have been well founded. The
fcene changing to the Park, Sir John enters before
his own houfe, fully perfuaded that he has difcovered his wife's paramour; juft at this inftant he
fees Beverley coming from his houfe, and giving
Robert a gratification for his trouble; when the
jealous lover perceives the jealous hufband, he accofts him with a degree of peevifhnefs which is an-

fwered

livered in the fame ftile : Here recrimination pleafantly enfues, and the puzzle of circumftances is
kept up in a pleafing manner ; each catches eagerly
at what flatters his own opinion, while jealoufy gives
applaufe that fhe makes them fuch ridiculous fools.

Stung to the quick, when Sir John leaves him,
Beverley declares that he will have one interview
with his falfe miftrefs to vent his mind, and then,
however painful it may be, renounce her for ever ;
here fhe enters with Belmont, and Clariffa, who are
the moft commode polite companions we know ;
for they come on without any bufinefs, fay little,
help to make out a laugh, and complaifantly leave
their friends to battle as long as they like.

Belinda feems inclined to coquette it with her
gallant, but neither her fmiles, nor fallies of wit,
can clear the wintry gloom of Beverley's brow ; it
fcowls heavily upon her till the ftorm burfts in his
pronouncing an everlafting farewel : At length, after
confiderable acrimony on both fides, by his mentioning the circumftance of her being feen in the
arms of a gentleman, fhews her his miftake, which,
from a fpirit of refentment, fhe determines to improve for the fake of additional mortification.

His declaration of love, and the regard he has
for her future happinefs, notwithftanding the bafenefs he thinks her guilty of, are marks of an ingenuous and delicate mind ; however, fhe properly
triumphs and keeps him on the fret till he almoft
becomes an object of pity ; his affeverations of never approaching her again are carried too far ; indeed the fcene wants curtailing, for it harps too
long upon one ftring. Belinda concludes the third
act with placing jealous lovers in the light DRYDEN

has done great wits, that it is within the pale of madnefs or juft on the edge of it.

At the beginning of the fourth act he feems to verify her remark by meditating in a manner almoft frantic, and upon receiving, by the hands of his fervant, a letter from her, the delirium rifes ; our author has here given a fine fcope for acting merit, but it is not eafily hit off : The infeparable pair, Clariffa and Belmont, come on while he is in a painful reverie, they roufe him, and recommend a reconciliation with a woman they think he cannot help loving ; he remains obftinate, yet drops feveral ex-preffions which plainly indicate that his heart bends that way ; the circumftance of her fainting fit, which gave rife to Lady Reftlefs's ftrange narration being explained to him, he is fhocked at the idea of his own brutal behaviour, and fears to approach the injured fair, but by the encouragement of friends re-folves to attempt the reconciliation he fo much wifhes : The pleafing difcovery of Belinda's inno-cence tranfports her lover into almoft as extravagant joy as her imaginary falfhood gave him pain, he goes off, and his dove-like friends follow.

Belinda mourning her lover's unaccountable tem-per appears next, enquiring of Tippet whether any meffage is come from him : Sir John enters, when by Belinda's charging his Lady with having weaned Beverley's affection from her, Sir John opens a frefh field of perplexity, by accufing Beverley with a de-fign upon his wife ; Belinda's regard makes her he-fitate for fome time, but on being affured by the Baronet that what he has faid may be relied on, fhe in her turn refolves to difclaim him.

Sir

All in the Wrong.

Sir John, soon after leaving her, appears in the Park, in expectation of Marmalet; a woman comes on masked, who, confessing great fear, begs admittance to his house; knowing that Lady Restless is not at home he admits her, and orders that they may be private. We next meet Tattle acquainting Beverley with the mischief his picture had occasioned; he wants to see Sir John for sake of explanation, but she advises him not to stay on any account, however the argument is ended by her seeing the Baronet conducting a woman in a mask. Beverley's suspicion takes alarm, and for the sake of discovery he consents to be put into a closet where he may overhear.

By the by, this listening is a most ungentlemanlike action, the worthless fruit of a mean, suspicious heart. Sir John leads forward his Mask, which proves to be no other than his own crooked rib; having gone something too far while he supposed her Marmalet, he tries what soothing will do, but she remains inexorable, and going for pen and ink, as resolving to give her brother an account of the disagreeable situation she is in, she finds the closet where Beverley lies concealed locked; this proves fresh cause of suspicion, and being laughed at by Sir John she grows more impatient. The Maid is thrown into confusion and pretends to know nothing of the key, but being forced to produce it, throws it on the ground and runs away.

On perceiving a man, her Ladyship screams out, and Sir John, at Beverley's unaccountable appearance, revives his jealousy; Beverley endeavours to apologize, but cannot obtain a hearing; he is beset both by Sir John and the Lady, whose mutual at-

tacks

tacks place him in a very difagreeable fituation; at
length Beverley threatening a duel if his picture is
not returned, the Baronet's courage fails him, and
he gives it up; after which the young gentleman
retires with a declaration, that when reafon can be
heard he fhall be ready to convince them of their
error. Sir John, glowing with fufpicion, renews
the verbal war with her Ladyfhip, in which, like a
true female, fhe maintains her part ably; threats
and reproaches of an angry nature are vented reci-
procally, and they conclude the fourth act with
very virulent terms.

Blandford, Sir William, and Belmont, meet us,
the former obferving that all matters relative to the
marriage are fettled, goes to call his daughter Belinda. From an intermediate conference between
Sir William and his fon, the latter difcovers an inclination to evade the match his father has provided
for him, and pleads the lady's averfion to it; the
old fellow grows warm and infifts upon the point,
which obliges Belmont to fay, if the Lady is willing he fhall be ready; but this condefcenfion he
only makes from an affurance that fhe will never be
brought to compliance; however in this he feems
greatly difappointed, for Blandford comes on proclaiming with joy his daughter's readinefs to obey;
fhe formally declares her fentiments to the utter
confufion of Belmont, the fathers go off to take a
cheering glafs and invite him to participate, after a
fingle queftion to Belinda he follows them.

She in a fhort foliquy declares that her determination is ferious, but Clariffa's claim to Belmont
ftriking upon her mind caufes fome impediment;
to her maid Tippet fhe vents her fpleen againft Beverley.

verly, defiring that all his letters, and a bracelet, may be returned, claiming her's in exchange; fhe gives one alfo to inform him that his falfhood has forced her into a compliance with the match her father has propofed.

The fucceeding part of this fcene fhews Belinda in a very natural pleafant view of love-fick agitation; juft as fhe is entering into the moft folemn refolutions never to fee his face again, a fervant acquaints her that Beverley requefts admittance, fhe orders him to be fhewn up, and bids Tippet retire. Her gallant at his entrance pleads pardon for his mifconduct, which fhe peremptorily denies, he folicits her acceptance of the picture recovered from Sir John, but fhe afferts it is come from Lady Reftlefs; when fhe mentions her marriage with Belmont, his fubmiffion and fupplication changes to very fevere retorts, which work her into tears, and drive her off with a farewel for ever.

In a fhort fcene with Tippet he fhews what faft hold fhe has of his heart, and goes off to find means of clearing matters; fhe returns, and having the fame feelings for him which he has for her, is perfuaded by the waiting-woman to feek an explanation from Lady Reftlefs, for which purpofe fhe orders a chair. Belmont enters and blames her for caufing him fuch perplexity, fhe pleads Beverley's falfhood. The gentle Clariffa appears, much warmed with a fuppofition that fhe has been much impofed on by Belmont and Belinda; when the laft mentioned lady goes off, Belmont wants to perfuade Clariffa that fhe mifconceives matters, but intimating that her behaviour feems the effect of jealoufy, her pride is hurt, and fhe leaves him abruptly, declaring

claring that Belinda shall have her thoughts upon paper.

Sir William enters to his son, declaring all is now ready for consummation : Belmont, by way of gaining time, gives a material reason for declining the match, no less than the lady's having a blemished reputation ; this alarms the old baronet. Blandford, full of the wedding, comes enquiring for his daughter ; being informed that she is gone to Sir John Restless's, he entertains some fear, and this circumstance corroborates Belmont's insinuation to his father ; they all go off in pursuit of her. Tattle conducts Beverley in ; a few speeches pass between him and Lady Restless, when Sir John rushes in with fresh complaint : Beverley attempts to discuss the point calmly, when Belinda enters, which occasions a very laughable jumble of jealousy. While their passions are in the full tide of recrimination, Blandford and Sir William appear, Lady Restless maintains perplexity, by charging Belinda with making her miserable. Belmont and Clarissa appear : Sir William, confirmed by what he hears of Belinda's blemished reputation, desires his son to take the lady of his choice. This occasions some rubs between the old gentlemen, and Blandford declares against any connexion with those who could slight his daughter.

Clarissa, without any point being cleared up, patiently suffers Belmont to take her hand. Belinda is offered to Beverley by her father ; Lady Restless says, if he will marry the object of her jealousy, she will be satisfied ; and Sir John says, that Belinda's consent will quiet his mind. This brings matters to an explanation, with regard to the picture ; but Sir John

2

and

All in the Wrong.

and his lady laying fresh charges against each other, he goes off to bring on conviction, and she follows to prevent his having a private conference with his confidante Robert.

All the characters go off, and leave Belinda and Beverley to make up their bickerings in a tender, natural, agreeable manner. The other characters soon return, when it appears, that Sir John and his lady, by what conviction we know not, are satisfied; the union of Belinda and Beverley is agreeably confirmed by Blandford's insisting upon it; the piece concludes with mutual assurances of regulating temper better for the future; the lady's concluding rhimes we dont admire.

Never did criticism toil through such a pantomimical jumble of incidents as this comedy, especially in the last act; and there is such a similarity in most of the scenes, that we have been extremely puzzled to find words for the account of them, without saying the same thing over and over again.

Time and place are very well preserved, but the plot is unpardonably intricate, and not sufficiently elucidated at the catastrophe; the four leading characters are exactly alike, save two being married and two single. From a natural impetuosity in Mr. YATES's temper, and his knowledge of the stage, great expectations might have been formed from his exhibition of the precipitate, weak, chimerical Sir John Restless, who catches at the shadow of offence, and entirely sets aside the reasonable investigation of the circumstances which pain his mind; not one critical idea could be formed but he fulfilled to a very particular degree of satisfaction; and we are surprized how Mr. KING has brought himself

All in the Wrong.

himself to such an exact equilibre with the original :
without borrowing from his predecessor any thing,
he equally gains and pleases our attention ; we cannot point out any precedence that should take place
between these two gentlemen in this play ; if any
preference must be given, the last mentioned perhaps may claim it, as having a more pleasing, though
not a more chaste utterance.

Beverley is a stranger object for a batchelor, than
Sir John is for a husband, captious, fretful, and
suspicious to an intolerable degree, so much that we
think Belinda's suffering such repetition of his infolent airs, and uniting with him at last, is an impeachment of her understanding ; love we know works
unaccountable effects, but we think the jealousy of
this play so strained and improbable, that to us it
seems carried to the last degree of folly.

The gentleman who first appeared in this amorous Quixote being retired from theatrical connections we are not at liberty to name him, but must
assert that his merit was inimitable ; Mr. CAUTHER-
LEY, oh la ! oh la ! oh la ! only serves to pain remembrance with a dismal contrast to what we have
seen. Belmont is such an insipid daudle, it would
be cruel to expect any thing from an actor in the
representation of him ; no body need wish to dif-
possess Mr. PACKER of him, and whoever does
will not, we imagine, have more merit ; Sir William Belmont and Blandford being equally insignificant may repose quietly enough in the somniferous
possession of Messrs. BRANSBY and BURTON, as
same a pair as e'er made audience nod.

The

The character of Lady Reftlefs is exactly fimilar to that of her hufband, a childifh fhadow-hun-
ter, a perplexing termagant, fond of mifery, and
conftantly in purfuit of it : Mifs Houghton, notwithftanding a lifp, and the Newcaftle mode of
pronouncing the letter r, had a very particular
merit in this turbulent Lady ; yet we have great reafon to be furprized why Mrs. Pritchard was not
the original, whofe acting in the Jealous Wife
gave fuch juft and general fatisfaction ; at prefent
the part is fupplied by Mrs. Hopkins with more
ability than fhe fhews in moft of her undertakings.

Belinda is very like, though not quite fo great
an oddity as her lover ; how Mrs. Yates could be
appointed her reprefentative is impoffible to fay, as
fhe never had, nor never will have, any degree of
comic expreffion : Mrs. Abington goes infinitely
beyond her, and feems to fill up the author's intention perfectly. Clariffa is too infipid for any actrefs to make a figure in, fhe impaired the real merit of Mrs. Palmer, and lies heavy on Mrs. W.
Barry.

Upon the whole, we muft condemn that hurry of
incidents, and that famenefs of character which we
find in this piece ; nor do we perceive any very obvious
moral ; the dialogue is eafy and fpirited, but not
enriched with fentiment ; it is almoft entirely a kind
of peevifh chit-chat : This comedy, had there not
been one previoufly called fo, fhould have been
named the Picture, for that is the axis on which
it turns ; this brings to mind a remark of Mr.
Quin's, at a confultation, what name to give the

SUSPICIOUS HUSBAND; his opinion being afked, Why, fays the cynic, I have always thought that a play fhould take its title from the moft ftriking incident or character; and, upon this principle, advife you to call it the LADDER and HAT; for, d---m me, if I fee any thing elfe in it worth notice. ALL in the WRONG is kept alive by buftle, and may exift upon the ftage, but is a very poor companion for the clofet.

B A R-

BARBAROSSA.

A Tragedy: By Dr. Brown.

OTHMAN, an officer belonging to Barbaroſſa's court, and a ſlave, open this piece: the former, being told that a ſtranger requeſts admittance, after a pretty account of the unknown perſon, deſires him to be conducted in. Upon Sadi's entrance, Othman approaches to embrace, and give him the moſt cordial ſalutation, which he declines in angry terms: from what enſues, it appears, that this honeſt Algerine, filled with indignation againſt Barbaroſſa, as murderer of their late good king, conſiders Othman, from his place and habiliments, as an abettor of the uſurper. His zeal, for ſome time, is deaf to reaſon; but, when Othman mentions that his ſtay at court was in pity to the Queen, and to watch ſome favourable opportunity of juſt revenge upon the tyrant, Sadi ſoftens. A melting picture is given of the oppreſſion Algiers labours under, and the ſad ſituation Zaphira is in from the murder of her huſband, the exile of her ſon, and being tormented with the amorous ſolicitation of him who has been the cauſe of all her woes.

Othman obſerving that aſſaſſins are diſpatched to find and deſtroy Selim, Sadi's impatience again breaks out, but is moderated by his cooler and more politic friend, who adviſes him to leave the court, which advice, hearing trumpets proclaim the approach of Barbaroſſa, he takes. The tyrant, on his

entrance,

entrance, aſks concerning the execution of five perſons, ſacrificed for what he himſelf had been guilty
of, and delivers himſelf in the haughtieſt terms of
ambitious pride.   Obſerving a penſive caſt in Othman's countenance, he demands the meaning of it ;
then mentions his ſurprize that young Selim ſhould
be a voluntary exile, when he might find protection
from him.

Aladin here brings intelligence that Selim is no
more, the circumſtance ſtrikes Othman ſo that Barbaroſſa perceives it ; however, he gives it a favourable turn.   The Prince thus diſpoſed of, another
care takes up the uſurper's thoughts, how to prevail
on Zaphira : for this he aſks the aſſiſtance of Othman, with promiſes of great reward if he ſucceeds,
and bids him go before the account of her ſon's
death has gloomed her temper.   His ſuppoſed friend
being gone, he indulges his ſatisfaction at Selim's
fate, and confers with Aladin, a very proper agent
of barbarity, deſiring him to ſpread a report that the
widowed Queen has at length conſented to become
his wife.

As he is going to viſit her, his daughter Irene
meets him ; perceiving her in tears, he checks the
untimely ſorrow ſhe wears.   She comes, as it appears, a ſuppliant from the Queen, to beg he wont
perſiſt in his command to ſee her ; this ſhe urges
very tenderly : when he ſpeaks of Selim's death,
her tears flow afreſh.   This enflames him, and he
demands the cauſe, which appears to be gratitude
for his having ranſomed her from a ſtate of captivity : inſtead of applauding her delicate ſenſibility,
Barbaroſſa is enraged that ſhe ſhould have received
freedom from his foe, and goes off, commanding
her

Barbaroſſa.

her not to acquaint the Queen, whom he reſolves to
poſſeſs, with Selim's fate.

Irene, ſtruck with her father's ſtern, obdurate reſolves, declares her intention of aiding Zaphira's eſcape, the firſt favourable opportunity. The humane attachment of this princeſs to diſtreſſed innocence is very amiable, and gives a moſt favourable
impreſſion.

At the beginning of the ſecond act, we meet Zaphira, bewailing her hapleſs lot, bereft both of
huſband and child, and enſlaved by their deſtroyer.
Upon Othman's appearance ſhe mentions her ſon's
fate ; being told that Barbaroſſa aſſumes the name
of king, and means to ſee her, ſhe execrates the
monſter, and ardently wiſhes ſome means of eſcape,
but as there is a ſtrict watch kept Othman deems
that impoſſible ; therefore, recommends external
acquieſcence, as the only method of gaining that liberty which may make her eſcape practicable :
however hard to put on diſſimulation in her caſe,
however painful to a mourning wife and mother,
ſhe, after many ſtruggles, to work the means of revenge, promiſes that her friend's advice ſhall be pur-
ſued. Barbaroſſa approaches, with ſoftened looks
and amorous ſalutation, which ſhe evades, by obſerving, that her heart cannot be weaned from the
firſt object of its regard, that ſhe could not return
his affection, and begs, if he really loves, a proof of
it, by giving her liberty to ſeek her father.

The uſurper endeavours to perſuade, by drawing
a pompous compariſon between his own powerful
grandeur, and the unſettled obſcurity of that ſtate
which ſhe wiſhes to be in : dead to all joys and
ſplendor, ſhe perſeveres ſo far in her requeſt, as to
kneel

kneel at his feet. This moves Barbaroſſa to reproach, which ſhe returns with great bitterneſs of
expreſſion : when, as a ſtroke of art, he offers to en-
throne her ſon if ſhe will marry him, her paſſion
riſes to its utmoſt pitch, and ſhe pours curſes on
him. Finding ſhe has been informed of what he
meant to keep from her knowledge, he ſays the report is not true ; however, ſeeing through and de-
teſting his deſigns, ſhe peremptorily declares againſt
his ſuit ; this draws threats from Barbaroſſa, which
ſhe replies to with ſpirited dignity.

Thus baffled, the tyrant ſoliloquizes in great perturbation, during which Aladin enters, to whom he
tells his diſappointment and diſtraction ; to calm
which, the convenient tool of royalty acquaints him,
that the murderer of Selim is arrived : he immediately deſires to ſee him, and Selim, under the title
of Achmet, is introduced. Upon receiving a ring
from the ſuppoſed ſlave, Barbaroſſa, after giving him
freedom, enquires how the affair was tranſacted.

His curioſity being gratified, he promiſes Achmet conſiderable reward, bids him go to the Queen,
and tell her that Selim, with his dying breath, re-
queſted to heal the wounds of his country, that ſhe
would ſhare Barbaroſſa's bed and throne : he alſo
recommends the ſtranger to Othman's care, and goes
off with Aladin to a banquet.

An anxiety of thought, perceptible in Othman,
occaſions Selim to enquire the cauſe of it, but
he obtains no diſtinct anſwer : the loyal Algerine,
fired with indignation, not only at his lawful
prince's death, but having the murderer before him,
throws off his aſſumed allegiance to Barbaroſſa,
and lays his hatred open ; this, we think, very in-
conſiſtent

Barbaroffa.

confiftent with the fcheme of policy he has laid down
for affifting Zaphira; however, it gives him an opportunity of declaring his friendly fentiments refpecting the Prince, who, with gradual caution at
length reveals himfelf.

Moft dramatic difcoveries, of this nature, are either trifling or improbable ; Selim's we take to have
a touch of both : for though Othman fays no time
can blot out the remembrance of his luftrous eye
and graceful features, yet he cannot recollect him
without adverting to a fcar, which the poet has very unaccountably called beauteous ; had he been
an Irifh author, this would have been named a bull.
Well, this ornamental fcar is produced, at which
Othman very properly exclaims, Am I awake ! and
recognizes the Prince immediately ; nay, fees every
lineament of his father's face in his countenance.
Selim mentions the manner of getting Barbaroffa's
ring, by which he has paffed unfufpected ; he afks
tenderly for his mother, and mentions the tyrant's
order for feeing her ; but Othman, fearful of difcovery, wifhes him to quit the court.

Secure in his difguife, he determines to ftay and
watch a fit opportunity of revenging his father's
blood ; that his defign may not appear romantic, he
fpeaks of having feen Sadi and Almanzor, who,
with a chofen band of citizens, have promifed to
ftorm Barbaroffa's palace. Othman gives precautionary advice, and Selim concludes the fecond act
with an interefting and very fpirited fupplication to
his father's fhade.

Irene, notwithftanding her father's harfh commands, holds Selim in tender regard ; and knowing
him through his difguife, expreffes, at the beginning

2 of

of the third act, anxious concern for his ſafety. He enters, and endeavours to avoid her, but ſhe avows knowledge of him, and with great generoſity of ſpirit, warns him from the court, taking on herſelf the taſk to tell the Queen he lives. When he mentions revenge, as a main motive of his ſtaying in the palace, her filial affection is alarmed, and ſhe utters ſtrong apprehenſions for her father. He urges Barbaroſſa's guilt, ſhe pleads herſelf his daughter, and again tenderly urges his departure, which he ſeems to acquieſce in, if allowed an interview with his mother. She retires, and leaves him to view his perilous ſituation, which he does with very becoming fortitude ; then requeſts from an attendant ſlave audience of the Queen.

Zaphira appears, who, as well as Othman, has ſtrangely forgot the features of her darling ſon : ſhe enquires reſpecting Selim's fate, he tells her that he was witneſs of it, and literally fulfils Barbaroſſa's commands reſpecting Selim's laſt requeſt : Zaphira fires with indignation at ſuch an inſult to her ſon's memory ; ſeeing and pitying her agitation, he changes his tone, and gives her a glimmering of hope that the prince is ſtill alive ; ſays he was his companion in exile, and ſpread the ſtory of his death to gain an interview with her, he bids her maintain her reſolution with becoming confidence, till a ſtroke can be ſtruck for her delivery, and ſends her off in a ſtate of much greater comfort than he met her.

Being alone he indulges that grief which in her preſence he was obliged to ſmother ; when Othman and Sadi appear, he aſks how the night wears, which they inform him approaches the mid-hour ; he communicates the purport of his interview with

the

the Queen, and is told his friends in the city burn
for the hour of action; mentioning that Irene
knew him, his friends preſs immediate departure,
but he determines to be near for the aſſiſtance of a
mother, threatened with violation. He deſires,
upon hearing how matters are concerted, that the
tyrant may be left for his particular vengeance;
Othman reminds him of Irene, but with noble
firmneſs he declares himſelf above the influence of
love in ſuch a cauſe. When the midnight watch
warns them to part, Selim gives a humane charge
to ſhed none but guilty blood; the Prince, in ſoliloquy, ruminates upon the awful circumſtances depending; he examines his heart, and emphatically
apologizes for working by underhand means, that revenge which he could wiſh to obtain by open and
honourable war. The author has laboured, and
not unſuccefsfully, to make this ſcene a ſolemn preparation for the great event that is in agitation; the
ſtillneſs of the night, the murmuring ſurge, the
moon riſing in blood, all call attention, to the
wiſhed for point.

Irene begins the fourth act with Aladin; it appears, that terrified by an ominous dream, ſhe has
deſired to ſee her father, who comes on in a very
churliſh mood at being diſturbed during his banquet; ſhe expreſſes her apprehenſion of lurking
danger, and relates her dream with ſtrong colouring, which Barbaroſſa treats with contempt.

Aladin comes on, and informs him, that a ru-
mour prevails of young Selim's being alive, and
in the city; though loth to admit fear, he orders
the watch to be doubled, and commands Achmet
to be brought before him; this alarms Irene, who

begs hard that he may not ſee Achmet, but the uſurper will have hís way, and · drives her off the ſtage in a ſtate of painful perplexity ; being alone, conſcious guilt riſes to his view, and ſeems to ſtagger his reſolution ; but knowing in his ſituation, the danger of remorſe, he reſolves to ſupprefs the feelings of conſcience. He demands of Selim, if he be really what he has repreſented.

This unexpected queſtion rather confounds the prince ; Barbaroſſa, with violent threats, aſks if Selim is not alive ; Selim, with a dagger's point at his breaſt, evades fate, by braving it ; however, the uſurper commands he may be ſtrictly watched, then orders the marriage writes, vowing, that Zaphira ſhall, during the current night, be joined to him in wedlock ; ſhe comes on and is queſtioned, whether her heart has relented, by perſiſting in refuſal, ſhe enflames him ſo that he calls his guards to drag her to the altar ; whether Mahometans have any altars we are not entirely clear ; theſe compulſive meaſures occaſion her to cry out for her abſent ſon. Selim hearing her voice, enters, Barbaroſſa orders him to retire ; Zaphira very oddly we think, prays his aſſiſtance, for what could the aid of a ſingle, unarmed ſlave avail againſt the determination of a monarch ſurrounded by guards ; however, Selim tries what ſolicitation will do ; finding that vain, he makes a final effort with his dagger ; Barbaroſſa evades the blow, and delivers him to the guards, when priſoner he avows himſelf the identical Selim ; this ſudden diſcovery of her ſon, and his deſparate ſituation, overwhelms Zaphira ; ſhe faints, and he, running to embrace her, they are torn aſunder.

When

When the Queen recovers, Barbaroſſa renews his order for her being forceably borne off; this again reduces Selim to his knees, the uſurper wiſhing to touch her heart in the tendereſt vein, orders her ſon to be borne to the rack; ſo ſevere a trial works her to compliance with the marriage; the Prince, with noble diſdain and unſhakeable reſolution, declines life, gained by ſo ſhameful a purchaſe; ſhe catches the noble flame, and both defying the tyrant's power, they are carried off ſeparately.

Aladin increaſes the confuſion and rage of Barbaroſſa, by giving certain intelligence of a conſpiracy in the city; he orders out ſpies to diſcover, if poſſible, the members of it, then commands Selim's immediate death, and goes off breathing threats, dreadful in their tenor.

At the beginning of the fifth act, we again meet him, enquiring whether proper precautions are taken, and obſerving, that the ſpies which were ſent out, have found no trace of tumult; the ſecond watch he dooms for Selim's final moment. Irene once more comes a ſuppliant to her father, and with tears offers up petitionary plaints, yet is treated with unuſual, or rather increaſed ſeverity; however the urgent occaſion, and the violent emotion of her heart, in favour of the man ſhe loves, oblige her to perſevere till her enraged ſire orders the guards to force her off.

Left alone, the perilous condition ambition has brought him to, preſents itſelf to his diſheartened mind; upon enquiring for Othman, Aladin ſays, that he is fled, and that much danger may be apprehended; the following line uttered in Barbaroſ-

ſa's

fa's fury is unpardonably vulgar, " Why then, may all hell's curfes follow him," this frefh alarm precipitates the Prince's fate, and the ufurper with moft vindictive ideas goes to fee him put to the rack, unlefs propofed conceffions mitigate his fentence.

Selim, furrounded by executioners, appears no further concerned than that his remains may not be treated with difrefpect; but that feems an unneceffary application, fince the great foe who robs him of life muft have equal power, with perhaps equal antipathy over his breathlefs body, that he has to the animated; Barbaroffa entering, orders him to be raifed from the ground, and afks if his life is not forfeited upon his own principles; the Prince defires him to take it; however, the tyrant, for Zaphira's fake expoftulates, till contemptuous refufal, and found of the fecond watch, end the fruitlefs conference, Selim is left to the rack, and they are binding him with cords when Irene's entrance gains him a fmall refpite. Far from upbraiding her with her father's cruelty, he treats her in the tendereft manner, and ftrives to foften that woe fhe feels, as fuppofing herfelf the means of his being difcovered, fhe begs forgivenefs, which he moft readily grants, and commits his mother to her care.

Juft as they are fixing him to the rack, a tumult is heard, which fills him with fpirit, and the guards with difmay. Aladin enters in confufion, and calls off the officers, &c. to affift Barbaroffa. Irene now again melts with tendernefs for her father's danger, and hearing the clafh of fwords goes off in a ftate of diftracted grief: Othman entering with a party frees

Selim

Barbaroſſa.

Selim, and gives him a ſword, with which he goes to ſeek his mortal foe.

The tyrant, like Macbeth, tied to a ſtake, knows not what ſtep to take. Othman encounters, and gives him a mortal wound, at which inſtant Selim enters. Seeing Barbaroſſa proſtrate, he regrets that his hand had not given the blow, and calls on the murderer, that he may awake the ſtings of remorſe. His words have the deſired effect, and when he finds the expiring monſter contrite, his generous temper takes ſo humane a turn, that he ſolicits heaven's mercy in his favour.

After the tyrant begs protection for his daughter, and draws his laſt breath, the Prince gives orders to ſtop all hoſtilities. It is an amiable ſtroke when Sadi moves that the body of Barbaroſſa ſhould be dragged about the ſtreets, for Selim to forbid ſuch inhumanity. Zaphira, filled with apprehenſions, enters, jealous of her ſteps, and fearful of every one ſhe ſees ; but ſoon perceives with joy the happy revolution of affairs. After mutual congratulations, and pious acknowledgment to heaven, Selim aſks for Irene, who, by Othman's order, has been taken care of. Zaphira pronounces her worthy to partake his throne, which he acquieſces in, and then concludes the piece, deducing its general moral in the following agreeable lines :

> Now let us thank the eternal pow'r : convinc'd
> That heav'n but tries our virtue by affliction :
> That oft the cloud which wraps the preſent hour,
> Serves but to brighten all our future days.

Though Dr. Brown has in a previous advertiſement, pompouſly paraded his ſteady adherence to

the

the ancient drama in this compoſition, yet, I believe, had he not mentioned it, no reader would
have found it out; he has indeed, been ſcrupulouſly
nice with reſpeſt to time and place, but vigour of
genius is wanting, and there is much more labour
than fancy : from the former he has deviſed a plot,
which preſents us with ſeveral ſtriking incidents,
and works on to a juſt, agreeable and inſtruſtive
cataſtrophe ; but being deficient of the latter, expreſſion in many of the ſcenes is ſo languid, that if
it does affeſt, it muſt be more through the merit of
the aſtor than the poet.

Barbaroſſa is an ample ſubjeſt for deteſtation to
work, not a ray of virtue can we perceive to light
his gloomy frame ; haughty, revengeful, luſtful,
and cruel. A wretch, eaten up with impious paſſions, and an entire ſlave to each of them ; a curſe
to himſelf, and a plague to human kind ; at leaſt,
that part of it which unhappily came within his
ſphere. There is ſuch a mixture of gloom, fire and
affeſted ſoftneſs, that it requires very uncommon
powers to give this part due force. Mr. Mossop
made it ſo conſpicuous, that we may juſtly ſay, as
the author no doubt formed the charaſter for him,
ſo nature formed him for it. We cannot deſcribe
how amazingly he improved his original, and
ſtrengthened many weak paſſages which muſt lie
heavy on performers of leſs ability. Alas ! Mr.
Bensley, Mr. Colman puts you as Marlborough
did John Duke of Argyle, upon all the moſt hazardous attempts : for heaven's ſake, reſign the ſove-
reignty of Algiers ; dont miſlead yourſelf, by thinking that goggling the eye-balls will give the idea of a
ſtern aſpeſt ; nor imagine, that puſhing one ſhould-

er before the other, and rolling like a Dutch long-
boat in a rough fea, can pafs for dignity of deportment.   We would moft humbly, in the fincerity of
friendly wifhes, advife you to change places with
Mr. CLARKE ; a prudent retreat is no fmall part of
generalfhip ; if the managers fhould threaten you
with a Chancery fuit for declining his mighty appointment, try if you cant get him to ftand the
roaft in a fimilar manner.

Achmet is an object as amiable as his vile competitor is horrid ; his fituation very critical, his undertaking noble, his filial piety unfhakeable, his honour inviolate, his love difinterefted, his friendfhip
warm, permanent and affable ; his difpofition gentle, even to foes, and his courage equal to any danger.   As a part, he is much better written than
Barbaroffa, yet many of his fpeeches want nerve,
which indeed Mr. GARRICK moft amply fupplied.
There are feveral breaks and paffages in this character, which feem in perufal to have very little
meaning ; yet he fent them thrilling through the
heart, and then brought them flowing from the eyes.

Mr. SAVIGNY, being as yet a very young performer, in point of practice, which is highly effential
to perfection, we muft, as far as impartiality will
admit, touch him with a lenient hand.   Whether
this part was chofen by himfelf, or recommended
by fome anxious friend, we can by no means approve it for a beginning ; there is fuch an intricacy,
fo many tranfitions, fuch a variety of manoeuvres,
commonly called ftage bufinefs, that two feafons, at
leaft, are neceffaay to cultivate properly even fuch a-
bilities as are naturally adequate to the undertaking.
                                                    The

The gentleman who has lately appeared, ſeems to ſpeak, bating the barbariſm of *furm* inſtead of *firm*, *ſturn* inſtead of *ſtern*, and being faultily emphatic upon *thy*, *thee*, aⁿ d *thou*, with propriety : the middle and lower notes of his voice harmoniouſly diſtinct, and either from nature or imitation, very like thoſe of Mr. GARRICK. We are told, that he has very extenſive powers, we wiſh it may prove ſo, but we could not perceive any proſpect of ſuch. In the midſt of firſt night fear, they will break out, though irregularly. Mr. BARRY and Mr. MOSSOP, ſhewed their excellent voices in their firſt attempts, though doubtleſs not ſo well as they have ſince exerted them.

Mr. SAVIGNY's countenance, from what we could diſcover, ſeems pleaſing and expreſſive, but wants thoſe ſtrong lines of expreſſion, which command a large audience. His perſon appears well propor-'tioned, for what there is of it ; and, if he would lay aſide that mode of holding his head over his ſhould-er, which ſeems to be caught from Roſcius, his po-ſitions and deportment would b more natural. Upon the whole, we are willing to allow him the beſt acquiſition by much, that our theatres have made ſince Mr. POWELL's commencement.

The dreſs of Selim is a very diſadvantageous one, and reſembles as a wit in one of the boxes obſerved, part of the Queen's Zebra's wardrobe : We wiſh Mr. SAVIGNY, who has good feelings, and pleaſing expreſſion, every improvement and acqui-ſition neceſſary to place him deſervedly at the head of his new profeſſion.

Sadi

Barbaroſſa.

Sadi has little to diſtinguiſh him, but a commendable ſpirit of loyalty; which he expreſſes in reſpectful terms, during the firſt ſcene. We remember to have ſeen Mr. DAVIES's performance of this part; it was ſenſible, and ſuitably ſpirited: We are in no ſhape pleaſed to find Mr. HULL undertaking this patriotic Algerine; declamation and paternal tenderneſs are his ſtile, not love nor fire.

Othman is alſo a faithful ſubject to a dead monarch, and his oppreſſed heir: Mr. HAVARD did him juſtice, but we think Mr. CLARKE much preferable; indeed, he has not ſuch dazzling rays of merit round him, as the original had to encounter.

Aladin is one of thoſe obſequious, execrable court jackalls, who are never happier than when providing prey for the lion authority; he has not one word to ſay that can render his villainy paſſable; Mr. GARDNER is rather better than Mr. MOZEEN was.

Zaphira is drawn with dignity as a Queen, conſtancy as a widow, and tenderneſs as a mother: through the whole piece ſhe claims reſpect and pity, when we dont ſee her, ſhe is neverthelefs kept in our view.

The dead are not ſo often flattered as the living; Mrs. CIBBER can now give no compenſation for praiſe; nor, if ſhe could, would it avail in this work; but let gratitude, as well as judgment, place her for the peculiar feelings ſhe raiſed, far before Mrs. YATES. Her tenderneſs was truly pathetic, and the reſiſtive parts delicate, her countenance a matchleſs index to the whole. Her ſucceſſor has a voice too full for ſoftneſs, and a countenance more expreſſive of diſdain than ſorrow; yet, as things go at preſent, the ſtage might rejoice if only one half of the capital parts could ſhew the merit ſhe has in this.

Miſs MILLER is more tolerable in Irene than any thing we have ſeen her in yet, though a poor, whimpering daudle from beginning to end ; we mean theſe laſt words of the character, and prefer the lady mentioned to Miſs MACKLIN.

From the tears it has drawn, we may conclude this is not a bad acting tragedy ; however, being upon the whole but a middling effort of genius, we think it meagre food for contemplation in the cloſet.

MUCH

MUCH ADO ABOUT NOTHING.

A Comedy: By Shakespeare.

LEONATO Governor of Meffina, begins this piece, perufing a letter from Don Pedro, of Arragon, by which he is informed of that Prince's arrival the fame evening; he queftions the meffenger concerning a battle which has been fought; this occafions honourable mention to be made of one Claudio, a young Florentine; Beatrice enquires for Benedick, and is tartly witty at his expence. The Prince entering with his fuit, falutes Leonato; Benedict happening to let fall fome words, Beatrice immediately attacks him, and a fhort altercation of quibbling raillery enfues, more pregnant with pleafantry than meaning. While they are playing the game of fnip-fnap, we find Don Pedro has accepted Leonato's invitation, to ftay a month or more at his houfe,

When all go off but Claudio and Benedict, the former afks the latter if he has noticed Leonato's daughter; after humoroufly giving his opinion of her, he obtains from Claudio a confeffion of love for the young lady; this he acquaints the Prince with on his return, who feems to approve Hero as an object worthy of affection: Benedick, from an affumed contempt of amorous feelings, puns and quibbles ludicroufly, not only upon the fubject of Claudio's paffion, but upon matrimonial connec-

tions

tions in general; his remarks occasion the Prince and lover to retort, by obferving, that he, for all his boafting will fall into the fnare; however, the confident batchelor thinks his freedom in no danger, and proclaims himfelf poffeffed of unfhakeable independance; Pedro fends Benedick off to acquaint Leonato he will attend his fupper.

Claudio being alone with the Prince, profeffes at large his affection for Hero, and that it may not feem a fudden ftart of fancy, declares, that he loved her before his going to the war, they have lately been engaged in; then follicits Pedro's affiftance in favour of his fuit, which is readily and cordially granted to him, for which purpofe the Prince, knowing there is to be a mafquerade, lays a fcheme for founding Hero's inclination; which is to affume the character of Claudio, and in that fhape to make ftrong declarations of love.

This fettled, they go off to make way for Antonio and Leonato; the former tells the latter that a fervant of his has overheard the Prince declaring a paffion for Hero, and that he intended mention of it to her during the mafquerade; this feems very improbable, there being no time for Antonio's receiving fuch a piece of information, as one party enter immediately upon the other's departure; Leonato, though he does not feem to lay much weight on the difcovery, neverthelefs, determines to acquaint his daughter with the matter, that in cafe it fhould be fact, fhe may be the better prepared.

When the old gentlemen difappear, Don John and Conrade come forward; from their converfation, it appears, that Don John is of a furly mifchievous difpofition; that he hates obligations, and would

would injure the Prince, his brother, who has lately reſtored him to that place in fraternal affection,
which his ill behaviour had forfeited. Conrade
adviſes him to a ſmoother mode of behaviour, but
villainy being the firſt fruit of his heart, he determines to purſue it. Upon being informed by Borachio of an intended marriage, he goes off with
the malevolent intention of diſturbing the peace of
thoſe who never injured him.

At the begginning of the ſecond act, Leonato
enquires whether Don John was not at ſupper;
mention of this gloomy blade, occaſions ſprightly
Beatrice to remark ſhrewdly upon the contraſt between him and Benedick; the following part of
this ſcene is made up of rhapſodical obſervations,
upon love, marriage, maids and batchelors, by this
loquacious lady; the maſquers coming on, Pedro
ſingles out Hero, who has been prepared by her
father; he ſollicits conference, but is baffled by her
anſwers; while they retire, other characters play
on each other; among the reſt Benedick and
Beatrice encounter, whoſe phraſes are bandied to
and fro with all the quickneſs and levity of a ſhut-
tle-cock: under cover, ſhe cuts him up to himſelf; after a dance, Don John comes forward with
Borachio, they miſtake Claudio for Benedick, and
acquaint him that the Prince is in love with Hero,
deſiring him to prevent ſo inadequate a connection;
when they are gone off, Claudio meditates upon
what he has heard with moſt ſtrange feelings of
jealouſy; the Prince had to him declared a deſign
of wooing Hero in his favour; yet now he is ſurprized to hear that what they had agreed upon has
been put in practice; nothing but the abſurdi-
ties

ties lovers are capable of, could possibly justify this.

While he is in peevish mood, Benedick comes on, and jestingly confirms his jealousy, which teizing of his ruffled temper, occasions a sudden retreat. Pedro approaching, is charged with having caught the affection of Hero, which he declares to be won in favour of Claudio; the Prince mentioning a quarrel Beatrice has to Benedick, he gives a very fanciful and humorous account of his own mef- fage by that volatile dame; juft as he has finished his account, she appears; seeing her, he haftens off, as if terrified at the thoughts of encountering so nimble and bitter a tongue.

When Pedro fays to Beatrice that she has *put down* Benedick, she makes a reply rather reprehen- fible, as raifing a grofs idea, " So I would not he should do me, my Lord, left I should *prove* the *mother* of *fools.*"

The Prince, perceiving a cloud on Claudio's coun- tenance, demands the reafon, to which he receives equivocal replies; Benedick is guilty of a vulgarifm when he fays the Count is *civil* as an orange, the name being *Seville*; at beft, like many others in this play it is a ftrained pun.

When Pedro declares that he wooed Hero for Claudio, Leonato gives her in form to the raptured lover; this difpofal of her coufin, fets Beatrice rat- tling once more; she is again blameable for reply- ing to Pedro as she does, when he fays, " shall I get you a hufband, I had rather have one of your *father's getting*". When she is fent off by her un- cle, Claudio's wedding is fixed for that day week, and by way of making the interval tedious to impatient

patient love, pafs more agreeably, Pedro propofes to attempt working Benedick and Beatrice into a violent affection for each other ; with this pleafant propofal the fcene concludes.

Don John enters with his hopeful affociate Borachio ; the former wifhing, at any rate, by any impediment to crofs Claudio's marriage ; to effect this purpofe, Borachio lays a villainous plan, through his intimacy with Margaret, Hero's waiting-woman ; for this infamous project John promifes the tool of his iniquity a thoufand ducats, and they go off to forward their execrable plan.

Benedick enters in Leonato's garden, with a boy, whom he fends for a book : In foliloquy, he expreffes furprize, that Claudio, who formerly ufed to laugh at love, fhould fall fo effectually into the fnare himfelf : He then proceeds to enquire, whether his own mind can be fo ftrangely altered ; and, with a very natural, pleafant degree of confidence, fuppofes fuch a metamorphofe impoffible. This fpeech is much in favour of the actor, and truly agreeable to the audience.

Seeing the Prince, Claudio and Balthazar approach, he retires behind an arbour : after a pleafing fong, they enter upon the fubject of Beatrice's love for Benedick ; perceiving that he liftens, all poffible fymptoms of violent affection in that lady are mentioned, which Benedick fwallows the more greedily, as being advanced and avouched by fo grave and venerable a character as grey-headed Leonato. The train of deception is admirably carried on through this fcene, and when Benedick is left alone to ruminate upon what he has heard, he

does

does it moſt humorouſly. He ſeems to fear ſome flaſhes of wit, if he ſhould appear ſerious in a love affair, yet argues himſelf into a favourable opinion. She enters, and invites him to dinner ; her words, though not kind, or even polite, he interprets favourably ; and concludes the ſecond act with reſolving to get her picture.

Hero, Margaret, and Urſula, open the third act. Hero ſends Margaret to draw Beatrice into the garden ; it appears, that the ſame deſign is now to be put in practice upon her, as Leonato and Claudio wrought upon Benedick, in the foregoing act ; for this purpoſe Hero inſtructs Urſula. Seeing Beatrice ſteal into a woodbine arbour, they proceed on the ſubject of Benedick's love for her, and anatomize her ſpirit of pride and coquettry pretty ſeverely : while they blazon him with the warmeſt terms of commendation. After they have exhauſted praiſe upon one, and ſatire on the other, they go off. From what Beatrice ſays, when alone, it appears, that their converſation has produced the deſired effect, and occaſioned her to think ſeriouſly of Benedick. This ſcene has conſiderable merit, but being exactly ſimilar to that which ends the ſecond act, cannot take equal poſſeſſion of an audience.

Don Pedro, Claudio, Benedick and Leonato, appear next : the Prince declares his intention of ſtaying till Claudio's marriage is conſummated ; then propoſes going for Arragon, and that Benedick ſhould go with him. This draws on ſome obſervations which charge Benedick with being in love, the Prince and Claudio mention ſeveral pleaſant ſymptoms to prove their ſuggeſtion : when Benedick

walks

walks afide to fpeak with Leonato, Don John enters, and charges Hero with being difloyal; this
naturally furprizes the Prince and her lover; who,
upon being offered ocular demonftration of her
licentioufnefs, jointly determine to expofe her, and
break off the marriage.

When they go off, we are prefented with Dogberry, Verges, and Watchmen. This fcene exhibits in the Conftable and his affociate, a very laughable picture of blundering, ignorant confequence;
the neglect and villainy of nocturnal guards, is very
well, and keenly touched upon: after giving the
watchmen charge to look fharply about Leonato's
houfe, Dogberry goes off. Here Borachio and
Conrade enter; thefe worthy gentlemen, not fufpecting eves-droppers, talk over the whole of the
plot againft Hero, how Margaret being fubftituted
for her, Claudio had fwallowed the deceit, and determined upon expofing his intended bride in the
temple; the watchmen having overheard this hopeful conference, take them into cuftody, and hurry
them off the ftage.

Hero next enters with Margaret, they converfe
about a wedding-fuit; Beatrice joins them, and
profeffing herfelf ill at eafe, Margaret archly puns
upon Benedick's name, by advifing her to lay fome
Carduus Benedictus to her heart. After fome pleafant raillery upon Beatrice's complaint, they retire
to drefs Hero for her nuptials.

In the next fcene we are entertained with a very
whimfical account which Dogberry and Verges
give Leonato of the two men the watch have taken
up; their roundabout, fuperfluous manner, is truly
diverting. Leonato, wearied with their verbofity,

defires them to queftion the culprits, and bring him
the examination. At the beginning of the fourth
act, we meet the bride, bridegroom, prieft, and all
the nuptial guefts. Upon the Friar's afking Claudio if he is not come to marry the lady, he anfwers
no; upon queftioning Hero, fhe replies in the affirmative; to the next interrogation, whether any
lawful impediment is known, Claudio replies in a
ftrain not very intelligible to the company, till he
explains the matter in fuch lines as we think worthy tranfcribing.

> She's but the fign and femblance of her honour;
> Behold how like a maid fhe blufhes here:
> Oh what authority and fhew of truth,
> Can cunning fin cover itfelf withal:
> Comes not that blood as modeft evidence
> To witnefs fimple virtue? would you not fwear
> All you that fee her that fhe is maid,
> By thefe exterior fhows? yet fhe is none,
> She knows the heat of a luxurious bed,
> Her blufh is guiltinefs not modefty.

So unexpected and heavy a charge, fupported by
the Prince and Don John, ftrikes Leonato to the
heart; and fo far overpowers his unhappy daughter, that fhe faints. When the accufers are gone,
the wretched father breaths forth his forrow in very
pathetic and bitter plaints; patience is urged, and
a vindication of Hero attempted by Benedick and
Beatrice, but Leonato feems from fuch reputable
evidence, to think the accufation juft. The Friar,
in a moft fenfible, humane, fanciful addrefs, takes
up the injured lady's caufe, who fpeaks of her own
innocence with melting modefty. Her father, upon a furmife that it may be the effect of fome bafe
design,

design, delivers himself with very emphatic spirit : the Friar, who prudently prefers moderate measures, desires that a report of her death, in consequence of slander, may be spread, in order to work out her exculpation ; or to give an opportunity, if guilt is confirmed, of secreting her from the world. To this salutary advice Leonato agrees. The other characters being gone off, Benedick and Beatrice remain, who both entertain a favourable opinion of Hero ; after urging him to espouse the cause of her cousin, a pretty entertaining declaration of mutual affection, comes from these whimsical lovers ; and Benedick, in compliance with his mistress's earnest desire, goes off, fully bent on challenging Claudio.

Dogberry and Verges, with their prisoners and others, next appear ; this examination of Conrade and Borachio, confirms the laughable idea we have already entertained of their consequential examiners : after much quibble, they are confronted by the watchmen, who unfold the affair of Don John's bribing Borachio with a thousand ducats to slander Hero ; this discovery being made, they are ordered to be carried before Leonato ; this part of the business falls to the lot of Dogberry and Verges, the former of whom, upon being called an ass by Conrade, makes some very risible remarks.

At the beginning of the fifth act, Antonio is comforting his brother Leonato, who replies to his consolation, in terms that we must offer to our reader's perusal, as truly beautiful, and strictly argumentative :

I pray

I pray thee ceafe thy counfel,
Which falls into my ears as profitlefs
As water in a fieve ; give not me counfel
Nor let no comfort elfe delight mine ear ;
But fuch a one whofe wrongs doth fuit with mine ;
Bring me a father who fo lov'd his child,
Whofe joy of her is overwhelm'd like mine,
And bid him fpeak to me of patience.
But there is no fuch man ; for, brother, men
Can counfel and give comfort to that grief
Which they themfelves not feel ; but tafting it,
Their counfel turns to paffion, which before
Would give preceptial medicine to rage,
Fetter ftrong madnefs with a filken thread,
Charm ach with air, and agony with words :
No, no, 'tis all men's office to fpeak patience
To thofe that wring under the load of forrow ;
But no man's virtue nor fufficiency
To be fo moral when he fhall endure
The like himfelf : therefore, give me no counfel,
For there was never yet philofopher
Who could endure the tooth-ach patiently ;
However, they have writ the ftile of gods,
And made a pifh at chance and fufferance.

Don Pedro and Claudio entering, the old man
accofts them in angry terms, which they wave,
though Claudio receives a regular challenge from
him, and both of them from Antonio. The Prince,
in palliative terms, laments Hero's death, but afferts,
that the charge which occafioned it was founded in
truth ; this, as he refufes to hear a vindication of
her, fends off the old gentlemen violently agitated
with paffion. No fooner do they difappear, than
Benedict, ripe for quarrel, comes forward ; they
joke with him, but find that he is thoroughly bent
upon a forceable vindication of Hero's blafted reputation ;

putation ; however, they jeer him, by giving the matter a ludicrous turn, and make mention of Beatrice. Benedick is neither to be frighted nor foothed, and leaves them, promifing revenge upon Claudio.

Dogberry and Verges here bring on the prifoners Borachio and Conrade, who make a full confeffion of their flanderous guilt to the Prince : this unexpected intelligence, as may be well fuppofed, ftrikes him and Claudio with forrowful aftonifhment. Leonato entering, after having been acquainted with the villainy, receives from Borachio a fecond confeffion ; however, in the zeal of refentment, he charges the injury his daughter has received againft the Prince and Claudio. After fome exculpatory addreffes upon their fide, he foftens, and propofes, as Hero is irrecoverable, that Claudio fhall marry a neice of his ; this being agreed to, they go off, after Dogberry, with farcical folemnity, has complained of being called an afs.

Benedick comes on with Margaret, whom, after fome quibbling, and not very decent fpeeches, he fends for Beatrice. When alone, he pleafantly defcribes his love-fick fituation : the lady comes on, when a very unimportant conference enfues, which ends juft as it begins : Urfula communicating the difcovery of Hero's innocence, they go off to hear it more at large. The next fcene at Hero's monument is, and we think juftly, omitted in reprefentation.

When the author brings us to Leonato's houfe, we find Benedick foliciting the Friar's matrimonial affiftance, upon which Leonato mentions the manner how he had been tricked into love. Pedro and
Claudio

Claudio appearing, according to appointment, Hero, under cover of a maſk, is brought on; when Claudio ſolemnly receives her at the Friar's hand, ſhe reveals herſelf to the aſtoniſhment and joy of her firſt intended huſband. The explanation of this ſeeming riddle being referred to another opportunity, Benedick and Beatrice, by the intervention of other parties, conclude their match, and ſo concludes the piece.

When we take a general view of this comedy, we muſt be ſurprized that SHAKESPEARE himſelf could make ſo much of ſo little; the plot has rather a romantic air, and is, in point of merit, but very moderate; the unities are not groſsly violated; the cataſtrophe is ſatisfactory, the language eaſy and ſpirited; many of the ſentiments diſcover fancy and good ſenſe, and the characters are well ſupported.

Benedick is a very pleaſant effuſion of genius, we have no reaſon to allow him any virtue, or to charge him with any vices. He is a humoriſt poſſeſſed of very laughable peculiarity, we dont often meet ſuch a perſonage in private life, yet we are glad to ſee him on the ſtage, eſpecially when repreſented by Mr. GARRICK.

In ſpeaking of our modern ROSCIUS, after what has already been offered, we muſt either limit our praiſe, or ſay over again what has been ſaid before: general ſuffrage has for many years authorized the warmeſt encomiums upon this great man in Benedick; it has been ſet down by many leading critics as his beſt comic character, but this opinion we cannot implicitly admit, notwithſtanding we are willing to allow the pre-eminence of his ſignificant

features,

features, the diftinct volubility of his expreffion, and his ftage manœuvres ; in the fcenes of repartee with Beatrice, his diftinct vivacity gives uncommon fatisfaction.   It is a character not fo well fuited to his age and figure as it was fome years ago, yet we have no idea of any performer now on the ftage who could render it fo agreeable as he ftill can.

We have attended Mr. KING's performance of, Benedick with much critical pleafure, and if we had never feafted upon Mr. GARRICK's fuperior merit, 'tis highly probable we fhould never have wifhed for any thing better.

Mr. LEE, if he had not laborioufly methodized good natural requifites into moft offenfive oddity, might have deferved confiderable reputation in this part ; as it is, though nature has fuffered fo much from palpable art, he has his admirers, and in fome few paffages really merits them.   It is painful to think that any man who does not want fenfe, fhould become fuch a clock-work actor, miftaking mecha-nifm for eafe, and ftiffnefs for propriety.   We have been tortured both in eyes and ears by Mr. SHE-RIDAN's barbarous attempts on this part.

Claudio is a gentle youth, who falls fuddenly in love, and gives up the object of his paffion with lefs feeling, in our apprehenfion, than he ought : there is nothing in the part which requires, or could fhew great abilities, yet it is much too important for Mr. CAUTHERLY's very feeble abilities, and was much better fupplied by the late Mr. PALMER, though in fome meafure a marrer of blank verfe.

Leonato is a very refpectable, uniform perfo-nage ; a fenfible, feeling father, who utters feveral fentiments decked with fuitable ftile, that do the author great credit. When warmed by the suppoſed guilt of his daughter, his expreſſions, if the actor does them juſtice, muſt affect every heart capable of impreſſion : we are ſorry to remark, that Mr. AICKIN is by no means capable of working this eſſential effect, or, if capable, has not been able to ſhew the leaſt trace of it ; he fails extremely in attempting to deſcribe the force and delicacy of paternal feelings.

Mr. BERRY went as much beyond the tender parts of Leonato, as the laſt mentioned gentleman falls below them. It is much to be wiſhed that old men of a ſerious caſt were put into abler hands ; the ſtage has had an irreparable loſs, in this particular, by the death of Mr. POWELL, eſpecially as Mr. Ross, whoſe capabilities might be very reſpectable in this view, manifeſts moſt weariſome negligence.

There is no point of excellence in which SHAKESPEARE has more diſtinguiſhed himſelf than in the variety and propriety of his characters : if we look through many pieces, eſpecially thoſe of the laſt twenty years, we ſhall perceive a diſguſtful ſameneſs of ſtile ; lords and valets, ladies and chambermaids, maintain nearly the ſame dialogue ; ſuch inſipidity SHAKESPEARE's good ſenſe, knowledge of nature, and powerful genius diſdained : a great number of ſtriking inſtances might be offered from his works, in proof of this aſſertion ; and, among the reſt, his Dogberry and Verges, who are as whimſically imagined, and as well ſupported, as any characters we know ; their ſolemn buffoonery and blundering importance, muſt be rich entertainment for the graveſt mind.

Mr,

Much ado about Nothing.

Mr. TASWELL, whofe drynefs of humour, quaintnefs of expreffion, a id laughable caft of features will never be excelled, gave every idea of Dogberry that the author feems to have meant; at prefent, Mr. PARSONS, though not quite equal in excellence to his humorous predeceffor, well deferves the warm applaufe he receives. Mr. HARTRY, who has a moft peculiar and happy countenance for the caricature of low comedy, is the beft Verges we remember to have feen; laughter feels fome injury from not having a little more of him. All the other male charaҿers in this play are fo immaterial, with refpeҿt to performance, that we deem ourfelves excufable in declining mention of them; and for the fame reafon two of the females only will come under confideration.

Hero is an amiable young lady, thrown into a painful and pitiable predicament; the part is pretty, but feeble; it requires an agreeable, though not a great aҿrefs. Having faid thus much, we believe our readers will readily concur in opinion, that it need not be more pleafingly fupplied than by Mrs. W. BARRY.

Beatrice feems to have engaged as much of our author's attention as Benedick, and is equally well fupported; as a child of whim fhe is extremely pleafant. Mrs. PRITCHARD was fo excellent in this part, and ftruck out fuch unifon merit with Mr. GARRICK, that her uncharacteriftic corpulence was always overlooked. Mrs. WOFFINGTON we have heard receive confiderable applaufe, which fhe well deferved; and though we could wifh to fee Mrs. ABINGTON's fuperior talents put into poffeffion of this part, we don't think ourselves unjuſtifiable in allowing Miſs POPE ſome ſhare of approbation.

MUCH ADO ABOUT NOTHING, ſupported by capable performers, will always pleaſe in repreſentation, and does not caſt any damp upon the great fame of its immortal author ; at the ſame time, we do not conſider it as making any addition thereto. It is undoubtedly an agreeable, ſpirited compoſition for the ſtage, but can never be of any great importance in the ſtudy.

THE

The REVENGE.

A Tragedy: By Dr. Young.

THIS piece opens with judicious folemnity. A night fcene, attended with elementary concuffions, lightning, thunder, wind, hail, &c. introduces Zanga, the captive Moor, who, from perturbation of mind, enjoys the ftorm. Ifabella, who appears to be his miftrefs, through tendernefs of regard, follows him into the lonely retreat of gloomy meditation; her folicitations and tears draw from him an elegant and fpirited acount of what has laid the foundation of his difcontent.

Hence, it appears, that being fon of a Moorifh monarch, at war with Spain, he fought in a battle where his father was killed, and he himfelf made prifoner. That becoming Alonzo's, the Spanifh general's flave, the victorious commander had given him as humane and friendly treatment as could be wifhed; but, upon fome flight occafion, in heat of paffion, gave him a blow, which to Moorifh tempers, proves an offence never to be forgiven.

Having painted the agony of his mind to Ifabella, who in vain urges patience, fhe tells him that an exprefs is arrived from Alonzo; having devifed fome means to damp the progrefs of that chief, he prays for favourable intelligence, and goes off to queftion Don Carlos concerning it.

Manuel

Manuel and Carlos are now introduced, by whom we find that Alonzo, notwithstanding Zanga's treachery, has obtained another compleat victory, attended with much flaughter of his foes. We are also informed, that Carlos was freed from a bondage among the Moors by that general, whom as a friend he had deputed as an advocate in love to the beauteous Leonora. We find likewife, that Alvarez, the young lady's father, from a love of wealth, countenances Don Carlos's paffion, knowing that he is in hourly expectation of a fleet immenfely rich.

Here the object of his affection appears, led by her hoary father, who, after warmly urging her acceptance of Don Carlos, leaves them to an amorous tete-a-tete; the lover preffes his fuit with much tendernefs, but her inclinations dont appear to wear that cordial condefcenfion he feems to wifh.

She evades his warmeft attacks, and leaves him to receive the triumphant Alonzo; who, upon his entrance, declares more fatisfaction in meeting his friend, than in the charms of fame and conqueft. After terms of falutation and reciprocal regard are interchanged, Zanga comes on, informing Carlos of news from the port, to receive which he goes off.

Alonzo being left with the Moor, opens the fecret feelings of his heart, which, furrounded by a blaze of glory, is yet wretched. He informs Zanga, that while he fhould have acted as the ambaffador of love for his friend, Leonora's charms had compelled him to become the principal; a faint exculpatory circumftance is mentioned, that having received no letters from Carlos, he concluded him dead; this mifcarriage in correfpondence, it ap-

2

pears, has happened through Zanga's treacherous, underhand dealing, to work his own finifter purpofes.

Seeing Leonora, the captivated conqueror goes off to meet her, which gives Zanga an opportunity of uttering fome lines, fraught with moft vindictive malevolence. When the lovers come on, a long, laborious, and, in fome places, laughable fcene enfues ; the whole purport of which, is a violent ftruggle of pride and love in the woman ; love and friendfhip in the man. Our author has here made an attempt upon the power of action, injurious to that power ; he has indulged his own imagination contrary to the probability, at leaft the reprefentable probability of nature ; for which reafon the laft fcene of the firft act is generally much and commendably curtailed on the ftage : at the conclufion, Alonzo gives us a moft unmeaning jingle of rhimes, founding much, meaning little.

The fecond act commences with Zanga and Manuel, informing the audience that Don Carlos's fleet is wrecked, and with it his fortune ; hence Zanga fuggefts Alonzo's union with Leonora.

Ifabella coming on, he makes enquiry of her concerning fome material circumftances, fends for his tablets, and ruminates, in an emphatic foliloquy, upon the connexion of circumftances ; wherein he difplays a fund of policy for deep intrigue.

He determines upon working Alonzo to a marriage with Leonora, from which he draws hopes of a tempeft that may wreck their peace ; fome lines he utters concerning that paffion which he is endeavouring to raife, being nearly equal to any we have

met

met in any author, it would be unpardonable not
to tranfcribe them.

> I have turn'd o'er the catalogue of woes
> Which fting the heart of man, and find none equal :
> It is the hydra of calamities :
> The feven-fold death—the jealous are the damn'd——
> Oh jealoufy ! each other paffion's calm
> To thee, thou conflagration of the foul,
> Thou king of torments ! thou grand counterpoife !
> To all the torments beauty can infpire.

Upon Alonzo's entrance, Zanga, with profound
artifice, congratulates him upon the certainty of
poffeffing Leonora ; the generous minded Spaniard, though he doats on the woman, ftill ftruggles
with the reftrictions of friendfhip. The artifices of
Zanga are mafterly, and at length determine Alonzo to confer with Don Carlos.

After his departure, the author has again furnifhed his Moor with fome lines of a mafterly nature ;
boldly imagined, copioufly arranged, and emphatically expreffed. Don Carlos comes in upon his
meditation, wrapped up in thought likewife. Don
Carlos moralizes, in foliloquy, with judgment and
feeling ; his fentiments, refpecting hope and human
happinefs, are founded in philofophical truth.

The Moor, warmly intent upon his evil purpofes,
preffes the melancholly lover to a refignation of his
miftrefs, in favour of Alonzo ; the voluntary facrifice of his deareft wifhes, though in defpair of their
ever being fulfilled, pains him fo much that he cannot comply ; therefore, requefts Zanga to prevent
an interview with his friend. This the Moor promifes,

mifes, yet goes off with a determination to bring it about.

Carlos again ruminates upon the inftability of temporal enjoyments ; his remark on the power of beauty is juft and pleafing. As he is going off, Zanga brings on Alonzo---Here a very delicate and pathetic fcene enfues, wherein the friends manifeft a cordial feeling for each other. Alonzo's diffidence works the defired effect upon Carlos ; who, at length, triumphs over the agony of his mind fo far, as not only to refign Leonora, but even to requeft his friend's acceptance of that happinefs which he has been difappointed of.

The general's mind is fo affected with this behaviour, that he retires, and Carlos concludes the act with a very defcriptive affimulation of his own cafe to that of Epaminondas, who lived with an arrow in his fide till victory was proclaimed, and then drawing forth the mortal fhaft expired.

The third act commences with Zanga, in a ftate of malevolent rejoicing, that his defigns are in fo fair a train : by what he fays to Ifabella, we find Alonzo's nuptials have been compleated, and that a letter, forged by him, as from Carlos to Leonora, had fallen into the bridegroom's hands, on whom it had wrought a very powerful effect. Zanga's defcription of Alonzo, upon perufal of the infamous fcroll, is mafterly painting.

When the general enters, teeming with jealous doubts, the Moor pretends to go off, that he may be called upon. After much preparation, which Zanga receives with artful furprize ; Alonzo communicates the letter : here the Moor's hypocritical attachment is exhibited in ftrong colours ; to give

the

the forgery freſh force, he ſhews the utmoſt concern for its contents ; then, under a friendly pretext, tears the paper. What follows in this ſcene, ſhews Alonzo to be of an open, unſuſpecting nature ; an apt ſubject for impoſition, and the Moor ſhrewdly villainous.

The traitor draws forth every collateral circumſtance which may increaſe the taint of his maſter's mind ; after which, with fair faced tenderneſs, he ſends off the unhappy, deluded huſband, to reflect upon a ſubject which he knows the more it is thought of, the more pain it gives. After putting a picture of Carlos into Iſabella's hand, that ſhe may place it in Leonora's chamber, to riſe up a corroborative proof of infidelity, a gleam of remorſe breaks in upon the traiterous gloom of Zanga's mind ; for a moment he feels compunction, and with great dignity of ſentiment, reflects upon the diſgraceful ſtate of mental depravation his antipathy has led him to ; however, his darling principle of revenge ſuppreſſes every idea of remorſe, and even renders infamy meritorious. This is one baſe effect of violent prejudices, which ſeldom fail to beautify the moſt culpable and horrid purpoſes.

At the beginning of the fourth act, we meet Alonzo labouring with increaſed perplexity ; he propoſes going to his wife, and by terrifying threats, to force the ſecret from her. This ſtep, ſo very dangerous to his hopes and views, the Moor artfully evades, by taking upon himſelf, with much ſeeming reluctance, the taſk of explaining matters. Juſt as he commences his artful tale, the author has introduced Leonora, without, in our apprehenſion, any purpoſe ; therefore, the omiſſion of her ſhort,

Revenge.

infignificant fcene, in action is judicioufly left out. The lady being difpatched, Zanga gives a formal account of what, in a garden by moonlight, he had feen pafs between her and Carlos. The picture wears fuch ftriking features of criminality, that Alonzo is even overwhelmed with conviction. When the confirmation of his wife's guilt is invincibly impreffed upon Alonzo's mind, fhe is again introduced, and reproves him for avoiding his friends.

By a disjointed, unintelligible mode of behaviour, he alarms her feelings, and fhe goes off, filled with very painful fenfibility. Zanga returns, and hearing his mafter talk of death, gives him joy of having facrificed Leonora to his juft jealoufy. Being informed that fhe ftill lives, he fets at work every engine of infinuation and diffimulation to affect her deftruction ; this point, at length, he gets determined, and even obtains Alonzo's commiffion to get Carlos murdered. This act ends with a fanciful, but bombaft fpeech.

At the beginning of the fifth act, we encounter the general, haunted with the imaginary ghoft of his murdered friend. Zanga comes on, and tells him, that his orders refpecting Carlos has been ftrictly fulfilled ; this intelligence fomewhat awakens remorfe ; however, having thus begun the work of blood, he determines to carry it on as far as his wife, and mentions the place he has appointed for this facrifice to jealous rage. The Moor, viewing his mifchievous plan in fo thriving a fituation, breathes out fome mafterly lines of emphatic exultation.

Leonora is next difcovered fleeping in an arbour, the fight of her occafions a tendernefs in Alonzo's mind, which he expreffes in an agreeable manner, but too florid and picturefque for the ftate of agitation he is in. At length, he works his paffion up to the fatal act, and even lifts his dagger to give the blow, but is ftopped by her waking : love here interpofes, and checks his rage, which extends no further than the utterance of fome incoherent fpeeches; fhe fooths him, and aims at explanation, but in vain.

Going off, he drops his dagger, at fight of fuch an object fhe is ftaggered, and, like a faithful wife, fears for her hufband's fafety ; however, when the bofom-fnake Zanga hints to her, that her life ftands endangered from Alonzo's jealoufy, with the true fpirit of confcious innocence, fhe determines to vindicate her own honour from fo foul a charge ; and to free him from a feeling, which fhe can hardly fuppofe him mean enough to indulge.

Alonzo returning, Zanga urges afrefh Leonora's guilt, but is fent off with a churlifh reproof. When the lady re-enters, fhe is accofted by her hufband in terms of very foft and tender refpect : their converfe, for fome time, promifes reunion, harmony and mutual fatisfaction ; but, upon her producing the dagger, takes quite a different turn. He is thrown into frefh agitation by feeing the inftrument of his jealoufy, which Leonora perceiving, fhe expreffes herself in fuch terms as warm him into a direct accufation of guilt : after fome violent altercation, the pride of flander rifes fo high, that fhe ftabs herfelf.

This

This act of fatal extremity ſtrikes Alonzo's affection deeply ; after apologizing for ſuicide in plauſible terms, ſhe is carried off, and Alonzo follows, poſſeſſed with the moſt horrid doubts. Zanga now comes forward, bent on filling up the meaſure of his revenge, by the moſt deſperate means ; which, upon Alonzo's return, he puts in practice, by an open and triumphant declaration of his villainy ; this has the deſired effect, and ſuperadds ſuch a weight of woe, that the unhappy victim of his implacable reſentment, faints under the load. At length, having with great, though falſe dignity of ſentiment, endeavoured to juſtify his cruel and treacherous proceedings, Zanga attempts to kill himſelf, but is prevented by Alonzo, and delivered as a priſoner to guards, who enter with Alvarez.

Upon hearing that Leonora is dead, the general puts a period to his own wretched exiſtence ; this ſtrikes the Moor with remorſe, which he utters in very generous and forceable terms. When Zanga is carried to the fate his crimes deſerve, Alvarez concludes the piece, with ſome rhimes which we cannot greatly approve.

The REVENGE, upon a general view, exhibits indiſputable marks of a powerful genius : the verſification is flowing and nervous ; the ſentiments noble and comprehenſive ; the moral, a warning againſt that hydra of calamities, jealouſy. Yet, if we ſcrutinize, we ſhall find a barrenneſs of incident, a palling ſameneſs in the ſcenes, and a weariſome length of laboured dialogue. There is alſo a moſt diſadvantageous and palpable ſimilitude to OTHELLO.

The

The characters are few, and of them only four deserve any notice. Alonzo is introduced to our regard as a brave and successful soldier ; yet, upon examination, we must consider him as a weak or a wicked personage : the former undoubtedly he is, and he borders close upon the latter, by first supplanting his friend in the business of love, and then authorizing his murder ; though, as a jealous Spaniard, with whom, as well as the Moors, revenge is virtue, he stands excusable.

In representation, he requires extensive and variable powers ; there are very difficult transitions in many passages, and he is a leading object for critical attention till his last scene, where he falls off most miserably.

Mr. RYAN was in voice and years, when we saw him, very unfit for the love scenes of this character; yet, in the jealousy and distraction, he struck out considerable beauties. Mr. HAVARD looked the part better, and was more characteristic in the tender scenes. Mr. REDDISH, though deficient in powers for the most impassioned speeches, has, we apprehend, more equality of merit, and is, upon the whole, more agreeable than his predecessors. Had Mr. GARRICK ever condescended to represent the Spanish general, he would, beyond doubt, have made him one of the greatest parts on the stage ; whereas, wanting such incomparable abilities, he ever has been but a kind of foil to Zanga.

Carlos, though a very poetical character, is sadly insipid ; Mr. Ross did him more justice than any other person we recollect. It was barbarous in the managers to load Mr. J. AICKIN with this part. In a proper stile, we entertain a very favourable

idea

Revge.

idea of this gentleman's senfibility; but, we are sorry to say, that his Don Carlos was a most somniferous exhibition: why might not the sweet swain, Mr. CAUTHERLY, whine through this unseasoned lover? though, to confess truth, the matter would in that case be very little mended.

Zanga is a finished villain, with some greatness of mind: we do not know any character more favourable to the actor; this is plainly evinced by considering that in a great variety of performers we have seen undertake it, every one has met and deserved considerable applause. Mr. QUIN, in the soliloquies, and last scene, acquitted himself with great ability, but wanted ease of insinuation, and was heavy in the other parts. Mr. SHERIDAN, with powers vastly inferior, was more in character upon the whole. Mr. HOLLAND was better than either, by mingling the merit of both, yet fell greatly short of Mr. MOSSOP, who most certainly stands in this part himself alone; as possessing and happily adapting an unequalled spirit, extent and propriety of expression.

Leonora has been rendered very agreeable by Mrs. BELLAMY, but we are inclined to prefer Mrs. BADDELY.

Auditors and readers, of florid conceptions, will be entertained with this play, both on the stage and in the closet; however, we are inclined rather to praise it as a poem than a tragedy.

The

The SUSPICIOUS HUSBAND.

A COMEDY: By HOADLEY.

RANGER, a young and volatile templar, opens this piece, juſt returned from the tavern, after a whole night's debauch ; he reflects with ſenſible pleaſantry upon tavern enjoyments : it is ſomething odd, that having from CONGREVE ſketched out ſuch a female as ſuits his inclination, he ſhould ſay, " Oh that I had ſuch a ſoft, bewitching fair, to *lull my ſenſes to their deſired ſleep* ;" falling aſleep is a bad compliment to a lady. After receiving ſome complimentary cards, he is encountered by a milliner, with whom he makes very free ; however, his amorous parly is interrupted by the abrupt entrance of Mr. Bellamy, who, perceiving what Ranger had been about, gives him a friendly rebuke for putting modeſty to the bluſh.

When Frankly comes on, a moſt indelicate idea is raiſed by his remark upon Ranger's looking ſadly ; we wiſh his queſtion and the anſwer totally expunged. The remaining part of this ſcene is filled up with very agreeable converſation, upon the ſubject of gallantry and the fair ſex ; by which each diſcovers the bent of his own mind, with reſpect to the ladies. The viſit is a mere chit-chat one, and ſeems to have no other meaning than opening the characters.

In

In the following scene, we meet Mrs. Strickland and Jacintha, by whom we are made acquainted with Clarinda ; and that Cupid's arrow has touched her heart, in favour of a young fellow she danced with at Bath. We also receive a hint of Mr. Strickland's gloomy state of mind. When that gentleman makes his appearance, we find, that as guardian to Jacintha, he has received a letter from Bellamy, foliciting his consent to marry that lady ; upon which subject he makes some churlish remarks, but at last consents to see the lover.

After Jacintha goes off, Strickland opens at large his suspicious temper, by expressing dislike to Clarinda, as a companion for his wife. His expressions are full of ill nature and asperity, insomuch, that the lady burst into tears, which soften him into a faint, aukward kind of an apology, with which he retires, leaving Mrs. Strickland in doubt of his motives for such behaviour, and surprize at the foundation of them.

We are now carried into the Park, where Frankly and Bellamy present themselves, the former disclosing to his friend the passion he has conceived for an unknown lady ; his account of the matter is pleasant and spirited. When Jack Meggot comes on, the subject gives way to his frothy, rhapsodical prattle : which, with very little meaning, is tolerably pleasant.

After the butterfly of fashion runs in pursuit of one of his favourite dilettanti, Frankly gives a favourable idea of his heart, though we cannot entertain any respect for his head. Our author has in the following passage, we apprehend, been guilty of unpardonable disrespect to the fair sex---" There is

a heart

a heart, *even* in a woman's breaft, that is worth the purchafe," why the emphatic word *even*, as if worth and generous feelings were more rare to be met with in the female, than the male fex. A moft il-liberal, as well as falfe idea.

The firft act ends with Frankly's determining to fearch out, if poffible, his fair incognita. At the beginning of the fecond, three ladies prefent them-felves, Clarinda, Jacintha and Mrs. Strictland ; the former being taxed with her Bath partner, fhe throws out fome fprightly obfervations upon gal-lants, and the manner of treating them. Jacintha's prudent and fettled notions of love are well op-pofed to Clarinda's levity ; fhe having met with a worthy and agreeable man, has given him unre-ferved poffeffion of her heart. Mrs. Strictland's unhappy fituation being mentioned, the gay lady re-commends refiftive behaviour, which the fenfible wife declines. To remove Strictland's uneafy ap-prehenfions, Clarinda goes off, with a refolution of leaving his houfe.

After two or three fpeeches, fhe returns in a great flurry of fpirits, having met her admirer ; the trick of letting him know where fhe lives is natural : a kind of pantomime purfuit enfues, till, at length, Frankly having houfed her, takes the advantage of an open door, and obtains a fhort conference with her, in which he fpeaks plainly as to the paffion he has conceived for her.

Her diffidence is delicate, and the lover makes no further progrefs than receiving information, that he will find or hear of her at Mr. Strictland's houfe. After he goes off, Clarinda makes an open confeffion to Mrs. Strictland of her captivated ftate.

ftate. Mr. Strictland, in foliloquy, expreffes much uneafinefs at the vifitors and meffages which come to Clarinda, as fuppofing his wife may have fome finifter concern in them. Seeing Lucetta, his wife's waiting-woman, he determines to examine her; but thinking fhe may deceive him, calls for Tefter, whofe fimplicity he thinks may be more fafely trufted than the chambermaid's cunning; however, upon confideration, he deems him too weak and fallible an object for confidence to reft upon, therefore again calls for Lucetta, to whom he addreffes himfelf with fuch whimfical caution, that fhe very artfully pretends to apprehend an attack upon her virtue; this, and her laughing at his perplexity, increafes it fo much, that he hurries her off; and makes a very forceable remark on the tormenting fituation of his own mind, fo painfully enflaved by fufpicion.

From Bellamy and Jack Meggot, in the next fcene, we learn, that if Jacintha, who has determined to elope, effects her purpofe, fhe is to be lodged at Jack's houfe. Frankly enters to them, on the wings of tranfport, at having found his Perdita; of whom, however, he can give no further account, than that he has feen and obtained leave to vifit her again.

When Jack Meggot retires, Bellamy acknowledges himfelf in the lift of lovers: pleafed with their fympathetic feelings, Frankly and he embrace, a circumftance merely introduced for Ranger to jeft upon their infipid fituation. His entrance rather interrupts their amorous ideas, as deeming him a heretic in love affairs; however, he delivers a letter from Jacintha to Bellamy, which informs the audience that fhe has planned her elopement. Ranger's advice of carrying her to a bagnio, however fmart, is rather grofs.

When Bellamy claims Ranger's affiftance, he calls himfelf a *damnable* unlucky fellow, we wifh he had found another epithet, for though it may be natural enough in a Covent Garden buck, it is reprehenfible on the ftage. Buckle, Bellamy's fervant, informs his mafter that Jacintha, having no other means of efcape, intends to defcend from her chamber-window by a ladder of ropes, and that fhe is to be difguifed in boy's cloaths : matters thus fettled, the fecond act concludes.

Bellamy, difguifed in a chairman's coat, begins the third act, before Strictland's houfe, to which fpot alfo love has conveyed Frankly. Lucetta, from below, informs Jacintha at the window, that fhe muft be very cautious, as her guardian is up and on the watch. Frankly, from what he imperfectly hears and fees, imagines that fome intrigue is going forward, therefore refolves to liften. While he is clofely attending Jacintha's motions, Clarinda enters, returning from a whift party, and overhears fome converfation between them. Jacintha, fuppofing it is Bellamy, throws down the rope ladder ; juft as fhe is going to defcend, Lucetta informs her that fhe may come down the back ftairs ; this change of fituations gives Clarinda an opportunity of detecting, as fhe fuppofes, her faithlefs fpark. He endeavours to exculpate himfelf, but fhe flounces into the houfe without affording him an idea of forgivenefs.

Here Bellamy enters, and feeing a man under his miftrefs's window, entertains jealous apprehenfions

of

of rivalfhip. Jacintha, in the hurry of her efcape, runs into Frankly's arms---How he immediately difcovers her to be a woman is not obvious. Bellamy's alarm increafes, and he gives the fuppofed rival an oblique challenge. No fooner are thefe characters off the ftage, than Strictland appears, in purfuit of his ward. To him fucceeds Ranger, who having more liquor than prudence in his head, feems eager to have what he calls a frolic.

Reeling along, he encounters the rope ladder, and in the flow of fpirits determines to mount it. Upon reaching the window, he fpies an agreeable woman, and very modeftly refolves to follow, determining to make an amorous attack upon her. Mrs. Strictland and Lucetta next appear; from fome words which the maid drops, Ranger difcovers that the lady's hufband is jealous, and from that circumftance draws favourable hopes refpecting his own defign upon her; when Lucetta, for delivering her fentiments rather too freely, is ordered to quit the room, our gallant templar prefents himfelf, in a manner not very delicate. His purpofe thro' the whole fcene is culpably licentious, and the lady's behaviour, as we think, much too tame for fuch an unpardonable intrufion.

Strictland's approach occafions Ranger to retreat precipitately; in his hurry he inadvertently drops his hat; it appears, that Strictland has recovered Jacintha, and fhe is brought on as his prifoner.

Having fharply reproved the young lady for her adventurous elopement, Strictland ftrikes his foot againft Ranger's hat, which, in his hurry, that gallant had dropped. Such an object found in a wife's dreffing room, might naturally alarm a man

lefs

less tainted with suspicion. Mrs. Strictland, bold in her own innocence, though with such an unfavourable circumstance against her, endeavours, with becoming spirit, to set her precipitate lord and master right ; who cannot, however, be reduced to any degree of reason, till wrought upon by a finesse which Lucetta suggests, that of Jacintha's owning the hat.

This turn is pleasant enough, and works the desired effect. A reconciliation, at least an aukward, temporary one, takes place between the married couple ; but the disappointed single lady is sent close prisoner to her chamber, with a declaration from her guardian, that in the morning she must be removed to the country.

The scene being changed, Ranger comes forward, groping his way in a dark chamber, bent upon seeking out game : Jacintha enters with a candle, whom, from appearance, he takes to be a boy ; however, by some expressions she drops in soliloquy, he discovers his mistake, and as she is going to attempt a second escape, by means of the ladder of ropes, which she supposes is still at the window, he presents himself : with humorous freedom he pays his devoirs in such pressing terms, that, being afraid, on Mrs. Strictland's account, to cry out, she is at length obliged to mention Bellamy's name ; this strikes Ranger, who plays her off agreeably, concerning her letter, which mentioned the plan of elopement.

Perceiving hereby that Ranger is in her lover's confidence, she readily agrees to his proposal of helping her from confinement, and conducting her to the man of her heart.

Act

Act the fourth begins with Bellamy and Frankly, the former rating the latter, as being, though without design, the occasion of his losing Jacintha. While he is in this critical state of temper, Lucetta comes in great confusion to enquire for Jacintha; he knowing nothing about her, the maid remarks, that Clarinda supposes her to be gone off with one Frankly. On this information Bellamy sends Lucetta to search for the lost fair one, and seeing a confusion in Frankly's face, which might very naturally arise in such a case, he draws, demanding what is called gentleman's satisfaction for the supposed injury.

Here Ranger opportunely enters, and ludicrously remarks, that they manifest a strange contrariety of behaviour---One moment hugging each other, and the next tilting. In the account he gives of his last night's adventure, some very pleasant misapprehensions arise, which bring on the alternate resentment of Bellamy and Frankly, against their merry friend; who designedly plays upon them the game of cross purposes, till he is both threatened and wheedled to give an explanation that may ease their anxiety.

This, however, he refers to Jack Meggot, which the sprightly prattle enters upon immediately, by informing them that Jacintha is at his house. This eases Bellamy's painful feelings, and Frankly's new raised jealousy subsides by being told, that the other lady Ranger had encountered is a wife. Each having mentioned a particular destination, the four gentlemen go off to make way for Mrs. Strictland and Clarinda.

The

The latter, we perceive, is preparing for a speedy removal from Mr. Strictland's house : he appears, and receives ironical, cold thanks, for the civilities she has received from him. Having conducted her off, he re-enters, expresses satisfaction at her departure, and then leads his wife off also.

Lucetta being left alone, states to herself the suspicious situation of affairs, and seems, from the hat, to think her mistress guilty. While she is thus meditating, Frankly comes, desiring to speak with Clarinda ; being informed that she has left the house, with warm persuasion, and a golden bribe, she promises to deliver a letter to her.

Strictland, alarmed by hearing a knock at the door, and a man's voice, listens. When Frankly goes off, he steals behind Lucetta, and snatches the epistle out of her hand ; reads it, and finding an apology for an unseasonable visit, he concludes it to be from the owner of the hat to his wife ; from mention of a companion at Bath, he supposes Clarinda to be an accessary. His jealous ideas thus confirmed, he storms at Lucetta, who desires him to look at the cover of the letter, a point his impatience had neglected.

By this he finds that it is directed to Clarinda : the maid, justly reproving his folly, he concludes that they are all confederates, that his wife is indisputably guilty, and that in consequence thereof, a positive separation must take place.

Clarinda next appears, crossing the stage in a chair, and goes into a lodging house : Ranger pursues her, and, by bribing the chairman, gains free access. The lady discovers who he is, and asks for a mask, under which she resolves to try her mad-cap cousin.

2

Upon

Suspicious Husband.

Upon his approach, he suppofes her to be a lady of eafy virtue, and as fuch, though with delicacy, makes his attack in very flattering terms, till being wrought up to a particular degree of rapture, fhe difclofes her face, and throws him into a laughable confufion ; however, he turns it off with agreeable addrefs, profefling a knowledge of her, though dif-guifed.

In their converfation Jacintha is mentioned, and Clarinda fpeaks of the hat dropped in Mrs. Strict-land's chamber ; this leads to a difcovery which Ranger avails himfelf of, that his coufin is Frankly's miftrefs. After receiving from her a kind of cate-chetical admonition, by way of retaliation, he a-larms her with a fictitious incident of Frankly's being wounded.

Here, by fhewing palpable concern for her lover, fhe convinces Ranger of her regard, and he teizes her pretty handfomely ; however, fhe at laft gets rid of him, and then determines upon enquiring fur-ther into the truth of fo interefting a circumftance.

At the beginning of the fifth act, we fee Strictland at one end of a table writing, and his wife at the other end weeping ; the purport of his letter is to acquaint Mrs. Strictland's brother in the country what a fifter he is like to receive ; the thoughts of being fo criminated affect her deeply. Hearing two foft taps at the door, her fufpicious hufband ftarts, and thinks to make fome difcovery againft her : upon opening the door, he fees Tefter, and enraged at his difappointment, ftrikes the undefigning fim-pleton, who, by way of vindication, declares, that his miftrefs had ordered him never to come in with-out knocking ; this is confidered as a frefh corrobo-

ration

ration of guilt. Upon reading a letter from Bellamy and his bride Jacintha, he determines upon going to Jack Meggot's, where an ecclairciffement is promifed, though he fuppofes all the parties combined to deceive him.

Soon after he goes off, Lucetta comes on, and acquaints Mrs. Strictland, that Mrs. Bellamy defires her appearance alfo at Mr. Meggot's, particularly as the young gentleman, Ranger, who was fo unexpectedly in her room the night before, is to be at the general rendezvous. We next meet Frankly, Ranger, Bellamy and Jacintha ; the former being informed that Clarinda is not only a lady of fortune and Ranger's coufin, but that fhe loves him, expreffes warm fatisfaction. In a fhort time the lady appears ; not feeing Frankly, her fears of his being wounded increafe ; a concern which fhe cannot hide is pleafantly rallied by the other characters : at length the men retire.

When the women are alóne, Jacintha, with much formality of countenance and phrafe, plays upon her friend's feelings, but immediately relieves them, by declaring, that her gallant has no wounds but thofe of love ; fhe then calls Mr. Frankly from his concealment, and leaves the enamoured pair to an explanation of their own concerns.

In a fhort tete-a-tete, the lover makes clofe approaches, while the lady fhews a delicate, but not an unkind refiftance. When they are both puzzled what to fay, Ranger appears, and laughingly points out the aukwardnefs of fpeechlefs love : he then comes to the decifive point of fettling matters ; at once afks his coufin if fhe has not given confent to make her lover happy, which queftion not being

answered

answered satisfactorily, he mentions the letter Mr. Strictland had intercepted, and goes off to bring proof of what he asserts.

When he is gone, Frankly confesses having given such a letter to Lucetta : matters now take a very tender turn, when they are again interrupted by the entrance of Ranger, Strictland, Bellamy, Jacintha, and Jack Meggot. Mr. Strictland being promised satisfaction in the affair of the letter, seems disposed to entertain a more favourable turn of mind. Clarinda, being persuaded that Mrs. Strictland's future happiness, in a great measure, depends on her agreeing to Frankly's solicitations, acquiesces. Strictland seeing her with the very person whose letter he had stopped, seems to apprehend his folly ; and, upon Frankly's openly declaring the matter, confesses his error.

Ranger here takes a pleasant advantage of the state of things to hasten Clarinda's marriage, by telling Strictland not to trust their declaration, unless confirmed by a positive match ; this being insisted on, the point is settled agreeably to all parties. Seeing Mrs. Strictland approach, Ranger, conscious of his own censurable indiscretion, takes alarm : the injured wife, perceiving her occasional gallant, points him out to Strictland, as the person who was in her chamber the night before ; to prevent serious resentment he recapitulates his adventure, and in the relation gives Strictland a severe reproof for his jealousy.

Finding conviction flash upon him from all sides, the reformed husband encounters his jealousy, and is reconciled to his wife with tears of joy. All matters being thus agreeably disposed, Ranger concludes the piece with a fenfible compliment to matrimony, when attended with fenfe and virtue.

No play has appeared with greater eclat for many years than the Suspicious Husband did at its firft appearance, nor is any comedy more likely to live from an uncommon vivacity of dialogue, variety and pleafantry of incidents. There are fome improbabilities in the plot, which occur in the third act, but they are rather pleafing than offenfive, and the defign is entertaining, though trifling.

Wit there is none and very little fentiment, yet nature need not be afhamed of our author's delineation, who has neither heightened her charms, nor caricatured her defects.

The denouement is moft fatisfactorily wrought up; the circumftances are fpiritedly and convictively explained ; as to the characters, let them fpeak for themfelves.

Strictland, who is confeffedly drawn from Johnson's Kitely, wants much of that nervous beauty which appears in the original, yet is not without merit; his jealoufy is well defcribed, and his fituations properly imagined ; his reformation is brought about by very powerful perfuafive ; and, at the cataftrophe, we have great reafon to believe he is cured of his folly.

To perform this part requires judgment and expreffion ; it has never been better done than by Mr. Bridgewater. Mr. Sparks, notwithftanding we only place him fecond, buftled through the jealoufy very well ; his fault was aiming at more than is neceffary. Mr. Berry, and the prefent poffeffor, Mr. Love, got to the other extreme, a moft drowfing infipidity.

Ranger

Suspicious Husband.

Ranger is a very pleasant and plausible rake, who commits many culpable actions, but without any fundamental, ill design; his clambering into a gentleman's house at midnight, is a very indiscreet joke; but to ballance his foibles, he seems to have friendship, generosity and honour, at the bottom.

Mr. GARRICK was his faithful, excellent representative; the volatile humour of the inconsiderate templar, was admirably described by this most metamorphosable actor; insomuch, that we well remember several young fellows, who, having more spirit than sense, attempted to imitate his Ranger in real life, for which both their bones and pockets suffered smartly.

Doctor HOADLY's jokes would not do retailed in such a manner; we laugh at transactions upon the stage, which would be very displeasing at home. Mr. LEE had undoubted merit in Ranger, but wanted that voluble spirit which places Mr. KING, in our opinion, next to Mr. GARRICK, and not far behind him. Mr. DYER has made several inadequate efforts, but for a London theatre has always appeared more like the sketch of a character than a real one. Would you, kind reader, believe so gross an improbability, as that Mr. SHERIDAN, not having the fear of murder before his eyes, should, with more than savage barbarity, mutilate poor Ranger? yet, true it is : upon this occasion, as well as many others, we were induced to wish, that, *as an actor,* he had studied that excellent admonition, KNOW THYSELF; a maxim quite as essential to public as private life, yet as little attended to in the former as the latter.

Frankly is a gay young fellow, susceptible of the tender passions; though he cannot obtain such ap-

plause

plaufe and attention as Ranger, he is neverthelefs more refpectable as a man ; he loves one object, and purfues her only. His fituations, though not very critical, are yet well difpofed ; and though he can never add much to a performer's reputation, yet, if there are adequate abilities, he wont injure them.

Mr. RYAN was the firft reprefentative we recollect of this character, and had a confiderable fhare of fprightly eafe ; but age and figure were both a-gainft him. Mr. HAVARD was genteel, but wanted life. Mr. PALMER had fufficient fpirit, but was rather coxcomical. As to Mr. JEFFERSON, we think the part above his cut.

Bellamy is a fober, regular gallant ; and we think he is juft as well fupported by Mr. PACKER, as by any body elfe. Jack Meggot was moft happy with Mr. WOODWARD ; and has no manner of reafon to complain of Mr. DODD. Mr. VAUGHAN's fimple Tefter cannot be mended.

Mrs. Strictland is an agreeable picture of what a wife fhould be, only we think her patience and con-defcenfion are carried rather too far : there is a commendable degree of pliancy in domeftic dif-putes, which often prevents extremities ; but, in this character, there is a cenfurable tamenefs.

Mrs. ELMY, who had a peculiar grace and hap-pinefs in making characters confpicuous, which fcarce any other actrefs could gain attention to, fup-ported the tafk of playing this part, for fuch it really is, with pleafing ability. Mrs. PALMER, though not equal to her predeceffor, was extremely amiable in this gentle wife ; and we are not at all difpleafed to find her in poffeffion of Mrs. W. BARRY.

Clarinda

Sufpicious Husband.

Clarinda we may perceive to be an object of the author's particular regard; she is furnished with a large fund of spirits, and a slight dash of the coquette; yet capable of a settled, sincere passion, without any tendency to imprudent actions. She likes to rally, and has a pleasant flow of expression, but never sacrifices delicacy at the shrine of licentious wit.

Mrs. WOFFINGTON was pleasant in Clarinda, but stiffened her too much with the affectation, both in deportment and delivery, of a fine lady. Mrs. PRITCHARD, by equalling her excellence, and avoiding her faults, took the lead considerably; there was a freedom and fire of expression in her performance, that we have never seen surpassed. Miss HAUGHTON was by no means unentertaining, yet far below either of these ladies; and Miss POPE, at present in a state of comparison, makes but a very moderate shift.

Jacintha, in the circumstance of her elopement, shews more of a romantic, adventurous disposition, than prudence; however, she has ardent love on one side, and confinement on the other, to plead her excuse; and the most rigid observer must be pleased that she effects her escape. When Mrs. WILLOUGHBY played this part, some years since, she gave us great pleasure, though an actress little known, and by few now remembered; by giving her the preference, we dont mean to deprive Mrs. JEFFERIES of the praise she deserves.

Lucetta is a short, unimportant chambermaid, yet well drawn, and useful to the play; Mrs. GREEN made every line of her tell; but, for Mrs. LOVE---oh! oh! oh!

We

Suspicious Husband.

We are forry, after a ferious, candid enquiry, into the nature and tendency of this play, to condemn fo agreeable a piece of entertainment. It is moft certainly calculated to exhilerate, but will it mend the heart? we fear not. Will it reft neuter, and leave the fufceptible mind no worfe than it finds it? we are apprehenfive, no. Ranger is certainly a gilded bait of vice, for youth, and vanity to fnap at; and all his tranfactions tend at leaft to inflame, if not to taint the imagination. On the ftage it is full of vivacity and laughter; in the clofet flimzy and uninftructive.

King

King HENRY the Fifth.

An Hiſtorical TRAGEDY: SHAKESPEARE.

WE have ſome where obſerved, in reſpect of our author, that he not only ſuccefsfully availed himſelf of hiſtorical ſubjects in general, but, with peculiar addreſs, turned to advantage, many remarkable characters and tranſactions of his own country ; which from a very natural and commendable partiality to our native ſoil, prove particularly intereſting to Britiſh audiences.

The poet's idea of that unexpectedly great monarch the fifth Henry, may be collected from his prologue to this play ; which, not only for the eſſential connection, but its ſublimity, ſhould always be ſpoken ; it is a noble apology for the groſs treſpaſſes upon time and place, which ſo often occur to ſhock nice and rigid criticiſm.

Ely and the Archbiſhop of Canterbury open this play, like true churchmen who love to hold faſt temporalitics, they conſult how to ward off a parliamentary attack upon a conſiderable part of their poſſeſſions ; they ſeem happy in having the king of their ſide, of whoſe reformation, from the diſgraceful follies of his youth, they give a very favourable account ; the royal favour ſeems to have been purchaſed by a politic propoſal of Canterbury's, to furniſh the king with a larger voluntary contribution than ever had been given by the clergy, to his predeceſſors.

In

In the fecond fcene we meet King Henry, furrounded by feveral noblemen; upon the Archbi-
fhop's entrance, his majefty afks his opinion, relative to the falique law of France; whether it fhould
or fhould not affect the Englifh claims upon that
kingdom; this propofition Canterbury anfwers
with nice political diftinctions, and decides in favour of England.

How the author could fuppofe any actor could
gain attention through fo long, laborious and intricate a fpeech, we know not : the prelate ftrongly urging war, is backed by the other nobles, when
Henry takes occafion to utter his apprehenfion that
the Scots may take a dangerous advantage of foreign hoftilities; this point is overuled by his coun-
fellors, upon which the king orders the ambaffador
of France to be called in.

During his audience, we perceive the Frenchman to be very pert, particularly in his mention of
the ton of tennis balls, fent by the Dauphin as an
ironical equivalent for the territories claimed by
England; the monarch's reply is pregnant with
truly royal fpirit, and becomingly denounces the
chaftifement of France for fuch prefumtuous infolence; the Ambaffador being difmiffed, Henry
urges fpeedy, vigorous preparation for the expedition; declaring that he will return the Dauphin's compliment at his father's door.

In the fucceeding fcene, we find a ftrange tranfition of characters; from the higheft rank in life,
we are immediately popped amidft the fcum of the
earth, Nim and Bardolph; we find, that the former has had fome quarrel with Ancient Piftol,
which the latter wants to make up between them.
They

Henry the Fifth.

They are foon joined by the fwaggering blade and Hoftefs Quickly; the quarrel is renewed, and a converfation in the flafh ftile enfues.

It is painful to think that fuch low, unintelligible jargon, fhould have been obtruded upon a ferious piece. The Hoftefs gives them an intimation, that their old leader, Sir John Falftaff, is at the point of death, and defires them to vifit him.

At the beginning of the fecond act we meet a chorus, which never fhould be omitted ; the tale of connexion is fine, and exprefled with nervous elegance. Exeter, Bedford and Weftmoreland, come forward, mentioning fome traitors who have been difcovered. The king, upon his entrance, addreffes himfelf to the culprits, in very gentle terms, defiring their opinion concerning the expedition : from this he leads them on to warm profeffions of loyalty ; at length, giving each a paper, they perceive their detection, and cannot conceal their confufion ; but inftantaneoufly acknowledge their guilt, and fue for mercy, which the king, upon their own principles, very juftly refufes ; for having fome fpeeches before propofed pardoning a man, who, in heat of liquor, had fpoken difrefpectfully of his majefty, thefe confcious villains exprefled difapprobation of fuch royal lenity.

After recapitulating in a mafterly, but rather too minute a manner, their ingratitude and treache-
he delivers them over to the courfe of law, and, with great humanity, prays for their acquittal. They are formally arrefted by Exeter, and behave with becoming contrition : they are borne to their fate, and Henry goes off with a fpirited refo-

lution of feating himfelf on the throne of France, or falling in the bold attempt.

In the next fcene we are placed amongft the raga-muffins, from whom we learn, that Falftaff is no more : the Hoftefs's defcription of his final exit is mafterly ; and, we doubt not, all lovers of the fat knight, feel, at this paffage, fome regret for the lofs of him. We are inclined to wifh that all his followers, who could only be fufferable through their connexion with him, had tripped off the ftage of life alfo ; but, as the author has chofen to retain them, we muft compound for their company, how-ever irkfome ; efpecially as they follow the king to France.

The grand monarch and his fon, the Dauphin, next appear, conferring with the Duke of Burgun-dy and Conftable, concerning the Englifh invafion. Henry's character is lightly treated by the volatile Dauphin, whofe opinion is controverted by the peers ; and even the French king feems to think him formidable, as having fprung from that victo-rious ftock which fhook the power of France, at the memorable, fatal battle of Creffy. A meffenger announcing the approach of ambaffadors from Eng-land, they are admitted to an immediate audience.

Exeter, on the part of his royal mafter, plainly and directly urges a renunciation of the French crown, in favour of Henry, under claim of his illuftrious anceftor, Edward the Third ; denouncing warlike compulfion in cafe of refufal. The Dauphin afk-ing what reply the Englifh monarch has fent to his meffage, receives threats of chaftifement. The French king, though fo roughly attacked, tamely promifes promises an answer on the following day ; and thus with the conference, ends the second act.

Here again we meet with a very essential, because explanatory and connective chorus ; after which King Henry appears before the gates of Harfleur, where he has begun hostilities ; the proposals from France not being equal to his vast ideas. His address to the assailants is truly heroic, and worthy a royal character, roused to vindictive measures. He leads them on to the assault with becoming dignity and resolution.

Here a scene follows, which is a strange and trifling intrusion upon the serious circumstances of affairs. Three captains, Scotch, Welsh and Irish, are introduced ; the two last enter into a dispute of some humour, though a very unseasonable one, concerning discipline. Hearing a parley sounded, they go off, and Henry appears again before the gates ; declaring, that he will no longer be trifled with, by the governor of Harfleur ; but, on refusal of surrender, will sacrifice the town to his just resentment.

The governor, despairing of succour, yields, and the victorious monarch enters his new conquest.

Catherine, a French princess of France, is next introduced, endeavouring to learn some English words ; sure there never was a more trifling and superfluous scene written. The French king, with his son, and several nobles, are now brought forward, descanting on the English spirit. Touched with shame at the unchecked approaches of so daring a foe, the monarch gives orders for a sudden and vigorous opposition.

We next meet Gower, an officer, and the Welsh captain, Fluellin ; who remarks, that a person of little note, Ancient Pistol, has shewed himself a man

of

of spirit: the Ancient immediately appears, and solicits the Welshman's interposition to save Bardolph, who has committed a robbery. The Cambobriton disdains such an office, and declares, he would not, in such a case, seek favour for a brother. This irritates Pistol, who goes off in a violent huff.

Gower explains his character to Fluellin, who, it appears, had no proof of his bravery, but his own boasting. Upon this discovery, and his contemptuous words, the Welshman determines to watch an opportunity of putting him to the test. Here Henry enters, and is addressed by the captain, with some compliments upon the Duke of Exeter's martial abilities. Upon his mentioning Bardolph's situation, the king properly declares, that such persons are fit objects of punishment; and declares against all exercise of cruelty and rapine, though in an enemy's country.

Mountjoy, as ambassador from the French king, enters, and, in an address of considerable spirit, delivers his master's defiance. Henry mentions the distressed, sickly state of his army; yet, with an exalted resolution, declares his purpose to advance to Calais, and his determination, if opposed, to fight his way.

We do not approve the national reflections thrown out by the king in this scene; they are uncharacteristic, both as to his understanding and station; the sum total of this audience is, that he will neither seek nor shun a battle. It appears, that the English monarch is reduced to a very ticklish and perilous situation, which however no way appalls his mighty heart.

The

The Dauphin, and peers of France, next exhibit themselves ; between whom a moft trifling converfation, upon the merit of horfes, enfues. When the prince goes off, his character is freely and flightly handled by one of the lords. In the latter part of this fcene, being informed that Henry is within fifteen hundred paces of the French camp, the fprightly and confident monfieurs divert themfelves at the expence of the English, whom they feem to confider as an eafy prey, and go off to prepare for certain victory.

Well met again, at the beginning of the fourth act, honeft chorus. Some part of this addrefs to the audience, as well as other paffages in the play, CIBBER has tranfplanted into his RICHARD THE THIRD. A moft pitiable picture is drawn of Henry's fituation, yet the author has taken particular care to fuftain the dignity of his character ; this painting is very political, as his future, wonderful victory, is thereby thrown into a more confpicuous and advantageous light.

His defcription of the king is fo mafterly and amiable, that we cannot avoid prefenting our readers with a part of it.

—forth he goes and vifits all the hoft ;
Bids them good-morrow with a modeft fmile,
And calls them brothers, friends and countrymen.
Upon his royal face there is no note
How dread an army has furrounded him ;
Nor doth he dedicate one jot of colour,
Unto the weary and all-watch'd night :
But frefhly looks, and overbears attaint
With chearful femblance and fweet majefty ;
That every wretch, pining and pale before,
Beholding him, plucks comfort from his looks.

After

Henry the Fifth.

After this very favourable impreffion is ftruck by the chorus, Henry appears, remarking, with fuitable compofure, to Bedford and Gloucefter, the danger they are in. Upon the entrance of an aged knight, Sir Thomas Erpingham, the king good naturedly obferves, that the foft pillow of peace is more adapted to his enfeebled age, than war's flinty couch ; however, the fpirited baronet returns a brief and pithy anfwer.

Henry takes a fhort leave of them, as wifhing to confult his own heart, previous to the impending conflict. When the peers have left him, the king, wrapped up in Sir Thomas Erpingham's cloak, is accofted by Piftol, who, in his pompous cant, pays Henry fome compliments ; but denounces heavy threats againft Fluellin, which the king banters pleafantly.

After Piftol goes off, Gower and Fluellin meet ; the latter, who greatly admires the Romans, defcants warmly on military decorum, he contends hard for filence in a camp ; and, upon being told that the French do not maintain any fuch referve, but are loud, very fenfibly obferves, that their diffipated and irregular folly, is no juft ftandard for foldiers, who regard reputation and fuccefs to go by.

Three foldiers, Bates, Court and Williams enter ; the latter accofts King Henry, demanding whom he ferves under ; he is anfwered, Sir Thomas Erpingham. A very fignificant conference enfues, wherein the foldiers exhibit melancholy ideas of their fituation ; the king reafons with them, and throws their danger upon the neceffity of invaded honour. Williams afferting, that a king who urges war,

war, has the lives and limbs of his fellow-creatures to anfwer for, Henry enters into a very cool, candid and rational exculpation of royalty.

There is confiderable inftruction, efpecially for militarians, to be collected from this fpeech : an obfervation that Williams makes, occafions the king to give a rebuke, which produces a challenge; Williams gives a glove, and Henry prefents him another. When the foldiers difappear, his majefty ruminates upon what has paffed, and juftly confiders the regal ftate, as a fountain of ever fpringing cares. Some lines he utters on this occafion, we muft tranfcribe.

> And what art thou, thou idol ceremony ?
> What kind of God art thou that fuffereft more
> Of mortal grief than do thy worfhippers?
> What are thy rents, what are thy comings-in ?
> O ceremony, fhew me but thy worth ;
> What is thy foul of adoration ?
> Art thou ought elfe but place, degree and form ;
> Creating awe and fear in other men ?
> Wherein thou art lefs happy being fear'd,
> Than they in fearing.
> What drinks thou oft inftead of homage fweet
> But poifon'd flattery ? oh be fick, great greatnefs,
> And bid thy ceremony give thee cure.

The whole of this fpeech is fine, but our fanciful author has run it to a length, beyond the power of any actor to fupport ; it muft, in fome places, hang heavy on expreffion, though every line pleafes in perufal.

Being informed that his nobles are impatient to fee him, the king defires they may be fummoned to

his

his tent; and, after a very pious ejaculation, though rather relishing of the proud Samaritan, who confidently boasted of his own good works, he goes off to meet them. In the next scene we hear the Dauphin, and other French chiefs, proudly vaunting their superiority over the drooping English; they hasten to the field, confident of success, and leave the stage for Henry and his party. There is an Iricism in this line of Westmorland's, *but* ONE *ten thousand of those men in England.*

The royal Briton, though conscious of the fearful odds against him, addresses his peers with heroic cheerfulness; and when Mountjoy comes with insolent proposal of a ransom, the gallant monarch declares they shall have none but his bones. After this scene the armies join in battle: while we are waiting and anxious for the great event, our author has unaccountably brought in a scene between Pistol and a Frenchman, he has taken prisoner; the whole of which is contemptibly farcical, and this passage very reprehensible, " Signieur DEWE should be a gentleman;" playing upon sacred terms, though by mistake, is no way allowable.

After this Bartholomew-fair dialogue, we learn from the Dauphin and Constable, that the victory has gone against France; however, they go off to make a final effort. Henry enters, when a pathetic account is given of York and Suffolk, who have fallen in the battle: hearing a fresh alarm, the English monarch gives an order, shocking to human nature, however justified by necessity; that is to kill all the prisoners.

While the decisive stroke of battle is giving, we are entertained with Fluellin's ludicrous assimulation of King Henry to Alexander; and when the monarch

monarch comes on, the ſame humorous captain laughably mentions his being a Welſhman. Williams, to whom Henry, in diſguiſe, gave a glove, is brought on; being queſtioned why he wears that token of a challenge in his hat, he aſſigns the reaſon; being ſent off for Gower, his captain, the king gives that glove he received from Williams to Fluellin, telling him, he took it from Alanſon in the battle, and that if any one challenges it, he muſt be a friend of Alanſon's; Fluellin receives it with particular ſatisfaction.

This ſeems a boyiſh, unmeaning circumſtance, in the king's conduct, to put two men in the path of quarrel; and the moment he has done ſo, diſpatches two of his nobles to prevent any ſerious conſequence. SHAKESPEARE has in this ſacrificed the dignity of his hero to a deſire of enriching Fluellin's character; and ſhewing Henry's liberality, by filling the glove with crowns for Williams.

After this frivolous, uneſſential point is ſettled, a herald recapitulates the loſs of the French, which appears to be prodigious! eſpecially when compared to that of the Engliſh. The king, as a man of ſound ſenſe and religion, moſt juſtly attributes the miraculous difference, to providential influence in his favour. The fourth act cloſes with Henry's order to embark for England.

At the beginning of the fifth act, we again meet our friendly chorus, who gives many ſubjects for imagination to work upon; without which the piece really makes a very disjointed and irreconcilable figure. The choleric Welſhman is preſented to us with a leek in his hat; which, according to

his own account, he wears for fake of Ancient
Piftol, who had flightingly mentioned that national
ornament : opportunely his antagonift appears, to
whom he gives terms of provocation, which the Ancient replies to by a frefh infult upon leeks ; this
occafions Fluellin to infift upon Piftol's eating that
he has in his hat. So fevere a tafk is contemptuoufly
declined· at firft, but a few ftripes caufe the boafting poltroon to comply, which however he does with
high founding praife.

The kings of England and France are next
brought to a friendly interview, which turns upon
the fubject of a pacific alliance, planned and urged
by the Duke of Burgundy : Henry obferves, that
the terms are before his Gallic majefty, and that on
his anfwer peace depends. The French monarch
defires time to reconfider matters, which is allowed,
and five Englifh nobles are authorized to fettle mat·
ters with him.

All the other characters being gone, a very infipid, aukward fcene of courtfhip enfues, between
Henry and Catherine, a princefs of France ; words
are played upon in a moft childifh manner : we fee
no reafon why Catherine fhould be the only perfon
in the French court who does not fpeak Englifh ;
and that Henry, though the French language was
not in his time fo fafhionable as at prefent, fhould
be ignorant of it when he claimed France as his natural, lawful inheritance. Had thefe abfurdities in
character ferved any ftriking purpofe, there would
have been fome degree of palliation ; but the whole
purport of four infignificant, word-catching pages,

is

is to acquaint us with the monarch's defire to make Catherine his queen.

After this interview, the French king comes on, and all articles being agreed upon, particularly the propofed marriage, the play concludes. We fee no reafon for introducing the laft chorus, as it is nothing but a piece of unneceffary, hiftorical information.

The principal event of this tragedy, renders the fubject dear to every Englifh mind, elfe we cannot find fo many fhining proofs of SHAKESPEARE's genius in HENRY the FIFTH, as in many of his plays : incidents are fadly crouded, and the laft act is lamentably languid ; the comic parts are a moft unnatural connexion, and notwithftanding we allow Fluellin to be well drawn, moft contemptible ; there is very little to ftrike in action, and as little to pleafure in perufal.

The Englifh monarch is drawn a moft excellent picture of what a king fhould be, wife, cool, politic, liberal, merciful and brave ; fond of fame, but not in an unjuft caufe. We have feen Mr. SHERIDAN difplay folidity of judgment in this part, though royalty was much injured by his external appearance, and harmony of expreffion violently wounded by the difcord of his voice. The juftification of a king, in cafe of waging war, he delivered better than any other perfon we have feen.

Mr. SMITH is, upon the whole, more pleafing, yet wants confequence and variety.

Mr. BARRY, in this part, fteps far beyond any degree of competition, within our knowledge ; his figure and manner happily unite to fill up our idea of the fifth Henry.

The

The other serious characters of this piece are too immaterial for recollection; however, we can venture to say, that we have seen Exeter and the Constable of France, well supported by Messrs. CLARKE and HULL ; nor have we any fault to find with Mr. GARDNER, in the Archbishop of Canterbury. Fluellin is a part of great oddity, and requires peculiar acting; we are inclined to think Mr. MACKLIN much more characteristic in this part than Mr. SHUTER.

Mr. THE. CIBBER made more of the popgun Ancient Pistol than possibly ever will be seen again, by a laughable importance of deportment, extravagant grimaces, and speaking it in the sonorous cant of old tragedizers, he exhibited a very entertaining piece of acting merit. Mr. DYER is nobody.

Mrs. PITT's Hostess is worth notice, though short of Mrs. MACKLIN, whose description of Falstaff's dying was inimitable.

AARON HILL, favoured the town with a piece on the subject of this play, in which he preserved much more dramatic regularity, and approached nearer the tender passions, but has rather eclipsed the blaze of genius. With all its irregularities, SHAKESPERAE's must take the lead considerably, as indeed he always will in a state of comparison ; for even his weakest, and most censurable efforts, have in them an affluent originality, beyond the reach of any other dramatic author.

The BUSY BODY.

A COMEDY: By Mrs. CENTLIVRE.

SIR George Airy meets Charles in the Park; the former appears to be a little uneasy in his mind, which the latter rallies him for pleasantly; insinuating, that a man poffeffed of omnipotent gold, may obtain any thing to lull unquiet feelings. Being told that the caufe is love, he feems to think Plutus a more powerful deity than Cupid, and that the blind God muft yield to the God of Wealth.

It appears, that Sir George's paffion is engaged by two ladies, one whofe face he has never feen, but is charmed by her wit; the other he has feen, and is captivated by her beauty, without having ever exchanged a word with her; Miranda, who is the ward of Charles's father, claims a preference. Sir Francis Gripe's avaritious character is opened, and his intention of marrying the young lady himfelf, for the fake of her fortune, difclofed to the baronet, who gains a promife of affiftance from Charles, to obtain the lady. Their conference is broke in upon by the appearance of Marplot, of whom a preparative picture is given. The forward blade, after having eagerly urged an introduction to Sir George, accounts laughably for a black patch which appears on his nofe. Having formed fome intimacy with the baronet, Marplot is afked by that gentleman to convey letter to Miranda; Charles juftifies his

readinefs

readineſs to go upon ſuch ſervices, but paints him
as a very blundering emiſſary.

Hearing buſineſs mentioned, Marplot's curioſity
riſes ; Sir George excuſes his ſtaying any longer in
the Park, by obſerving, that he has an appointment
with Sir Francis Gripe. Whiſper coming on, acquaints Charles that Iſabinda can't meet him in the
Park, but that her rigid, jealous father, will certainly go out in the afternoon ; he then goes to
know the hour. Here Marplot is ſadly mortified,
at not knowing the purport of his meſſage, and determining to find out the occaſion of Charles's a-
brupt departure, follows him.

Miranda coming out of her chair, meets Patch,
of whom ſhe enquires for Iſabinda ; and is told,
that her father, Sir Jealous Traffic, has detained
her at home ; this knight's ridiculous attachment
to the formal and tyrannical cuſtoms of Spain, is
here ſet forth. It appears, that Patch, though
really Iſabinda's friend, has gained ſo much of the
father's confidence, that he truſts her in the ſtile of
a duenna, with the care of his daughter.

The waiting woman, who had formerly ſerved
Miranda in that capacity, takes the liberty of enquiring about a common report, that Miranda is
going to be married to her guardian ; to this the
lady replies, that ſuch a report is neceſſary, though
not founded in truth. She then acquaints us, that
ſeeing a man ſhe likes, is the motive of her coming
into the Park : Sir George appears to be the man,
and comes forward in conference with Sir Francis.
Miranda and Mrs. Patch, ſtand aſide and liſten.

We find, that the young knight is bargaining
with the old one, for a limited interview with his
ward ;

Busy Body.

ward ; in confideration of the fum of one hundred guineas, he confents to a conference of ten minutes, with this provifo, that he fhall be prefent all the time ; the old blade chuckles at having taken the baronet in, and leaves him. During their fcene, two remarks drop, one from the lady, and the other from the maid, not very delicate.

After Sir Francis retires, Miranda, under cover of a mafk, comes forward. Seeing his incognita, Sir George folicits a view of her face ; this is denied, and he undergoes fome fpirited raillery, which he fuftains, and replies to in an agreeable manner. Being brought to a fituation rather critical, and fearing a difcovery, fhe fuggefts a method of getting off ; which is by promifing, if he will turn his back, to let him know her meaning, who fhe is, and her place of refidence ; this he complies with.

She retires gradually, confeffing, that he has infpired her with a very tender paffion for him, then fhe rhimes herfelf off. The baronet, pleafed with his conqueft, hopes fhe may prove handfome, and promifes the behaviour of a gentleman. Hearing no voice found, he imputes the paufe to her modefty, but begs fhe will proceed ; receiving no anfwer to repeated folicitation, he turns round, and expreffing fome chagrin at being fo jilted, concludes the act with fix very flimzy lines, which we may juftly ftile profe baftardized into hobbling, unnatural verfe.

At the beginning of the fecond act, we meet Sir Francis, telling his ward, with triumphant fatisfaction, of the bargain he has made with Sir George. She, to forward her own defigns, feems to relifh the circumftance highly ; and pays the old

old fool fome compliments, which caufe him to think, that he has fecured a place in her heart. She makes a propofal to him, which, in the flow of good humour, fhe hopes he may comply with ; that is, if he will give her poffeffion of her own fortune, fhe will marry him the day after.

The danger of this he is aware of, and declines the propofal ; finding herfelf difappointed, fhe tacks about, and mentions a fcheme fhe has formed to baffle Sir George, which is to maintain ftrict filence, and not anfwer a word he fays. This pleafes the old knight greatly ; however, his fatisfaction is rather damped by the appearance of his fon Charles, who pleads hard, refpecting his neceffitous circumftances, but without any effect.

While the father and fon are parlying, Marplot enters, who, obferving Charles's melancholy face, afks Sir Francis for a hundred guineas, for which the curmudgeon gives him an order on his clerk. When Marplot goes to receive his money, Sir Francis makes a propofal to Charles for mending his circumftances, that is by marrying Lady Wrinkle, whofe age and deformities are fufficiently compenfated for, by her having forty thoufand pounds. The young man's declining this propofition, occafions the old one to drive him forth with very harfh terms. No fooner is he gone than Marplot returns, counting his cafh ; when he miffes Charles, he hurries out after him, for fear of lofing fome fecret. Sir George Airy being fhewn in, Miranda is called ; Sir Francis fets his watch, and the interview immediately begins.

Sir George's attack upon the lady's inclinations is warm and fignificant ; the old centinel, who

keeps

Busy Body.

keeps watch, throws in some interruptive lines, but is by threats kept out of ear-shot. The lady's unaccountable and invincible silence, causes the enamoured baronet to teach her signs, by which she may answer such interrogations as he may chuse to propose.

There must be a mistake in the printed copy, where Sir Francis says there are *three quarters* of an *hour* gone, because the time specified was *ten minutes*. Sir George having settled the mode of reply, he proceeds to offer his questions; her answers are some favourable, others doubtful. At length, tired with his unsatisfactory state, he tries another method, which is to speak both for her and himself; and, in her behalf, produces a letter, which he reads and kisses rapturously. In the heighth of his pleasing emotion, Sir Francis acquaints him, that the time is expired, and giving Miranda the guineas, sends her off.

Sir George's imperfect audience occasions Gripe to chuckle, which nettling the lover, he throws out a prognostication of cuckoldom, and both the characters clink themselves off the stage with some Grub-street lines. It is astonishing how actors, or public taste, could bear such frequent intrusions upon sense and nature; rhimes were, I suppose, found to be clap-traps, and consequently gained some degree of estimation; but why are they not now rejected in the old plays, as well as the new ones.

We are next introduced to Sir Jealous, who we hear lecturing his daughter, in favour of Spanish reserve and gravity. Patch, with politic address, backs his opinion, and insinuates, that Isabinda is rather prone to levity and resistance; in consequence of this, he gives the maid a frefh authority and charge to lock her up, till the arrival of one Signior Babinetto, whom he expects hourly from Spain.

Whifper, who has watched Sir Jealous going out, haftes to the door, where he meets Patch ; fhe informs him that Ifabinda is now alone, and defires him to acquaint Charles. Juft as he is going off, he meets Sir Jealous, whom fufpicion has brought back : the knight queftions him very roughly, as to what bufinefs has brought him near his door. This puzzles the valet ; however, he ftarts a whimfical apology, of having loft his lady's lap-dog, and afks Sir Jealous if he has found the creature ; by this device, he gets clear of the choleric old blade, who neverthelefs feems to have fufpicion of fome defign.

Charles and Marplot next prefent themfelves, and are foon joined by Sir George, who appears in the dumps : on afking Marplot if Miranda's filence proceeded from her folly, he juftifies her title to wit, by mentioning, that fhe has often rallied him till he had not a word to fay for himfelf. Whifper enters, and by fpeaking afide to his mafter, ftirs afrefh the inquifitive faculties of Marplot, who is a mortal enemy to all referve : his ftroke of defiring Sir George to afk Charles what his fervant has been faying, is droll and in character. When Charles and the baronet propofe going different ways, Marplot has fo ftrong an inclination to difcover what the former is about, that though he is roughly refufed the privilege of going with him, he follows directly.

3

At

Busy Body.

At the beginning of the third act, Charles appears at Sir Jealous Traffic's door, and is introduced by Patch : juft as he enters the houfe, Marplot fpies him ; and, by way of friendfhip, determines to watch him out again. The lovers being met, they lay a plan for their own happinefs, and to defeat Sir Jealous's defigns. An alarm of the old knight's approach, throws them into extreme confufion, amidft which it is determined, that Charles fhall effect his efcape from the balcony ; this fettled, they part.

Sir Jealous now appears in the ftreet, and breathes out fuch terrible threats, in cafe of finding a man in his houfe, that Marplot, who overhears, in zeal for Charles's fafety, and to prove his courage, accofts the knight ; and threatens, if any mifchief is done his friend, he will retaliate it feverely. This difcovery roufes Sir Jealous into fuch a paffion, that he belabours the poor, unlucky, blundering intruder, moft unmercifully. Still folicitous for Charles, he cries murder ; the lover defcending from the balcony, perceives who it is that's raifing the tumult : here Marplot improves the miftake he has made, by boafting of what he has done ; but, upon getting a hearty fhake by the collar from enraged Charles, he conceives his errors, and, drooping like a dog that had loft his ears, retires lamenting his ill luck ; but not without fome hopes of gaining fuch intelligence for Sir George, concerning Miranda, as may bring him into favour again.

Sir Jealous, full of conviction that a man is in his houfe, though not to be found, enters with fervants, enquiring if they have fearched every where : Patch ftill preferving his confidence, he renews his

orders

orders for locking up Ifabinda, then goes to renew his fearch. The maid comforts her miftrefs with the idea of gaining at laft the man fhe wifhes, and they retire.

Sir Francis meets his lovely ward in the next fcene, and fhe plays him off fo admirably, that he thinks her his own beyond a fhadow of doubt. Marplot enters to them, who mentions Sir George's hundred pounds, and upbraids Miranda with cheating him of it : warm words arifing, Sir Francis bids the inquifitive meddler get out of his houfe. Upon hearing Miranda declare that fhe will take her guardian for better for worfe, Marplot banters the idea till he is threatened with the knight's cane, but havingfo lately feltone, he defifts. Miranda, with great addrefs, fends an affignation to Sir George, by bidding him keep from his old haunt, the garden gate, at the hour of eight. Her meaning is grofsly miftaken by both the old fool and young one, and her opennefs increafes the old fwain's confidence, who leads her off, full of joy, with a Latin quotation.

The fcene now changes to a tavern, where Sir George and Charles are difcovered over a bottle : the baronet offers his friend fome confolation, to free his fpirits from that gloom which his late mifcarriage has occafioned. The waiter mentioning that Mr. Marplot defires leave to wait on them, they defire him to be admitted : on his appearance, the unhappy adventurer puts on a face of confeffion, and endeavours to apologize.

When Sir George enquires after Miranda, he gives a very unpromifing account, and declares her fettled determination to marry Sir Francis ; to

which

which alfo, he adds her warning about the garden gate. Sir George does not immediately perceive her meaning, but, after a few fhort fpeeches, catches it; and thanks Marplot for fo pleafing a piece of intelligence. His fatisfaction puzzles our Bufy Body.

In order to take fo unlucky an object out of the way, Charles urges Marplot to go with him; he is pleafed at being forgiven, but fufpecting, from Sir George's behaviour, fomething that de does not underftand, he refolves upon going to Sir Francis Gripe's, that he may ftand a chance of finding it out.

The firft fcene of the fourth act is before Sir Jealous's door, where Patch receives a letter from Whifper for her miftrefs; and defires him to acquaint his mafter, there will be a fair opportunity for paying a vifit to Ifabinda, by means of a ladder of ropes: hearing the old man, fhe hurries the valet off; and, in her confufion, drops the letter: no fooner does fhe difappear, than Sir Jealous comes on; he perceives the billet, which, upon opening, he finds to be hieroglyphically infcribed. This unintelligible object caufes frefh fufpicion, and a glimpfe he got of Patch's tail fweeping by, throws fome part of it on her.

A fervant entering, Sir Jealous enquires for fome company he had invited; being told that they will all wait upon him, he countermands the invitation; calls for his butler, and orders that fupper may be brought into his daughter's chamber. Ifabinda and Patch are thrown into ftrong perplexity about the letter, which cannot be found. The maid running out to fee if fhe had dropped it by the

the way, is met at the door by the butler, whofe
bufinefs being afked, he fays it is to lay the cloth
in that room, for his mafter's fupper. This circumftance fuggefts to the young lady fome frefh
mifchance : the old man approaches, ftops Patch,
and queftions his daughter about the letter ; fhe
pleads ignorance, and the chambermaid, to make
up for her blunder, invents an affertion, that the
paper is hers ; declares it was given her as a charm
for the tooth ach, and throws herfelf into violent
agitation at the misfortune of its being opened, as
the magic power is thereby deftroyed.

This bait takes with the old knight, and Ifabinda, collecting fome fpirit from the fuccefs of it,
accufes her father of feverity ; to which he anfwers,
that Signior Babinetto's arrival, will free her from
all parental authority. Supper being placed on
table, he afks the young lady to partake ; which,
from her ftomach being already too full, fhe declines. He next defires, that as fhe can't eat, fhe will
entertain him with a tune on the fpinnet, while her
maid fings a fong; both thefe requefts, through confufion, they are fo unable to comply with, that one
plays, and the other fqualls moft miferably out of
tune, which provokes the old man to threats.

While they are endeavouring to proceed, Charles
bolts in upon the wings of rapture ; but feeing Sir
Jealous, retires haftily, though not fo foon but that
he is perceived : to cover his retreat, the women
cry, a ghoft ! a ghoft ! and throw themfelves acrofs
the door. Having given the lover time to efcape,
they make way for the impaffioned knight, who
rufhes into the clofet, bent on difcovery and deftruction.

He

He foon returns, and not having found the main
object of refentment, lets his wrath wreak itfelf
on the females ; his daughter he locks up in a clofet, and then drives Patch out of doors. In this
exiled ftate fhe meets Charles, and acquaints him,
not only of Ifabinda's imprifonment, but alfo that
her deftined Spanifh hufband is expected on the
following day, and is to confummate the nuptials
with all poffible expedition.

In the midft of Charles's diftraction, Patch fuggefts his perfonating Babinetto, and furnifhes him
a letter, by counterfeiting which, he may gain
credit with Sir Jealous, who knows nothing more
of the young Don, than what occurs by corref-
ponding with his father. This politic hint revives
the lover, and they go off to concert matters, by
which room is made for Sir George, who appears
at the garden gate ; through which he is foon conveyed by Scentwell into the houfe.

Miranda, in foliloquy, apologizes for a feeming
breach of delicacy, in bringing Sir George to vifit
her in a clandeftine manner, but the juftification
fhe offers is very allowable ; fuch' a guardian as
her's would juftify any young woman for taking all
fteps, but vicious ones, to defeat his loathfome defigns upon her perfon, and knavifh views upon her
fortune.

The baronet advances with polite rapture : in
the conference which enfues, we find Miranda fo
prudent, that fhe wont gratify her inclination by a
violent attack upon circumftances, but determines,
before fhe leaves Sir Francis's houfe, to take the
writings relative to her fortune along with her.
Sir Francis's unexpected return obliges Sir George

to

to make a precipitate retreat behind the chimney-board; it appears, that Gripe's return has been occasioned by Marplot's perfuading him, that Miranda had certainly fome fatal, barbarous meaning, in the blunderbufs. Sir Francis defires Scentwell to throw an orange peel behind the chimney board, this fhe evades, by defiring to eat it; but that being refufed, Miranda defires the board may not be removed, as fhe has a monkey, which being very wild, might do mifchief, if let out.

Marplot immediately expreffes ftrong curiofity to fee what he calls, aptly enough, a miniature of man; however, he is forced to defift by threats, and Sir Francis goes off to vifit his rich neighbour at Epfom, from whom he expects a large legacy.

While Miranda attends her guardian to his coach, Marplot lifts up the board, when out bolts Sir George, and thropples the frightened, inquifitive blade; who, in his confufion, defires the baronet to break fome china, as an apology for the uproar he has made.

Sir Francis and Miranda returning, Marplot frames a ftory of the monkey's efcape, for which he receives a fevere rebuke from the old fellow; who, after ordering fearch to be made for the little favorite, goes off again to profecute his journey. Miranda upbraids Marplot, who accounts laughably for his mifapprehenfion.

Sir George returns, when Marplot begs to be excufed, and is, upon his fubmiffion, forgiven. Patch enters, and acquaints Sir George, that a friend of his wants affiftance: on being told that it is Charles, he determines to wait on him, but declines Marplot's company, who expreffes great de-

fire

fire of going also ; and to prevent him, infifts he may ftay with Miranda, fo concludes the fourth act.

At the beginning of the fifth, we meet Miranda, telling Patch that fhe has taken a bold and hazardous ftep, by venturing upon a hufband, whofe difpofition fhe is not fufficiently acquainted with : after ordering Scentwell to pack up her jewels, fhe is going to leave the houfe ; at which time moft inopportunely, fhe meets Sir Francis, who having found himfelf fummoned upon a fham meffage, has declined the continuation of his journey.

Scentwell entering abruptly with a diamond necklace in her hand, occafions fome confufion ; but Miranda paffes it off with ready addrefs, and turns the matter quite off, by telling him of Ifabinda's approaching marriage with a Spanifh Don, to which fhe is invited : the amorous guardian, hoping that the fight of matrimony may whet his ward's appetite for a fimilar feaft ; he promifes to go, and receiving an equivocal declaration from Miranda, that if ever fhe marries, it muft be in the courfe of that day ; he leads her off with terms of moft triumphant joy.

Sir Jealous next appears, who being told by a fervant that Signior Babinetto is arrived, receives, and brings Charles, attended by Sir George, as Mr. Meanwell, forward : after fome attempts at Spanifh, which Sir Jealous is very imperfect in, the converfation is continued in Englifh. Sir George, with great art, as a deputed guardian to the young Don, and many plaufible arguments, urges an immediate marriage ; which the father feems very well inclined to, after being fatisfied in one point ;

that is, why no mention has been made in the introductory letter of thofe five thoufand crowns, which were to be fettled on his daughter, in cafe of her becoming a widow.

This unexpected circumftance occafions fome hefitation ; but Sir George anfwering that the value of that fum is configned to his care, for the propofed purpofe, in various kinds of valuable merchandize, Sir Jealous is fatisfied, fends for Mr. Tackum, who, as it appears, is ready.

The angry father goes off, and drags on his daughter, who folicits hard againft a forced marriage, but to no purpofe, fhe adheres to her refolution ; after much threatning, and many violent remonftrances from Sir Jealous, Sir George undertakes the perfuafion, and by privately communicating who the apparent Spaniard really is, gains her to the defired point. Her rapture, which breaks out a little untimely, is reftrained ; the father, heartily rejoiced at this unexpected and fudden converfion of his perverfe child, gives her with tears of fatisfaction, to Don Diego, and they all go off, highly fatisfied, to the celebration of thofe nuptials which the young couple fo eagerly wifh, and Sir George has earneftly laboured to promote.

Marplot, without adverting to his former blunders, which have brought him into fuch difagreeable fituations, now runs headlong into a frefh fcrape ; and having heard that Charles has borrowed a Spanifh habit, determines to enquire about him at Sir Jealous Traffic's. Pat to his purpofe, a fervant comes out of the houfe, of whom he afks if tnere be a gentleman in a Spanifh habit at his mafter's ; from the minutenefs of his enquiry, and

3   faying

faying he thought a friend of his might be there in
difguife, the footman fufpeas a poffibility of impofition, and calls his mafter.

When Sir Jealous comes forth, he accofts Marplot churlifhly, demanding his bufinefs ; on mention of a Spanifh habit, he is fuppofed to be a
friend of Babinetto's, and is queftioned as fuch,
but not being able to give any intelligent account
of who or what he wants, the old gentleman grows
warm, and perceiving that he is the perfon who had
threatened him with half a dozen mirmidons, he
frightens poor Marplot in fuch a manner, that he
comes to an explanation about Charles, which a-
larming the father, he calls in to ftop the marriage.

This noife brings out Sir George, with his fword
drawn ; feeing Marplot, he finds out the fource of
evil incidents, which, to confirm, the buftling Bufy
Body calls the baronet by title and name, which
unfolds the deceit, and an attempt is again made to
ftop the marriage ; however, Sir George ftanding
centinel between the door and him, orders it to go
on : finding himfelf foiled, he wreaks his vengeance
on Marplot, who once more feels the difcipline of
his cane.

At this crifis Charles and his bride enter ; foon
after them Sir Francis and Miranda come forward.
Sir Jealous accufes Gripe with being acceffary to
cheating him of his child ; Sir Francis being defired to open his purfe in favour of Charles, he declines any concern with him as a fon, and declares
his fettled connexion with Miranda.

Here Sir George fteps in, and claims the lady as
his ; this, fhe confirms, and, as it appears, has not

only

only taken care to get her own writings, but Charles's too, relative to an estate left by an uncle, which the Jew, his father, kept from him. Thus totally over-reached, Sir Francis leaves them with great heat of passion : after his departure, matters take a more favourable turn, and Sir Jealous, with a commendable share of good sense, cools into good humour.

The several parties being agreeably disposed of, Marplot asks, what reparation he is to have for the hard usage he has received ; forgiveness of his blunders, and a promise from Sir George, that his guardian shall give him his estate, and make him happy. Thus the piece concludes, a very incontestible moral being deduced from past transactions in three lines : if we search for solidity of sentiment, or purity of language in this comedy, our enquiry will be fruitless ; yet there is a pertness of dialogue, and a womanish whim of incident, that must ever tickle the lighter passions, and keep attention upon a pleasing bent.

As to the characters, they are natural and well chosen ; as will appear upon their being separately examined. Sir George is a fine gentleman, with elegant ideas, lively feelings, and a large estate ; he meets with a woman he likes, and spares neither money nor pains to obtain her honourably. One circumstance is odd, that he never once mentions his fair incognita after the first act : the author might easily have discovered to him that Miranda was the person, and a good scene might have been struck out, of her rallying him upon the masked lady ; however, this is a very pardonable lapse.

Mr.

Busy Body.

Mr. PALMER, was in this gay baronet too much of the fop, indeed, it was so natural to him, he could not shake it off. Mr. SMITH has sufficient vivacity, without diminishing essential elegance; we never desire to see the part better supported than by this gentleman.

Sir Francis Gripe we find so complete a son of avarice, as warmly to wave every principle as a father, guardian, or man, to the insatiable love of gain; his preposterous amour is more founded in wealth than regard; his situations are pleasant, and render him rather an object of laughter, than of the contempt he really deserves. Mr. YATES, a great favorite of ours, for strict adherence to nature in his proper cast, was remarkably chaste in this character, which he played upon the most critical principles; and, certain it is, that though Mr. SHUTER may make the galleries laugh more, by a luxuriance of humour, yet he never can be so correct.

Mr. PACKER has done the inoffensive Charles for many years inoffensively enough; we have seen Mr. CLARKE exhibit him, but think the part far beneath his abilities; and, as to Mr. HULL, who goes on for him at present in Covent Garden, we never wish to meet him in any but the graver parts of comedy, many of which he would support in a very respectable manner. Why is not Charles given to Mr. LEWES, who ought to be brought forward in such a light, till practice and improved merit make him fit for a more favourable one.

Sir Jealous Traffic is extremely well contrasted to Sir Francis, as his folly does not arise from a bad heart, but a deficient head; violent regard for his daughter, makes him anxious for her happiness, and a mistaken a miftaken notion of the means to prevent any finifter accident, makes him feem cruel, when he really means well ; there is an open bluntnefs of expreffion about him, which Mr. LOVE is very characteriftic in, and we think Mr. DUNSTALL equally happy.

Marplot, the main engine of this piece, is a very well conceived caricature of nature, adequately drawn, and prettily finifhed : notwithftanding a Bufy Body in private life, is a very mifchievous and obnoxious character, yet Mrs. CENTLIVRE has contrived to prefent us with one fo inoffenfive and laughable, that we believe many of the audience would be glad of fuch an acquaintance to exhilerate their fpirits occafionally : we remember many performers in this character, Mr. MACKLIN very dry, infipid and faturnine : Mr. THE. CIBBER, egregioufly comical, extravagant and incorrect : Mr. BROWN, by fome thought a good actor, though certainly the worft that ever was feen, faint, indefcriptive and laborious : Mr. GARRICK, lively and expreffive, but too mechanical : Mr. KING, fpirited and picturefque, with rather too much fenfibility : Mr. WOODWARD, every thing the author or fpectator could wifh, poffeffing every beauty his competitors could boaft, and exhibiting a fuitable naivéte above them all.

Miranda has nothing blameable, but being a little too forward in her love affair ; fhe feems to have good fenfe, fteadinefs and generofity. Mrs. PALMER was very unequal to the reprefentation of this part, yet, being an amiable actrefs, paffed off without giving offence, Mrs. BULKLEY mended the

matter,

Bufy Body.

matter a good deal, but we are much inclined to place Mifs MACKLIN firft.

Ifabinda was very improperly given to Mrs. MATTOCKS, who is much fitter for Patch ; however, fhe reprefented the young lady in a refpectable manner : Mifs PLYM was well fuited to the part, as is Mrs. BAKER.

Patch fhould always be in the hands of Mrs. GREEN, though we have feen Mrs. PITT fhew acting merit in the character, and Mifs MINORS perform it extremely well. We readily admit this play to a ftage exiftence, but we think it fcarce worth any body's purchafe for the clofet; notwithftanding it is free from the heavy charge of licentioufnefs, which juftly lies againft fome abler compofitions.

King

King HENRY the Fourth.

An Historical PLAY: SHAKESPEARE.

THE King, attended by his son, Lord John of Lancaster, and other peers, gives us to understand, that the play opens with a newly commenced peace ; yet from what Westmoreland says, we find that a general calm is not established, notwithstanding a decisive victory gained by Piercy, over the Scots. Mention of this young nobleman occasions Henry to paint, with strong feeling, the disreputable contrast between Hotspur and his son, the Prince of Wales : nothing further material occurs in this scene, except that Piercy has refused to deliver up the prisoners taken in battle. In the next we meet Prince Henry and Falstaff ; the latter enquiring what time of the day it is, is rallied by the Prince for demanding any information concerning a circumstance so totally immaterial to his irregular course of life ; the fat knight retorts, by painting his royal companion as graceless as himself. This is very natural, for the dissolute always endeavour to level other characters with their own ; or, if possible, to make them worse.

This scene is chiefly made up of a quibble of words, yet is sensible and entertaining. When Poins comes on, there is a fine equivocal turn in Falstaff's character : some few lines before, we find him bent on a new course of life, but, upon mention

tion of a robbery, which is likely to produce defireable fpoil, he hears the matter, and joins in it, with great glee; wifhing that the Prince may be an affociate, he goes to Eaftcheap.

After the knight has waddled out of fight, Poins propofes a fcheme of amufement, that is, to rob Falftaff, Bardolph, Peto and Gadfhill, after they have acquired the booty : to this projeft the volatile Prince agrees readily ; the mode of proceeding is fettled, and Poins retires to provide neceffaries.

When alone, Henry, though linked with fuch a diffipated crew, and feemingly involved amidft the depths of iniquity, makes fome glorious refleftions; wherein, his fpirit as a man and a royal charafter, break brightly forth.

The obfervation that his latter years will fhine more bright by a comparative view with the gloom of his former ones, is not a very allowable apology for joining in a courfe of life, which, in his own conviftion, is held defpicable ; however, the foliloquy throws a plaufible glofs on his charafter, and prepares us agreeably for the reformation he fuggefts.

In the next fcene we meet the King, highly nettled at being croffed, as it fhould feem, by Hotfpur, and his relations. Upon Worcefter's attempting an apology, he is forbid the prefence : after a palliative introduftion, delivered by Northumberland, Hotfpur enters upon his own defence, concerning refufal of thofe prifoners which the King had demanded : his addrefs is very peculiar and fpirited ; his contraft of the rough foldier's charafter, to a perfumed, effeminate peer, is finely imagined, and happily expreffed.

VOL. II.　　D d d　　King

King Henry, however, confiders his reply as equivocal, and founded on provifo, that Mortimer, a fubject hateful to majefty, fhould be ranfomed. Hearing an imputation of Mortimer's revolting, Hotfpur, with charaĉteriftic impatience, contends this point warmly with the King, and maintains his brother-in-law's charaĉter, both as a fubjeĉt and commander. This altercation roufes Henry to fome fevere terms, and a pofitive infinuation, that further difobedience of his orders, will be attended with difagreeable confequences.

This peremptory threat occafions a flow of paffion, which vents itfelf on Hotfpur's fide, in a very glowing ftile. Being forbid even to fpeak of Mortimer, ftings fo home, that every trace of patience is obliterated; and, with the utmoft heat of temper, he charges ingratitude and tyranny againft the King. After fpending the fire of his refentment in frenzied ftarts and bitter reproaches, he condefcends to hear fome cool and politic advice from his coufin Worcefter; who points out fome vindiĉtive meafures by the path of rebellion, which he deems very praĉticable, from powerful difcontents which agitate many leading charaĉters of the realm.

Piercy's expeĉtation warms from this view, fo confonant to his defires, and he concludes the firft aĉt with a wifh, formed by wounded pride, and a kind of military enthufiafm.

At the commencement of the fecond aĉt, two carriers are introduced, throwing fome very low refleĉtions upon their quarters and accommodations. After having informed us of their ftation, and that they are going to continue their journey, they make room for the Prince and Poins, who having removed

moved Falftaff's horfe out of his reach, the puffed knight comes on, almoft breathlefs with fatigue, calling for them, and defcribing his own cumberfome, painful fituation : when they appear, he afks, partly in a paffion, and partly foothing, for his horfe. Gadfhill and Bardolph giving notice that the monied travellers are at hand, they take their ftations ; while Henry and Poins retire to put on their difguifes.

Hearing a furious noife of " ftand, down with them," &c. the travellers drop their cafh, which the valorous Sir John and his mirmidons have no fooner taken, than it is taken from them again by the Prince and Poins, in buckram fuits. This jocular defign being happily executed, the victorious couple go off, enjoying their cheap conqueft.

Hotfpur, in foliloquy, now prefents himfelf, perufing a letter, on which he makes fome whimfical comments, as the contents are matter of excufe from fome defireable partifan, whom he expected to join in his enterprize. In the following fcene with his lady, which, by the bye, is very immaterial, he difcovers much peculiarity and flightinefs of temper ; fhe, with a kind of childifhnefs, endeavours to wheedle from him, the caufe of manifeft perturbation, which, neverthelefs, he declines communicating, and in a manner we think unneceffary ungenteel, though bluntnefs feems to be a material part of his character.

We are now tranfplanted to the tavern in Eaftcheap, where the Prince and Poins appear, ftill enjoying their adventure. Henry, in the flow of fpirits, boafts an intimacy with a parcel of drawers, and with Poins's affiftance, plays upon the fimpli-

city

city of one, in a manner that might very well become a Bartholomew-fair droll, but is too meanly
farcical for the stage, though it seldom fails of a
laughable effect.

After this unmeaning piece of buffoonry, Falstaff and his crew are introduced: the knight sets
forward with a furious exclamation against cowards,
not forgetting to compliment himself, as being one
of the only three honest, valuable men in England.
At length, he broadly insinuates, that Henry is a-
mong the list of cowards, but, upon getting a rebuff from the Prince, readily and humorously re-
tracts his meaning, yet continues the insinuation:
having mentioned taking a prize of a thousand
pounds, and its being most violently forced from
him again, he enters into a very curious account
of his own valorous resistance, wherein such circumstances and contradictions occur, as must di-
late the rigidest features.

After he has gone through the detail with most
entertaining prevarication, the Prince enters upon
his account, which reduces Falstaff to a dilemma
apparently inextricable; yet with invincible effrontery, and quick address, he exhibits a masterly
stroke of equivocation, by observing, that he knew
it was the Prince who attacked him, and out of
respect to the blood royal, would not make any
resistance.

Just as this point is discussed, the Hostess enters
in a violent hurry, acquainting the Prince, that a
nobleman of the court desires to speak with him:
Falstaff is deputed to give him an answer, which
charge he speedily fulfills, and upon return, gives
some hints of the civil commotions which are on
foot.

foot. The Hoſteſs again enters, and acquaints them that the Sheriff is at the door, demanding entrance, to ſearch for ſome men who have committed a robbery. Falſtaſt, conſcious, claims protection ; he is ordered behind the arras, and the Sheriff admitted, who, being queſtioned of his buſineſs, declares it : the knight being plainly pointed at, Prince Henry ſcreens him, by aſſerting his abſence upon buſineſs; and that he will himſelf undertake to anſwer any charge that may be brought againſt the ſuppoſed guilty perſon.

The magiſtrate being diſpatched, and danger with him, Falſtaff is heard ſnoring : the Prince orders Poins to pick his pocket, from whence he extracts nothing but papers ; one of which, being read, proves a curious tavern bill, thê principal article of which is an enormous quantity of ſack. Henry declares his intention of going to court in the morning, and ſays, he will not only provide for Poins, but procure Falſtaff a company of foot. With this ſtrange intention the act concludes, ſtrange, we ſay, becauſe however flighty the Prince might be in his general conduct, we cannot ſuppoſe, that in ſo ſerious and critical an affair as civil war, he would put a proved poltroon, a known ſcoundrel, into commiſſion : but the author found it neceſſary, ſo without any ſcruple or apology, he has ſacrificed royal prudence and decorum, to the preſervation and enlargement of his favorite character.

At the beginning of the third act, we find ourſelves in the preſence chamber at Windſor : the King having deſired his nobles to retire, lectures the Pr. of Wales with much paternal feeling, and eloquent energy ; his ſpeeches, though fine and pithy, are
beyond

beyond doubt, too laborioufly long for the actor's expreffion: his fon's vindication of himfelf, and promife of future actions, fuitable to his dignity, fhow a fpirited fenfibility, which melts the King into a cordial reconciliation, who immediately gives him an honourable command, and appoints the day for his marching to meet the rebels.

Sir John and Bardolph fucceed this royal interview; the former complains that he finds himfelf in a confumptive ftate, and therefore feems inclined to repent of his diffolute courfes; but, upon Bardolph's blaming him for fretting, reverts again to vice, and jefts upon the red nofe of his Bacchanalian follower. Seeing the Hoftefs, our fat knight mentions his having his pocket picked, which irritates the lady much, as being a heavy charge againft the credit of her houfe: a warm altercation enfues, in which they both difplay confiderable abilities.

He afferts having loft a feal ring, worth forty marks, which fhe declares the Prince had often told her was copper. This occafions Sir John to utter fome heavy threats, but, upon feeing Henry, he turns the fubject off; however, Mrs. Quickly refolves to have it handled, and to that end tells the Prince, that Falftaff had threatened to cudgel him. This caufes a frefh and very laughable altercation, in which the knight is confiderably embarraffed; however, his old and conftant friend equivocation ftands by him, till Henry flafhes conviction, by declaring, that he was the caufe of this exaggerated robbery, which produced nothing but tavern bills, and a halfpenny worth of fugar-candy. This explanation, after a conceffion from Falftaff, brings all matters to a right underftanding; the Prince

acquaints

acquaints his fat favorite, that he has procured him a charge of foot, then gives Bardolph fome difpatches for Lord John of Lancafter.

From the two conclufive lines of this act, we very plainly perceive that Falftaff is much better inclined to a tavern than military operations.

Hotfpur, Worcefter and Douglas, begin the fourth act, in Shrewfbury: the former compliments the latter with generous terms of efteem. A meffenger brings fome letters, and the difagreeable intelligence, that ficknefs prevents Piercy's father from joining perfonally the common caufe. Worcefter feems to think his abfence a great damp upon their enterprize; however, Hotfpur, with unbateing fpirit, thinks it will reflect greater credit upon their daring attempt. Sir Richard Vernon informs them of the powerful preparations which are moving forwards, to make head againft them. Piercy enquires particularly after the Prince of Wales, which gives Sir Richard an opportunity of defcribing him and his warlike companions, with very beautiful imagery. This fires Hotfpur, who longs to enter the lifts againft fuch gallant opponents, though unaffifted by his father and Glendower.

Sir John and Bardolph now appear upon their march to Coventry: having difpatched his follower for a bottle of fack, the knight, in foliloquy, gives a moft diverting account of the foldiers he has picked up; his infinuation of mifufing the king's prefs money, we believe fits many a recruiting officer. Prince Henry coming on with Weftmoreland, afks whofe fellows they are that come after, and make fo wretched a figure. Falftaff acknow-

ledges

ledges them to be his, and humoroufly confiders them as merely food for powder, confequently good enough for that purpofe.

Hotfpur, Worcefter, Douglas and Vernon, again come forward, debating whether they fhall give battle the fame night, or refer it to another day. Piercy's impatience wifhes to feize the earlieft opportunity, and Douglas fupports his opinion ; Vernon and Worcefter diffent. After reafons urged on both fides, it remains ftill an undetermined point ; when Sir Walter Blunt addreffes them on embaffy from the king, who fent by him fome plaufible offers of pacific redrefs, in cafe any real grievances can be made out. In Hotfpur's reply, which is nervous and circumftantial, he accufes the king of ambition, duplicity and ingratitude, not to be trufted ; however, he defires a night to confider the royal propofition, and promifes to fend a categorical reply by his uncle Worcefter in the morning.

Our author has judicioufly concluded this act with probable ideas of peace, which bring on more forceably the operations of the next.

King Henry, at the beginning of the fifth act, gives audience in his camp to Worcefter, who recapitulates the caufes of complaint, which his majefty treats with contempt. The Prince of Wales, perceiving that all hopes of accommodation are vanifhed, and that war is to be the arbitrator, with a gallant generofity, propofes to reft the general difpute upon a fingle combat between him and Hotfpur. This pleafes the King, his father, highly ; however, with humane condefcenfion, he once more offers, upon fubmiffion, to decline hoftilities, nay,

even

even a renewal of royal favour, to his rebellious opponents.

There is a moft centemptible piece of ftage buffoonery introduced here, which ought to be repulfed, not laughed at ; we mean Falftaff's fitting upon the fame drum with the King, and tumbling down when Henry gets up; SHAKESPEARE's luxuriant humour needs no fuch pitiful refources. Falftaff's foliloquy, where he inveftigates the meaning and value of honour, is as laughable an apology for cowardice as ever was penned.

Worcefter, from a fuppofition that the King's fmooth propofitions are founded in fallacy, declines acquainting his nephew with them ; and, on Hotfpur's appearance, mentions fuch aggravating terms as precipitate a battle. Vernon's defcription of the Prince of Wales's challenge, is delicate and generous. On being told that the royal army comes forward, Hotfpur and party go off to meet them, with a truly martial fpirit. Here alarms are heard, and Sir Walter Blunt is flain by Douglas. A good deal of the fkirmifhing introduced by SHAKESPEARE, is properly omitted in reprefentation.

The fat knight has another foliloquy, and though horribly frightened, preferves his humour ; the giving him a bottle of fack in a piftol holfter, is whimfically characteriftic. While Hotfpur and the Prince of Wales are engaged, he comes on vapouring, but feeing Douglas, falls down as if dead. When Hotfpur has yielded his breath to his victorious competitor for glory, the generous conqueror pays an expreffive and pathetic compliment to his qualifications : feeing his old companion Jack prollrate, proftrate, he fpeaks of his fall with friendly though ludicrous regret.

The coaft being clear, our prudent knight gets up, rejoicing in his own fafety, and applauding the means of it. The fight of Piercy, though dead, touches him with frefh panic ; however, he collects refolution enough to make him fure, and giving him a wound in the thigh, declares his refolution to claim the honour of killing him. Here the Prince of Wales returns, with his brother Prince John of Lancafter. Seeing Falftaff with Hotfpur on his back, he is furprized, and is ftill more fo at Sir John's afferting himfelf to be the conqueror of Hotfpur ; however, he good-naturedly inclines to countenance his humour, and the knight lugs off his honourable burden.

King Henry, after fentencing Worcefter and Vernon to death, declares his intention of purfuing rebellion through all its haunts, and thus the play concludes.

Though we do not hefitate to pronounce tragi-comedy to be the moft heterogenious production that ever entered the human imagination, yet we muft contend that our author has in this piece made it as pardonable and probable as a union fo unnatural would admit. In the tragic fcenes there is great dignity and fire of expreffion ; in the comic ones, unparalleled pleafantry. The plot, though void of unities, has a face of regularity, and keeps attention agreeably employed through the whole.

As to characters, we find Henry cool, politic and refolute, well fuited to his elevated ftation ; in per-formance, little more is requifite than importance

I.   of

of deportment, and propriety of declamation. Mr.
SPARKS, in the former was ſtiffly mechanical, in the
latter, irkſomely laborious ; yet ſhewed more merit
in the firſt ſcene with Piercy, than any other performer within our notice. Mr. GIBSON, is undoubtedly a burthen to himſelf in this part, conſequently can't ſit very light on the eyes, ears or feelings, of an audience. Mr. BANNISTER is better
than either.

The Prince of Wales is totally made up of light
and ſhade, his diſſipated ſtate and ſhameful companions, render him an object of contempt ; but his
martial ſpirit, when called upon, and his real courage, ſo happily tempered with generoſity, preſent
him to view a very eſtimable character. As a rake
he is pleaſant, as a hero ſtriking ; in the tavern
a trifler, but in the field important. Mr. RYAN
had an eaſe in this mad-cap prince, which
preſented him in a very agreeable manner. Mr.
PALMER did the comic part well, but was egre-
giouſly deficient in the ſerious ſcenes. Mr. CAU-
THERLY is boyiſh at firſt, and inſipid at laſt. We
do not recollect any perſon better calculated to do
the character general juſtice than Mr. SMITH, he is
well adapted by nature to give us an idea of the
gentleman and prince.

Hotſpur is marked a very peculiar character,
exactly anſwering our author's deſcription of a ſol-
dier in AS YOU LIKE IT, "jealous of honour, ſudden
and quick in quarrel :" an enthuſiaſtic admirer of
fame, who enters the liſts of rebellion, rather from
ill founded reſentment than any ambitious view ;
however his cauſe deſerves cenſure, the original motive of it admits of ſome defence ; while his ſpi-

rited

rited conduct commands applause, and his fall demands pity from every generous mind.

A martial figure, with great voluble powers, are
the requisites for this character ; we have heard one
Mr. DELANE much spoke of, but have too faint an
idea to corroborate report. Mr. BARRY we often
attended with great pleasure, his externals pleaded
powerfully for him, and he shewed many capital
strokes ; but in the last scene of the first act, was remarkably deficient ; the breaks and transitions
wanted essential spirit and variety.

Mr. MOSSOP has power well suited to Hotspur,
but having less ease and more sameness than Mr.
BARRY, is consequently less pleasing. Mr. SMITH,
who indeed is seldom any thing but Mr. SMITH,
can never do the gallant Piercy justice ; had Mr.
GARRICK martial consequence, his other requisites
would surpass all competition.

The other tragedy parts we don't sufficiently recollect for criticism ; indeed, they afford no great
opportunity for conspicuous merit to shew itself.

Falstaff is, beyond doubt, one of the most luxuriant productions that ever sprung from human
imagination ; a character so inimitably drawn,
that by the force of irresistable humour, we are led
not only to forgive the unprincipled knight, but
even to view him as an object of singular regard.
There is not a sentence he utters but feasts atten-
tention. The author has in this part shewn most
powerful originality, and Mr. QUIN was in
the representation of him a true disciple of Momus ; his comely countenance, his expressive eye,
his happy swell of voice, and his natural importance of deportment, all united to make up a
most

moſt characteriſtic piece of acting. To point out one ſtroke where ſuch uniformity of merit adorned the whole, may ſeem ſuperfluous ; yet it would be ingratitude to the remarkable pleaſure we felt from unuſual excellence, not to mention that paſſage, where Falſtaff's lies about the battle and buck-ram men, are pinched ſo cloſe, that he has no no refuge but the very unexpected one of pretending that he knew the concealed aſſailants, and therefore conſidered the whole matter as a joke. There was in this place ſuch a glow of feature and expreſſion, as we ſhall never ſee equalled.

Mr. Berry was a deplorable falling off, as heavy and unmeaning as a bare repetition of the words would admit. Mr. Shuter's common fault, that of being too comical, lies much againſt him in the corpulent knight. Mr. Love is certainly correct, and ſtands next in our idea to Mr. Quin. His figure, features, eyes and manner, are agreeable to criticiſm ; but we wiſh him a little more animation, a little of that luxuriance which Mr. Shuter has too much of. Poins is well ſupplied by Mr. Packer.

It is almoſt needleſs to ſay any thing of the ladies, they are ſo trifling : Lady Piercy is the very ſimpleton of tragedy, totally uſeleſs, and unentertaining ; we have ſeen Mrs. Woffington, Mrs. Bellamy, Mrs. Hamilton, and Mrs. Palmer, daudle on for this part, without being able to diſcover any ſuperiority of merit, ſo very inſipid is the compoſition ; indeed, were it not to compliment Hotſpur, an indifferent actreſs would ſuit it better than a firſt rate one ; becauſe the former would probably take ſome pains, while the latter muſt undoubtedly deſpiſe ſo ungracious an undertaking.

The

The Hostess, for what she says, is well delineated ; Mrs. MACKLIN made her appear to great advantage, and we are sufficiently pleased with Mrs. PITT, and Mrs. BRADSHAW.

From what we have said it will evidently follow, that the author of this play, though he has manifested great abilities in the composition, for want of female characters and familiar incidents, has greatly abated the success of it on the stage ; few ladies have the same relish for Falstaff's rhodomontades that Queen Elizabeth had. In the closet it must ever please substantial taste.

The MOURNING BRIDE.

A TRAGEDY: By CONGREVE.

WE are told that the ingenious parent of this tragedy, was four years finishing it, an old adage, signifying, that too much cookery spoils the broth, here strikes us, and we wish it may not be verified by the present object of consideration ; but as we have hitherto avoided anticipation of judgment, let examination first take place, and candor, as heretofore, decide.

The MOURNING BRIDE begins with some very happy lines, spoken by Almeria. By the scene between her and her confidante Leonora, which is too diffuse and prolix, we find, that the Princess's father, Manuel, had deposed King Anselmo, to whose son Alphonso, she had been married unknown to her father ; we are also informed, in a very poetical, but unnatural manner, that Alphonso, flying with his bride from Manuel's fury, was wrecked, and in her idea lost for ever ; hence Almeria's distress, which she expresses emphatically.

Shouts of triumph are heard : after Almeria's resolving to visit the tomb of Anselmo, Gonzales enters. From him we receive a pompous account of King Manuel's triumphant entry : the Princess hears of her father's success with cold indifference ; the old statesman hints his son Garcia's devotion of

heart

heart for Almeria, but that subject is interrupted by the victorious monarch's approach.

Manuel seeing his daughter and her train in the sable weeds of mourning, while splendor and joy gild every other part of his palace and kingdom, considers her singularity as a mark of disrespect, and checks her in severe terms. She apologizes, by saying, she keeps that day as the anniversary of her deliverance from shipwreck. This vague excuse, rather irritates than softens the King, who orders her from his sight, enjoining a change of dress. We think this order should be complied with in the remainder of the play, as certainly a person of Manuel's violent temper, would have resented in express terms, a fresh instance or continuance of disobedience; we don't remember to have seen this point observed upon the stage.

As the Princess is going off, Garcia puts in his claim; which Manuel confirms, by giving his daughter's hand, and appoints the next day for their nuptials. This sudden, irresistible stroke, overwhelms Almeria with a fainting fit, by which she gets clear for the present.

Alonzo here acquaints the King, that his lovely captive Zara, the Moorish Queen, is arrived. Before her entrance, some intimation is given of Osmyn's character. Zara is received by her conqueror, not only with benevolent, but amorous politeness, which she receives with haughty reserve; however, the monarch resolving to persevere, frees her with his own hand, then addresses Osmyn, who replies with enigmatical sullenness.

Zara

Mourning Bride.

Zara, fearful of any ill confequence, apologizes for him, by imputing his concern to having loft, in the confufion of battle, a valued friend called Heli. The King orders fearch to be made for him, and concludes the act with a rapturous declaration of his paffion in fome tolerable lines, if they did not rhime.

The fecond act begins with Garcia, Perez and Heli, in fearch of Ofmyn; they get fight of him gliding acrofs the Ifle of a Temple. Heli intreats to follow his friend alone: when they are gone off, Almeria and Leonora come forward; the latter feels very natural, womanifh fear, at being amidft fo awful and terrifying a fcene; but the former, made defperate by grief, feems to enjoy the horrors of fo gloomy a place. Having gained the tomb of Anfelmo, fhe perceives, with furprize, the iron and marble gates open: after making an addrefs to the grave, as a refuge from care, and confequently the feat of peace, fhe mounts her fancy in very bombaft terms to ftarry orbs, milky ways, liquid light, and feats of blifs; mere poetical trumpery, when thus made ufe of.

After feveral emphatic repetitions of Alphonfo's name, he, in the habit and character of Ofmyn, rifes from his father's tomb; fo unexpected an object ftrikes the Princefs with aftonifhment, that brings on another fainting fit: he endeavours to call her fenfation back, while Heli enters unobferved by him. At length, being reftored and convinced of her hufband's identity, terms of the moft endearing nature are interchanged; but our author has certainly rendered the fcene heavy, by extending it too far: he feems to have confulted the indulgence of his own genius, more than nature and the eafe of attention.

Perceiving Antonio, known by the name of He-li, their fatisfaction is confiderably encreafed: while they are employed in mutual congratulations, upon fo unexpected a meeting, Leonora perceives fome perfons in fhining garments croffing the Ifle, whom Heli difcovers to be Zara and Selim: her ill-placed paffion for Ofmyn is mentioned to Al-meria, and he requefts, for mutual fafety, that the Princefs may retire, which fhe does.

Previous to Zara's entrance, Ofmyn reflects up-on the penury of fight, which only admits exterior objects, and thofe through neceffity. This is not unnatural for a lover's extravagant ideas, but though common fenfe admits the great latitude and fuperiority of mental perception, we are not to throw a kind of philofophical contempt on fuch refined organization as the fource of vifion: but love and reafon fo very feldom meet, that this paf-fage, though it might be fpared, neverthelefs ftands in fome meafure juftifiable.

Zara, urged on by her violent paffion for the noble captive, purfues him even to the gloomy re-gion of death. Seeing him in a ftate of deep, and to her regardlefs contemplation, fhe upbraids him with flighting the affection fhe has fhewn for him, and urges fome powerful proofs of love. In this fcene, the lady difcovers more romantic warmth than delicacy of feeling, and cafts off every trace of becoming pride: fhe offers, through her influ-ence over Manuel, to give him liberty, which, knowing her terms, he declines. This roufes her to the rage of a difappointed female, tinctured with jealoufy,

jealoufy, and fhe refolves to irritate Manuel againft him.

Juft at this crifis, the amorous monarch enters ; who, hearing that Ofmyn dares to be a rival, orders him to prifon and punifhment : then concludes with a boyifh obfervation, that love is the main fpring of life.

At the beginning of the third act, we meet Ofmyn, a prifoner, ruminating upon the tranfition from his father's tomb to an ignominious dungeon. He reads a paper, found in his cell, which, by the by, is very unnaturally thrown into blank verfe : this fcroll appears to be a tender, fupplicatory addrefs to heaven, from his deceafed father Anfelmo, for his deliverance and protection ; one word being torn off, caufes an abrupt conclufion, and Ofmyn moralizes on that circumftance, in a ftrange, perplexed manner.

At laft, he comes upon the point of eternal juftice, which, notwithftanding the profeffed privilege of thinking, he leaves juft as he finds it : we agree with our author, that thought precedes the will to think, but cannot own that error lives, ere reafon can be born ; or that reafon, though a fallible, can juftly be deemed a mere twinkling light, fooling the follower.

Whitfield himfelf, nor any other enthufiaft, could have given a more unworthy picture of human nature's foremoft attribute : Heli comes opportunely to break this chain of falfe, or, at leaft, partial philofophy.

Obferving that he has gained admiffion by Almeria's influence over the guard, Ofmyn enquires how fhe is, and whether he may hope to fee her :

being

being anfwered affirmatively refpecting the laft
point, he expreffes fears for her purfuing misfortunes in his perfon.   The following comparifon of
himfelf to chaff, is abominably far fetched :

> One driven about the world like blafted leaves
> And chaff, the fport of adverfe winds ; till late
> At length imprifon'd in fome cleft of rock,
> On earth it refts, and rots to filent duft.

Heli offers friendly confolation, and acquaints
him, that there are diforders ripening in the ftate,
which hang as a ftorm over the head of Manuel,
and promife fair in Ofmyn's favour.   This raifes
the noble·captive's fpirits, and, for a moment, he
fancies himfelf at the head of a conquering army ;
which idea of exultation is foon turned into rage,
on· feeling the reftriction of his chains : his friend
judicioufly recommends a moderation of fuch violent
feelings, and advifes, at leaft in appearance, an a-
batement of his averfion to Zara ; adding a defire,
that he may caft his main hopes upon providence.

Heli going off, Ofmyn, in foliloquy, accufes himfelf for queftioning the impartial care of heaven, in
temporal difpenfations ; and, at the fame time, bla-
zons his father's piety in that refpect.   We are
forry to find in a fpeech of fuch moral and religious
intention, the Book of Prefcience mentioned ; as it
immediately draws the thinking mind into an idea
of predeftination, which we deem the moft uncomfortable opinion that human nature can fuftain.
The paffage we here object to, reminds us of four
lines in one of DRYDEN's plays, which feem to us

the

the oddeft flight of fpeculative fancy, that ever was committed to paper :

> If fate be not, then how can we forefee ?
> Or how can we avoid it if it be ?
> Whether we drive, or whether we are driven,
> All ill belongs to us ; all good to heav'n.

What a fpacious and intricate fcope of fpecula-tion, do the two firft lines propofe ? how vague and unfatisfactory a come off, do we find the two laft exhibit?

Zara entering, covered with a veil, is miftaken by Ofmyn for Almeria, and therefore tenderly ad-dreffed : upon perceiving his miftake, he manifefts furprize, which betrays feelings no way confonant to the Moorifh Queen's wifhes. This caufes her again to upbraid him, though in tender terms ; at the fame time, fhe pities his mournful fituation, and feems painfully to confider herfelf as the caufe of it : his reply is generous, but his exculpation of her, by bringing in *fate* as the fource of his woes, is blameable.

Expreffing a wifh that he had not been a flave, particula:ly at fuch a time, the enamoured Queen promifes, ere the rife of morn, to procure him li-berty : the account fhe gives of love forcing his eye-balls abroad, at the dead hour of night, is a ftrained, unnatural effufion of fancy.

When Zara retires, Ofmyn pronounces a fhort eulogium upon her internal virtues, and external charms ; yet concludes with confidering her, from the violence of paffions, as an object more to be feared than loved : here Almeria appears, whom he receives with the utmoft tranfport, though in-

cumbring

cumbring chains damp his tender feelings ; to be a captive without probable hope of enlargement, ftings his heart. The Princefs ftrives to footh his pangs, yet is too fenfible of them to check her melting fympathy.

Several fpeeches which occur between this diftreffed pair, are totally in the bombaft ftile ; particularly where Ofmyn puts in practice that contemptible ftage trick, dafhing on the ground ; and the defcription of the effects defpair is like to have on him, is highly offenfive. In fhort, this whole fcene, though of pathetic tendency, is an impofition upon nature ; equally injurious to humanity and common fenfe.

While they are funk into a ftate of undifcerning grief, Zara re-enters, producing the King's fignet for Ofmyn's liberation : being requefted by Perez, Captain of the Guard, to ftop till the Princefs is retired, her Moorifh majefty catches the gleam of jealoufy. Ofmyn perceiving her, conducts Almeria off, returning thanks for the condefcending notice fhe has been pleafed to take of an unknown captive.

Zara fees through his diffimulation, and addreffes him in terms which are a very fmall degree above Billingfgate ; for which we think the author highly blameable, fince a royal character, though as fubject to the unruly paffions as thofe of lower ftation, fhould ftill maintain a fuitable dignity of fentiment.

After indulging her fury in reproaches, fhe orders the guard, not only to confine him more ftrictly, but to watch that he makes no attempt at felf-deftruction. Then concludes the act, with an obfervation, which we take to be very well grounded ; that there is nothing more dangerous than love

3

turned

Mourning Bride.
turned into hatred, nor any thing more vindictive
than an amorous, jealous woman fcorned.

Zara and Selim open the fourth act; by what
paffes between them, we find that fhe has deeply
incenfed the King, and that Manuel's rage has received frefh fuel from fome accounts of a revolt
amongft his troops, and the flight of Heli, with
fome other perfons of diftinction. Being told that
the fate of Ofmyn, even for immediate execution,
is figned, the Queen relents, and refolves to defer
his death. The agitations of a female mind in love,
are here well defcribed; the turbulence of rage
and hate give way to fofter paffions, which fo circumftanced we believe natural enough, even in a
virago.

Puzzled to find probable means of faving the
man fhe loves, we hear her threaten the eunuch
Selim with inftant death, unlefs he fuggefts fomething for her purpofe : at this exigence he advifes
her not to difcover any change in favour of Ofmyn,
but to requeft that execution may be done upon
the noble prifoner in private, and by her mutes,
as fuppofing the royal guard to be bribed. Here
Manuel comes forward, dooming fome rebellious
leaders to death : by what Gonzales intimates to
the King, we find fome imperfect information has
been received that Alphonfo is ftill alive; by comparative circumftances Zara difcovers that Ofmyn
is Alphonfo.

This caufes frefh anxiety, as his fate feems inevitable; however, fhe refolves, at all events, to attempt his prefervation : for this purpofe, fhe urges
the neceffity of his death, and frames a deceptive
tale, importing that fhe knows of a triple league
between

between Alphonſo, Heli, and Oſmyn. This gains Zara confidence with Manuel, who readily falls into her ſcheme of having him put to death by the mutes, and ſeems highly ſenſible of the obligation conferred by the zeal ſhe ſhews for his intereſt upon ſo important an occaſion. Orders in conſequence of this arrangement are given, that no perſon ſhall have admittance to the Captive Moor, but ſuch perſons as have authority from Zara.

In the recollection of her jealous feelings, ſhe throws in a ſuſpicious hint, that even the Princeſs muſt not be allowed to viſit him. Gonzales, with the true penetration of a practiſed politician, ſuſpects the Mooriſh Queen's ſincerity, from ſo particular and ſo emphatic an interdiction. Upon hinting the matter, Zara inadvertently ſlips out that ſhe had heard of an interview between Oſmyn and Almeria: this fires the King's reſentment, to which ſhe gives an artful turn, and retires, under pretence of preparing her miniſters for the execution of Oſmyn. No ſooner is ſhe retired than Gonzales mentions his doubts in explicit terms to the King, who for ſome time conſiders her as a ſanguine friend ; but being awaked from the lethargy of confidence, at length ſees with the eyes of unprejudiced caution, and fires at the thought of his daughter's diſobedient infidelity.

At this unlucky criſis the diſtreſſed Princeſs comes before her father, who indulges his rage, and loads her with reproach for the myſterious and ill-timed grief ſhe wears ; his paſſion throws her into ſtill greater confuſion of mind, and this her intemperature he concludes to be proof of ſome hidden, dangerous guilt. At length, the King's mention
that

that he knows *who* Ofmyn is, throws her into a ftate of mental agony, bordering on defperation, and fhe drops fome hints refpecting her hufband; which, but that they are deemed the offspring of diftraction, muft caufe the ruin of all her deareft hopes.

Another convenient fainting bout is introduced, which rather checks the fubject. After fome disjointed flights on her fide, the King orders her to be taken care of as an infane object; when her father retires, Gonzales endeavours to footh Almeria's grief, which increafes to fuch an height, that fhe explains at full the fecret of Ofmyn's being Alphonfo; then impelled by the force of a frenzied imagination, runs off, fuppofing fhe hears herfelf fummoned by the mournful found of Alphonfo's dying voice.

Gonzales finding a firft hufband in the way to impede his fon's progrefs to royalty, by marriage with the Princefs, deliberates how he may beft work his own ambitious views for the aggrandifement of his family: he fears to tell the King of the difcovery he has made, leaft paternal feelings fhould work him to a reconciliation; the captive Queen he alfo apprehends danger from, on account of her fecret attachment.

At length he refolves, without opening his defign any farther than by ordering Alonzo to procure him the drefs of a mute; with this, and an intimation that Alphonfo muft be flain, he concludes the act, afferting alfo his refolution to place the crown at all events on Garcia's head.

At the beginning of the fifth act we meet the King, rather difturbed that Zara, nor any of her

attendants are to be found. Juft as Perez is giving an account how Ofmyn is bound to earth with
double chains, a mute appears, who, on fight of
Manuel, retires precipitately. Alonzo is difpatched
to feize him, on account of his having difcovered
fuch diforder, and concealed fomewhat in his bofom; Alonzo quickly returns with a paper, and
information that the mute had ftabbed himfelf on
its being forced from him.

Upon perufal of the paper, it appears that the
King is moft violently agitated : turning fhort,
and perceiving Perez to be within ear-fhot, he firft
reproves him for fo prefuming a fituation, and then
charges him with not only being privy to the difguife of Alphonfo, as Ofmyn, bvt alfo of Almeria's
intercourfe with him, and Zara's attachment in
proof of which latter charge he reads fome paffages
of the intercepted letter.

The injured officer pleads his fervices, as deferving better ufage, but obtains no other return than
the unkingly one of a blow ; after which he is ordered to drench his dagger in Alphonfo's heart; this
he ftartles at, but promifes, on a threat againft his
own life, to perform. Enraged majefty then gives
way to an after thought, and propofing to confront
Zara, orders the cell where fhe intends feeing Ofmyn to be darkened, intending to be himfelf robed
in Alphonfo's habit, and laid proftrate as the captive is, that fhe may have no idea of deception till
conviction flafhes upon her.

Seeing the Queen approach he avoids an interview, and retires. Zara perceives him, and draws
apprehenfion from his enflamed looks : we wifh, at
fuch an anxious period, fhe had not ftepped afide for
the

3

the affimulation of his eye to the dog ftar, which al-
lufion would be forced and fuperfluous in any character, but is egregioufly wrong for a *Moorifh* lady,
fince in that country they have not fuch ideas of
aftronomy as we have, even among the men, and
the females are totally ignorant of every fcience, the
moft familiar; therefore, mention of an abftrufe
one here is peculiarly abfurd, but our author feems
determined to wrap her up with fimilitudes this
feene.

Suppofing Selim deficient in fome of his proceedings fhe upbraids him, while he, in a very moral ftrain, juftifies himfelf under the idea of mortal
imperfection. Two mutes, with that common tragedy appurtenance, a bowl of poifon, are ordered
to attend this wrong-headed Queen, which, as fhe
hopes, and is determined to fet Alphonfo free, we
don't fee occafion for, unlefs it be to prepare the
audience for death. Gonzales next enters to the
prifon, difguifed and alone; he furveys the manfion of mifery, he perceives the inner door to be
unbarred, and enters with murderous intention.

Garcia comes on at this critical point of time,
calling eagerly for his father; Gonzales foon returns, chafed at the interruptive clamours, however it appears he has done the deed of death.
When Garcia mentions the city is all in confufion,
and that Ofmyn is fled with Perez to the foe, Gonzales afferts that part of the intelligence is falfe,
as his poinard reeks with the Moor's blood. To
prove this affertion, Garcia goes into the cell, and
returning inftantly proclaims his father murderer
of the King.

This

This dire miftake throws them into the utmoft confufion, and the old ftatefman wifhes to atone it with the facrifice of his own life ; however, as things are circumftanced, they refolve to conceal Manuel's fate, and for this purpofe Alonzo is or-, dered to fever his head from the dead trunk. This done, they go off to oppofe the infurrection.

Zara, teeming with gloomy fentiments and fatal refolutions, comes forward, attended by Selim and her mutes : the ftill horror of the fcene affects her, fhe fends the mutes to tell Alphonfo that fhe waits him, and orders Selim to acquaint the King fhe has done what he commanded. When the mutes return, with unufual terror in their eyes, fhe enquires the caufe, which they difclofe by opening the back fcene. Perceiving the horrid, headlefs trunk, and from the garment fuppofing it to be Ofmyn, fhe indulges deep grief, though it appears that fhe came refolved to die, and to carry the object of affection to the grave with her.

While fhe is in the utmoft agony of mind, Selim enters, and telling her the King is no where to be found, fhe ftabs him. The faithful eunuch, wifhing to fave his miftrefs, warns her not to drink the poifon, and is going to inform her that Alphonfo is alive, but death checks him in the inftant of information. Zara proceeds to finifh her weary life, but the author has run her into a fad miftake; being a Mahometan, fhe fhould not talk of her fpirit's meeting Alphonfo's in a future world, for in that faith women are not allowed immortality.

No fooner is the unhappy Queen expired, but Almeria and her confidante enter; the Princefs alfo comes to feek the object of her affection ; up-

on

Mourning Bride.

on feeing the headlefs trunk her grief rifes to a diftracted height : viewing the fatal cups, fhe determines to end her cares ; at the moment fhe is going to drink the poifon Alphonfo enters, and fnatches her from the gaping jaws of fate ; the furprize of joy overpowers her, and fhe faints for the third time.

The conclufion of this play draws a very moral inference, juftly obferving, that though virtue may labour under occafional chaftifement, yet perfeverance in rectitude cannot fail of reward. The MOURNING BRIDE has been, at different times, fupported by very able performance, and has drawn many brilliant audiences, yet we cannot help thinking it one of the worft living tragedies : it is apparently laboured, the fentiments in general ftrained, the verfification in many places monotonous, and the plot equivocal.

In point of characters, we find the King a weak, bluftering, tyrannical object ; a credulous lover, and a harfh father. His paffions, efpecially in the fourth act, are laughable, and the device which occafions his death, farcical ; he is altogether the moft ungracious load that ever lay heavy on the fhoulders of a performer. The higheft merit that can be attained is to pafs through him inoffenfively, and in this view we have feen Mr. SPARKS. Mr. BERRY rumbled him out in a moft difgufting manner: why he fhould be impofed upon Mr. J. AICKIN, we cannot conceive, unlefs to prejudice his merit in public opinion ; his brother's general caft and ftile of acting, fhould have royalized him in this play.

Ofmyn is defcribed to us as a hero, but appears in no other light than that of an affectionate,

conftant

conftant hufband. His fituations and embarrafs-
ments raife fenfations of pity, but being totally out
of the fourth act, and fo immaterially concerned in
the firft and fifth, he becomes a very imperfect hero
for reprefentation.

We have feen Mr. SHERIDAN make Gothic attempts upon this part, for which he had not a fingle requifite : an infufficiency of figure, diffonance
of expreffion, and limitation of voice, conjoined to
overfhadow every trace of merit. Mr. BARRY was
happy enough to be the very reverfe of the forementioned gentleman ; his love, grief and rage,
were all expreffed by very adequate powers. Mr.
GARRICK, we think, in the foliloquies, and the
fcene with Heli, outftripped every competitor ; but
the Moorifh habit proved rather too much for his
figure, and the amorous paffages did not flow from
him with that natural fincerity, of which Mr. BAR-
RY gave us an ample and very pleafing idea. Mr.
MOSSOP is much too mechanical and boifterous, he
cannot fhake off the bafhaw ; he fhould never attempt any thing in the amorous ftile, but that ful-
tanic hint of dropping the handkerchief. Mr.
HOLLAND ftiffened his deportment into a degree of
aukwardnefs, and tortured the tones of his voice
into an irkfome degree of diffonance. Mr. INCH-
BALD has prefented himfelf in Ofmyn this feafon
with a very flender degree of credit, being in every
refpect much worfe than any we have named, except Mr. SHERIDAN. Gonzales, like moft ftatef-
men, of all ages, moves upon that ruling principle
felf-intereft, and aggrandifement of his family. As
a part he ftands in a ftate of mediocrity, neither for
or againft the actor : we remember to have feen
him

him well done by Mr. HAVARD ; and Mr. PACK-
ER, who may be ftiled the *Pack-horfe* of DRURY
LANE, does him fufficiently well.   Mr. HULL has
abilities, if required, to render the part refpectable.
As to all the other male characters, we fhall leave
them to their own infignificancy.

Almeria, who gives name to the play, is amiable
in her principles, and pitiable in her circumftances ;
the author has run her a little into the romantic
ftrain, but fhe has the happinefs of opening the play
with two of the beft lines in the whole piece.
There is a variety of acting in this part, yet her
royal highnefs is undoubtedly too much upon the
whine : no perfon whom we have feen had equal
capabilities to Mrs. CIBBER for this part ; Mrs.
BELLAMY, though inferior in requifites, muft not
be placed far behind ; her painting of diftraction
was more faint, but love and tendernefs fhe always
expreffed with admirable feeling.   Mifs MACK-
LIN, about feventeen years ago, by the inftruction
of, and playing with Mr. GARRICK, fupported Almeria through a confiderable run, with much credit, and really ftruck out feveral beauties ; but her
feelings, though correct in tragedy, always wanted
the animation of expreffion ; her voice was too
thin and contracted.   Mifs YOUNG, whom we confider as a rifing actrefs, has fhewn ability in the
part, but we object to this lady's frequent attempts
at what fhe can't execute ; ftriving to excel is, no
doubt, a laudable ambition, but as a performer
fhould not overftep the *modefty* of nature, no more
fhould he or fhe ftrain the *powers* of nature ; it is
better to be a little below, than above the point of
rectitude.

Zara

Zara is, beyond difpute, the moſt indelicate Queen that can well be imagined ; ſhe is vicious and mean, grofs in ſentiment, and vulgar in ex- preſſion. Had ſhe been more delicate in the for- mer, and more reſerved in the latter, ſhe might have attracted ſome degree of humane concern ; but, as ſhe is, good ſenſe and decorum muſt frown through the four firſt acts, while ridicule attends her and the head-ſhaking miniſters of death in the fifth. The author's peculiar unhappineſs in the cataſtrophe of this leading character, is plainly evinced by an obſervation we have repeatedly made, that ſcarce any degree of merit can ſave ex- piring Zara and her diſmal attendants from being laughed at.

Mrs. WOFFINGTON's figure and deportment were well adapted to the captive Queen ; but the vio- lent, as well as tender paſſions, grated abominably in her diſſonant voice. Mrs. PRITCHARD was ma- jeſtic, but rather too corpulent ; in ſpeaking and acting the part, ſhe ſhewed correct and fine preſer- vation of character. The amorous paſſages were indeed not ſo harmonious as might be wiſhed, but in the jealouſy ſhe made ample amends.

We remember to have ſeen Mrs. CLIVE make a laughable aſſault upon Zara, which was nearer burleſque than could well be imagined. Had it not been to excite curioſity upon her night, it would have been one of the moſt unpardonable at- tempts that ever was made : excluſive of a voice dreadfully unfit for ſerious ſpeaking, her perſon rendered all the King's amorous compliments ludi- crous ; and juſtified Ofmyn's coldneſs, admitting

he

he had no other engagement to warp his inclination.

It is amazing that a principle of felfifhnefs fhould caufe people of great merit and good circumftances, for the fake of a few pounds, to exhibit themfelves in a contemptible point of view. Mrs. HOPKINS, who now apologizes for moft of the above excellent comedian's parts, makes rather a better figure in Zara, yet is bad enough, heaven knows. We have now got to the end of our remarks upon this laborious tragedy, and, without any hefitation, venture to pronounce it, though capable of drawing tears when well acted, the worft compofition that any man of equal genius to Mr. CONGREVE ever produced.

LOVE MAKES A MAN;

O R,

The FOP's FORTUNE.

A COMEDY: By CIBBER.

THE piece now offered to view took its origin
from two plays of BEAUMONT and FLETCHER,
which we think the Laureat should have owned;
but cannot find any trace of such justice and modesty in his prologue: two old dons, Antonio and
Charino, open this play, talking upon a marriage
between one of Antonio's sons and Charino's
daughter; the choice of who shall be his son-in-
law, and other matters being agreed upon, Sancho
enters and presents a letter from Carlos to his father Antonio; soon after Clodio's valet appears,
and in broken English announces his master's
speedy approach.

The brothers next come forward; when Clodio's vivacity, opposed to Carlos's stiffness, makes
a favourable impression upon Charino; who though
old seems fond of festivity; the Beaux's remarks
upon his brother's formal university air improve
the prejudice in his favour; Clodio retires to
change his dress, which gives Antonio an opportunity to consult Charles's inclination or ideas respecting matrimony; being desired to become a

man

man of the world, the abftracted fcholar feems to
point out books as the moft valuable and comprehenfive enjoyment; when told that he fhould
marry for fa'e of an heir to continue the family,
he defires that care to be caft upon his brother,
and feems ambitious of nothing but exalted knowledge.

This throws the matrimonial fcheme entirely
upon Clodio, who returns and entertains the two
old dons with a very whimfical and pleafant account of the French princes and princeffes he has
been familiar with in Paris, the father, and propofed father-in-law enjoy his rhapfodical volubility
fo highly, that Charino propofes immediate introduction to his daughter Angelina, which Clody
gladly accepts, and they go off highly pleafed
with each other.

Sancho, who has overheard the defign of fettling
the greater part of his mafter's inheritance upon
Clodio, determines to acquaint don Lewis, Antonio's brother, with the matter; the cynical old
blade entering juft at this point of time, and defiring to fee Charles, Sancho opens the matter to
him by degrees; upon hearing it he denies credit
to the tale till Antonio, who comes on with a lawyer, confirms the truth of it; this caufes don
Lewis to ufe fome very angry expreffions againft
Clody, and favourable ones in refpect of Charles;
his admiration of and regard for literary knowledge, though he knows nothing at all of the
matter himfelf, further than that Greek has a lofty
found, is humouroufly imagined.

There is a very grotefque and diverting oddity
throughout this fcene, and the firft act concludes

with a furious declaration of don Lewis's againſt the proceedings of his brother, and the hopes of his younger nephew.

Sancho is preſented at the begi'ning of the ſecond act in anxious ſollicitation for his maſter's interest, but the poſitive father, bent on his own determination, cuts the matter very ſhort; then calls all his ſervants to prepare the wedding entertainment: Carlos from his ſtudy hears an unuſual buſtle, the noiſe of which diſturbs him; on ſeeing Sancho he aſks the meaning of it; being told it is the cooks, he lays by his book, then enquires about his younger brother's knowledge of languages; the marriage being mentioned, Sancho gives a luſcious deſcriptiòn of Angelina, ty way of warming his maſter's numb'd feelings.

Upon hearing that all his birthright is to be ſettled upon Clody, he bears the intelligence with philoſophic patience. While he is in this ſtate of cold reſignation, the original of Sancho's picture comes on and immediately ſtrikes the ſcholar's wondering eyes; from ſome ſenſible replies he receives proof of her underſtanding, but finding himſelf touched more than he could wiſh, he retires.

The thought of his calling for an Ovid is very characteriſtic and pretty; Clody, don Lewis, Antonio, and the lawyer, now come forward; upon being bid welcome, don Lewis afreſh expreſſes his diſpleaſure, particularly againſt Clodio; concerning whom he ſpeaks to Angelina in very whimſical terms; tired with being fretted, he goes off and returns immediately to Charles in his ſtudy; with whom he parleys about his ill-timed negligent indifference;

Love makes a Man.

difference; at length he perſuades him to go and wiſh his intended ſiſter joy. Antonio enters with the lawyer to get Charles's ratification of his intended ſettlement, which he promiſes to execute; but wiſhing to do it in preſence of the lady, they retire for that purpoſe.

Charino, Angelina, Clody, a lawyer and prieſt next appear; don Lewis hints again to Angelina his diſlike of her match. Carlos enters with his father, and confeſſes upon the ſecond view of his purpoſed ſiſter, thoſe affectionate ſenſations which dawn'd at the firſt ſight of her.

Upon ſaluting Angelina, he expreſſes himſelf with all the warmth of rapture; ſhe ſympathizes, which occaſions him to declare that he could wiſh his brother happy with any other beauty: here Antonio and Charino interpoſe, while don Lewis encourages his nephew's amorous feelings, and ſeems determined to defend his claim.

The interruptions of Clody, and the replies of don Lewis, are very laughable; there is ſomething pleaſingly delicate in Carlos's readineſs to ſacrifice his own views and happineſs, to the lady's real inclination if againſt him. At length finding, as far as modeſty will permit, that ſhe pronounces him the man of her heart, he reſolves to ſupport the privilege of encouraged love; and being rouſed by a challenge which Clody gives, he decides the matter by diſarming his confident coxcombly brother, and carrying off the lady.

Her father highly enraged purſues, and the vanquiſhed Clody is left in a very whimſical ſituation; here the plot takes a romantic and unpardonable turn; finding that don Lewis, Carlos,

and

and Angelina have got on board ſhip, the two fathers and Clody reſolve to purſue them; thus affairs are ſtated at the concluſion of the ſecond act; between which and the beginning of the third, we are ſafely, though not very probably, conveyed to Liſbon, where we encounter don Duart the governor, and Elvira, ſiſter to the former.

From what paſſes we find the don is a moſt furious creature, violently prone to quarrel on ridiculous, chimerical notions of honour; being adviſed to a moderation of temper, he flounces off with a degree of brutal paſſion : here a ſcene follows which is generally omitted, but we think neceſſary for explanation of the plot; as by it we know how Angelina has come on ſhore, and by what means ſhe is placed in Louiſa's houſe.

In the next ſcene we meet Louiſa and Honoria returning from veſpers. From what the former drops, it appears that her devotion has been interrupted by the ſight of a moſt engaging young man; here don Lewis and Carlos enter; the former mentions their narrow eſcape from drowning, and their impoveriſhed circumſtances; the latter ſeems to think theſe matters of trivial concern, compared with the loſs of his miſtreſs.

His tenderneſs impreſſes Louiſa, ſhe reſolves to ſet a watch upon his ſteps, and for the preſent, under cover of a veil, gives him a purſe to relieve their neceſſity; don Lewis, at ſight of the gold, concludes her ſome woman of great fortune in love with Charles; and upon very mean, mercenary principles adviſes him to caſt aſide the remembrance of his firſt love, for ſake of the emolument which preſents itſelf; however Charles untouched

Love makes a Man.

touched with the avarice of age, and conſtant in his affections, rejects ſo unworthy a propoſition, reſolving to ſearch for his loſt Angelina.

Antonio and Charino appear next upon a hot ſcent of the run-aways; Clody joins them in the utmoſt anxiety for the loſs of a favourite ſnuff-box; this concern for ſo trifling an object, when the loſs of a daughter and bride claims notice, ſeems to abate Charino's favourable opinion of his deſigned ſon-in-law.

The old fellows go off on their purſuit, Clodio ſtays behind looking for his toy; while he is thus employed a page, preceding don Duart, orders him out of his maſter's way, the don himſelf coming up Clody banters him with pleaſantry; a blow given, brings on a tilting match, wherein Clodio wounds and brings his violent antagoniſt to the ground.

There is ſomething ungenerouſly cruel in Clodio's ludicrous remark of " having never fenced better in his life;" a man of real courage, and Clody though a fop might be ſuch, will never exult over a proſtrate, much leſs an expiring foe; an alarm being given by the page, and in conſequence a hue-and-cry raiſed, the conqueror finds it prudent to ſeek ſafety in flight; accordingly he eſcapes by a precipitate retreat from the officers of juſtice, who upon ſeeing don Duart think he has only received his deſerts; however they take up the body in order to convey it to his ſiſter's.

Don Lewis and Carlos now enter, having had ſome notice of Angelina; Carlos is forced by Louiſa's emiſſaries into a chair, and don Lewis violently dragged after him, with a gag in his

mouth;

mouth; the next scene places us in Elvira's chamber, where we find the young lady preparing for devotion, and very oddly ordering *all the lights* away, as, according to her own meaning, she can meditate without light.

Clodio having perceived the door of this lady's house open, in the hurry of flight makes it a refuge, and steals into the chamber where she is; being heard by her, she most unaccountably enters into conversation with a strange man, in the most suspicious circumstances, whom she cannot even see; we are at a loss to know whether she shews most folly or resolution in her behaviour; if the latter it is not very delicate or characteristic.

Immediately upon confessing that the officers are at his heels for having killed an antagonist, though in self-defence, she by a violent stretch of humanity pities, and affords him protection; she indeed palliates her proceeding by an observation that her rash brother may want such indulgence; no sooner is Clody placed in a secure retreat than his pursuers enter with don Duart's body.

Here Elvira receives a violent shock from the sight of a dead brother, and the instantaneous conviction that she has taken the murderer under her care; she indulges proper concern, but determines to keep her vow of protection to the unknown person. Clodio interprets this very undeserved, and culpable favour as a proof that she has a tender for his person; but how he could suppose that, as she has never seen him, we cannot tell; after the governors are gone she calls Clody forth, and desires him to take advantage of the

night

night for his escape; this he gladly complies with, but intimates a future design upon his protectress.

The succeeding scene carries us to Louisa's house; that lady enquires whether her orders have been obeyed; being told that the gentlemen are secured, she orders that all passages of egress may be shut up, and a strict silence observed; upon Carlos's enquiring why he has been forceably conveyed he knows not whither, Jaques declines a reply, and leaves him with his uncle, whom he finds gagged on the floor, and whose dumb language he does not understand.

Jaques however returns and releases don Lewis; Charles and the old man upon seeing each other feel some comfort, though both of them are puzzled to find out what the treatment they have met with proceeds from; while they are expressing a mixture of doubt and apprehension the servants re-enter with an entertainment, the sight of which seems to remove every disagreeable sensation from don Lewis's mind; he refreshes himself very heartily, but cannot persuade Charles to partake; after supper it is intimated that he must retire, he obeys with a kind of whimsical reluctance.

The old don, suspicious of somewhat extraordinary, gropes his way to a window, from whence he sees Louisa encounter Charles; this fair dame with very little reserve, nay we might say licentiousness, confesses and urges her amorous inclination; she presents him with jewels as a token of affection, and uses every method of tender persuasion but in vain; the constant and disinterested lover rejects her proposals and flies her temptations precipitately; this naturally enrages her, and don Lewis, who has wished an accommodation of matters agreeable to her defires, determines to try if he can't talk her into good humour; but his attempt is made in such fulsome, though laughable terms, and is so far unfuccefsful, that Louisa orders him to be again gagged, tied neck and heels, and thrown into a garret.

Carlos enters endeavouring to find a way for his escape but cannot effect it; in his progress from chamber to chamber he accidentally gets into that where Angelina is alone, meditating upon the ænigmatical behaviour of the people she has got amongst; Carlos seeing a lady alone hopes to make her a friend, his voice strikes Angelina's ear with a well known sound, she turns upon him and fills him with joyful astonishment; Jaques who has unperceived traced Carlos's steps, goes to inform his lady of the interview he has been witnefs of.

He soon returns with Louisa, who hears their mutual declarations of love, and also hears some severe strictures upon herself; finding an escape meditated, spurred by jealoufy, disappointed love and pride, she takes preventive meafures; however not time enough to hinder Carlos from getting over the garden wall; the lady feels this incident strongly, but finds some comfort in the idea of his returning within an hour, when she refolves that vengeance shall wait and intercept him.

The next scene introduces us to Clodio and Duart who meet in the street; it appears that the latter has been seeking after the former; to what end will appear by what follows: a converfation ensues, rather general than particular, and a bottle of wine is called for, we think a little oddly, in the ftreet; Clody's account of gallantry in different nations is certainly licentious, and in our idea vulgar; he may divert diffipated minds, but cannot be acceptable to good fenfe and delicacy.

His duel with don Duart falls in as a part of difcourfe, but why he fhould mention fo dangerous an incident to a perfect ftranger is very irreconcileable; when don Duart confeffes a thorough knowledge of the affair, he feems alarmed; but gives up apprehenfion at an affurance that he is free from all danger; why don Duart fhould give Clody a purfe, and why a man of his figure fhould accept of it, is not eafily accounted for, however thus we find it; and Clodio in the fullnefs of confidence, manifefting a very weak and uncautious head, communicates to his new friend Elvira's humane protection of him, which his vanity interprets love.

Don Duart feels very juft refentment at fuch behaviour as his fifter's appears to him, and undertakes to carry a letter that he may come more particularly at the real feelings of Elvira; thus concludes the fourth act.

At the beginning of the fifth, we perceive the lady, laft mentioned, in a ftate of deep mourning and profound melancholly; don Duart enters in difguife and delivers the letter; in order to effect that juftice for a brother's death which her rafh vow of protection prevented, fhe feems to receive the addrefs of her gallant favourably; to draw him within her power fhe expreffes to the meffenger rapturous wifhes for his appearance, and propofes anfwering his letter; this behaviour fills the brother with rage, which however he fuppreffes till more

fubftantial

fubftantial proof of her unnatural hypocrify can be made out.

We next meet Louifa and Jaques; fhe enquires if Angelina is feized; being anfwered in the affirmative, fhe orders that when the ftranger is taken alfo, immediate intelligence may be brought to her; fhe has a fhort foliloquy expreffive of her refentment at being flighted for one fhe calls a girl; at the end of which intelligence is brought that the cold object of her affection is feized; Carlos directly appears in a ftate of captivity; after a few lines of upbraiding, Louifa vindictively orders a door to be opened which fhews Angelina in the Turkifh ftate of a bow-ftring, on the point of being ftrangled; the fituation of Carlos and his innocent miftrefs here grows very pathetic, while Louifa's tyrannical exultation over their diftrefs renders her for fome time a very hateful object; at length melted by the fupplications of the man fhe has improperly fixed her defires upon, fhe difmiffes the bravoes, and reftores the unhappy lovers to mutual affection and peace. This is an unexpected and pleafing turn, but rather deficient in probability; for if CONGREVE's maxim, which we are apt to admit, be right; that

"Earth has no plague like love to hatred turn'd;
"Nor hell a fury like a woman fcorn'd."

This favourable turn of affairs feems brought about unaccountably; yet be it as it may, it has a fatisfactory effect upon the audience, and foftens the difagreeable view of a female monfter, which hitherto Louifa has invariably appeared.

Carlos having returned thanks for deliverance, enquires after his uncle don Lewis, who is ordered

in;

in; the old gentleman, upon feeing Charles, forgets his paft ill treatment, and enjoys the pleafing circumftance of meeting his nephew; feeing Louifa he begs excufe for his freedom at a former meeting; being introduced to Angelina he expreffes his fatisfaction in very whimfical terms.

The governor is here introduced, who comes to fearch for Carlos and Angelina upon the oaths of their purfuers; Louifa befpeaks his favour for the lovers, which he promifes; Charino now comes forward, with Antonio and Clody; he appears in a violent heat, demanding of juftice, while Antonio acknowledges a reconciliation to Charles's proceeding, and gives the young pair his bleffing: this irritates Angelina's tefty father a-frefh; fhe interpofes with modeft, emphatic perfuafion, which however he makes no immediate reply to; don Duart enters and prefents Clodio with the anfwer to his letter; finding it kind, he refigns all claim to Angelina, and invites the company to his wedding with the lady Elvira.

The fcene now changes to her houfe, where all the characters foon appear; Clodio approaches her in terms of fpirited nothingnefs, and introduces the whole company to her; when matters are at the point of an agreeable conclufion, Elvira calls the officers of juftice whom fhe has placed in waiting, and demands from the governor juftice on the murderer of her brother; here circumftances are thrown into confufion; Charino finding Clody's dilemma, receives Charles as his fon-in-law; and don Lewis with great humour, though very little humanity, diverts himfelf at his unhappy nephew's expence, till don Duart's difcovering himfelf gives

a pleafing

a pleafing explanation, and renders all the parties agreeable to each other.

After painfully toiling through this piece, which is highly offenfive in many places to criticifm, we are to exprefs aftonifhment that a perfon fo well acquainted with the drama, both as a writer and a performer, fhould have plunged into fuch unjuftifiable irregularity : even in hiftorical tragedies, where importance of events and dignity of characters may in fome fhape apologize for a breach of the unities, violent trefpaffes are not admiffible; how much lefs fo in a reprefentation of private life, where only common tranfactions are exhibited; but the laureat feems to have ftudied character alone in this play, and confideration will fhew that he has in his favourite point rather caracatured than followed nature.

The two old gentlemen, Antonio and Charino, are very whimfical fathers; the former wants to have one of his fons married by way of continuing the family; which of them fulfils this natural duty he does not feem to care, and upon Charles's declining a connection fo inconfiftent with his abftract ideas, very tenderly attempts to ftrip him of his birthright.

Charino is violently fond of his daughter, wants to fee her happy, yet never confults her inclination refpecting the moft material concern of human life; he takes a fancy to the oftentatious, unmeaning rattle of a fpirited coxcomb, and immediately fets him down as a moft defireable fon-in-law; without any other recommendation than a vivacity, and that rather licentious, feldom agreeable to declining age, there being nothing material in the representation reprefentation of thefe two characters, and indeed many more parts of this play, we cannot charge our recollection with any but the three leading ones.

Don Lewis is a very extraordinary creature, he feems to have good nature, but then it appears to be merely founded upon the fpirit of oppofition ; he is peevifh and pofitive, more of a humorift than an object of efteem ; many of his expreffions, though grofs, are laughable; the mode of performing this part is a cynic drynefs of expreffion, which we are apt to think Mr. Macklin hit off more happily than any other performer we have feen; he was extremely pleafant without being comical; his retorts upon Clodio were inimitably contrafted ; Mr. Yates is no lefs chafte and correct; but wants an equal degree of force : Mr. Shuter manifefts a glow of uncharafteriftic good nature, and plays off too many variations of feature; he feems too fenfible of his own humour, and palpably chuckles where he fhould leave that totally to the audience.

Clodio is made up of rhapfodical volatility ; he appears to have no idea beyond the character of courage and volatility ; he feems ready to addrefs any woman, or to fight with any man : intrigue, marriage or duelling are all alike to him ; he is thrown into a variety of whimfical fituations, and muft be allowed a moft favourable part for any actor who has fuitable capabilities.

Notwithftanding Mr. The. Cibber muft have collected many advantageous ideas from the original, his father, and author of the piece; we never could think him fufficiently poffeffed of negligent fprightlinefs ; he too often mixed the formal elegance

gance of a Foppington, and funk the coxcomb in the man of fafhion; he had alfo an unpardonable fault which difgraced many of his principal characters; that was making ludicrous faces, more adapted to Abel Drugger than any clafs of gentility: to Mr. WOODWARD's Clody we give a great preference; as, to us, his figure, deportment and expreffion, fill up every fatisfactory idea; he makes ufe of fome theatrical manœuvres, which feem more calculated to catch the million than critical judgement, but as they are upon the whole innocent baits to gain applaufe, we do not think it neceffary to particularize them. If pleafing the majority be the actor's moft profitable confideration, as certainly it is, this gentleman may be defended in moft, if not all of his outré ftrokes; the theatre frequently verifies what Cimberton remarks;

" Nature's too fimple, of all art bereav'd;
" If the world will, why let it be deceiv'd."

Mr. KING has every pleafing and effential requifite for Clody, but we never had the fatisfaction to fee him perform it.

Carlos, as a ftudent, is moft formally pedantic, totally unacquainted with life; as a lover, enthufiaftically amorous and romantic; he has courage when called upon, and appears not only conftant in his affection, but commendably difinterefted in his love; he is, through the former part of the play, a fubject of efteem, in the latter an object of pity; we refpect though we cannot admire.

As a part he is not very favourable to the actor, as fome of his fcenes are incumbered with a tedious famenefs; Mr. DEXTER, who had very much of the gentleman in his appearance and expreffion,

filled

Love makes a Man.

filled up this part fome years ago with very pleafing ability, yet we muſt give a preference to Mr. Ross's requifites, ere his perfon increaſed beyond the idea of a ſtudious life; Mr. BENSLEY is leart enough, but wants the foft flow of expreffion, and philofophical compofure of look, which ſhould picture Carlos; he is too auſtere in the beginning, and too boiſterous where the paffions come in : we remember one Mr. W. GIFFARD marching on for this part fome fifteen years ago at Covent-Garden, who had fo much of the antique paternal pompofity ſtamped on his performance, that in fome places he might have paffeJ for Alexander; in others for Bajazet; now Cato, then Caftalio, all exaggerated : fuch grofs violations of nature, fuch an unharmonious gallimaufry of acting, fure never was feen, and can hardly be conceived.

Elvira and Angelina are very lukewarm ladies, efpecially the former, who is much more of a fool than a philofopher; if any thing can be made of Angelina in reprefentation, Mrs. BULKLEY's talents appear well adapted to make the burthen agreeable.

Louifa is as contemptible a female as we know; grofsly licentious, and naturally cruel in her temper; indeed ſhe foftens at laſt, and throws off the monſter; but we think that fince fo unworthy a female was introduced, it would have been but barely confonant to public juſtice to have puniſhed her in fome manner fuitable to her culpable behaviour; inſtead of which, ſhe is allowed to huddle up an advantageous match with a worthy man, who has addreffed her for years : Mrs. HAMILTON did this lady great juſtice; we may fay entered too far into the author's meaning, for it is blameable to exhibit offensive pictures of nature in strong colours.

When we look back upon this piece, we must again censure and lament Mr. CIBBER's hardiness to venture and work upon so pantomimical a plot, highly improbable and grossly irregular; the sentiments, in many parts of this comedy, convey gross ideas; many of the scenes are too long, others totally insignificant: the dialogue is natural and sprightly, though void of wit and elegance; the moral very vague, lying wholly in this, that the passion of love will inspire a man to rouse up principles of reason and action, which, till he feels that passion, lie dormant in his breast: what utility is inculcated hereby, we know not; but this we know, that young minds may be prejudiced by the capital figure in this piece of theatrical painting.

Upon the whole, if an audience chuse merely to laugh, the FOP's FORTUNE, when well performed, will gratify that wish; but we cannot by any means recommend it to perusal; if in the closet it escapes tainting the mind, which we doubt, it may be safely asserted, that no instruction can be derived from the piece.

The DISTRESSED MOTHER.

A Tragedy: By Am. Philips.

ORESTES, the fon of Agamemnon, in character of ambaffador from feveral Grecian ftates,
opens this piece meeting moft unexpectedly, and
with much joy, his faithful friend Pylades, from
whom he had been feparated by a ftorm at fea;
his appearance and fplendid retinue occafion friendly congratulation upon the apparent favourable
reverfe of fortune; but we find that an amorous
feeling damps any pleafure which might be derived from the eminence of his ftation.

Pylades expreffes furprize and concern at this
painful weaknefs, efpecially as he fuppofed his
princely intimate long fince freed from fuch an ef-
feminating bondage. By Oreftes's exculpatory explanation, we find that Hermione, daughter of
Menelaus, who has betrothed her to Pyrrhus king
of Epirus, is the object of his affection; we alfo
learn, that he had endeavoured to fhake off the
influence of her charms, but being unluckily deputed a public minifter to the court of his rival,
where he cannot avoid feeing the princefs, love
flows in upon him with a returning and refiftlefs
tide.

The fubject of his embaffy is rather ftrange and
difgraceful to his employers; a vindictive demand
of Aftyanax, Hector's fon, who, with his mother
Andromache, are captives at the court of Epirus:

Oreftes

Oreſtes in this ſcene ſhews himſelf a man of very violent paſſions, and therefore ill calculated for public truſt; a gleam of hope breaks in upon the agitated lover, on being informed that a preference ſhewn to Andromache by Pyrrhus, occaſions Hermione to turn her thoughts from the cold monarch to her firſt lover's tranſports.

Here Pyrrhus enters to give audience; when Oreſtes delivers his addreſs, in as manly, nervous, and plauſible terms, as the ſubject of it will admit; a great ſhare of dignified humanity breaks forth from Pyrrhus in his replies; his determination to guard the fatherleſs and widow, amidſt every peril, would manifeſt true magnanimity of mind, but that we find an amorous inclination at the bottom of it; after many remonſtrances, the ambaſſador ſounds Pyrrhus reſpecting Hermione; the monarch's anſwer is doubtful, however he ſends Oreſtes upon the agreeable errand of ſeeing the idol of his heart.

Upon Phœnix's obſervation to Pyrrhus, that he is encouraging a rival, he expreſſes a deſire of being freed from the Princeſs, at any rate; here Andromache and her confidante Cephiſa approach; the former being addreſſed by Pyrrhus, ſhe weepingly turns the diſcourſe to her ſon Aſtyanax: mention of him occaſions the king to tell her what the Grecian ſtates demand; ſhe claims protection, which he promiſes, but taxed with a proviſo of having his love returned.

His propoſitions are ardent and flattering, but the royal widow's inflexible attachment to the memory of her firſt lord, thwarts his views and ſollicitations, inſomuch that he ſhews reſentment, but

gives

Diftreffed Mother,

gives her time for confideration; defiring fhe may vifit the child, and reflect while fhe is embracing him, whether to become a queen, and fave her darling boy, or remain deaf to intreaty, and lofe him by an obftinate perfiftance in widowhood.

Andromache in a fhort, pathetic foliloquy, founded more on mafculine heroifm than maternal tendernefs, feems to refolve upon his fate, and expreffes a determination to fhare it; thus ends the firft act.

Hermione begins the fecond with her attendant Cleone, whom we perceive to be a partner of her bofom fecrets; it appears that the princefs had re- fufed an audience to Oreftes, but by perfuafion now agrees with his requeft; a point of confufion, wrought by her fenfe of the unworthy treat- ment fhe has given him, occafioned the refufal, and a fpark of pride that he fhould find her in a foreign court, neglected by the man to whom fhe is be- trothed, ftrengthens her diftrefs of mind; being irritated againft Pyrrhus by Cleone, fhe determines, amidft the warmth of jealous refentment, to take the advantage of Oreftes's ambaffy, and, under his care, once again to feek her father's kingdom.

This princefs, though fomewhat juftified by the idea of a rival, triumphs rather too vindictively over the unhappy mother and her diftracted fon; her paffion for Pyrrhus appears very warm, though her fenfibility perceives and allows the merit of Oreftes. Here the ambaffador makes his appear- ance, and paints his fuccefslefs, yet unabating paf- fion, in very emphatic terms; hearing that Pyr- rhus refufes to deliver up Aftyanax, her jealous refentment kindles a-frefh, and fhe cheers her lover's

drooping

drooping fpirits with fome tender expreffions; but upon being told by him that Pyrrhus neglects her charms, wounded pride confeffes impatient feelings, and Oreftes falls under blame for fuggefting an idea fo mortifying to beauty.

After feveral ftruggles and changes of paffion fhe refolves, unlefs Pyrrhus delivers up the captive boy, to return with Oreftes; this gives the prince fingular fatisfaction, as he cannot fuppofe compliance from the monarch; Pyrrhus approaches, and to the ambaffador's great aftonifhment, confents to the demand made by the Grecians. Thunder-ftruck with fo unexpected a change, Oreftes makes a confufed, and indeed very uncharacteriftic reply; the agitation of his mind is much increafed by Pyrrhus's declaration, that he will, on the fucceeding day, receive Hermione as his bride, and from Oreftes, as reprefentative of her father. Pyrrhus having gained a momentary triumph over his prejudice in favour of Andromache, boafts of it in fuch a ftile that his bofom counfellor Phœnix, who fees with the difcerning eyes of unimpaffioned age, feems to think his ftruggles like thofe of a lion in the foils, which only ferve to entangle him more deeply; the ftatefman expreffes his doubts, which the royal lover deems ill grounded, though he is obliged to flip out an acknowledgement, how difficult it is to root up a fettled attachment from the heart; the fecond act concludes with a fimile too flowery and poetical for an agitated mind.

At the beginning of the third act we meet the two friends, Pylades and Oreftes, the latter violently lamenting his wayward fate, the former endeavouring, by cool perfuafion, to appeafe his paf-

fions;

ſions; which however hurry on to the deſperate and unjuſtifiable extremity of bearing his miſtreſs off by force: being made ſenſible how contrary to his ſtation and public faith ſuch an act would be, he requeſts Pylades to take charge of Aſtyanax, while he reſolves to undertake the enterprize alone; but rather than ſuffer this, his faithful companion reſolves to ſhare the enterprize however dangerous and culpable.

This point ſettled, Hermione enters, and is acquainted by Oreſtes that Pyrrhus has conſented to eſpouſe her; though ſhe doubts the principle on which the monarch's ſudden change is founded, yet ſhe appears extremely willing to embrace it. Oreſtes goes off with a ſeeming reconciliation to the circumſtance, upon which, like a true woman, ſhe ſeems nettled that her old lover ſhould ſo tamely yield his hopes to the new one; however the approaching gratification of her real inclination diſſipates the tranſient cloud into ſmiles of joy, and ſhe breaks into a rapturous elogium on the heroiſm of her intended bridegroom.

Andromache here with untimely grief comes upon the princeſs, and in very moving terms ſollicits her interpoſition in favour of Aſtyanax; to which ſhe makes a cold and rather diſdainful reply, that concludes with an inſulting taunt, the offspring of a little, rather than a great mind, which latter ſpecies maintains dignity even in reſentment.

Soon after Hermione retires, Pyrrhus enters enquiring for her; perceiving him diſtant, Andromache's fears for her child increaſe, and for ſome time ſhe wants reſolution to addreſs him on the
subject;

subject; this he interprets coldnefs tinctured with pride; fhe makes a motion to retire, which occasions him to mention, with fome degree of ruffled temper, the furrender of her fon; fo heart-wounding a circumftance gets the better of modeft, timid referve, and fhe fues for pity.

Pyrrhus fuftains her fupplications for fome time with unmoved firmnefs; at length, touched with her plaints, he orders their attendants to withdraw, then explains the ftate of his own heart, and his political concerns; tells her he is ready to fend away Hermione, even at the utmoft peril of vindictive nations, if fhe will become partner of his bed; he retires with again, and finally, fubmitting to her choice, meeting him in the temple, or lofing her fon for ever.

Brought to this painful dilemma, fhe recapitulates fome very powerful motives for declining a marriage with Pyrrhus, who was a main agent in the deftruction of her former hufband Hector, his family and country; however maternal feelings at length prevail, fhe gives up every other confideration to the prefervation of her fon, and then rhimes herfelf off with more jingle than meaning.

At the beginning of the fourth act we again meet the diftreffed mourner confirming the refolution juft mentioned, and hinting to Cephifa fome fecret defign which demands her confidence: matters thus fettled, fhe goes off to be robed for royalty, and feems for the prefent to wear a heart fomewhat lightened of its mortifying load. Hermione now prefents herfelf with a countenance full of fullen and vindictive forrow; it appears fhe has heard of the intended nuptials, and enquires for

Oreftes,

Diſtreſſ'd Mother

Oreſtes, who enters almoſt on the word; revenge for the flignt ſhe has received is inſtantaneouſly propoſed, which Oreſtes ſeems ready to undertake by open force of arms, but her impatience from jealous rage infiſts upon immediate ſatisfaction, even in the temple.

He very juſtly remonſtrates againſt a proceeding ſo contrary to the law of nations, as for him to make an aſſault upon a monarch who has hoſpitably and honourably received him in the confidential ſtile of an ambaſſador ; however, the reſult of this conference ſhews, that a truly jealous woman is not to be perſuaded by reaſon nor humanity, and that a man totally enſlaved by love is liable to commit the moſt unjuſtifiable actions, under perſuaſion of the object he adores.

After Oreſtes retires to execute the dire command Hermione has enjoined, ſhe triumphs in the idea of vengeance, but ſeeing Pyrrhus approach, immediately ſoftens from her ſanguinary purpoſes, and ſends Cleone after Oreſtes ; a ſhort ſcene enſues between her and the monarch, when being again enraged by his coldneſs, ſhe goes off with threats of fatal tendency.

Phœnix after her departure expreſſes fear of his maſter's ſafety, while Pyrrhus, intoxicated with love, has no apprehenſion but for the ſafety of Andromache and her ſon : the intended queen, decked in the magnificence of bridal garments, next appears ; however the mental gloom ſeems invariably fixed, and we perceive that external grandeur, often the caſe, is but the covering of internal ſorrow.

Diftr ffed Mether.

She relates with feminine credulity a dream, from whence she forms the gloomy resolution, which was very common in her days, of ending her cares by suicide, after she had secured Astyanax's life by fulfilling her promise to Pyrrhus; this may have a portion of heathen heroism and delicacy in it, but wants our idea of true resolution, which makes it cowardice to fly cares by such means, and maternal tenderness, which will encounter any difficulty to watch the tender years of an infant offspring, she concludes the fourth act with assimilating herself to a victim going to sacrifice, a sentiment very trite, but well enough applied to her situation.

Act the fifth commences with Hermione in soliloquy, full of horrors at having doomed the object of her affection to death; there is great variety of acting merit in this speech, and the agonizing throws of a mind torn between love, jealousy, revenge and repentance, are pictured strikingly by the pencil of nature. Cleone comes to the aid of her unhappy mistress, and rouses up her vengeance, by describing Pyrrhus's progress to the temple, and the mortifying satisfaction which shone in his countenance; borne beyond every degree of calm reflection, or patient sufferance, she indulges the most ungovernable passion, and renews her vindictive threats with double fury. Upon the entrance of Orestes, who informs her that according to her wish and express order Pyrrhus had been slain at the altar; a most striking, and we think natural, turn of mind affects the princess; she hears the manner of Pyrrhus's fall with a kind of sullen distraction, then breaks forth

in

Diſtreſſed Mother.

in the fullneſs of paſſion againſt Oreſtes, for having ſo readily obeyed the precipitate order of unthinking jealouſy ; the ambaſſador vainly endeavours to vindicate his proceeding, while ſhe leaves him with moſt virulent terms of reprobation.

In ſoliloquy he reflects upon himſelf for being hurried by love into ſo unjuſtifiable an action, eſpecially for one ſo ready to accuſe him of the miſchief occaſioned by herſelf ; Pylades entering urges the prince to a neceſſary retreat : loſt to all feelings for his own ſafety, he determines to remain at all events with Hermione. Hearing from his friend that the unhappy fair one has expired on the corpſe of the deceaſed monarch, his reaſon gives way to accumulating horrors, and at length reſigns its throne to the moſt furious diſtraction ; a variety of unconnected images diſtract his ideas, till at length nature yielding to ſuch heart-racking ſtruggles, he is borne off void of all ſenſibility.

Phœnix enters with guards ſeeking the Grecian aſſaſſins who have fled ; Andromache comes forward, who declares that vengeance ſhall be taken of the faithleſs Greeks ; then gives orders for the funeral of Pyrrhus, and concludes the play with that common, but moral inference ; that the innocent, however oppreſſed, meet when they leaſt expect it, effectual comfort and relief.

To conſider this tragedy at large, we find it critically regular, both in the plot and connection of ſcenes, which perhaps takes from it a portion of ſpirit that plays better ſupplied with buſineſs maniſeſt ; it is ſo thin of characters, that a ſameneſs creeps through many paſſages ; the verſification is ſufficiently ſmooth, without an enervating mono-

tony,

tony, and the ſentiments are elevated without ſuch an indulgence of fancy as ſhocks nature; however at the cataſtrophe we perceive a fault, which is, leaving the audience in doubt concerning the fate of Oreſtes; as we have no ground to form an idea of what becomes of him, whether he dies diſtracted or gets back ſafe to Greece.

As the author has not ſcrupled to violate real hiſtory in the fate of Hermione, he might as well have fixed that of the prince: we are alſo of opinion that the boy Aſtyanax might have been introduced to conſiderable advantage, as a real perſonified object muſt ever influence an audience more than an ideal character, witneſs the ghoſt in Hamlet, who makes a much greater impreſſion by appearance than the previous deſcriptions of him, though awful and emphatic can do; we hope it will not appear an Hiberniciſm to mention a ghoſt, where perſonification is hinted, ſince thoſe chimerical children of the brain are cloathed with corporeal ſemblance.

In point of characters we find that Pyrrhus, who has been a victorious proſelyte of Mars, like many other military heroes, ſacrifices the dignity of his mind to the charms of Andromache; nay, he gives up common honeſty by a breach of his plighted faith to Hermione; his paſſion is obſtinately fixed, neither danger from abroad nor his own reflection can deter him. In performance he is a good, but not a great part; while in view he commands attention and reſpect, but he takes leave of the audience in an imperfect and unconſequential manner; he melts from our view without affording the leaſt reaſon to think we ſhall not ſee him again.

Dignity

Diftrefjed Mother.

Dignity of appearance, and placidity of expreſſion are eſſential to the repreſentation of this character; Mr. QUIN poſſeſſed the former, but rather in a brutiſh degree, and the latter he was totally deficient in; he neither looked or ſpoke the lover. Mr. BARRY has done the part with more merit than any other perſon we remember, and ſatisfactorily fulfilled every idea we could form of it; he looked like a man that might well engage Hermione's affection, and ſpoke like one who muſt melt the heart of Andromache, had not grief rendered it callous to all other feeling. Mr. DIGGES ſupported it in a manly becoming manner; we know not any perſon now at either houſe, who would not be trifling or heavy in it.

The character of Oreſtes, as a man, makes a mean figure, though as a lover ſeverely diſtreſſed, he engages ſome concern; he ſeems willing to betray his truſt as an ambaſſador, and then turns aſſaſſin in obedience to his ungovernable paſſion; he has many rapid and violent tranſitions, which offer an actor fair opportunities of diſplaying capital powers to advantage: Mr. RYAN, though very uninteresting through the four firſt acts, threw more fire into the fifth than any of his competitors we remember; his painting of the diſtraction was truly fine, and the following words in particular he expreſſed inimitably: " I ſhiver----oh, I freeze." Mr. BARRY was uniformly reſpectable through the character, but wanted that quick fire of expreſſion ſo requiſite in many paſſages; Mr. MOSSOP is too boiſterous in expreſſing the paſſions, and toils through the whole piece in a moſt painful manner, incumbered with a ſtiffneſs of deportment incompatible

patible

patible with real dignity. Mr. Powell was languid, totally unequal to the princely Greek ; Mr. Holland had fufficient powers, but moft rude and indigefted ; his mechanical formality, and ungovernable violence, rendered his performance in general, either infipid or offenfive ; Pylades and Phœnix are in point of acting merit below criticifm.

Andromache, in our view, appears rather a romantic than a natural character ; however the author has made her favourable to the actrefs, and very interefting to the audience. Mrs. Cibber was undoubtedly herfelf alone in the Distressed Mother ; her feelings were deeply pathetic, and her expreffion entirely adequate ; Mrs. Bellamy difplayed confiderable merit, but was not equal to her great cotemporary and competitor, though confiderably beyond any other lady who has come within our notice ; Mrs. Barry we have not feen, but think fhe has requifites and judgment to do Andromache great juftice.

The Grecian princefs is placed in very odd circumftances, and indeed her conduct feems full as odd as her fituation ; love is extremely capricious, and often runs the wifeft heads into actions either very ridiculous or highly culpable. Hermione's violent affection for Pyrrhus may therefore apologize for the inconfiftencies which form her character ; but her making fuch a fool of poor Oreftes, and her infulting the diftrefs of Andromache, are ftrong indications of a fubtle, ungenerous, felfifh mind ; in action fhe muft be very confpicuous, giving full fcope for the difplay of every capital tragic attribute.

Mrs.

Diſtreſſed Mother.

Mrs. WOFFINGTON, in point of voice, was not equal to the paſſions of this part, but filled up every other idea with pleaſing and forceable ability. Mrs. FITZHENRY, had ſhe not been a ſervile copy of the above-mentioned lady, would have given much ſatisfaction; but juſt and impartial criticiſm muſt ever frown upon ſecond-hand acting: if it was diſpleaſing in no other view, this alone would render it ſo, bringing to recollection the merit of an original, which muſt ever ſtrike more than the happieſt imitation.

Mrs. HAMILTON, an uncertain, excentric actreſs, was not without ſome excellence in perſonating Hermione; Mrs. PRITCHARD, bating figure, did the princeſs peculiar juſtice, but upon the whole we are well diſpoſed to give the capabilities of Mrs. YATES, conſiderable preference to any who have gone before her.

The Frenchified regularity of this play, which ſome very able, but over-nice critics admired at its firſt coming into the world, is in our apprehenſion an enervating circumſtance; the characters are too confined, and but indifferently diſpoſed; Mr. PHILLIPS was happy in being perſonally acquainted with thoſe eminent geniuſſes who ſhed ſo great a luſtre on QUEEN ANNE's reign; from their partial friendſhip a much more reputable account was given of this tragedy than it deſerves; for beyond all doubt it is heavy in repreſentation, and languid in the cloſet.

Here we take leave of particular pieces, and ſhall now enter into more general criticiſms on compoſition and action; hitherto we have religiouſly
adhered

Diſtreſſed Mother.

adhered to our original principle of impartial in-
veſtigation, both of plays and performers; we
have not praiſed the dead to cut up the living, but
very freely pointed out alternately, excellencies and
errors as they have appeared; not one ſyllable in
the DRAMATIC CENSOR has been dictated by
friendly attachment or private pique; by fear of
reſentment or hope of reward; this aſſertion we
defy any perſon mentioned to contradict with reaſon and truth.

We wiſh the STAGE, as a noble and uſeful in-
ſtitution, increaſe of ſucceſs, and all the diligent,
deſerving ſons of THESPIS reward; our cenſure is
not meant to prejudice but improve performers who
are not too ſelf-ſufficient, and our praiſe is offered
as an incentive to emulative merit.

The character of an actor, though more reconciled at preſent than ſome years ſince to ſocial
eſteem, is yet by many held in a prejudicial and
painful light, without the ſhadow of reaſon; for if
a player is in private character a good man, his profeſſion cannot prevent him from being an eſtimable
object; if every profeſſion was to fall under legiſ-
lative and general interdiction, on account of ſome
diſſolute and diſgraceful members, what would become of even the moſt reſpectable degrees of life?
is religion leſs ſacred, becauſe ſome who wear cano-
nicals are not only a diſgrace to their cloth, but
even to human nature? is law leſs reſpectable, becauſe there are among its profeſſors wretches who
ſacrifice every idea of juſtice to avaricious, mercenary views? is phyſic leſs worthy attention, becauſe ſome of its practitioners vend poiſonous
noſtrums? is the army leſs honourable, becauſe

an

an unavoidable mixture of fools, knaves, and cowards, frequently fhows itfelf.

If there is an alloy in all human actions, and every ftation of life, why fhould an uncharitable irrational mark of reprobation be ftamped upon the fons of the Drama; thofe words in our moft extraordinary penal act, refpecting the ftage, " *gain, hire,* or *reward,*" are the ftrangeft fuggeftion that ever entered the human brain; if pecuniary advantage is to reflect difcredit, what fituation in this great ftage of life is exempt? if, as we have fomewhere found it fenfibly remarked, dramatic entertainments are either contemptible, or pernicious, why fhould not the writers as well as performers be ftigmatized; yet on the contrary, we find authors treated with the higheft refpect, while the poor actors are vilified, except where liberality of mind, and gentility of education, refcue them from fuch difagreeable and irrational treatment.

When we come to confider the powers and diverfity of dramatic action more particularly, we fhall perceive that a performer, to come near critical propriety, muft poffefs an intelligent mind, many agreeable qualifications, ftrong feelings, and at leaft a decent, if not a good, education.

There have indeed been inftances of fome performers who having very faint imperfect ideas of their own, became by infinite pains tolerable organs to convey thofe of others in an agreeable manner, but where one of thofe parroted machines arrives at any ftability of merit, twenty fall to the ground.

There is nothing more eafy, or more common, than for a managerical fineffe to preponderate againft public judgment; an admiration of novelty is a Britiſh characteriſtic ; this induces the audience to give every new performer a favourable reception ; ſuch commendable good nature is anticipated by preparatory puffs, and corroborated by twenty or thirty pounds worth of well diſpoſed orders, who are to furniſh the deceitful and tranſitory ſtamp of noiſy approbation. The object of this approbation fancies the applauſe deſerved, grows conſequential, and never aims at improvement, but falls in public opinion as faſt as it riſes in its own.

This, among many others, is a point of high reproach againſt the managers ; let young and riſing merit work its own way, take care that the party of an envious veteran does not nip the ſwelling bud ; but, at the ſame time gentlemen providers for public taſte don't palm upon us Dutch plaice for turbot, or necks of beef for ſirloins ; don't grapple at ſo many thouſands a year, but let your benefactors ſatisfaction keep ſome decent kind of pace with your own weighty emoluments ; a paltry take-in is below men of ſenſe ; impoſitions are beneath men of honeſty.

A SHORT

A

SHORT DISSERTATION

ON

Theatrical Management.

AMONGST the many fimilitudes which have been applied to a Theatre, down from a kingdom to a cook's-fhop, the former ftrikes us moft; we view it as a little but intricate ftate, where he who provides fhould, like the monarch of a political conftitution, feek without any prejudice for or a-gainft individuals, after merit; which, when found, ought to be cherifhed and rewarded : regularity of bufinefs, and propriety of decorations, are mattters of effential concern; but mechanical ftiffnefs in the one, which too often appears, and glare in the other, not only offend but miflead judgment.

A manager as caterer for public tafte, fhould ftudioufly avoid adulterating that tafte with fpecious trifles, fplendid nothingnefs; Sadlers Wells would be laughed at fhould they attempt tragedies, and Comedies; why then fhould Royal Theatres trefpafs on the prerogative of buffoonery? we remember a prologue of Mr. GARRICK's, wherein he was re-markably fevere on harlequinades, yet, by fome un-accountable influence, he foon entered warmly into

an

an emulative exhibition of those exotic unmeaning whims which he had so justly condemned.

How much credit would have beeen reflected on his name had he banished such illegitimate bantlings of the drama, such incongruous medleys from the stage; to say that his own sterling merit, supported by so excellent a company as he then had, could not have defended the breach of common sense against the patched coat and wooden sword, is paying national taste a miserable compliment; indeed matters are now gone so far that according to the common proverb, we may soon hope to see them mend, since it is absolutely impossible they should be worse.

Is it not equally astonishing that Mr. COLMAN, who has given some pleasing proofs of genius, ever since he has assumed the reins of theatrical government, should have laid down the quill (for MAN and WIFE, and the OXONIAN, we esteem as nothing,) to mix with carpenters, projectors, &c. in the fabrication of snip snap changes, Witches, Demons, Mother Shiptons, paltry ballads, face making, tumbling, jumping, and all the wild &c. of pantomimical mummery; poor RICH, as knowing no better, was at least pardonable, if not commendable, for he gave the public what he loved himself; what excuse can be made for those who furnish their audience with such stuff as they must necessarily and naturally despise? there is but one, and that shamefully awkward; that their sole motive is to get money, and if nonsense can obtain that golden aim with more ease and advantage than elegant instructive compositions, vanish genius, what have we to do with thee! no, let dulness wave her

leaden

leaden fceptre, and lay the piercing eyes of criticifm faft afleep, while our purfes fwell with golden harveft.

But is the genius of writing alone hurt by thefe dumb burlefques upon the dignity of human reafon? no, the genius of acting is ftill more deeply wounded, as may be plainly evinced; in an eftablifhed winter-theatre, it ufed, and ought to be the rule, to have every diftinct caft of playing fupplied by perfons who kept uniformly in that tract; now we find the hero of to-night, often more properly to-morrow night, performing a character of no confequence, inftance Meffrs. HURST, and PALMER, at Drury Lane, and many others at each houfe, who occafionally mount aloft; this is certainly œconomical, though not commendable; for the managers hereby get two or three performers for the price of one; and are freed not only from the weighty charge, but alfo the painful confequence of men really meritorious.

Befides, if one, two, or three, of the ftop-gaps either retire of themfelves or are taken off by death, their places are eafily filled by fome of the thirty fhillings a week tribe, who fnatch greedily at an additional guinea to become capital, and bind themfelves three or four years for a penurious pittance.

There is another refource for recruiting, which, though private emolument may have occurred, has thefe three or four years paft afforded very little public entertainment; I mean collecting from itinerant companies people who have aftonifhed villages and market towns for years; of whom there is not the leaft hope of improvement; and
fhoving

fhoving them on under the artful fhelter of a firft appearance; each of thefe adventurers is engaged at fuch a rate, that the attraction of a firft night, generally pays his, or her whole falary for the feafon; if criticifm withers all hope the firft attempt, there is no lofs but to the unhappy individual, who meets condemnation; if they exift three, four, or half a dozen nights, which *orders*, and *paragraphs* may eafily effect, the managers are fure to gain; and then the neglected objects may fink as faft as they can, to make way for others equally infipid, but lefs known, and therefore more attractive.

That this game has been moft induftrioufly played of late, and with confiderable fuccefs, is evident to the fhame of London audiences, who, by afferting their own judgement and dignity, fhould prevent the practice of kidnapping performers who might live decently in the country, to render them defpicable and obnoxious in the capital.

There is one circumftance of power which we apprehend contributes to render the fituation of our patentees rather uneafy to themfelves, as well as prejudicial to genius; we mean the reception or rejection of new pieces; we lay it down as a pofitive rule that, in duty to the public, each houfe, if furnifhed with fo many fhould produce fix new plays, and as many after pieces every winter; if fo many are not furnifhed and approved, they cannot be expected from the managers; but if they *are* produced, no Mother Shiptons, no Jubilees---mere cufards of folly, fhould be ferved up fuch a multitude of fucceffive nights; fuch an opening would give every dramatic writer a fair chance; and that intrinfic merit alone fhould prefent itfelf without the inftructive,

2 dogmatical

dogmatical recommendations of titled blockheads, which is at prefent almoft the only path to admiffion; that men of liberal education might not be taxed with the mortifying neceffity, of tedious and fervile attendance, let a DRAMATIC SOCIETY, or INQUEST, for the examination of every new piece, that may be fent for their infpection, be eftablifhed; let the authors be under the ftricteft obligation not to difclofe themfelves till the fate of their productions take place, let that be determined by a majority of votes, and let the feal of the inqueft be an undeniable recommendation to the managers, whom we would fo far indulge as to be conftant members of the fociety.

Upon this plan we are confident more plays, and with much more credit, would annually appear; genius would then apply itfelf in a becoming manner, and feldom fail of due reward.

That we may not feem too hard upon managers, we cannot avoid obferving that the third and fixth night, with the advantage of Printing, muft be a very adequate reward for any play, fuppofing it to coft the author twelve months application ; and if any production of that kind takes more than half the time, we are ready to believe it will prove laborious, and unpleafing.

As to dreffes and fcenery, thofe indifpenfible paraphernalia, they have been extremely well attended to, and elegantly fupplied for the laft feven years, in fo much that we may truly fay the ftage has proportionally improved in decorations, as it has declined in acting merit; it is now for the moft part fplendidly infipid; we have the robes and proceffions of tragedy, but want her fpirit; how juft an application

tion in this fenfe, may be made from Ophelia " *fee-ing what we have feen, feeing what we fee.*"

It was certainly well fuggefted by Mr. FOOTE, in his occafional prologue, that " *Taylors are deemed the only poets now*" and if we add that carpenters are the chief actors for bringing money, we fhall not exaggerate much, but this will ever be the cafe till public fpirit throws juft and neceffary contempt upon fuch frippery exhibitions as nature and reafon mutually blufh at; nor will fuch impofitions be eafily fuppreffed till avarice is alarmed and frighted in her fordid den behind the curtain, by the tremendous and irrefiftable voice of public clamour.

A SUMMARY

A

SUMMARY VIEW

OF THE

Moſt Known DRAMATIC WRITERS.

HAVING offered ſome hints to abate that rancorous prejudice which attacks the character of a player; that illiberal cenſure which ſtigmatizes the profeſſion, as not only obnoxious to moral rectitude, but contemptible in ſociety; it becomes a duty to offer our readers ſome remarks upon theatrical authors, with this reſerve, that our criticiſms upon them muſt rather be general than particular.

Mr. POPE has ſtiled an honeſt man the nobleſt work of God. This is perhaps an exaggerated compliment to the human ſpecies, eſpecially if, as the Chriſtian faith directs, we allow the exiſtence of beings much more refined, much nearer the purity of abſolute perfection, than we in a ſtate of frail mortality can come; in the ſame light we conſider Mr. ADDISON's aſſertion, that a good tragedy

is the nobleft work of man. However thus much
advantage we may derive from his opinion, that a
play founded on virtuous principles is a valuable
acquifition, and that the author of it may be deemed an ornament as well as a friend to his country.

The moral rectitude of Mr. ADDISON never has
been called in queftion, his writings are all chafte
and inftructive; his circumftances were independant of emoluments as an author, therefore we
may very juftly infer, that his approbation of the
ftage proceeded from cool, difinterefted, impartial,
conviction; that it was worthy countenance, not
merely as an amufement, but as a fchool of improvement; that it has been proftituted to very unworthy views by fome men of great abilities, muft
be acknowledged, fo has the pulpit by fordid fcep-
tics, and wild enthufiafts; fo have the courts of
juftice by venal judges, and corrupt practitioners;
in fhort plays and players may reduce their plea of
reputation to one fingle obvious point, where reafon
readily and powerfully fupports their caufe; if in
common, with every circumftance and ftation of
life they manifeft an alloy, fure they cannot merit
general condemnation for not being totally free
from blame.

It is very remarkable, that not one of the hot-
mouthed preachers, or bedlamite authors who have
declaimed and wrote againft the ftage, ever offered
more than a diffufe, unfupported, malevolent charge,
that the inftitution is diabolical; if they are poffeffed of any arguments to make good this gloomy
affertion, they take care never to let them flip into
public

I

public view, leaft inveftigation fhould prove them to be the froth of fermented malice.

It is, in vain to contend any point with wretches whom avaricious views, or obftinate ignorance, fortify againft all approaches of reafon ; animals in the human fhape, who cover wolfifh hearts with the inoffenfive femblance of fheep, who endeavour to render the paternal difpenfations of providence ineffectual; who change the comfortable fmiles of religion into the moft mortifying frowns; who pretend that mifery here is the fafeft road to happinefs hereafter; who would break the fpirit, and reftrain the faculties of man, under pretence of rectifying his mind; who would upon the whole prevent or fupprefs the moft laudable, and effential ordinations of fociety, to make the great and multitudinous ftage of nature, one deplorable, unvarying fcene of flumbering infipidity, frenzied difcontent, or tragic exhibition.

The mimic ftage derives from fuch foes much more credit than prejudice; wherefore to their own dulnefs, hypocrify, or avarice, we leave them, not forgetting in Chriftian charity, to wifh every pitiable or deteftable character, a fpeedy and entire reformation.

SHAKESPEARE, who has by general confent, been ftiled father of the Englifh drama, firft prefents himfelf; his characteriftics in tragedy are fupporting and purfuing all the paffions which agitate, adorn, or difgrace human nature to their utmoft extent; a ftrict and moft praifeworthy adherence to uniformity of character, both in conduct and language; he never finks an elevated perfonage in dialogue, nor raifes a low one by improper dignity of phrafe;

variety

variety and ftrong contrafts feem always in his view, he well knew the force of his own genius and fought fubjects fuitable; his choice of hiftorical plots was highly judicious, as a more extenfive field than any other, a field in which fcarce any other author has ranged, with fuccefs, except BANKES, whofe well chofen fubjects made the worft writing that ever efcaped poetical pen bearable.

Though we fhould have been forry to perceive the trammels of criticifm, on SHAKESPEARE's fire-eyed Pegafus, yet we rather wifh that he had not fhown fo total a contempt for probable regularity; he certainly might have obferved fome bounds, without any prejudice to his imagination, and we particularly lament thofe difguftirg fcraps of fafhionable buffoonery which occur in, and difgrace, many of his beft pieces: in comedy we find him fanciful and pleafant, his characters are rich and pleafing, though obfolete; his plots in general good, though irregular, moft of his cataftrophes fatisfactory; his converfation nervous and pointed, but in fome places rather ftiff; faults frequently occur, but they are hid amidft a blaze of beauties; and it may be truly faid of this author, that criticifm reluctantly ftumbles upon his blemifhes, having fo rich a fund for praife and admiration.

DRYDEN, as a tragic writer, encouraged bombaft ideas and pompofity of verfification, aiming more at the marvellous than juft pictures of nature; however his ALL for LOVE has merit, and there are fome mafterly ftrokes in the character of DORAX, in DON SEBASTION; in thofe fcenes of ŒDIPUS, faid to be written by him, we difcover great merit, and may juftly conclude, that his plays in rhime

were

were the effect of a fervile compliance with falfe tafte, occafioned by very unfavourable circum-ftances, which perverted his genius, and enflaved his opinion; indeed his principles appeared, upon every occafion, fubfervient to pecuniary advantage.

Notwithftanding there are fome well imagined whimfical characters in his comic writings, the deteftable licentioufnefs with which they are loaded, renders them obnoxious, and we could wifh them funk in oblivion; a diffolute court will ever taint public entertainments, as well as private conduct; and it feems DRYDEN's peculiar misfortune to have written in a reign when vice was patronized by the higheft authority; a reign which wanted the honeft indignation and keen fatire of a JUVENAL to chaftize and expofe its infamy.

BEN JOHNSON, though ranked fo high in literary fame, does not appear to us deferving of fo honourable a ftation; his tragedies are the moft ftiff, uncouth, laborious, unaffecting, productions we know, fpun out to an intolerable length, by tedious, uneffential, declamatory paffages, tranflated from the claffics; three of his comedies have juftly received the ftamp of general approbation; VOLPONE, SILENT WOMAN, and EVERY MAN in his HUMOUR; yet even in thefe nature feems rather carricatur'd, and there are many blamable intrufions upon delicacy of idea and expreffion; the remainder of his works might have dubbed any man, lefs lucky, with the title of a bad writer, and we are perfectly of opinion that naming him with his great cotemporary, is pairing authors as poulterers do rabbits, a fat and a lean one.

OTWAY

OTWAY was peculiarly happy in a full and un-
rivalled poffeffion of the true Pathos; in his two
plays of VENICE PRESERVED and the ORPHAN, the
audience are never left to a ftate of indifference,
but tied down by a fucceffion of interefting ftrokes
to a moft feeling, fympathetic attention; his verfification is the moft unaffected and natural for dialogue of any we know; but the whole of his reputation fhould reft upon the two pieces we have
mentioned; his other productions, of the ferious
caft, are very meagre, and his comedies not only poor,
but infamous; it feems to have been a fettled
maxim with OTWAY, to fhow the moft unfavourable pictures of human life, yet, by a kind of bewitching power, he annexes pity to the diftrefs of
fuch characters as fhould rather fall under contempt.

ROWE deferves the praife of being chafte, moral,
and pathetic; he has evidently inftruction conftantly in view; his merit, fave one unfortunate attempt upon comedy, is more uniform than that of
any other writer; it is true he does not rife within
many degrees of SHAKESPEARE's peculiar elevation, but at the fame time, he never finks fo low,
and it is not an exaggerated compliment to fay of
him, as LORD LITTLETON has done of THOMPSON,
that he never wrote a line which, dying, he might
wifh to blot; his FAIR PENITENT and JANE SHORE,
keep the ftage moft conftantly, though we think
his TAMERLANE rather fuperior, and his AMBITI-
OUS STEP MOTHER equal to either; one, and only one,
fault we find with this amiable author, which is,
making all his characters fpeak in exactly the fame
ftile, furnifhing them with too rich, too fanciful a
ftrain

ſtrain of expreſſion, and frequently making the poet take place of the character.

Lee poſſeſſed great fire of imagination and much tenderneſs; but we need no other information than peruſal of his pieces to know that his brain was frenzied; Theodosius notwithſtanding many ſtrange extravagancies, is ſufficient to fix his claim to poetical merit.

The muſes beſtowed ſmiles of peculiar favour on Mr. Addison, but his poem of Cato hardly gives him title to the ſtile of a dramatic author; if he was really writer of that pleaſing, natural, ſimple, comedy, the Drummer, we readily admit him, and wiſh he had favoured the world with more productions of a ſimilar kind.

Thompson ſeems to have been much better calculated for eaſy poetry than theatrical compoſition; yet his plays ſtrongly manifeſt a knowledge of nature, a moral delicacy of judgment, and great ſtrength of expreſſion; but they are wanting in point of buſineſs, incidents are too thinly ſcattered, and his ſcenes frequently fall from their length, he does not appear to have known, or conſidered, the effect of repreſentation, and criticiſm may eaſily diſcover that he wrote more for the cloſet than the ſtage.

From all we can collect of this reſpectable author, we may conclude that he was ſo tenacious of a virtuous tendency, he never could have been prevailed upon to flatter depraved taſte, as Dryden did.

We recollect a circumſtance in his life, which, though foreign to our plan, muſt be pleaſing to every generous mind; a very ſtrict cordial intimacy
ſubſiſted

subsisted between THOMPSON and QUIN, the former, who was often in low circumstances, invited his friend to dine with him at Kew, where he then lived; after the hospitable repast was over, the author, who was as remarkable for modesty as genius, with much hesitation told the player he wanted fifty pounds, and would esteem the loan of that sum as a great favour. QUIN, with his usual roughness, replied, look ye JEMMY THOMPSON, this is an odd invitation of yours; you have given me a good dinner, and I have done it justice, but did not think I was to pay so confounded dear for it; this brutal rebuff silenced the diffident bard, and not a syllable more was then mentioned of the matter.

Next morning THOMPSON received a letter from his churlish friend to this effect, JEMMY QUIN informs JEMMY THOMPSON that he hates the word *lend*, but if the inclosed bit of paper is of any use, shall be happy: here a bank note for two hundred pounds unfolded itself, and in a postscript were these words; my wine merchant will this day send you a hogshead of his best claret, which I will come and help you to demolish, as often as health, leisure, and inclination, will permit; there was a considerable share of oddity in this action, but it is better to do good, even ungraciously, than to neglect drooping, oppressed, merit ; and it is no small addition to Mr. QUIN's character, that he afterwards reproved his friend sharply for making the matter known.

DOUGLASS HOME, we title this author from his first piece, because not one he has written since possesses any tolerable degree of dramatic merit; he enjoys some share of genius; his descriptions are

in

in general picturesque, and sometimes pathetic ;
but upon the whole, he traces the more powerful
passions languidly ; his characters want variety, his
plots are barren, and his catastrophes very imperfect ; his language is sufficiently chaste and flowing,
but wants vigour, and many scenes drag through a
dull uninteresting sameness ; church persecution has
made many nations bleed in every age ; however
the austere presbytery of Scotland forced this gentleman's pen and circumstances into a situation
which they could never have reached without such
illiberal oppression ; it may be truly said this bard,
like parsley, has vegetated the better for being trod
upon, and though we cannot admit, yet we cordially congratulate him on his peculiar success.

Dr. Brown, author of Barbarossa, rose in our
opinion above the last mentioned gentleman, yet
his Pegasus was animated by false fire, and often
puts us in mind of the flying horse which seems
ready for the most rapid motion, yet always stands
still : It is his first play, also seems to have exhausted all the dramatic merit he possessed, though Mr.
Garrick's powerful merit forced Athelstan on the
town for some nights ; it certainly is a most incongruous, wretched, piece of stuff : The Doctor was
much more of a prose writer than a poet.

Moore, author of the Fables for the fair sex,
has left us one tragedy, which, being written in an
unusual stile, and upon a very unfashionable subject, does not preserve the station it has a right to
claim ; for we are bold to pronounce it a most
striking and instructive picture of nature, especially as she is depraved in Great Britain at present,
though perhaps he has tinctured his piece towards

the latter end with too high a colouring of horror.

The GAMESTER certainly attacks one of the most pernicious national vices that can prevail, and the familiar profe dialogue renders it more intelligible to all degrees of an audience: Some critics feemed to think it loft confequence and politenefs for want of being expreffed in meafured fyllables. Indeed it is no wonder that the boxes in general fhould be afraid to view the horrid confequences of tranfactions they themfelves are fo devoted to, and fo deeply involved in ; however, we give the author great praife for all and every part of this play ; in the comic ftile he was delicate and fpirited ; his aim in writing feemed to center in the production of fomething ufeful, therefore his deficiencies, which were but flight, fhould not be mentioned.

MURPHY, by picking up materials from the French and fome of our own writers, has manufactured feveral praifeworthy pieces in both the ferious and gay ; the latter feems moft his talent, but he has fo excellent a knack of pilfering, that no author ever feemed to maintain a greater equality in the contraft ftiles ; without one grain of originality he has pieced together feveral plays that muft pleafe, by a very extenfive knowledge of theatrical action, and its effects ; he has compofed tragedy without poetry, unlefs ftrained and multiplied metaphors deferve the name, and comedy without wit ; he ranks well amongft living authors, but let the dead call out for their own, and like the bird with borrowed feathers you would foon perceive him in a ftate of poetical nakednefs.

HOOLE,

HOOLE, a fuccefsful tranflator, who has to his own confiderable emolument plundered Metaftafio of two flimfy morfels, which are well enough calculated to flip down and relifh with palled appetites, but have nothing in them truly fubftantial for vigorous critical digeftion; they feem made for the actors who are too weak to bear up a heavier tafk, and the actors appear calculated for them, which greater abilities could make nothing of; fo far a happy junction: But what muft tafte, and thofe fine feelings we have had gratified, exclaim when they are forced to be patient with fuch acting, and fuch compofition.

We now come to authors who have chiefly profeffed themfelves votaries of the comic mufe, and firft mention CONGREVE, not only in point of time, but, as we think, of merit; no man who ever wrote for the ftage has fhewn more capital, more correct, or more pleafing delineations of life; his characters are beautifully contrafted, his language pointed, his wit brilliant, his plots amazingly regular and pleafingly intricate, his fcenes variegated, and his difpofition of the whole mafterly; two faults, one of a very heavy nature, countervail his extenfive merit, his flafhes of wit are too frequent, often too much for the perfon who utters them, his dialogue rather profufe, and a moft abominable vein of licentioufnefs runs through the whole; virtue reluctantly peeps in, while vice with brazen front bolts forward unblufhing, unreftrained: Had this author written under the commendable reftrictions of this age, his luxurioufnefs would have been brought within better bounds. His pieces muft give great pleafure either in action or perufal, but

are

are like the sweet scented rose, with prickles beneath, which while it gratifies one sense wounds another; it is with reluctance we pronounce the sentence of moral justice which condemns his four comedies to oblivion, as pernicious; but we doom his tragedy to contempt, with the full satisfaction of critical propriety.

FARQUHAR is not so rich, but more natural than CONGREVE, his plots are not so laboured and correct, yet are full as agreeable; his characters are all well selected from the volume of life, pleasingly grouped, and well disposed of at the catastrophes; some scenes are rather improbable, as Tom Errand's getting into Lady Lurewell's chamber and stripping before her; besides some others which we could point out; however they are introduced with a degree of whim, which renders them excusable; no doubt the STRATAGEM and RECRUTING OFFICER are far before any other production of his, yet the remainder are not without very great unforced pleasantry.

CIBBER, the laurelled CIBBER, though he had no claim even to the smallest sprig of a poetical tree, has nevertheless by way of attonement, for his doleful birth day odes, furnished the stage with some agreeable pieces; there is a vivacity and pertness discoverable peculiar to himself; his comedies are not very original, yet are they in general very laughable; they had the essential support of most capital acting at their first appearance; else we think they might have sunk into the Lethean stream; the much boasted CAARELESS HUSBAND is, no doubt, remarkable for elegance of dialogue and character; yet it is a very drowsy exhibition.

By

By what we have heard of the laureat's concern in
the PROVOKED HUSBAND and CONSCOUS LOVERS,
we are inclined to allow him the praife of an able
helpmate; we alfo think he ftole judicioufly, and
knew the ftage fo intimately, that he could not fail
much in dramatic compilation; but as to natural
genius, look at all his tragical attempts, except
RICHARD the THIRD, and fee what deplorable fpec-
tacles; however he was a manager, a firft rate actor,
had the ever blooming wreathe, good falaries, and
an annual butt of fack, with which marks of diftinction let him reft in peace, while we who furvive
confider him as much more fortunate than deferving, a circumftance not tied down to any age or
clime.

VANBRUGH, as an artichect, was accufed of having a very phlegmatic tafte; in writing he appears
to poffefs exactly the contraft; fpirit, propriety,
and character; he feems to have known life well,
and has in his dramatic compofitions made good
ufe of that knowledge; his language is free, his
fcenes well difpofed, incidents pleafant, and plots
regular; his play of the PROVOKED WIFE, notwithftanding a ftrong vein of humour, is fcandaloufly
licentious, even as it is now performed; how much
more fo when he adopted the character of a clergyman for rioting, beating the watch, &c. we are
furprized, however great Mr. GARRICK may be in
Sir John Brute, that he conttibutes to keep alive fo
cenfurable a piece; its merits are, or ought to be,
totally funk into its infamy.

There is a grofs error in character which this
author in particular feems fond of, and many have
followed him; that is making Spanifh fervants
fmart,

smart, humourous, fellows; so very free with their masters as even to jest upon their most serious concerns; now however such an idea may have been suggested even by national novel writers yet certain it is that the Spanish pride, for which the Dons in particular are so very remarkable, would never suffer such instances of pert familiarity from their own domestics, whom they consider as animals of a quite different, nay, a despicable species; there is nothing more incumbent upon authors than distinguishing the different spheres of life properly, and giving each a language suitable to his station.

Mrs. CENTLIVRE had a pretty, whimsical talent of composition, and some originality; but her productions are more of froth than solidity; they may divert but cannot improve, and often, for want of decency, shame a female pen.

SOUTHERNE, as a tragic writer, made very powerful attacks upon the tender passions, and is remarkably free in his versification; his comedy is not without spirit, humour, and character; but the infectious taste of Charles's reign, rendered it gross enough for the entertainment of a brothel.

KELLY, as a grave chaste writer deserves praise, but we cannot perceive any marks of strong genius, or lively conception; the spirit of party has been most illiberally prejudicial to this gentleman, but we hope it will pursue him no further.

BICKERSTAFF, this author, with great propriety, we may call the *dramatic cobbler*; for he, figuratively speaking, patches, soles, and heel pieces very well, though he cannot make a new piece of work; he should never attempt any thing out of the Opera stile, as well adapted music may soften many errors;

his

his fentiments are trite, his characters common, and his language moft fhamefully incorrect; his laft piece had an unhappy title *'Tis well its no worfe*; a critical wag, juftly obferved that it was a mifnomer, for it fhould have been called, *it cannot be worfe*; the conclufive lines fpoken by Mr. KING, were fuch an inftance of deficiency both in rhime, and reafon, as fcarcely was ever offered before to an audience; had Mr. DIBDIN compofed them, perhaps the harmonical repetitions, for which his inimitable mufic is fo remarkable, might have melted nonfenfe into captivating found; what are CONGREVE, FARQUHAR, HANDEL, ARNE, or ARNOLD, to this matchlefs author, and as matchlefs compofer.

CUMBERLAND, a moft fortunate jumbler of incidents; who haphazard, throws them together, difdaining probability, and lets them fucceed each other as they may; an author who had modefty enough, in his admirable prologue to the BROTHERS, to accufe all authors of plagiarifm, yet is himfelf made up of nothing elfe; no writer ever more glaringly verified SOLOMON's remark, that there is nothing new under the fun, however he feems to have got poffeffion of the town, and we are in fome meafure glad of it; as perhaps he may be incited to amendment; befides it is better even the fhadow of merit fhould meet with fuccefs, than any portion of it go unrewarded.

GARRICK has employed his pen rather extenfively, and if he had let alone at leaft two thirds of his Prologues we fhould gladly have allowed him a better place as an author than we can do; he has introduced fo much of the ludicrous, and played fo repeatedly on the fame ideas, that criticifm, though it may be forced to laugh, muft be much offended. In one he ftiles himfelf a Prologuefmith, we wifh he had wrought up more fteel, and rejected much of the drofs he has forged into rhime; when the advantages of fpeaking are withdrawn, we fear they will not be deemed any addition to the writer's name. Pope's to Cato, and feveral of Dryden's, will laft in the eftimation of found tafte, as long as fuch pieces are read.

Thus much our impartiality obliges us to fay at the fame time, we moft gladly allow this gentleman warm praife for his alterations, and judicious amendments of feveral plays, befides the production of fome very pleafing originals ; his perfect knowledge of the ftage makes him mafter of difpofition ; he has fpirit and correctnefs, but feems, in our idea, much better fupplied with tafte than genius, with humour than wit : we fee him prefixed, in a kind of poetical partnerfhip, to the CLANDESTINE MARRIAGE; we know not what part he had in that comedy, but readily admit that the compofition does him and Mr. COLMAN great credit.

FOOTE, this writer we ftile the dramatic noun fubftantive, who ftands entirely upon his own bottom ; whofe peculiarity of genius, ftrength of judgment, knowledge of life, felection of characters, application of fatire, vivacity of fentiment, and terfenefs of dialogue, place him diftinct from any other writer, paft and prefent. There is one point worth obferving, which is, that though he often appears negligent in working up his cataftrophe, yet he ftudioufly, and in the moft agreeable manner, impreffes moral inferences upon fuch of his audience

ence as chufe to think; and thofe who only come to laugh, receive no taint from vitiated ideas. The charge of perfonal feverity that has been levelled againft him, muft, upon a moment's confideration, fall to the ground; for if there are fuch knaves, fools, hypocrites, and coxcombs, as he prefents to public view, there is no doubt but fuch are fit objects of fatire, and ought to feel her keeneft lafh.

COLMAN, as we called the laft mentioned author a noun fubftantive, we are induced to ftile this gentleman a noun adjective; for by his productions, ever fince he has feparated from Mr. GARRICK, we receive melancholy proofs that he cannot ftand alone. His JEALOUS WIFE, no doubt, gives him claim to a very honourable ftation in the dramatic lift, but we have great reafon to apprehend he had fome powerful affiftance in compofing that play; however, we imagine, that fenfible of his own intellectual decay, or natural weaknefs, he has fhrewdly appealed to the affiftance of pantomime, and turned his pen into a wooden fword, for the patch coat conjuror. Mercy deliver us! what a tranfition for even common fenfe to make, unlefs urged by the moft preffing neceffity? how would JOHNNY RICH exult, take fnuff, and ftroke his cats, were he alive again, to fee an author facrificed at the fhrine of fpeechlefs mummery, before which he had fo many years proftrated his empty noddle? how would he rejoice to fee the Nine Mufes fwallowed up by MOTHER SHIPTON, as greedily as the Dragon of Wantly devoured houfes and churches? would the voracious old lady had been buried in a real Yorkfhire coal-pit, never to have appeared again, rather than have metamorphofed our pretty little managerical play-wright, into a headlefs bantling of her's.

Though laft, not leaft in love, WILLIAM WHITE-HEAD, Efq; come forth, the verdant wreath frefh nodding on thy brows; reft birth-day odes, they are no objects for us; indeed, we read them not, therefore cannot fay but the fack, or its equivalent, may be well earned. As a dramatift, this gentleman is as much upon the medium as any writer we know; his tragic ftrains will never make any body cry, nor will his comic ones ever raife a laugh; however, though he cannot reach abfolute praife, he efcapes pofitive blame. His fentiments are juft and commendable, his dialogue polifhed, but a dreadful foporific languor drowfes over the whole, throwing both auditors and readers into a poppean lethargy. His laft Trip, that to Scotland we mean, was unluckily imagined; there could not be a worfe clime for the production of humour. Thus we take leave of authors, and now proceed to the laft point of inveftigation, their public agents, the performers.

THEA-

THEATRICAL REPRESENTATION

A N D

P E R F O R M E R S.

To give a juft delineation of nature for the
ftage, either in compofition or action, claims very
peculiar and powerful talents ; wherefore it is more
a matter of furprize, that fo many fhould arrive at
decency in both, than that fo few fhould attain excellence in either. Of the former, we have already
fpoken as far as our plan feemed to admit ; of the
latter, we fhall now deliver our fentiments on the
fame principle, with unchecked freedom, and we
hope with fome propriety.

Mimic reprefentation of the incidents and characters which fill up this great ftage of life would
be almoft an unfurmountable difficulty, if every
fpectator was a competent judge of the feveral
claffes ; but criticifm being for the moft part confined to one fphere, by individuals, though feelings
are pretty general, falfe colouring and difproportion
often go down. We remember the circumftance,
feveral years fince, of an intelligent countryman,
who was carried to fee the STRATAGEM, in which our

Englifh

English Roscius was to do Archer. The persons who accompanied this natural critic, had previously given this great actor his due praise ; however, they left the rustic to find him out. His sensations being properly operated upon, he discovered, that brother Martin was a woundy comical blade, and gave him, as well as Scrub, a hearty tribute of laughter ; but being told it was Garrick, he would not give credit, because, said he, a *great* man would never wear a livery ; however, in the last act, where Archer was dressed like a gay and blooming bridegroom, he readily admitted the truth. From this and a multitude of instances which might be advanced, it is demonstrable, that though nature has strings of sympathetic unison, when judiciously touched, yet her feelings are often checked or perverted by external prejudices, wherein the eye supercedes the heart.

It is an odd remark, but it may be fully justified, that the blind in general are much better judges of tones than those who see ; that the dumb and deaf are the ablest judges of action ; and the reason obviously is, their being confined to the perception of a single sense.

Theatrical representation should undoubtedly be considered and conducted as the water colour painting of life ; for, as oil scenes, though finished by the most accomplished masters, would melt away to an undistinguishable glare of sameness by the rays of an artificial light, so, in the same situation, animated characters must be sustained with more forceable strokes than we meet in real life ; but then those strokes should be tempered so to the distance, that to an audience they may feem no ftronger nor fainter.

The natural mode of exhibiting tragedy, and indeed comedy alfo, no doubt, owes its rife to Mr. Garrick ; for, before him, it is agreed on all hands, that not only blank verfe was fwelled to a moft difguftful monotonous pompofity, but even common profe dialogue was verfified by utterance. It may feem ftrange, but we aver it to be true, that Mr. Delane, who had many fine requifites for a great actor, ufed to tell Boniface " I have heard your " town of Litchfield much commended for its ale," in as confequential a manner, and as regular a cadence, as he ufed in Pyrrhus, when replying to the embaffy of Oreftes.

We have one capital living inftance of what is called the old way, we mean Mr. Wignell, of Covent Garden, who is, to borrow from the title of Tom Thumb, the moft tragical tragedian that ever tragedized on any ftage. We heartily wifh, to fhew what nature in reprefentation is, and what fhe is not, and alfo to prove that the general approbation of Mr. Garrick's mode is not founded upon fafhionable acquiefcence, that the aforefaid gentlemen were to play Jaffier and Pierre, or Dumont and Haftings, in contraft, then would arife a conviction in favour of propriety, which muft imprefs the moft rufticated obfervation ; however, Mr. Wignell may certainly claim nature at fecond hand, fince cuftom has fo far wrought upon him, that he is the fame off as on the ftage ; and always, in either cafe, appears no other than himfelf.

In ftage oratory there is amazing variation, and great part of this depends upon the performer's

happy

happy conception. We cannot enter minutely into a fubject, which, properly difcuffed, would fill a
volume; therefore, only fome general outlines can
be offered. All unimpaffioned declamation fhould
be delivered in a full, diftinct, level, tone of voice,
fo modulated as juftly to mark the cadences, according to the ftops : all exclamations, whether of
grief or rapture, violence of rage, or climaxes of
furprife, fhould be expreffed by upper notes ; and
all paffages of gloomy rage, defpair, revenge, &c.
by the lower. In point of emphafis there is a tafte
as well as propriety ; the former of which arifes only from a thorough knowledge of the author, and a
refined ear ; the latter, by itfelf, will ever appear
ftiff and mechanical. There may be inftances
where fuperior judgment may affift inferior, refpecting a difficult paffage ; but marking every emphafis in a performer's part, as we have heard of
the late Mrs. Ward, and fome others, is enflaving
ideas wretchedly, reducing the performer to almoft
the ftate of wood and wire ; leading-ftring actors
and actreffes may be paffable, but can never be
great. There is one remarkable peculiarity which
we are inclined to cenfure highly, yet modifhly a-
dopted on the ftage at prefent, particularly at Covent Garden: a kind of uneffential emphafis hunting,
that lays powerful ftrefs upon words which by no
means require it, lifting up the conclufive word of
a period, which moft erroneoufly gives force, not
only to perfons but particles, almoft wherever they
are met by, my, the, you, thou, thy, &c. we wifh this
was fo reformed as to obferve where antithefis,
which chiefly governs the emphafis of thefe and fuch
like

like parts of fpeech, authorizes additional force of expreffion.

Breaks and paufes, fuch as occur in HAMLET, LEAR, MACBETH, and other plays of Shakefpeare, are very difficult to execute happily. This is a point very obvious, as they never fail, when well fupported, to give warm and general approbation; they not only give variation to the voice, but alfo an agreeable tranfition to the features.

Stage deportment fhould be free, and void of all affectation; folemnity of ftep, by breaking half way, the old mode, or dragging the hind foot with a kind of flide, are both unmeaning and ungraceful; ftooping, unlefs where neceffary, maims a figure much, and difpleafes the obferving eye; turning too often from the perfon fpoken to, for fake of difplaying figure, by traverfing the ftage, is a breach of decorum, not only inconfiftent with civility but reafon; and looking from the object of converfation, to take a view of the audience, or, as we have too often feen, to falute an acquaintance, is reprehenfible to the laft degree, difrefpectful both to the actor on the ftage, and to the public; fpeaking or not, a performer fhould never lofe fight of character, yet many we have viewed waking as it were from a reverie juft when alarmed by their cue.

As action is the life of public fpeaking, we think it fhould be moft induftrioufly cultivated, and that rather by a ftudious, rational, enquiry into motions of eafe, grace, and explanation, than the reflection of a looking-glafs. Shakefpeare's general rule, let the action fuit the words, the words the action, is concife, comprehenfive, and juft; as is alfo his interdiction againft fawing the air. We think that a

fet

set of drawing, to shew all the variations of action in the different situations of character, would be highly useful, not only a rich subject for describing all the passions of the features, but all the positions of the body; we wish Mr. Garrick to be the subject of such a design, for such sized prints as would come at a price suitable to general purchase; but it is a matter of too great fatigue to be ever hoped for; however those capital pieces, in which we have seen his excellence described, justify our wish.

Attitudes, we mean those of a picturesque nature, should never be obtruded upon unimportant passages; a constant display of such is the peculiar province of Pantomime; but when they are called for, they should be executed with all spirit and exactness; the extent of figure being consulted; for what may appear graceful in a large, may be the contrary in a small one, and what may well suit the latter, will often render the former puppet like.

If there is a just feeling, all movements of the features will be just, although more strongly described in some than in others; but the disposition of body and limbs may yet be very awkward and unpleasing; which is frequently verified by country actors, and sometimes by those in town; it is certain that those who understand action least use it most; willing to do something clever they undo, and misapply most egregiously; we remember amidst a multitude of instances, an actor well received in Jaffier, who speaking this line, "how I could pull thee down into my heart;" so far anticipated propriety of motion, as to clap his hand to his breast at the

2   word

word *pull*, and throw it from him at the word *heart*.

Mr. Barry has often offended us, with clafping his hands five or fix times in a fpeech of as many lines; this is a proper, and becoming action upon many occafions, but, too often ufed, difgufts: Mr. Palmer imitates this particular fault, with great induftry; upon the whole it is much to be lamented by all admirers of the drama, that performers don't make themfelves better acquainted with different ftations in life; that they don't rather ftudy characters than gallantry and diffipation; that they don't collect and lay down for themfelves fome rules, not play fuch a precarious game of hap hazard, right and wrong, as they do now; which occafions them to commit ten faults for the difplay of one beauty; afk three fourths of them, why they do fo, and fo, the reply is, Mr. Garrick, Mr. Barry, Mrs. Yates, or Mrs. Barry, do fo; let me afk thofe complaifant, cloying imitators, why they don't get the identical dreffes of thofe gentlemen and ladies they fo implicitly follow; the garments without taking meafure, will probably fit them as well as the modes they affume; for fhame fons and daughters of Thefpis, fearch into, and improve, your own talents, capability is not fo much wanting at prefent as originality; work for that jewel, and you'll obtain reward; do not all old men of Drury Lane hobble miferably after Mr. Garrick's Lear, nor young men of Covent Garden monotonize after Mr. Smith's every thing.

In the courfe of this work we have often experienced and lamented what we forefaw at firft; the unavoidable neceffity of multiplied repetitions; fo

many fimilar circumftances relative to both performers and plays, that we have found ourfelves deprived of language to exprefs our ideas differently;
this however we hope will find excufe and we
fhall go forward without further mention of an in-
convenience infeparable from the undertaking.

Mr. Garrick, whom we are to confider merely as
an actor, is indebted to nature for an almoft
matchlefs fignificance of feature, enlivened with
eyes peculiarly brilliant; from an amazing flexibility
of countenance, he can exprefs the moft contraft
feelings; fimplicity, mirth, rage, grief, defpair,
and horror, with nearly equal excellence; hence
his Abel Drugger, Benedick, Ranger, Hamlet,
Macbeth, King Lear, and feveral other characters,
have no equal, poffibly never had; what may lie
in the womb of time we know not, but think it
would not be a very extravagant prophecy, to fet
him up againft any future excellencies taken in a
general view; great, no doubt, he is in both depart-
ments, the fock and bufkin; however, though
that eminent genius, Sir Jofhua Reynolds, has placed him equally between both, we have no fcruple
to pronounce him moft confpicuous in the latter; in
light fcenes he exhilirates, 'tis true, in a very peculiar
manner; but in the graver and more impaffioned
ones, he leads the heart captive as he pleafes, and
roufes feelings of a much more important, difficult,
nature, than can arife from comedy; with her he is
very pleafingly fportive, but with her fifter afto-
nifhingly powerful.

His peculiar excellencies are, an harmonious, diftinct, voluble, and extenfive voice; without any
unnatural fnaps, the laft word of all his periods, is

as intelligible as the loudeſt; in all ſudden tranſitions his correctneſs, force, and judgment, are ſcarcely to be deſcribed; in his ſoliloquies he happily avoids that abſurd method of ſpeaking ſolitary meditation to the audience; he appears really alone.

His defects, for every light has its ſhade; is ſhortneſs of figure, which however by art he evades, as much as poſſible, by not only diſpoſing it to the greateſt advantage, but alſo by taking care to ſhift ſituations ſo often, that the eye can hardly have time to find out, and dwell upon the defect; though graceful in motion, and very much ſo in attitude, he never could picture dignity, nor attain what is called the fine gentleman, a character indeed too languid for his active powers; though generally correct in modulation, and almoſt invariably ſo, in expreſſing the ſenſe of his author, there is a reſpirative drag, as if to catch breath, and ſome unneceſſary pauzes, ſeemingly for the ſame purpoſe, which we have often been under a neceſſity of ſilently objecting to; and the ſame ſort of cenſure ſhould have ſufficed ſtill, but that we ſet out with a poſitive reſolution to be juſt, and having thus far maintained it, we muſt continue to the end.

The leading figures ſhould be more minutely inveſtigated than thoſe who have leſs advantages; we have often regretted an adulteration of language, by changing the *e* and *i* into *u*; this gentleman, and ſeveral after him, have pronounced *ſtern*, *ſturn*, *mirth*, *murth*, *birth*, *burth*, which is really rendering our language, already ſufficiently diſſonant, ſtill more ſo; our Engliſh Roſcius we could never admire in declamation, indeed he has kept pretty clear of it, and we heartily wiſh that, for ſake

of

of his fame, Benedick, Ranger, Archer; Don Fe-
lix, or any thing in that juvenile ftile, may not hereafter ferve to fhow his advance in life; it is not
enough to fay he is *greater* than *any body elfe*, in the
true cordiality of heart, we form a hope, that he
will not in any future feafon appear *lefs* than *himfelf*,

Mr. Quin found his deficiency, and retired, but
rather too late by fix or feven years; however what
he performed in that period wanted neither freedom
of figure, nor much limitation of years.

In the courfe of thofe obfervations we have already made upon this gentleman, we have attacked
the public reputation he obtained, with afperity,
but could not avoid it, as his tragedy, bating fome
paffages in Cato, Brutus, Zanga, Tamerlane, and
Bajazet, was intolerable; he often ftruck out a
beauty, but was upon the whole fo unnaturally
confequential, fo monotonous and heavy, that criticifm recollects moft part of his performance with
pain, his comedy, from a cynical roughnefs, and
where it wanted a mellow jocundity of humour, was
truly pleafing, and it is fcarce any exaggeration to
fay, we fhall never fee the OLD BATCHELOR,
SPANISH FRYAR, PLAIN DEALER, and MASK-
WELL, half fo ably fupported,

His figure was graceful and important, his countenance open, regular, and authoritative, his
eyes expreffive, and his voice diftinctly fonorous;
but affectation of utterance hurt the latter, and
falfe confequence of deportment often rendered a
good perfon ridiculous; his action was often burlefque, feldom graceful, or well applied; we have
mentioned this gentleman, as we fhall fome other
deceafed

deceased capital performers, because they come within our own æra, and may furnish such as never saw, or do not remember them with comparative ideas.

Mr. Barry, in the meridian of life, possessed most shewy, and agreeable externals, he could not fail to prepossess a female audience, at first sight, in his favour, and even male critics must have felt considerable recommendation from so much elegance of appearance, and harmony of countenance; his voice might justly be called, the pipe of love, and in his eyes dwelt a languishing softness which set him above all competition in soft sensations; his paternal feelings were refined and pathetic, but his declamation trifling; his climaxes unequalled, yet too frequently called upon; he often seemed at a loss how to dispose of his hands, but was, when requisite, happy in attitude; indeed his heighth, and expanse of limbs, were particularly advantageous to him in this point; in all his performance, execution seemed to rise far above judgement; we have been extremely concerned to see such a decayed remnant of what we once thought fabricated by nature with peculiar grace, crippling about this last winter, under the chill of public neglect, and the irksome pains of a shattered, enfeebled, constitution.

Look back twenty years, who would have formed an idea of this lamentable decline, or, at least, that there would have been a necessity for exposing it; however jocose Mr. Garrick, in his occasional epilogue for the theatrical fund, may be, he must have his joke in such compositions, respecting decayed actors wanting half a crown or a pot of porter; we seriously lament that any conspicuous ser-

vant

vant of the public fhould come to live upon charity, and are certain that no perfon of either fex,
who has filled for twenty years, or more, a firft,
fecond, or third rate, with refpect, need want fuch
an irkfome, though benevolently calculated refuge;
want of œconomy is in all ftations pernicious, but
in none more fo than the theatrical.

Mr. Sheridan, who does not come in improperly
here, mounted the ftage at an early period, with the
advantage of a good education and natural underftanding, which gives him a juft title to the ftile of
a fenfible man; he appeared too at a time when the
Dublin ftage was an Augean-ftable of theatrical
filth; no wonder any degree of merit fhould then be
received; add to this, that he was bred in the Col-
lege, which gained him countenance and protection from his fellow ftudents; fo that the public,
having nothing better to regale upon, and feeing
him over and over again, like thofe very collegians
who think, from ufe, mutton the beft eating, Mr.
Sheridan became a ftandard difh, till the introduction of more luxurious theatrical dainties removed
him to London, where he was never even fairly
relifhed; no performer ever conceived his author
better, or marked him more correctly, but his organs of delivery were fo diffonant, fo imperfect,
his manner fo ftudied, his perfon fo trifling, and his
action in general fo extravagant, that his defects
greatly out-number his merits.

It is matter of much concern that, as a performer, he had not been confined to very few parts; as
the conductor of a theatre he had great requifites,
fpirit, knowledge, and integrity; genteel, generous,
and juft, to his performers; but rather unhappy in

a

a taint of courtly attachment, which drew on him a ruinous popular prejudice; his study of oratory rendered him more stiff and disagreeable as an actor.

We most sincerely wish he had wisely considered his own interest, and made, as he might have done, a genteel independant provision for the present and future days; he has made some little attempts in the dramatic way, as a writer, but so trifling as not to deserve mention; his treatise on education, and his lectures on elocution, do him credit, not only as an author, but as a man.

Mr. Moffop, in point of literary knowledge, and strong natural parts, stands very high in the theatrical list, nor are his public talents, in some respects, exceeded by any; his externals are not very favourable, his countenance is not exceptionable, nor yet striking; his eyes, otherwise well calculated for a stage, are injured by a nearness of sight, which occasions him often to contract and wink them; his action, by too much use of the left hand, is uncouth; his attitudes forced, and his deportment rather pedantic than graceful; his voice has power almost without end; full, harmonious and variable; his feelings are fine, and generally just, yet his enunciation is so incumbered with unnecessary multiplied emphasis, that he often appears in the painful situation of a man gasping for breath.

This gentleman has been but an unfortunate manager, and we wish for his own sake, as well as that of the English stage, which has been, and is deplorably supplied in his stile, that he had never left London; from his medium time of life he may be esteemed with all faults, the tragedy sheet anchor at present; but never let the luring jade, comedy, decoy

coy him into the circle of ridicule, or contempt, with her enticing smiles; she was not made for him, nor he for her.

Mr. Ross! perhaps the most ungrateful son of nature that she ever produced; possessed of exceeding good requisites, save an unmeaning countenance, has by matchless neglect sunk himself almost below notice; industry and perseverance might by this time have set him foremost in public esteem, whereas we find him very little used, and less spoken of, so early, we imagine as the age of forty: his voice is pleasing and extensive, his feelings, when properly called upon, have spirit, and pathos; his person, before corpulence enlarged it, was very agreeable, his deportment and action free, his utterance easy, yet pointed and distinct; even now, if he would promise, and keep his word, to take pains with Jaffier, Castalio, Essex, &c. we should see him with much more pleasure than any other present performer; we never wish any thing more agreeable than his Lord Townly, and young Bevil *have* been.

Mr. Smith, a meritorius contrast to the preceding gentleman, recommends himself to managers and familiarizes himself to the public, by an uncommon share of assiduity; the talents he has are not spared but often through necessity, misapplied, as we have shewn in the course of our remarks; we could wish him totally devoted to genteel, sprightly comedy, as his expression and feelings never do justice to the more important passages of passion, and his declamation loses due effect from levity; we believe, not only from our own, but very extended critical opinion, that scarce any performer ever played so much, to affect the heart so

little

little

little; but an agreeable perfon, genteel carriage, engaging countenance, and a diftinct, fmooth, powerful, voice, though monotonous, carry him refpectably.

Mr. Reddifh, in point of pecuniary advantage and ftation, is on the ftage at a very lucky time, but we cannot fay fo much in refpect of critical fame; for though a very ufeful performer, he never was defigned to be a great one, he ever fhould have been in Mr. Havard's line, and that only; his expreffion is not always a juft comment upon his author; his feelings are not adequate to violent paffions, which has occafioned us more than once to fmile at his efforts in Alexander; the beft character he plays of any force and variety is Edgar, level fpeaking feems beft fuited to his voice and manner, his perfon is manly, but neither genteel nor confequential; his tones are diftinct and agreeable enough, but too limited for climaxes of material extent; we were fhocked at the malevolent irony of fome news paper remarks in the *Ledger* fome time fince, which faid this gentleman, in many capital parts, was fecond to none but Mr. Garrick; how could he have provoked any writer to advance fuch an abfurdity, or how could any writer, unprovoked, attempt to damn him with fuch falfe praife?

Mr. Savigny we wifh not to fpeak of, as we are under an indifpenfable neceffity of ufing Obadiah Prim's words, who, when afked what he diflikes about Sir Phillip Modelove, replies, thy perfon, thy manner, thy every thing; if neceffity had forced this gentleman on the ftage we fhould have lamented him fincerely, but as it is, we are rather induced to wonder at, than condemn the devotion of fuch trifling requisites to theatric action; a diminutive person, without any grace, and a voice that has not one tolerable note above the level of a common conversation; there is an evident aim at, and very faint, therefore disagreeable, similitude to Mr. Garrick, that is, to his greatest dificiencies: we heard a sort of a critical pun uttered on seeing this performer in Cyrus, which may not be unworthy notice; if, says a wag, Mr. Savigny's razors touch a beard no better than his features, and utterance, do the passions, it must be torture to be shaved by them.

Mr. Powell, though alas! no more, must not pass unnoticed; his person was no way striking, yet of good size and proportion; his face rather vacant, but pleasing; his voice harmonious, and pathetic; his address genteel, but his action limited, and inexpressive: in old men, where his features were rendered more expressive by art, and where the feelings seemed natural to him, he perhaps never had a superior but Mr. Garrick, 'tis true he took, or rather was obliged to take, too large a field of action, and sometimes get out of his depth; but almost in every point of view, he was much better than any thing he has left behind him.

Mr. Holland, as a tragedian, made up of stiffness, dissonance, and violence, respectable in figure, and powerful in voice, both which he misused abominably; as a comedian, in the Plain Dealer, Sir William Evans, and that stile, he deserved the praise which was lavished on him in other parts that he did not do half so well: he strutted several years in Mr. Garrick's shoes, slip-shod, and was, with all his faults, a great loss to the theatre, as may appear from viewing the dreadful partition of

his

his characters amongst--- oh la!---in pity let us sink the names.

Mr. Aickin, we have no objection to either in respect of person, .or voice, but lament his being lifted above the proper sphere, and wish he would restrain that immoderate violence which Out-Herods Herod, he is much better calculated for a second than a first light, and would be a great gainer if he exchanged some of his superfluous fire for a degree of his brother, Mr. J. Aickin's natural ease.

Mr. Bensley, if this gentleman was but half as great a favourite with the public as he is with the manager, he would be happily stationed; but very partial advantages cannot effect this; his person is slight, his features contracted and peevish, his deportment falsely consequential, his action mostly extravagant, and his voice rather harsh; we always view him most favourably in a Turkish dress, though he can never make a Turkish countenance, his features being much more of the Chinese cast.

Mr. Clarke is very respectable in appearance, and performance; he is as seldom out of his latitude as any one we know, and if he never mounts a great height, he never sinks much below a proper level, he is literally a good, chaste, actor, but sometimes rather phlegmatic.

Mr. Cautherly a tragedy school-boy; effeminate, and insipid throughout the piece: a decent Lovell, in the Clandestine Marriage, nothing further, everlastingly the same, soup for dinner, soup for supper, soup for breakfast, and so on.

Mr.

Mr. Packer, and Mr. Jefferson, two useful and inoffensive performers, the latter confiderably better than the former.

Mr. Hull, very capable of fupporting paternal characters, with propriety, and feeling, as he has often evinced to public fatisfaction; but never more fo than on a late occafion, when he played Leonato, at Drury Lane; this gentleman always convinces a fenfible auditor, that he thoroughly underftands his author; had nature given him executive requifites equal to his judgement and affiduity, he would have been a capital pillar of the ftage; what he is poffeffed of he exerts with judgment and modefty.

Mr. Palmer, is what may be called a handfome figure, yet greatly injured by defective carriage, particularly a moft unpardonable ftoop; his voice is loud, but made up rather of rumbling than of perfect tones, which he ufes fo lavifhly in tragic ftrains, as to offend delicate ears; in comedy he has very pleafing talents, as witnefs his Lyar, Loader, Brufh, &c. he has been, by the neceffities of the ftage, pufhed rather beyond his mark, which is apt to prejudice a young performer.

Mr. Bannifter, very capable of Henry the Fourth, and parts in that caft. Mr. Kniveton, a very tolerable comedian, but for tragedy, hufh. Mr. Moody, the beft teague that ever the ftage produced, and an actor of merit in other views. Mr. Vernon, an exceeding good comic performer, though merely ufed as a finger, which we profefs not to judge off. Mr. Dodd, the theatrical cockatoo, fpirited and pleafing in the coxcomb-ftile. Mr. Love, the bloody murderer of blank verfe, but a good Boni-

face

face, Cacafogo, and a refpectable Falftaff; not a-mifs in Sir John Brute.

Mr. King, in the comic walk of acting, has for fome years fhewn more force, and variety, than any cotemporary; his figure is fmart, eafy, genteel, his countenance pleafing, his features archly expreffive, his eyes fpirited, and fignificant, his voice diftinct; his utterance remarkably voluble, and his action well adapted.

Mr. Woodward, who has fuffered lefs impair from time, than any man in public life of his ftanding, is amazingly great in *outré*, and whimfical, characters, far beyond competition: in the fop ftile he is alfo himfelf alone; his perfon is genteel, his deportment pleafing, but rather too picturefque, too ftudied; comedy has fet her feal upon his features, and laughter dwells in his eye; we have feen this gentleman lately with as much, or more, pleafure, than we did twenty years ago; his vivacity is ama-zing.

Mr. Yates, a very juft comedian, who is feldom beholden to trick for applaufe; his forte we have always thought is old men, yet we admit his Sharp, and Brainworm, to be inimitable.

Mr. Shuter, a luxurious performer, who has great humour both in looks and expreffion, but wants chaftity of character, and diligence; the former often runs him into buffoonery, the latter into imperfectnefs, and nonfenfe. Mr. Parfons has not fo much fun, but more correctnefs. Mr Wefton, the unparalelled eldeft born of fimplicity, whofe Dr. Laft and Mawworm, muft unbend the moft rigid brow.

3

We

We shall conclude male performers with Mr. Foote, who, as he never has attached himself to a sphere of general action, we must merely consider in his own pieces; in which he acts with the same inimitable spirit that he writes; as his ideas and characters are truly original, so is his representation of the parts he plays; his forceable merit has been substantially proved by the amazing sums he has drawn at different periods, but particularly the last four summers successively; if any other proof was necessary, we could furnish a very strong one by offering to comparative view the impotent, disgustful, illiberal, attempts that have lately been made upon his pieces, at both houses, by some theatrical quixote's, to their own utter disgrace, and indeed that of the managers; his pointed rapidity, his peculiar significance, and his laughable transitions, supported with unbating fire, and uncommon whim, set him above all efforts of imitation; and it may be said of him not only as an author, but as an actor, that he snatches graces beyond the reach of art.

The lower members of each theatre, whom we have not mentioned, nor could not without being tedious, certainly in general deserve the compliment of being much fitter for their humble stations than the leaders are for theirs; the rank, and file, rather shame their field officers.

Mrs. Woffington had an elegant, pleasing, appearance, and great comic spirit, but there was a peculiar taint of affectation, not suitable to a real fine lady; she always seemed too conscious of her personal charms, therefore too seldom threw off self to assume character, hence arose a sameness that we could not approve; her tragedy exhibited some

strokes

ftrokes finely imagined, and well executed, but upon the whole, fhe wore the bufkin with a very ill
grace; fhe appeared to more advantage in mens
cloaths, than any other female we have faw, and
was not only very pleafing, but very characteriftic,
in that difficult undertaking, Sir Harry Wildair;
fhe was relieved by death from the near approaching neglect of both public and private admirers; her
voice was the greateft defect fhe laboured under.

Mrs. Cibber, was very agreeable in her perfon,
happy in the difpofition of it, more happy in a fet of
features uncommonly expreffive, and moft happy
in a plaintive, mellow, powerful, voice, fhe had no
turn at all for comedy; in grief and diftraction, no
idea could go beyond her execution; and her Ali-
cia, Conftance, &c. muft ever be remembered with
admiration; yet after all fhe had a relifh of the old
ti-tum-ti, which often gave us offence.

Mrs. Pritchard was graceful and engaging, capable of commanding not only refpect but regard;
her merits were very general, nearly equal both in
the grave and the gay; it is not eafy to conceive
one and the fame perfon fo capital in Lady Macbeth, Jane Shore, Beatrice, and Catharine, fhe
had good feelings, but blubbered in grief; her voice
was rather coarfe, but well modulated, and her
perfon too corpulent, yet fo well deported as to
carry off its fuperfluity with eafe; her equal will not
adorn the theatre, thefe many years.

Mrs. Bellamy trod clofe on the heels of Mrs.
Cibber, fhe had, we think, the more amiable countenance of the two, though it was not marked with
fo much fenfibility, her perfon though fmall, was
very fatisfactory, and her expreffions of rapture, beyond

yond any thing we have ever heard; she came somewhat nearer comedy, than her great competitor, but
never deserved much praise in that stile.

Mrs. Barry has great advantage over the first, and
last mentioned ladies, as being far beyond either in
comedy, and not much behind them in tragedy; she
is graceful, genteel, spirited, and feeling; but from
a defect in her eyes, not so descriptive in countenance, as might be wished.

Mrs. Yates, in the present clouded, theatrical
hemisphere, shines a constellation, but we think
her merit very confined; a good person, regular
but haughty features, and powerful voice, carry her
well through rage, and disdain; but she is deficient
in tender feelings, and hurries the forceable ones to
a degree of violence, which criticism must condemn;
we are sorry to differ so much from public opinion,
which seems so warm in this lady's favour; she has
not a trace of comedy about her.

Mrs. Abington has all the advantages of Mrs.
Woffington, with more variety and more pleasantry;
she is beyond a doubt our best comic actress, and
fully deserves the favour she enjoys. Miss Pope
has considerable merit, in smart voluble comedy,
but is not totally engaging as to her person. Miss
Macklin had extensive, spirited, abilities, but is on
the decline. Mrs. Bulkley, and Mrs. Baddely, are
both pretty women, and agreeable actresses, where
nothing great is wanting. Mrs. Mattocks, a very
useful actress, but rather under-acts tragedy, and
over-does comedy, singing we take no notice of.
Miss Catley nothing of a speaker: Mrs. Fitz-
gerald, very little better. Mrs. Gardner, in Mr.

Foote's

Foote's pieces excellent. Mrs. Green, a very good fubftitute for Mrs. Clive. Mrs. Hopkins, a very bad one. Mrs. Clive, peculiarly happy in low humour; who with a moft difagreeable face, and perfon, was always the joy of her audience, when fhe kept clear of any thing ferious or genteel. Mrs. W. Barry, a very tolerable fecond Woman. Mifs Miller, nothing but partial managerical favour could have produced, or fupported, this Lady.

Thus the DRAMATIC CENSOR takes cordial leave of the reader, confcious of many faults, not without hopes of fome merit; and wifhes, that if any other work, upon this plan, and fubject, fhould hereafter be ftarted, there may be more fubjects for praife, and fewer for cenfure.

We cannot difmifs this volume, without gratefully acknowledging the general encouragement with which the public have honoured our critical purfuit, and the felf approbation we feel from having preferved one uniform fpirit of impartiality through the whole, agreeable to our free and unbiaffed judgment. As a candid review of the ftage was the only motive for this undertaking, and a fecond edition is now preparing for the prefs, we take this opportunity of foliciting the affiftance of the ingenious in general, in order to render the work as perfect and pleafing as poffible. At the fame time, we hereby promife, that whatever alterations

terations we may be favoured with, if not convenient to incorporate them into the body of the work, fhall, at leaft, appear in notes with the author's name, if required, by which the public may form a proper judgment of our performance, and eafily perceive the complexion of our principles: fuch correfpondents as favour us with any improvements, by fending their addrefs to the publifher, fhall have a fet of the new edition, handfomely bound, fent to them gratis, as foon as it is publifhed.

END OF THE SECOND VOLUME.

AN

ANSWER to our late CORRESPONDENTS.

AFTER thanking A. B. and E. M. for the friendly correspondence with which the Dramatic Cenfor has been indulged, we declare ourfelves happy in the idea of affiftance; for a fecond edition, every remark for enrichment, or correction, fhall be carefully attended to, every judicious alteration adopted, and every poffible ftep taken to make the work complete; we lament the indifpofition of our friend E. M. and are to regret that a fimilar impediment among ourfelves, prevented this number's appearing in due time; we have at prefent no fixed refolution, of extending the Cenfor beyond the limits at firft propofed, fhould fuch a defign take place, timely notice will be given for correfpondents; A. B. and E. M. with other friends, may reft affured we have not been fo incivilly curious as to employ the leaft thought in finding out the real names of thofe perfons who only fign initials.

INDEX

To the DRAMATIC CENSOR, VOLUME II.

ANSWER